C000225030

HARDPRESS.NET
HOME OF HARD-TO-FIND BOOKS

The Life of George Washington
by F. T. Headley

Copyright © 2019 by HardPress

Address:
HardPress
8345 NW 66TH ST #2561
MIAMI FL 33166-2626
USA
Email: info@hardpress.net

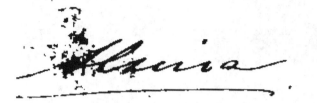

BOOKS;
lers;
SOWERBY,
LIFAX.

THE COTTAGE LIBRARY.—HALIFAX.

Royal 32mo. Cloth. Lettered. Uniformly Bound.—Nearly all of them are also got up in a superior style, in various Coloured Cloth, and elaborately ornamented.

BY THE AUTHOR OF THE "BASKET OF FLOWERS."

Basket of Flowers, &c
Christmas Eve, &c.
Eustace, the Christian Warrior, &c.
Godfrey, the Little Hermit, &c.

A Book that will Suit You
Æsop's Fables. 100 Cuts
Anna Lee; or the Maiden, the Wife, and the Mother
Arabian Nights' Entertainments
American Receipt Book
Anecdotes of Napoleon
A Wreath around the Cross
Baxter's Saints' Rest
Beams of Silver
Berquin's Children's Friend
Bloomfield's Farmer's Boy, &c.
Bogatzky's Golden Treasury —Morning
Bogatzky's Golden Treasury —Evening
Boy's Own Conjuring Book
Brown's Concordance
Bruce's Travels in Abyssinia
Buchan's Domestic Medicine
Buffon's Natural History
Bunyan's Pilgrim's Progress
Bunyan's Choice Works—1st Series
Bunyan's Choice—2nd Series
Bunyan's Choice—3rd Series
Bunyan's Holy War
Burns' Poetical Works
Byron's Select Works

Byron's Choice Works
Byron's Childe Harold, &c
Cabin Boy's Story
Captain Canot, the African Slaver
Cause and Cure of Infidelity
Chapone, Gregory, Pennington, and Dodsley
Children of the Abbey
Christ's Famous Titles. Dyer
Christian's Every Day Book
Clarke's Scripture Promises
Clater's Every Man His Own Farrier
Clater's Every Man His Own Cattle Doctor
Coleridge's Poetical Works
Comic Album & Comic Minstrel
Crotchet (The)
Cowper's Poetical Works
Cooke's & Seaforth's Letter Writers
Cook's Voyages
Cooper's Last of the Mohicans
Cooper's Pilot
Cooper's Sea Lions
Cooper's Spy
Cooper's Deerslayer
Cottage Gardener
Cottager's Key to the Holy Scriptures
Culpeper's British Herbal
Culpeper's Every Man's Doctor
Daily Comforter
Death-bed Triumphs
Dialogues of Devils
Diprose's National Song Book
Domestic Cookery

Don Quixote (Adventures of)
Don Juan. By Lord Byron
Dodd's Beauties of Shakspeare
Dodd's Beauties of History
Dodd's Discourses to young men
Doddridge's Rise and Progress
Dryden's Poetical Works
Dryden's Virgil
Engli...
Eveni...
Farm...
Fashi...
Fathe...
Fern...
Finne...
Flowe...
Foxe'...
Georg...
Glory...
Hei...
Golds...
and
Good...
Gulliv...
Heave...
Heave...
Heave...
Henry...
Herve...
Herbe...
Histo...
Hung...
Kinke...
Lamp...
Cun...
Language & Poetry of Flowers
Law of Kindness, and Kiss
for a Blow
'Lena Rivers, by M. J. Holmes
Life of Wellington
Life of Napoleon Bonaparte
Life of Washington
Life of Cromwell
Life & Exploits of Robin Hood
Life of Baron Trenck
?... ...v. J. Fletcher
... ... Fletcher
...ev. John Wesley

Life of Joseph & Death of Abel
Life of Christ, by Bromley
Lives of Highwaymen and
Robbers
Lives of Pirates & Sea Robbers
Longfellow's Poetical Works
Longfellow's Song of Hiawatha, and other Poems
... Jesus
...han, by Miss
...ev. T. W.) Light
...Valley
...the Rev. T. W.)
...m Lebanon
...r. Adam Clarke
...ical Works
...Rookh, &c.
...) Poetical Works
...ntertaining An-
...e Wise and Good
...a Convent, and
...k
...Udolpho
...d Miseries of
...Invisible World
...Woods
...he.) By the Au-
...e, Wide World
...Baron and Castle
...s
...e Insurgent Chief
Pamela; or Virtue Rewarded
Patent Sermons, by Dow, Jr.
Planter's Daughter (The)
Pleasing Instructor
Poe's Tales of Mystery, &c.
Poetical Keepsake
Popular Song Book
Pope's Poetical Works
Pope's Homer's Iliad
Pope's Homer's Odyssey
Power of Prayer (The)
Quarle's Divine Emblems
Queechy, by Eliz. Wetherell

Ex-Libris Biblioteca Central de la Diputación Provincial Barcelona

Rays of Gold
Ratcliffe's Mrs. The Italian
Ratcliff's (Mrs) Romance of the Forest
Reciter for the Million
Religious Courtship
Rob of the Bowl
Roderick Random (Adventures of)
Rose Clark, & other Sketches, by Fanny Fern
Ruth Hall, &c. by Fanny Fern
Sabbath Musings. &c.
Sacred Garland—First Series
Do., do.—Second Series
Sandford and Merton
Scarlet Letter, by N. Hawthorn
Scottish Chiefs, by Miss Porter
Scott's (Sir W.) Lady of the Lake
Scott's (Sir W.) Lord of the Isles
Scripture Truths Illustrated
Shady Side, by a Pastor's Wife
Shelley's Queen Mab, &c
Shelley's Choice Works
Shipwrecks & Disasters at Sea
Simpson's Plea for Religion
Simpson's key to the Prophecies
Smith's Bread from Heaven
Smith's Early & Latter Rain
Smith's Good Seed for the Lord's Field
Smith's Light for Dark Days
Smith's Sunny Subjects for all Seasons
Smith's The Book you will Like
Smith's Pearls from the Ocean
Smith's Food for Hungry souls
Smith's Fruit from the Tree of Life
Smith's Good News for All
Smith's Rills from the Rock of Ages
Smith (Life of the Rev. James) of Cheltenham
Smith's Book that you Want
Smith's The Book that will Suit You
Smith's Gleams of Grace

Smith's Glad Tidings of Good Things
Smith's Sacred Poetry
Smith's Believer's Daily Remembrancer : or Pastor's Morning Visit
Smith's Believer's Daily Remembrancer ; or, Pastor's Evening Visit
Smith's Manna in the Wilderness
Smith's Messenger of Mercy
Smith's Sabbath Reading ; or, Profitable Portions for the Lord's Day
Smith's Spiritual Poetry
Smith's the way of Salvation Set forth ; and Guide to God and Glory
Smith's The Voice of Mercy in the House of Affliction
Smith's The Church as it Ought to be, & Refreshing Dew Drops
Smith's The Love of Christ, and the Railway Companion
Sprig of Shillelah
St. Clair of the Isles
Stephens' Travels in Egypt, &c
Sunday School Reciter
Sunny Memories of Foreign Lands
Swiss Family Robinson
Tales and Stories of Ireland
Tales of Battles by Sea & Land
Tales of Fairy Land
Tales for Rich and Poor, containing Rising in the World, Retiring from Business, Keeping up Appearances. By T. S. Arthur
Tales of Married Life—Lovers and Husbands, Sweethearts and Wives Married and Single. By T. S. Arthur
Temperance Tales—The Broken Merchant, The Drunkard's Wife, &c., &c.
Tempest and Sunshine

LIFE OF GEORGE WASHINGTON.

EX LIBRIS ESCORNABOV

2

W Banks & Son Edin.

LIFE
of
WASHINGTON

HALIFAX,
MILNER & SOWERBY

THE LIFE

OF

GEORGE WASHINGTON.

BY

J. T. HEADLEY,

AUTHOR OF

"WASHINGTON AND HIS GENERALS," "NAPOLEON
AND HIS MARSHALS," "THE SACRED
MOUNTAINS," ETC., ETC.

HALIFAX:
MILNER AND SOWERBY.
——
1866

BIBLIOTECA

PREFACE.

THE appearance of this Life of Washington almost simultaneously with that written by Washington Irving, would naturally require some explanation. It will be sufficient for me simply to state that the present work was written, and all but two or three chapters *printed*, before Mr. Irving's work was even *announced to be published.* It was commenced nearly three years ago, and issued in numbers in Graham's Magazine. The series was concluded last March. My design was to popularize the Life of Washington by confining myself to events and incidents intimately connected with him and his movements, and thus make the work less voluminous than it would be if it embraced a more detailed history of concurrent events.

Recent collections of documents throwing new light on the war of the Revolution made such a work desirable. Mr. Lossing by his researches has exhumed a vast amount of interesting matter. All of Rufus Putnam's papers and correspondence and diary have also been put into my hands, which shed an entirely new light on some of the most interesting events of the Revolution, and movements

of Washington.   The reader will, therefore, find a vast
number of facts in this work which have never before
appeared in any Life of Washington, but which add greatly
to the interest which surrounds his character.   The Histo-
rical Societies of different States have also yielded me, by
their valuable collections, much aid.   Their efforts for the
last few years to gather and preserve old documents and
letters, which were fast passing away, have added greatly
to the material for any work connected with the Revolution.   The amount of my indebtedness to these new sources
of information will be readily perceived by the reader.   As
to the rest, I have consulted the usual authorities on that
period of our history, a list of which would be too long to
give in this place.

CONTENTS.

—oo—

CHAPTER I.

CHAPTER II.

CHAPTER III.

CHAPTER IV.

CHAPTER V.

CHAPTER VI.

CHAPTER VII.

CHAPTER XIII.

CHAPTER XIV.

LIFE OF WASHINGTON.

———*oo*———

CHAPTER I.

Birth and Death of Great Men—Ancestry of George—Loss of his Father—Sent to District School—Early History—Appointed Surveyor—Forest Life—Goes to Barbadoes with a Sick Brother—Appointed Major over the Militia—Sent a Commissioner to the French—Account of his Perilous Journey.

NATURE is not lavish of prodigies, and when she gives us one in the human species, men are always expecting she will indicate it by some outward sign. A lioness must cast her whelps in the streets when a monster is born—some convulsion of the earth, or strange appearance in the heavens, give token when a great soul has arrived on the earth, whose life is to change the current of history. We love to associate mysterious phenomena with strange and mysterious men. When Cromwell's stormy spirit was passing from this troubled sphere, the enraged winds and waves strewed the English coast with stranded vessels. As Napoleon lay struggling in the last throes of mortal life, the sea rose with a thundering sound over its barriers, as if striving to reach the spot where the great sufferer lay.

But no such violent changes of nature heralded the birth or accompanied the death of Washington.

15

Serenely like the sun, as if in harmony with the universe, he arose on the world—so bright and undimmed he moved over the firmament, and without a cloud to dim his splendour sunk gloriously to rest.

We take a deep interest in the childhood of great men, for we wish to detect, if possible, indications of their future greatness, and trace the mental processes by which they reached their elevation. Our curiosity in this respect is rather excited than gratified by the meagre accounts that have come down to us of Washington's early days. There are many traditions, all in harmony with his general character, but not substantiated as matters of history. His manly refusal to tell a lie to escape punishment, his generosity in winning a prize, by his superior strength, for another, and his love of the right exhibited in more instances than one, are so many floating traditions, which may or may not be true. The retired place of his birth, and the stern character of the times and men that surrounded his earlier years, would naturally cause his boyish conduct to pass unnoticed, leaving to the mother alone the pleasing task of hoarding up all his noble traits and generous deeds.

The ancestor of George held the manor of Sulgrave, Northamptonshire, England, which was granted to him in 1538. His grandson Lawrence had several children, two of whom* (the second and fourth) emigrated to Virginia in 1657. They bought plantations in Westmoreland, on the Potomac, and became successful farmers. John Washington entered into active service against the Indians, and rose to the rank of colonel. He had two sons and a daughter. The elder son, Lawrence, married Mildred Warner, by whom he had three children, John, Agustine, and Mildred. Agustine, the second son, married Jane Butler, by whom he had four

* John and Lawrence—the eldest, William, married a half-sister of George Villiers, Duke of Buckingham.

children, two of whom dying in infancy, left only Lawrence and Agustine. His wife also dying, he married in 1730 Mary Ball, by whom he had six children ; George, who was born in Westmoreland county, February 22, 1732, and Betty, Samuel, John, Agustine, Charles, and Mildred. The latter, however, died in infancy. While George was yet very young, his father removed to an estate which he owned in Stafford county, where he died in 1743. To each of his sons he left a plantation of several hundred acres. To George, at this time eleven years old, was reserved the estate on which he then lived. Four children, younger than he, constituted a large family of almost infants, to be brought up by the widowed mother. But she was a woman of uncommon character, combining in harmonious proportions all those qualities necessary to make the best and noblest of our species—a good and true mother. George was her eldest born, on whom she was to rely in her old age, and she watched his early development with that solicitude a pious mother only knows. She saw in him those generous and noble traits which afterward distinguished him—marked with pride his manly scorn of a lie, his hatred of wrong and oppression, whatever the forms they took, and his enthusiastic love of the great and the good. But she saw also a bold and impetuous nature, which, when thoroughly roused, was not easily laid—a fearlessness and recklessness of danger, that made her tremble, and it was with prayers and earnest teachings, that she sought to place that nature under the control of reason and the law of right. Around that bold and passionate heart she cast ligature after ligature, woven from truth and duty and conscience, and bound them with maternal fondness there, till even its wildest throbbings could not rend them asunder. Right well and faithful was her work done. It stood the fiery trials of youth, the storms of battle and the temptations of ambition;

and when at last, conqueror and hero, he leaned his head, covered with honours, on her aged shoulder, and wept as he bade her farewell to take his place at the head of the republic which he had saved, she reaped the fruit of her labours. How little she knew what destinies hung on her instructions, as that boy stood by her knee and listened to her counsel. With his passions cultivated instead of restrained, and his reflective faculties and conscience kept in abeyance by his strong impulses, he would have made a great and brilliant man, but never have become the founder of more than an empire and the beacon light of the world.

At this time only thin populated and widely separated settlements were scattered through Virginia, so that no colleges or high schools had been founded. Parents, therefore, who wished to give their sons a classical education, were compelled to send them to England. If they could not afford to do this, they had to fall back on a private tutor, or a district school in which only the common rudiments of education were taught. To the latter George was sent, and it was well that it happened so. However valuable a thorough education is, the mission George Washington was to fulfil required that he should be wholly one of the people. He could not have been educated in the universities of Europe, without at the same time coming under influences, the whole tendency of which would be to unfit him for the place assigned him by Heaven. Here, amid our primeval forests, in constant intercourse with the hardy settlers, trained in the rough life of the pioneer, and representing in himself the love of the soil, the fearless independence and self-reliance of the people, he became their true representative and leader.

At thirteen years of age we find him sitting in one of those humble school-houses in a Virginia clearing, which still form one of the most distinctive characteristics of our country. Full of lusty life, his shout rings over the fields as he bounds away from his pursuers, or his laugh mingles with the rollicking group, as they wrestle and leap and toss the bar in boyish rivalry. One of his graver sports was to arrange his playmates in companies, and, placing himself at their head, march and countermarch them or lead them to the charge in mimic battle. Bold and athletic, he soon acquired influence over his companions by his physical strength, while, by his probity and love of justice, he caused himself to be referred to as arbiter in all their quarrels. His hand dealt swift punishment on acts of meanness and oppression, for he would no more suffer wrong than do it. In school he was as much marked by his application and acquirements, as he was out of doors by his strength and agility. His taste in books was uncommonly grave, and he reveals at this early age the systematic subjection to wholesome rules under which he ever after placed all his conduct. He formed little manuscript books, into which he copied the forms used by men in transacting business, such as bonds, bills of exchange, notes of hand, receipts, etc. Selections of poetry are scattered along, evidently not such as a boy would naturally prefer. They were simply religious maxims, and doubtless had been hoarded from his mother's teachings.

He made also a large collection of rules of behaviour, which reveal a remarkably matured mind in one so young. Many of them would not be comprehended by a boy of thirteen, much less have arrested his attention and be set aside as guides to himself: such as "Gaze not on the marks and blemishes of others, and ask not how they came." "What you may speak in secret to your friend, deliver not before others." "Let your recreations be manful, not sinful." "When you speak of God, or his attributes, let it be seriously and in reverence." "Honour and obey your natural parents, although they be poor." "Labour to keep alive in your hearts that little spark of celestial fire called conscience."

It is certainly extraordinary to see a mere child thus reduce his life, as it were, to system, and shape all his conduct to rules of morality. The foundation of a well-balanced and virtuous character, thus early established, could not but result in a noble and complete structure. In his case the tree obeyed the inclination of the twig to perfection, and he grew up a striking example of the power and benefit of right early training. Virtues planted so deep in the heart are proof against the fiercest storms and severest temptations of life.

He had a decided taste for mathematics, which soon led him from the simple rules of arithmetic, into geometry, trigonometry and surveying; and he spent much of his time in surveying the lots around the school-house.

A fiery nature, that loves excitement and danger, joined to a mathematical taste and science, always gives a strong character, for it shows a union of the imaginative and reflective faculties, of energy and discretion, impulse and great accuracy—a union which in itself is power. Bonaparte exhibited these traits of character in an extraordinary degree, making him both rapid and exact—quick as the lightning's flash and as certain of its mark.

How different are the ways by which Heaven reaches results from those pursued by man! The wisest statesmen of France and England were absorbed in the affairs of this continent, and its fate depended, in their estimation, wholly on the wisdom of their management and the strength of their armies, while around the form of a lad of thirteen, in a Virginia school-house, clustered its entire destinies.

Young Washington was not quite sixteen, when, with his education completed, he left school and launched forth into active life. The treaty of Aix la Chapelle, to the completion of which had been given the thought and effort of the wisest diplomatists in the world, had just closed. Around it had gathered the attention of all Europe, but men were mistaken, the destinies did not hover about that imposing convention, but attended the footsteps of this unknown lad, as he passed through the forests of his native land.

On apparently trivial matters often hinge the greatest issues. Lawrence, the elder brother, having served as an officer in the English navy under General Wentworth and Admiral Vernon, in the expedition against the West Indies, he through them obtained a midshipman's berth for George. The latter was delighted at the prospect thus opened to him, and immediately began to make preparations for joining his vessel. His mother, however, wavered; she could not trust her first-born, her prop and stay, to the dangers and temptations of a naval life, and took it to heart so grievously that the project was finally abandoned. Once locked up in the British navy, and he never could have become the leader of the revolutionary army.

After George left school he went to his brother Lawrence, living at Mount Vernon, and passed the winter in studying mathematics and in practical surveying. He here became acquainted with the family of Lord Fairfax, whose daughter Lawrence had married, and through them was introduced into the highest circles of society. This eccentric but highly-cultivated nobleman took a great fancy to young George, and resolved to employ him in surveying large tracts of wild land which he owned in the interior. The young surveyor accepted his proposals, and, setting out in March, before the snows had left the summits of the Alleghany, entered the forest and passed an entire month amid the mountains. The third day out, after working hard till night, he sought shelter in a miserable hovel standing alone in the midst of a clearing. On retiring to bed, he undressed himself as usual, and jumped in. To his amazement, however, he discovered that his bed con-

sisted of nothing but straw matted together, without
sheets, and covered with a single dilapidated blanket,
loaded down "with double its weight of vermin."
His escapade from the straw was made with more
alacrity than his entrance, and, dressing himself, he
laid down outside.   This was his first lesson in
frontier life, and he resolved after that to sleep out
under the clear heavens.

   Pushing his difficult way to the Potomac, he found
the river swollen by the melted snows of the
Alleghanies, and rolling such a turbulent flood that
it was impossible to cross it.   Waiting two days for
the waters to subside, he then swam his horses
across and kept up the Maryland side, and in a
drenching rain-storm made forty miles, "over the
worst road ever trod by man or beast."   Halting
for a day and a half, till the storm broke, he came
upon a party of thirty Indians, returning from a war
expedition.   Following the custom of those days, he
gave them some rum, which so exhilarated them
that they resolved to entertain him with a war-
dance.   Building a huge fire, they gathered around
it, and, to the din of their wild music, treated the
young surveyor to a scene as novel as it was picturesque.

   Thus day after day he kept on, and at length
crossed the first ridge of the Alleghanies and entered
on an almost untrodden wilderness, and commenced
his surveys.   Scattered Dutch settlers, that could
not speak a word of English, collected as he passed,
and the men, women and children, with their un-
couth language, streamed after him to watch the
mysterious process of surveying.   They gathered
together round his camp-fire, and made the night
hideous with their grotesque appearance and half
savage behaviour.

   Young Washington, only sixteen years of age,
sitting by his camp-fire, its ruddy light flinging into
bright relief the encircling forest, whose trunks, like

columns of some old dimly-lighted cathedral, receded away in the gloom, surrounded by these half-savage children of the wilderness, would make a good subject for a painter. One night a violent storm arose —the trees rocked and roared over head, and the wind, dashing down amid the embers, whirled them over the straw on which he lay, setting it on fire. In a moment the camp was in a blaze, and, but for the sudden waking of one of the men, Washington would have been wrapped in the flames. Sometimes the wind would suddenly shift, blowing the smoke full on the sleepers, when they would be compelled to bivouac out amid the trees.

Having accomplished the task assigned him ably, he obtained the appointment of public surveyor, and for three years, excepting the winter months, passed most of his time in the wilderness. It was the same succession of hardships and exposures. To-day swimming rapid streams, to-morrow drenched and chilled, picking his way through the dripping forest—now reclining at the close of day on some slope of the Alleghanies, and gazing off on the autumnal glories of the boundless solitude, as it lay bathed in the rich hues of the setting sun; and again, pitching his tent, beside his lonely camp-fire, whose light paled before the flashes that rent the gloom, while the peals of thunder that reverberated along the cliffs seemed trebly fearful in that far-off wilderness, he passed through scenes calculated to make a heart naturally bold impervious to fear, and an iron constitution doubly insensible to fatigue. A better training to impart self-reliance and coolness in the hour of peril, and indomitable energy, could not have been furnished, while those moral qualities which, amid the false tastes of more cultivated life, might have sickened, could not but be strengthened by these long and glorious communions with nature. God sent Moses forty years in the wilderness before he would allow him to lead his chosen people to the land of Canaan.

So did Washington pass a long novitiate amid the solitudes of his native country, the better to prepare him to lead the children of freedom to peace and security.

How little he imagined, as he stood on some ridge of the Alleghanies, and looked off on the sinking and swelling forests beyond, that in a short time those solitudes would be filled with the hum of cities, and that on those very summits would meet from either side the shout of millions on millions of free people, sending still higher, in reverence and transport, his own great name to the skies. Of all the gorgeous visions that flitted before his youthful imagination— of all the strange and marvellous destinies that the young heart will dream of, none were so strange and marvellous as that which actually befel him.

During all this time he was a slave to that tender passion to which the strongest of our race, in the midst of their power, have fallen helpless victims. Its object, history and issue, remain in obscurity. He has left only here and there a memento of the inward struggle. An occasional sonnet to his low-land beauty, a melancholy tone pervading his letters at this time, show that he suffered deeply, but whether from rejected love, or from the effort to subdue an affection which circumstances forbade him to cherish, is not known.

In a letter to a friend, after speaking of the plea-sures he derived from correspondence with those he loved, he says, " My place of residence, at present, is at his lordship's (Lord Fairfax,) where I might, were my heart disengaged, pass my time very pleasantly, as there is a very agreeable young lady in the same house, Colonel George Fairfax's wife's sister. But that only adds fuel to the fire, as being often and unavoidably in company with her, revives my former passion for your lowland beauty ; whereas, were I to live more retired from young women, I might, in some measure, alleviate my sorrow by burying that chaste and troublesome passion in oblivion, and I am very well assured that this will be the only antidote or remedy."

This lowland beauty was all the world to the young surveyor for awhile, and how he succeeded in driving her at last from his heart, does not appear, but probably more exciting scenes effaced the impression which he would not allow to be kept fresh by personal intercourse.

That Washington was something more than an able and faithful surveyor, is evident from the great confidence reposed in him by the government. We have not the complete history of the boy-man. He must have exhibited more extraordinary qualities than appear on the surface, to have been chosen, as he was at this time, though but nineteen years of age, commander of one of the districts of the province which had been set off in order to organize more effectually the militia, to resist the depredations of the Indians. His title was that of adjutant-general, with the rank of major.

Young Washington had now got into the profession best suited to his tastes, and he immediately commenced studying military tactics, and practicing the sword exercise, until he became familiar with the one, and very skilful in the use of the other. He had, however, hardly begun his military service, into which he entered with all his heart, when he was compelled for a time to abandon it. His brother Lawrence, who had been for some time slowly sinking under a pulmonary disease, was advised by his physician to seek a warmer climate. Not wishing in his delicate state of health to go alone, he took his favourite brother, George, with him, and sailed for Barbadoes in September, 1751.

They were five weeks in making the voyage. Change of climate, however, wrought no permanent change for the better in the invalid, and after staying a few weeks on the island, he resolved to return to

Bermuda. In the mean time, George was seized with the small-pox, and he lay confined for three weeks. Immediately on his recovery, he was despatched by his brother to Virginia, to bring his wife to Bermuda, to join him there. His passage home was a long and stormy one. He was absent in all four months. His brother, finding that he continued to grow worse, wrote home, requesting his wife not to join him. He lingered on till summer, when he came home, and rapidly sank into the grave.

George being left one of the executors of his brother's property, which was very large, his time for awhile became almost exclusively occupied in taking care of it. Mount Vernon, with other estates, had been left to the only surviving daughter, but in case she died without children, they were to go to George.

In the mean time Governor Dinwiddie had divided Virginia into four military divisions, and appointed Washington, whose commission had been renewed, over the northern. This division covered a large territory, which he was required to visit at stated intervals. The militia in the various sections were mustered to receive him when he came, and he reviewed and instructed them, as well as the officers, in the duties of their calling. Very tall and finely formed, he was at this time the impersonation of a fine military character, and carried all the enthusiasm of his ardent nature into the profession so congenial to his tastes, and so in accordance with his love of excitement and adventure.

The French and English were at this time contending for the mastery of the continent. The latter occupied the Atlantic slope, while Canada was in possession of the former, who were making vigorous efforts to control the western lakes and rivers south to the mouth of the Mississippi, and thus shut up the English east of the Alleghany Mountains. Intelligence was soon received that they had already crossed over from Canada, and were erecting fortifications and establishing posts along the Ohio. This was crowding close upon the Virginia province, while, at the same time, it unsettled the Indians, hitherto at peace, so that an ominous cloud was gathering on the frontier. England had anticipated this state of things, and sent over orders to have two forts built on the Ohio, and despatched thirty cannon, with ammunition, to defend them. The French, however, had outstripped the slow movements of their rival, for they had already commenced a line of military posts, to extend from New Orleans to Canada. Their claims to this vast territory were based on the right of discovery and the stipulations of European treaties to which England acceded, viz., that France should retain all her actual possessions in America. By an extraordinary construction the latter insisted that having discovered the Mississippi river, she had a right to all the territories through which its waters flowed. Equally absurd with this claim was that of England, who based her right on Indian treaties, although the tribes with which she made them had no more power to cede away the land west of the Ohio, than they had the west of the Mississippi. On their vague assertion that they had at some former time conquered it, although the present savage occupants yielded them no allegiance, and denied their pretensions, the English made a treaty with them, including vast territories occupied by other independent tribes. The Indians might well be astonished at the turn things had taken, and be puzzled to know what course to pursue. They asked Mr. Gist, who had been sent by Governor Dinwiddie to trade with them, "*whereabout the Indian lands lay, as the French claimed all on one side of the Ohio, and the English all on the other.*" The claims of both England and France rested on a miserable foundation enough; but, so far as the two nations were concerned, the latter had clearly the advantage. It was evident, however, that *might* was to settle the question.

As a first step, Governor Dinwiddie resolved to send a commissioner to the French commander on the Ohio, and demand why he invaded his British majesty's dominions, and what he proposed to do. To undertake this, through nearly six hundred miles of forest filled with Indians and crossed only by trails, required a man of no common intrepidity, fortitude, energy, skill and daring.

There needs no stronger proof of the high estimation in which young Washington, then only twenty-one years old, was held, than the selection of him to perform this hazardous mission. The oldest frontiersman might well have shrunk from it, for it would task the hardihood and endurance of a man trained a life-long in the woods,

His instructions were, to proceed at once to the Ohio, and, assembling the neighbouring Indian chiefs at a place called Logstown, explain his visit, and request an escort of warriors to the French post. After delivering his message and demanding an answer, he was to ascertain, as far as possible, the number, position, and designs of the French.

Thus fortified with instructions, he set out on the last day of October, and, after a journey of fourteen days, reached Will's Creek, the utmost verge of civilization. Here he found Mr. Gist, an old and experienced backwoodsman, and engaged him as a guide. With a French and English interpreter, two Indian traders and two drivers, making in all eight persons, he left the haunts of the white man, and striking an Indian trail, stretched through the wilderness. Floundering through swamps, swimming deep rivers, and straining up the steep mountains, the little company kept on its difficult way, and at length reached the junction of the Alleghany and Monongahela. Washington's quick eye saw at once the advantages of the place, both for a fortification and a depôt for provisions, and by his advice a millitary post was afterward established there.

Pushing on to Logstown, he assembled a few Indian chiefs and made them a speech. Among these, one called the Half-King was the most distinguished. Persuading him, with three other Indians, to accompany him as guides, the young major started for the French fortification, a hundred and twenty miles distant. St. Pierre, the commander of the post, an old man and a knight, received him with marked urbanity. He promised to take Governor Dinwiddie's communication into consideration, and after two days gave his reply, declaring it was not for him to discuss treaties, but obey orders, and he should not leave his post until commanded to do so.

During this time Washington was examining the fort, making drawings of the works, and noting down the number of cannon and men, and strength of the post.

It was now the middle of December; the heavy and incessant rain-storms had turned into snow, obliterating the path and covering the forest with one vast winding-sheet. Fearing that the snow would become so deep that the horses would break down in their long journey across the wilderness, he sent them back to Venango, to wait there and recruit, while he made the passage down the river in a canoe.

The French commandant used every artifice to detach the Half-King from Washington, and not succeeding, determined to detain him till the latter was gone. But the young major, feeling how important it was to keep as allies the tribes over which this chief had influence, was resolved not to leave without him. Winter was deepening, and he was anxious to be off, and he remonstrated with the French commandant on the unfair course he was taking. But every appeal of the straight-forward Virginian was met with the bland smile and courteous denial of a true Frenchman. Being pushed, however, to give a reason for the detention of the savage chief, the wary old knight replied that the latter was waiting for the present of a gun promised him next morning.

The Half-King, having at length obtained his gun, prepared to leave; but the French commandant, still intent on retaining him, endeavoured to get him drunk. Washington, however, never left the Indian's side, and by plying him with appeals and remonstrances, and pressing on him the necessity of keeping his sacred promise, at length had the satisfaction of seeing him depart.

Embarking in a single canoe, they pushed out into the turbulent river, and started for Venango, one hundred and thirty miles distant. It was a perilous voyage, for the stream was swollen and filled with uprooted trees and driftwood, that were hurled along the rapid current on which their frail vessel danced like a feather. As night closed over the forest the canoe was hauled on shore, a fire built, and the party bivouacked on the icy bank till morning. With the dawn the boat was again launched, and went flying down the stream, requiring all the vigilance of eye and hand to keep it from being wrecked. Now they would shoot straight towards a rock, around which the water foamed and boiled in fierce eddies—again glance away from a cliff, against which they threatened to dash, and at last grounded on a deceitful shoal, compelling the whole party to disembark in the icy water. The savage king and the tall young envoy had to wade along, side by side, dragging the boat for half an hour over the pebbles before they could get into deep water again, and then, chilled and dripping, continue their voyage. At length they came upon a barricade of ice, stretching completely across the channel. Around this the canoe had to be carried for a quarter of a mile. They were a whole week making this hundred and thirty miles.

Having at last reached Venango, Washington bade

the Half-King good-bye, with much advice not to let
the fine speeches of the French detach him from his
frendship to the English, and next day struck into
the wilderness. The horses, however, were feeble
and emaciated, and being overloaded with provisons
which the party were obliged to carry with them,
soon began to show symptoms of giving out. In
order to relieve them as much as possible, Washington gave up his own animal for a pack-horse, and,
dressed in an Indian hunting-shirt, waded on foot
through the forest. But the cold becoming intense,
and the soft snow freezing hard, through which the
horses floundered with difficulty, it was evident they
could not proceed ; so after the third day, he left them
and the party in charge of Mr. Vanbraam, and with
Mr. Gist alone set out for the distant colonies. The
tall, handsome, and athletic young Virginian, in his
closely fitting Indian costume, his pack on his back,
his knife in his belt, and his trusty rifle in his hand,
presented a fine contrast to the brawny backwoodsman by his side, as they passed through the primeval
forest together. At the approach of night they kindled a fire, and scraping the snow from a fallen tree
for their table, and cutting 'pieces of bark for plates,
ate with a keen appetite their coarse supper. Then
wrapping themselves in their blankets, with the snow
for their couch, and the sparkling wintry heavens for
their canopy, they lay down to sleep. With the first
streakings of dawn they were again afoot, and through
the blinding storm and under the trees that swayed
and groaned in the fierce December blast, strained
up the steep mountain sides, or threaded the dark
gorges with unflagging spirits and undaunted hearts.
On approaching a spot called Murdering Town, upon
a fork of Beaver creek, they met an Indian, whom
Gist was sure he had seen at Venango, and whose
appearance was suspicious. He, however, seemed very
friendly, was loquacious, asking many questions
about the party behind, their horses etc., and when

they would be along. Major Washington wished to go the shortest routes to the forks of the Alleghany, and asked the Indian if he would be their guide. He readily consented, and taking the major's pack started off. But after travelling eight or ten miles, Washington declared that his feet were sore, his limbs weary, and he must halt. To this the Indian objected, grew churlish, and offered to carry Washington's gun, if he would go on. He said the Ottaway Indians occupied the woods, and if they laid out they would be scalped, and urged them to go to his cabin, from which he declared he just then heard a signal gun, where they would be safe. They kept on for awhile, but Washington's experienced eye soon discovering that they were going the wrong course, he became uneasy and remonstrated with him. The latter, to pacify him, hearkened a moment, and then declared he heard two whoops from his cabin. Washington then went two miles further on, when he declared that at the next water he came to he would halt. Before they reached it, however, they emerged into an open space, on the even snow surface of which the bright moonlight lay. The Indian was some distance ahead, but kept his wary eye on his victims, and, as they stepped from the deep shadow of the forest into the clear light; suddenly turned and levelled his rifle. The next instant a quick, sharp report rang through the woods. Washington immediately cried out to Gist, "Are you shot?" "No," replied the latter, and sprang towards the savage, who had leaped behind a big oak, and begun rapidly to reload his piece. Washington reached the treacherous guide at the same time with Gist, but, instead of seizing him, stood by and saw him ram home a ball without manifesting any suspicion, pretending, on the contrary, to believe that he considered the shot as a signal to those in his cabin. Gist then told Washington he must kill the traitor on the spot. The latter objected —he could not consent to murder the poor wretch there in cold blood, richly as he deserved such a fate. Gist replied that he must then be got away, and they travel all night.

Their position had now become critical; that rifle shot might have had a double purpose—to send one of them to his long account, and at the same time be a signal to companions near by, whose wild whoop might at any moment break on their startled ears. They, however, took the Indian with them, till they came to a little run of water, where they compelled him to make a fire. The guns were stacked against a tree, but either Gist or Washington always stood by them. The keen savage saw he was suspected, and grew uneasy. He still declared, however, that his cabin was but a little way off, and he could soon reach it. Gist then gave him bread, and told him to go home and fetch them some meat in the morning, while they, as they were tired, would encamp where they were. The fellow was glad to get off, and shouldering his rifle, disappeared in the forest. Gist followed him stealthily some distance and then returned. The two adventurers then went on about half a mile and built a fire. By its light they set their compass, took their course, and started forward. Knowing that the Indians, if really in pursuit, would take their trail as soon as it was morning, they kept up a tremendous pace all night. Nor did they slacken it at day-light, except to snatch a mouthful of food, but, weary and sore as they were, travelled all day. Two days and a night on the stretch, without a path to guide them, was terrific work; but it was a matter of life and death, and they never halted till dark, when they struck the Alleghany river. They had expected to find this frozen over, and put it between them and their pursuers before stopping; but the ice extended only about one hundred and fifty feet from either shore, while the channel between was swollen and angry, and loaded with huge fragments of ice which had broken loose

from above.   This abrupt termination of their journey, was heart-sickening enough; and as the two
weary travellers stood on the ice-bound shore and
gazed on the appalling spectacle, they felt that the
crisis of their fate had come.   There was no escape,
and if the savages continued their pursuit, they must
fight them there, whatever their numbers might be.
Nothing, however, was to be done, and wrapping
themselves in their blankets, they lay down upon the
snow and listened to the grinding, crushing sound
of the ice as it drifted down in the gloom.   The ear
was constantly turned to catch the sound of approaching footsteps, while the lonely cries that rose from
the forest combined to render the night long and
dreary.   At daylight they rose from their unquiet,
fitful slumbers, and began to prepare a raft, on which
they could float across.   With but "one poor hatch-
et," to hew down the trees, they commenced their
arduous task.   Its tiny strokes made feeble echoes
along that wintry stream, and it was night-fall before the raft was completed.   They then slid it on
the ice to the edge, and, as it fell heavily in the water,
jumped upon it.   Caught by the current, it was
whirled rapidly down.   They had not proceeded far,
however, before the descending fragments of ice so
pressed upon and jammed it against other pieces,
that it began to sink.   Washington immediately
struck his setting-pole heavily into the mud at the
bottom, to arrest the raft till the ice crowded by.
But the weight of the ice and raft together was so
great, that, when the latter came in contact with the
pole, Washington, who had grasped it firmly, was
jerked over, and fell in ten feet water.   He, however,
succeeded in getting hold of one of the logs, and held
on while the whole mass swept together down the
stream.   Their position was now perilous in the extreme—in the middle of the channel, carried resist-
lessly forward by the current and the ice, they could
reach neither shore.   Fortunately they drifted near

a small island, when, as a last resort, they both
abandoned the raft and made for it. Here on this
mere rock, with an angry and turbulent river on
either side, with no materials to construct a new
raft, with no fire, wet to the skin, they were compelled to pass the long winter's night. To add to their
discomfort, the night set in intensely cold, and it
required the most unwearied efforts and constant
exercise to keep from freezing. As it was, Mr. Gist's
hands and feet were both frozen, and Washington
escaped only by his great powers of endurance, inherent in his constitution, and strengthened by his
long exposure in the woods and mountains. The
frost, however, which well-nigh deprived them of
life, proved their salvation, for it formed a bridge of
ice between the island and eastern shore sufficiently
strong to bear them. Crossing cautiously on this,
they the same day reached a trading post of Mr.
Frazier, near the spot where afterward the battle of
Mononghaela was fought. Here they remained
several days, to procure horses with which to continue their journey. In the mean time Washington
paid a visit to queen Aliquippa, residing near, who
had been very much offended that he did not stop to
see her on his outward journey. An ample apology,
an overcoat, and a bottle of rum, especially the latter,
restored her good humour.

Leaving this trading post the second of January,
Washington continued his journey on horseback.
The intense cold, followed by rain storms, melted
snow and swollen rivers, combined to render the
termination of his route as painful as the middle
portion of it, but after fifteen days of hard labour, he
reached Williamsburg, having been absent in all
eleven weeks. He had accomplished the task assigned him to the letter, and performed one of the most
extraordinary expeditions on record. It is imposси-
ble, at this time, to conceive all the difficulties that
beset it. But whether we take into consideration
the time required to complete it, the country through

which it led—a vast, untrodden wilderness, crossed by mountain ranges, intersected by swollen rivers, and filled with lawless savages—or the season of the year selected—mid-winter—when the difficulties of the way were increased ten-fold by the deep snows, frosts, and sudden thaws, and incessant storms, or the long and dreadful exposures, borne without flinching, it certainly stands without a parallel in the history of our country. From first to last Washington had shown himself a most extraordinary young man. A mere stripling of twenty-one, he exhibited all the energy, self-reliance, endurance, tact, and courage of the most experienced man and veteran. As one in imagination beholds him in his Indian dress, his pack on his back, his gun in his hand, stealing through the snow-covered forest at midnight, or plunging about in the wintry stream in the struggle for life, or, wrapped in his blanket, sleeping beside the ice-filled river, lulled by its sullen roar, he cannot but feel that he beholds a being whom angels guarded through the terrible training which can alone fit him for the great duties and trials that await him.

Washington was highly complimented for the manner in which he had executed the commission that had been entrusted to him. His journal was printed and copied in the colonial newspapers. The English government at home had it reprinted, for it possessed peculiar value, inasmuch as it was the first clear exposition of the designs of the French on this continent, and the first reliable information respecting their past movements. Washington had ascertained, not only how matters stood on the Ohio and the lakes, but also obtained accurate information of the number and strength of their posts and garrisons at the mouth of the Mississippi. The extraordinary character of their claims, demanding all the territory washed by the Mississippi and its branches, aroused the English government to the necessity of immediate action.

CHAPTER II.

Washington sent against the French—Hostilities of the
latter—Fort Duquesne—Difficulties of the March—Dangerous Explorations—Message from the Half-King—
Night March—Attack on Jumonville—Feelings of Washington in his First Battle—Final Results of it—Fort
Necessity—Battle of Great Meadows—Washington Capi-
tulates—Resigns in disgust his Commission—Tart Refusal
to join the Army under Governor Sharpe—Accepts
Braddock's Request to act as Volunteer Aid—Is taken
Sick—Joins the Army—Battle of Monongahela—Bravery
of Washington—The Retreat—Death of Braddock—
Washington reads the Funeral Service—Burial by Torchlight—Scenes around Fort Duquesne—Demoniacal
Jubilee of the Indians—Washington at Mount Vernon—
Disgust with the Government—Appointed Commander-
in-Chief of the Virginia Forces—Head-quarters at Winchester—Inroads of the Indians—Terror of the Settlers—
Sternness of Washington—False Rumours—Difficulty
with Captain Dagworthy—Goes to Boston to refer it to
Governor Shirley—Reception on the way—Falls in love
with Miss Phillips of New York—His Return.

IMMEDIATELY on the return of Washington, Governor Dinwiddie called his council together and laid
before it the letter of the French commander, and the
report of his commissioners. It was resolved at once
to repel this invasion of the king's dominions by
force of arms. To effect this, an enlistment of two
hundred men each was advised, who should proceed
without delay to the Ohio, and erect a fort on its
banks. If there were not a sufficient number of
volunteers to make up the quota, drafts were ordered
to be made on the militia. Washington was appointed commander of this small force, the chief object of which was to bisect the operations of the
French, and prevent them from completing their
chain of posts from Canada to New Orleans. He
was stationed at Alexandria to enlist recruits and

despatch forward the cannon for the fort which the Ohio company had agreed to build.

The Legislature met in February, 1754, but the feelings of the members were not all in harmony with the warlike spirit of the governor—indeed some of them declared they could not see what right England had to those lands. The loyal old governor "fired at this," to think that "an English Legislature should presume to doubt the right of his Majesty to the back of his dominions." Ten thousand pounds, however, were voted for the defence of the colony, which gave the governor great satisfaction, but his ire was again roused when commissioners were appointed to superintend the disbursement of this fund. He nevertheless went diligently to work, and ordered four more companies to be raised, making six in all. Colonel Joshua Fry was appointed commander of these, with Washington raised to the rank of lieutenant-colonel, his second in command. The governor was authorized to call for two independent companies from New York, and one from South Carolina. These were immediately sent for, and in the mean time the cheering news came from North Carolina that she would soon have a force in the field to help to repel the common invader.

Washington having completed two companies, in all one hundred and fifty, self-willed, ungovernable men, left Alexandria in April, and marched for the Ohio, where he was ordered to complete the fort there which a party of men, under Captain Trent, were erecting, and to make prisoners, kill and destroy all who interrupted the English settlements. His march was slow and difficult, and before he reached Will's Creek, the French had descended from Venango, and summoned the force under Captain Trent to surrender. The latter was absent, but Ensign Ward, then in command, agreed to give up the fort if he was permitted to retire with his troops. The trees were felled around the fort, which they named Du Quesne, barracks of bark were thrown up, and before the smoke of the burning trees had scarcely cleared away, corn and wheat were springing up, and the first foundation of Pittsburgh was laid.

Immediately on the reception of this alarming news, Washington sent off expresses to the governors of Virginia, Pennsylvania and Maryland for reinforcements, and then called a council of war. Beset with difficulties, liable at any moment to be surrounded and cut off, he nevertheless resolved to push boldly forward, and, if possible, reach the Monongahela and erect a fortification. With his little force swelled to three hundred men, he entered the forest and began to cut his way through the wilderness. This was slow and tedious, for all the deep streams had to be bridged, the swamps filled up, dug-ways made along the sides of the mountains, and a grade and smoothness obtained sufficient to allow the passage of baggage-waggons. Reaching at length the Youghogany, a halt was made, till a bridge could be built across the stream. Being told here by some Indians that the river was navigable to its junction with boats, Washington took with him five men and proceeded down, to ascertain if it were so. The navigation of the stream proved extremely perilous, for he got entangled amid rocks and shoals, and was borne through dangerous rapids. At length, however, he entered a gorge made by two high precipitous mountains, where the stream, compressed between the cliffs, became very deep, and, ceasing its tortuous course, flowed in a straight, rapid current on. Borne swiftly and smoothly along, Washington proceeded for ten miles, when he came to a fall. This abrubtly terminated his explorations, and he returned to his army. He had scarcely reached it, when a string of wampum was received from his old friend, the Half-King, telling him that the French were advancing, and saying, "Come soon, or we are lost, and shall

never meet again.   I speak it in the grief of my
heart." Washington immediately ordered the troops
under arms, and pushed forward.   Without tents,
scantily supplied with clothes and provisions, en-
camping under the open sky, pelted by the rains,
fording the streams, and wearily dragging their
cannon after them, they marched slowly on, while
insubordination and complaints swelled the evils that
encompassed the young commander.   On the 25th
another message was received from the Half-King,
saying, "Be on your guard; the French army intend
to strike the first English whom they shall see."
The same day a second messenger entered the camp,
reporting that the French were but eighteen miles
distant.   Ignorant of their number, or from what
point they would attack, he hastened to the Great
Meadows, an open plain between two ridges, covered
with grass and low bushes.   Near the centre, where
it was about three hundred yards wide, and beside a
rivulet that flowed through it, he hastily threw up
an intrenchment, and prepared to meet the enemy.
As he looked around and saw what a broad interval
lay between his rude works and the covering forest,
he felt satisfied with the spot he had selected, declaring it was a "charming field for an encounter."
In the mean time he sent out some men on the
waggon-horses to reconnoitre, and all eyes were directed toward the forest, in constant expectation of
seeing them burst into the opening, bringing the
enemy with them.   But they returned without seeing any traces of the invaders.   In the night, however, the sentries became alarmed, and fired their
pieces.   In a moment the little camp was in commotion, and the troops stood to their arms till morning.
Soon after day-light a single man was seen moving
across the plain toward the fort.   This was Gist,
who reported the French near by.   The day wore on
without further cause of alarm; but at nine o'clock
at night the camp was again thrown into a state of

excitement, by the arrival of a messenger from the Half-King, who lay with his warriors about six miles distant, reporting that the French detachment was close by him. It was pitch-dark, and the rain fell in torrents, but young Washington, as he stood by the fire listening to the statement of the swarthy messenger, forgot both, and instantly selecting forty of his best men, started for the camp of the Half-King. Utter blackness filled the forest, and it was impossible to keep the right direction. Stumbling over the rocks and fallen trees, the little band staggered about in the darkness, the pattering of the rain-drops above, and their constant dripping on the foliage below, the only sounds that broke the surrounding stillness, save when the musket-barrel of some poor fellow, tripping in the gloom, rung against a tree or rock, or the low words of command fell from their intrepid leader, as he felt his way toward his first battle. They wandered about in the woods all night, and did not reach the camp of the Half-King till sunrise. A short council was then held, in which it was resolved to send forward two Indian scouts to ascertain the precise locality of the French. Following up the trail, these soon discovered the enemy concealed among the rocks. Streaming along in Indian file, Washington, with his savage allies, at length came in sight of the party. The latter, immediately on discovering the hostile approach, seized their arms and prepared to resist. "Fire!" cried Washington, and at the same moment discharged his musket. A rapid volley followed, and for fifteen minutes it was sharp work. Jumonville, the French commander, and ten of his men were killed, and twenty-two taken prisoners. The remainder fled. Washington had but one man killed and three wounded. It was his first battle, and the excitement was naturally great. In speaking of it afterward, he said, "I heard the bullets whistling, and believe me, there is something charming in the sound." In this first trial he showed the metal he was made of, and although the speech smacks of bravado it reveals the ardour and enthusiasm, without which the soldier never excels in his profession.

Probably there never before turned such vast consequences on a single musket-shot as on that fired by Washington in the commencement of this skirmish. Its echo went round the globe; it was the signal-gun breaking up the councils and diplomatic meetings of Europe, and summoning the two greatest powers of the world to arms to struggle for a continent. It began the long war which drove France out of America, and made a warlike people of the colonists, who were jealous of their rights. When the revolutionary struggle afterwards commenced France was but too glad to help to despoil England of the rich possessions of which the latter had robbed her, and saw with undisguised pleasure an independent government rise on these shores. But the French army, in helping republicanism, became republican, and scattered the doctrine of human rights throughout France. Her bloody revolution was the result. Met by the feudalism of Europe, it went rolling over the French borders, deluging the continent in its rash flow. The shout of the oppressed masses was heard rising amid the dim of battle, and the low and threatening under-tone of their mutterings makes monarchs at this day turn pale on their thrones, while the end is not yet.

What a long and frightful train of events that shot set in motion. When the news reached France, it threw both government and people into a state of high excitement. War had begun, and the name of Washington was heard for the first time in the saloons of Paris, and loaded with opprobrium. His attack was declared base and wicked, and Jumonville was regarded as the victim of assassination. A poem was written to commemorate his sad fate, and

Washington was looked upon as no better than a robber. It was asserted that Jumonville was on a peaceful mission, and had begun to read the summons he bore, when Washington fired upon him. This was false, and expressly declared so by the latter. The fact that Jumonville was entrusted with a summons commanding the English to evacuate the territory, does not make his mission a peaceful one. Besides, he did not advance like one on a friendly errand, but lay skulking about with an armed force. Washington, when sent by Dinwiddie to the French, took only necessary guides. If with a body of troops, he had laid for days about the fort, and when assailed had made no effort at explanation, but continued to fight till overpowered, it would have been perfectly absurb to pretend that he was on a peaceful mission. Still, French writers denounced Washington unsparingly, and to this day pronounce his attack unlawful and wicked. But the blame, whether much or little, rested on Governor Dinwiddie, not on himself, for the former had directed him to drive the French from the English territory, and he had been sent out with an armed force for that express purpose. He could not have done otherwise than obey the orders of the government. The fact that war had not been declared could make no difference, for the French had already commenced hostilities, by investing an English fort and forcing the garrison to capitulate. To expect Washington to sit still and see a second taken without striking a blow, would be absurb.

The latter, knowing that as soon as the news of his attack on Jumonville should reach Fort Du Quesne, a heavier force would be sent against him, retired at once to his little fort, which he named Fort Necessity.

But while compelled to prepare for the exigencies growing out of a superior force in his front, he had also to contend with the insubordination of his troops,

especially the officers, whose pay had been reduced
so low, that it would not meet their necessary expenses, and who, indignant at the meanness of the
government, declared they would go home and leave
the army to take care of itself. Washington, in this
dilemma, put on the "hypocrite as far as he could,"
and endeavoured to convince them it was better and
more honourable to remain where they were, while
at the same time he wrote to Governor Dinwiddie,
stating the feelings of the officers, and remonstrating
boldly against the insane policy which made them
inferior to the king's officers. He declared, so far as
he was concerned, it was not the smallness of the pay
that made him indignant, but the injustice and dis-
honour of this invidious distinction, while in fact the
services he and his fellow officers were required to
perform, were enormous and hazardous in the extreme. "For my own part," said he, "it is a
matter almost indifferent whether I serve for full
pay, or a generous volunteer. Indeed, did my circumstances correspond with my inclinations, I should
not hesitate a moment to prefer the latter; for the
motives that have led me here are pure and noble."
Here in the midst of the forest, liable at any moment
to be struck down, by an act of executive authority,
he nevertheless kindles into stern indignation against
the wrong committed by that authority, and demands
a recognition of those claims of his officers and men,
which he deems to be just and honourable.

While thus surrounded by a murmuring army—
threatened by a superior enemy, and destitute of the
necessary provisions for his detachment, he received
word of the death of his senior in rank, Colonel Fry,
at Will's Creek. He was now commander-in-chief.
But soon after, an independent company from South
Carolina arrived, commanded by Captain Mackay,
who, having a royal commission, ranked Washington. Here a new difficulty arose, and had not
Mackay been a thorough gentleman, it would have

been a serious one. The latter, however, contented himself with a mild refusal to obey the colonel's orders, and with his one hundred men encamped by himself. Washington, foreseeing the embarrassment in which this divided command would place the entire force, wrote to Governor Dinwiddie to settle the difficulty by a direct explicit order. The latter refused to take the responsibility of deciding on so grave a matter as who should command four hundred men; and Washington, in order to avoid a quarrel, determined with his troops to leave the fort, and advance to the Monongahela, while Captain Mackay remained at Fort Necessity. The nearest practicable route to Gist's settlement, thirteen miles distant, was through a terrific mountain gorge. Compelled to hew and dig a road that would admit the transportation of cannon, beset by friendly Indians, delayed by their troublesome councils and importunities, and deceived by spies, he occupied two weeks in making this short march.

Having at length arrived there, Washington sent out scouts, who kept him informed of all the movements at Fort Du Quesne. Being at length convinced that large reinforcements had arrived from Canada, he called a council of war, to determine what course should be pursued. At first it was resolved to make a stand where they were, and a fortification was commenced, and a messenger despatched to Mackay to hasten forward. The latter, like a true soldier, immediately marched to their relief; when another council was called, in which it was decided, that the enemy being in such heavy force, it would be more prudent to retreat. This was no easy matter, and at the same time drag nine swivels over the rough road that lay between the settlement and Fort Necessity. There were but few horses, and those comparatively worthless, so that soldiers were compelled to man the drag-ropes. To set a good example, and encourage and render cheerful the men, Washington gave up his own horse to carry the public stores, and paid the soldiers for transporting his necessary baggage. By dint of great labour they got back to the Great Meadows in two days. They could, however, go no farther, for they had been without bread eight days, and, weary and half-famished, found only two bags of flour at the fort. The want of horses and provisions, together with the news that two New York companies had twenty days before arrived at Alexandria, and hence must now be very near them, induced Washington to order a halt, and begin to intrench himself as best he might where he was. An express was sent to these New York companies to hurry forward, and every effort put forth to strengthen the impromptu works of Fort Necessity.

At length, on the morning of July 30th, a musket-shot was heard, and soon after a sentinel, who had been wounded by the enemy, came limping in. Scouts who had been sent out returned breathless with haste, saying that the enemy, nine hundred strong, was only four miles distant. This was stirring news, and Washington immediately drew up his little band of four hundred outside the trenches, and gave the orders not to fire till the enemy was close enough to let their volleys tell. At eleven o'clock the French approached, but halted when six hundred yards distant and commenced firing. Washington, after receiving their fire for some time, and seeing that they had no intention of attempting to carry the works by assault, as he expected, marched his men in again, and told them to fire when and how they pleased. That little breast-work was soon blazing with the irregular volleys. The French however remained at such a distance, and were so sheltered by the trees, that but little execution was done. The rain fell in torrents all day, drenching both armies and filling the trenches round the fort with water. This, however, did not cool the combatants, and a sharp fire was kept up the whole day, and, as twilight deepened over the dripping forest, its dark arcades were lit up by incessant flashes. But at eight in the evening the French called a parley, and requested an officer to be sent to them. Vonbraam, a Dutchman, being the only man that could speak French, was despatched, and soon returned with a paper containing articles of capitulation. Washington and his officers knew it would be impossible to hold out long against their adversaries, for the latter could starve them into submission in a short time, and, as the terms proposed were honourable, he accepted them. He and his band were allowed to march out of the fort with drums beating and colours flying, and retire without molestation to the settlements, taking everything with them but the artillery. Washington, on the other hand, agreed to restore the prisoners taken in his attack on Jumonville, and not build any more forts west of the mountains for a year. These articles, when they were afterward published, were severely criticised. They contained things Washington should not have consented to, and of which he was entirely ignorant at the time of the capitulation. The Dutch interpreter had intentionally, or through ignorance, deceived him. When he returned with the articles of capitulation it was raining so heavily, that a candle could with great difficulty be kept burning while he gave a free translation. Under the circumstances a written translation could not be made, and Washington had to depend on the faithfulness of the verbal one. In this nothing was said respecting the erection of forts *"west of the Alleghanies,"* but the specification on the point was rendered *not to attempt building or improvements on the lands belonging to the French king.* To this general promise there could be no objection, as no limits were designated. Again, in the written articles the "*death of Jumonville*" was called an "*assassination;*" while the interpreter used the *former* expression in translating them.

Twelve of Washington's command were killed and forty-three wounded. The former he buried in the forest, and with the latter took up his weary march back to the settlements.

The governor and council approved his course, and the House of Burgesses, when it assembled, passed a vote of thanks to him and his officers.

Washington rejoined his regiment at Alexandria, where he was ordered to fill up the diminished companies and march to Will's creek, to join Colonel Innies, who was then building Fort Cumberland. In short, the ardent governor had planned a winter campaign, in a country where there were no roads, no supplies, no forts, expecting to be carried forward by troops without arms, ammunition, provisions or tents. Washington told him the thing was absolutely impossible, and the order was countermanded.

The Assembly when it met voted twenty thousand pounds for the public service. This with ten thousand sent over by the English government, put Dinwiddie in funds again, and he set about enlarging the army, by the addition of ten companies of a hundred men each. These were to be independent, and the officers of them to rank with those of the same grade in the Virginia regiment, while the highest officers of the latter were reduced to captains. Resenting this degradation as a personal insult, Washington threw up his commission and left the army.

Shortly after, Governor Sharpe of Maryland, being appointed commander-in-chief of the forces destined to act against the French, solicited Washington to take his place again in the army, hinting that he might retain his old commission. The latter took fire at this, and wrote a tart reply to the governor, saying, "If you think me capable of holding a commisson that has neither rank nor emolument annexed to it, you must entertain a very contemptible opinion of my weakness, and believe me to be more empty than the commission itself."

It was with deep regret that he gave up his profession, for he was exceedingly attached to it, and was ambitious of military distinction. He did not, however, long remain idle, for the next spring [March 15th, 1754] General Braddock arrived from England, with two regiments of regular troops. These were expected to crush all opposition and sweep the French from the frontiers. Washington, who had thus far effected all that had been done, was requested by Braddock to form one of his staff, holding his former rank in the army. To this he acceded, solely, as he avowed, for the purpose of saving his country; for he expected no emoluments, whatever the result of the expedition might be, as he had resolved to accept no commission from Braddock.

The march of this army of more than two thousand men was looked upon as the forerunner of the certain destruction of the French, and a subscription paper was actually circulated in Philadelphia to raise money for the celebration of the victory on its return.

Washington joined it at Winchester, and was received in a flattering manner by the officers. The army then started for the interior, and reached Will's creek about the middle of May. Soon after Washington was sent to Williamsburg to procure money. On his return the main body was put in motion, advancing slowly, dragging its artillery with difficulty over the uneven roads, and stretching for four miles through the forest, as if on purpose to invite an attack. Washington urged on Braddock the necessity of greater despatch, and began already to feel uneasiness at the unwieldiness of this straggling army; he even gave up his own horse to assist in transporting the baggage.

At last he was taken sick with a fever, which raged more or less for fourteen days. At the expiration of that time, he endeavoured to overtake the army. Unable to sit on a horse, he rode in a covered waggon, but the jolting so distressed him that he was compelled to stop on the road, under the charge of a guard. His restlessness under this delay was very great, and nothing but the solemn promise of General Braddock that he should be brought up before the attack on the French at Fort Du Quesne was made, quieted him. To have the finishing battle to take place and he not present, was a thought he could not endure.

At length, though in a weak, exhausted condition, he came up with the army, on the last of June, at the Great Crossing, a few days before the battle of Monongahela. On the morning of the 9th of July, Braddock forded the Monongahela, just below the junction of the Youghogany, and moved in beautiful order, to the sound of stirring music, along the bank of that quiet stream—the scarlet uniforms of the soldiers contrasting richly with the wealth of green on every side. As Washington's eye fell on this military pageant, new to him, and saw nearly two thousand bayonets flashing in the morning sunbeams, and moving in steady undulations over the plain, as to the tread of a single man, while the summer forests echoed to the roll of the drum and bugle blast, his young heart kindled with enthusiasm, and he declared it was the most glorious spectacle he ever beheld.

About noon the army again waded the Monongahela, and began to move over the triangle toward the forks of the two rivers, where, seven miles distant, they united to ford the Ohio. A detachment of three hundred and fifty men, under Lieutenant-Colonel Gage, was sent in advance, attended by a working party of two hundred and fifty more. Braddock followed with the artillery, the main army, and baggage. The French had selected an admirable place for an ambuscade. A gentle slope, gashed by two ravines that extended from top to bottom on either side, covered with trees and long grass, furnished a secure hiding place, while at the same time, it enabled them t pour a double flank fire on the ascending force.   Sud denly, while Gage was moving up this gentle slope, along a path only twelve feet wide, a close and deadly volley smote his uncovered ranks. Volley after volley followed in quick succession, and encircled with fire, rolling on them from an unseen foe, the soldiers broke and fled down the hill. Falling on the artillery and baggage, struggling up from below, they threw these into confusion also. Braddock endeavoured in vain to restore order. The fire, which seemed to issue from the bowels of the earth, closed on them closer and deadlier every moment, and the ranks melted away like frost-work. The Virginian regiment wished to take to the trees, and fight the Indians in their own fashion, but Braddock forbade them, and endeavoured to form close columns, which only allowed death to traverse his ranks with more rapid footsteps. Confused by this new mode of fighting, and by the unearthly yells of the Indians, the regular troops lost all discipline—they fired wildly, without seeing the enemy, and would not obey their officers. A few discharges of grape up these ravines would have forced the enemy from their place of concealment, or a single steady charge of bayonets, scattered the Indians in affright. But neither was done, and for more than two hours those bewildered troops were held by their officers to that fatal spot, only to be shot down. Braddock had five horses killed under him in succession, and, at length was hurled to the ground by a ball through his lungs. The officers struggled bravely, charging together like common infantry, to stimulate their followers to bear up against the storm, and presented a spectacle of devotion on that ill-fated field. Braddock's two aids were borne wounded from the battle, leaving Washington alone to distribute orders. Here his military qualities shone forth in great splendour. Though pale and feeble, he forgot his exhausted condition in the excitement of the moment, and with his fine face lit up with the fire of enthusiasm, he galloped through the disordered host, his tall form presenting a constant mark to the sharp-shooters, whose bullets rattled on every side like hail-stones around him. Men were falling on every side, almost entire companies at a time, yet reckless of dan-ger he spurred his steed over the dead and dying alike, straining every nerve to save the battle and the army. Two horses were shot under him, but he rose each time from the earth unharmed. Four balls passed through his coat. An old chief singled him out and bade his young braves do the same, but after striving in vain to hit him, became alarmed, and told his men to desist from firing at one who was plainly under the care of the great Manitou. Cool and self-possessed the young aid stood like a rock on that turbulent field, and to see him endeavour to stem the panic and dis-order, one would have thought he had been tried in a hundred battles, than of being, as he was, in his first field fight.

Of eighty-three officers, sixty-three had fallen; while half the entire army was stretched on the field. Of three Virginia companies, only thirty men were left standing, and scarcely a single officer re-mained unwounded. Washington saw his brave Virginians thus uselessly sacrificed with a bursting heart. But faithful to the orders given them, they formed a glorious example to the cowardly regulars, on whom threats, entreaties, and the noble devotion of their officers were alike thrown away. At length the turbulent mass turned in flight, and over the dead and dying, and over their own cannon, went streaming along the road like a herd of frightened animals. All the provision and baggage, even the general's private papers, were left behind in the panic. Washington rode hither and thither, endea-vouring to rally a rear-guard, but was borne help-lessly along in the living torrent. Braddock was carried from the field in a tumbril, but being unable to bear the motion, was transferred to a litter and hurried forward. All day long he never spoke, but at night he seemed to rouse for a moment, and ex-claimed in amazement, "*Who would have thought it?*" Reaching Dunbar's camp, the panic was com-municated to the garrison there, and burning the public stores and baggage, and destroying the artil-lery, the entire army fleeing from its own shadow streamed on through the forest. Life was fast ebb-ing away from the stunned and discomfited general, and he lay in a half stupour; as if struggling with some dreadful dream. At night he at length roused again, saying, "We shall better know how to deal with them another time." But he had done with all future time, and was already entering the calm world where the sound of battle never comes. The litter on which he lay was set down, and his remaining officers gathered sadly around it. As a last token of gratitude to his young volunteer aid, for his noble devotion and heroism, he gave him a splendid charger and his own body servant. A brief farewell—a faint grasp—a weak struggle—and Braddock lay a corpse in the forest. A grave was hastily dug in the centre of the road, to conceal it from the Indians, into which, with his sword laid across his breast, he was lowered. Young Washington read the funeral ser-vice by torchlight over him, the deep tones of his voice interrupted only by the solemn amen of the surrounding officers. The motionless torch-bearers—the encircling forest, with its dimly lighted corri-dors—the long line of receding bayonets flashing in the light—the uncovered officers—the open grave, and beside it the pale face of the sleeper, combined to form a scene at once picturesque and most solemn. A mark was left to designate the spot, and the army again defiled through the wilderness. Alone, the defeated warrior lay in his rude grave, safe from the mortification and anguish that awaited him in the settlements and in the army. The place of his burial can still be seen, a little off from the national road, and about a mile from Fort Necessity.

All this time a far different scene was passing around Fort Du Quesne. The Indian allies of the French were frantic with joy, for never before had they reaped such a rich harvest of white men. The slope up which Braddock had attempted to force his way, was literally crowded with the dead and wounded, the scarlet uniforms of whom contrasted brightly with the green grass over which they were sprinkled. The tomahawk was soon crushing through skulls in which brain still throbbed with life, and the scalping-knife glancing around the heads of those already dead. At night the woods surrounding the fort exhibited a perfect Pandemonium. The exultant yells and frantic movements of the Indians as they danced and shouted together, shaking their bloody arms and knives above their heads, the heavy explosions of the cannon from the fort, mingling in with the incessant discharge of small arms without, combined to form one of the most frightful exhibitions the eye ever rests upon. The next day the savages painted themselves in the most gaudy colours, and, dressed in the scarlet uniforms of the soldiers, and the rich apparel and chapeaux of the officers, paraded around the fort in ludicrous ostentation.

The English army at length reached the settlements, sending consternation and affright through the colonies, and Washington retired to Mount Vernon.

It was well for Braddock that he reposed in the forest, for it would have been worse than death to have met the deep and utter condemnation of the people. But from the general obloquy that fell on nearly all connected with this ill-fated expedition, Washington was not only exempted, but received laudations innumerable. His gallantry, his chivalric bearing, and his miraculous escape, were the theme of every tongue. Said Davis, a distinguished clergyman, in referring to this defeat in a sermon, " I point out that heroic youth, Colonel Washington, whom I *cannot but hope Providence has preserved, in so signal a manner, for some important service to his country."* A remarkable prophecy, as thus uttered from the pulpit. "Who," said Lord Halifax, in a letter to a friend, "is Mr. Washington? I know nothing of him, but that they say he behaved in Braddock's action as bravely as though he really loved the whistling of bullets."

·Either Washington's conduct during this campaign has been most imperfectly given, or he at this early age possessed that strange power over others, which later in life formed one of his great characteristics. He was only a provincial officer and a volunteer, and it was not merely because he behaved gallantly in battle, like all the rest, that his dying commander bequeathed to him his faithful servant, or that his superiors selected him as the most fitting officer to act as chaplain. His bearing, language, actions, all must have possessed extraordinary attractions.

Disgusted with the ignominious termination of Braddock's campaign, still feeble and wasted from his five weeks' fever, followed, as it had been, by such exhausting labours and mental anxiety, Washington hailed the quiet retreat of Mount Vernon with the pleasure that the tost mariner greets the sight of land. Nothing but a frame of prodigious strength, and a constitution to match it, could have carried him through what he had undergone. But on the tranquil shores of the Potomac, his health gradually recruited, yet for a time he seemed little inclined to enter again the stormy scenes into which he had been thrown for the last two years. He was now but twenty-three years of age, and yet had passed through vicissitudes and trials sufficient for a lifetime.

He was not, however, long allowed to lay becalmed in the bay where he had sought shelter. His conduct in the battle of Monongahela, coupled with his former services, made him the most marked military man in the colony, and pointed him out as the proper leader of its forces.

The Assembly was in session at this time, in Williamsburg, and several of the members, one being his elder brother, wrote him, requesting his presence there, as it would facilitate a plan they had formed to get him the appointment of commander-in-chief of the forces of the colony. To these invitations Washington replied, that if there were no other reasons to prevent his complying, his health alone would be a sufficient excuse, as it was with the utmost difficulty he could ride over his different plantations. To his brother he wrote that he was always willing to render his country any service he was capable of, but never upon the terms he had done—impairing his fortune, and ruining the "best of constitutions," and receiving nothing but neglect in return. Said he, "I was employed to go a journey in the winter, when I believe few or none would have undertaken it—and what did I get by it? *My expenses borne!* I then was appointed, with trifling pay, to conduct a band of men to the Ohio. What did I get by that? Why, after putting myself to a considerable expense in equipping and providing necessaries for the campaign, I went out, was soundly beaten, and lost them all! Came in and had my commission taken from me, or in other words, my command reduced, under pretence of an order from home! I then went out a volunteer with General Braddock, lost all my horses, and many other things. But this being a voluntary act, I ought not to have mentioned it, nor should I have done it, were it not to show that I have been on the losing order ever since I entered the service, which is now nearly two years." A sorry picture, truly, of his past experience; and the young and fiery commander, now thoroughly aroused, will have nothing more to do with a government so reckless of his rights and so destitute of common justice. His

indignation at the course it has pursued, at length
finds utterance, and he will no longer be made the
plaything of power.

To Warner Lewis, another member who had written him on the same subject, he declared he would
never accept the command if tendered, unless something certain was secured to him, and he was allowed to designate who should be his subordinate officers.
He would not again put himself in positions where his
life and honour depended on the behaviour of his officers,
unless he could have the selection of them.   A small
military chest, he also considered indispensable to the
proper management of military affairs.

In the mean time, however, his appointment had
been made out.   Forty thousand pounds for the public service ; three hundred pounds to Washington,
and appropriate sums to the subordinate officers.   It
was resolved to increase the Virginia regiment to
sixteen companies, and grant to Washington all that
he had demanded, besides giving him an aid-de-camp
and secretary.   As soon as the news of his appointment reached him, he set off for Williamsburg, notwithstanding his feeble health, to consult with the
governor about future operations.   He was too sick
to ride a hundred and sixty miles to beg for office, but
not to fulfil his duties when given him.   He was too
sick in the Alleghany mountains to have travelled
back to his home, where he could find comfort and
good nursing, but not too sick to hurry forward to
the battle of Monongahela, and rage like a lion over
the lost field.   He never was too sick to do his duty
or to save his country.

Having settled upon a plan with the governor,
Washington immediately made every department of
the military organization of the state feel his energy.
Fixing his head-quarters at Winchester, he sent out
recruiting officers to fill up his regiment, the estimates
of which he sent to the governor, and then once more
turned his horse's head toward the Alleghany moun-

tains, which from boyhood had been the scene of his thrilling adventures.   Once more, elate with hope, he entered their rugged passes, and going from post to post, visited every one on the frontier from Fort Din- widdie, on Jackson's river, to Fort Cumberland. He observed every thing, learned every thing to be gained, and issued orders to each in turn.   He then started for Williamsburg, to consult with the gover- nor, but had proceeded only part of the way when he was overtaken by an express declaring that the In- dians had suddenly burst upon the settlements, mur- dered the inhabitants, blocked up the rangers in small fortresses, and were spreading devastation and terror on every side.   He immediately galloped back to Winchester, summoned the militia, called on the recruits to hasten to head-quarters, and soon had a respectable force under his command.   The report, however, was exaggerated, but nothing could allay the terror of the inhabitants, who swarmed in droves across the valley between the Blue Ridge and the Alleghanies; many not stopping till they had put the last mountain barrier between them and the enemy.

The colonies, at this early period, were so tenacious of their liberties, that very little power was given to the commander over the militia or civil authorities. The evil of this Washington soon felt in the insub- ordination of his troops, and the stubborn refusal of the settlers to assist him in transporting his men and baggage.   He was compelled to impress waggons and men into the service, and enforce every order by his " own drawn sword" over the head of the delinquent, or by the bayonets of a party of his soldiers.   This so exasperated the inhabitants that they threatened to blow out his brains.   He, however, by his strong arm, kept down both open mutiny and rebellion, and pushed forward his plans with all the energy he pos- sessed.   Meanwhile [Oct. 11th, 1755,] he wrote to the governor, detailing the difficulties under which he laboured, and requesting that more power should be delegated to the commander-in-chief.

While things were in this disordered state, there came on Saturday night an express, panting with fear and exhaustion, announcing that a party of Indians were only twelve miles off, driving the frightened inhabitants from their dwellings. Washington immediately strengthened the town-guards, and ordered the troops to be armed, while he sent out two scouts to give notice of the approach of the savages. At daylight a second express arrived, "ten times more terrified than the former," declaring that the Indians were within four miles of the town, "killing and destroying all before them;" that he had heard the shrieks and cries of the murdered. The whole place was immediately thrown into the wildest commotion. Washington, hastily collecting forty men, sallied forth, and marched rapidly toward the place where this scene of carnage was transpiring. As he approached it he heard the firing of guns, and shouts and horrid imprecations. But on advancing nearer he discovered that all this uproar was caused by "three drunken soldiers of the light-horse," who, in the midst of their debauch, amused themselves by uttering blasphemies and firing their pistols in the air. Peremptorily ordering them under arrest, he marched them back to town. On his arrival he met the spies sent out the night before, who reported that the party of Indians first discovered consisted of a mulatto and negro, whom a child had seen hunting cattle. The child had told her story to her father, the father to the neighbourhood, and the inhabitants, terrified out of reason, had abandoned their homes and fled to a place of refuge. The next day other scouts, who had been sent farther on, returned with letters from the outposts, stating that the Indians had gone off. They were supposed to be about one hundred and fifty in number, and had in their raid into the distant settlements, killed and taken prisoners about seventy men, and destroyed several plantations and horses.

The panic of the inhabitants at those massacres reached almost to frenzy, and they crowded the roads across the Blue Ridge, so that it was with difficulty a company of rangers could effect a passage.

But the Indians having retired, Washington repaired to the seat of goverment, and, by dint of perseverance, prevailed on the assembly to pass a bill giving power to the commander to hold court-martials and punish mutiny, desertion and disobedience. Having accomplished this he returned to head-quarters in better spirits, and began to prepare for an early spring campaign. Sometimes at Alexandria and again at Fort Cumberland, going from post to post, and placing everything on the best possible footing that his means allowed, he passed the latter part of autumn and the first half of winter. His duties were laborious and harassing in the extreme, and he here had an admirable training in the school of patience, which enabled him afterward to bear with the meanness, dilatoriness, and inefficiency of Congress.

In the mean time an event occurred, which shows to what a ruinous point the petty rivalries and jealousies of officers, and the spirit of insubordination had reached in the colonies. At Fort Cumberland was stationed a Captain Dagworthy, who had been put there by Governor Sharpe of Maryland. Having held a royal commission, he considered himself superior in rank to any provincial officer, and hence refused to pay any regard to Washington's orders. This, of course, the latter would not submit to, and wrote to Governor Dinwiddie for express orders on the subject. But the wary governor remembering that he himself had formerly sanctioned this very assumption of rank of the regular commissioned officers over the provincials of higher grade, and reflecting, too, that the fort was in the province of Maryland, whose governor he knew upheld the captain, he refused to give any orders. He did not hesitate, however, to intimate pretty clearly that Washington had better arrest the refractory captain. But the latter was not thus to be caught, and wrote back that his authority must be confirmed, or he should at once resign his commission. As a last resort, it was proposed to refer the matter to Governor Shirley, in Boston, who at this time was commander-in-chief of the British forces in the colonies. Washington was appointed bearer of his own petition, and on the 4th of February, accompanied by his aid-de-camp Captain Mercer, and Captain Stewart, set out on horseback for Boston. That a paltry captain, commanding only thirty men, should thus arrest the military operations of a whole state, and send the commander-in-chief of its forces five hundred miles, in the dead of winter, on horseback, to settle whether he should obey orders given for mutual benefit and the common good, seems, at this day, quite incomprehensible. But this peculiar sensitiveness respecting individual rights, though often exhibiting itself in absurd forms, was nevertheless necessary to the development of that spirit of resistance to the encroachments of the mother country, which afterward secured our independence.

Accompanied by his two subordinates, the young colonel took his long, cold, and dreary journey northward. The report of his chivalric and gallant character had preceded him, and he was every where received with courtesy and honour. Valuable acquaintances were formed and useful knowledge gained. Mr. Beverly Robinson, a strong loyalist, and in the Revolution afterward a Tory, received him at New York as his guest, and entertained him with rare hospitality. A sister of Mrs. Robinson was staying in the family at the time, whose beauty and winning manners soon took captive the chivalric heart of the young southern colonel. He had forgotten his lowland beauty, and when he bade adieu to the hospitable mansion of Mr. Robinson, to prosecute his journey to Boston, he felt that he had left a large portion of his happiness behind him.

Having obtained full and ample authority from Governor Shirley, he returned to New York, and was again placed under the influnce of Miss Phillips' charms. Lingering here as long as duty would permit him, he at length turned his reluctant footsteps southward. Whether he gave the lady any indications of his passion, or whether he resolved to wait till more leisure would furnish him a better opportunity of renewing his suit, does not appear. At all events, he was deeply in love, and could not leave until he had confessed it to a friend, and engaged him to keep watch of her movements, so that if any rival appeared he could be informed of it at once. In a short time a young officer, one of Braddock's aids and an acquaintance of Washington, became a suitor of Miss Phillips. Washington's friend immediately wrote him of the dangerous state of affairs, and told him, if he wished to win the lady, he must come on at once. But whether the duties of his command detained him at home, or whether, having ascertained the name of his rival, he was too magnanimous to endeavour to supplant him, was never known. She, however, passed away with the "lowland beauty," leaving the young colonel to forget his passion in the exciting scenes of the camp.

Reaching Williamsburg about the time of the meeting of the assembly, he set about arranging with the governor a plan for the summer campaign. The want of artillery, means of transportation, etc., rendered offensive operations impossible, and it was resolved simply to defend the frontier already occupied by British outposts. The jealousy of the separate states preventing them from uniting in a common campaign against the French, Virginia, which was most threatened, was left alone to defend her extensive borders. A bill was therefore passed to raise the army to fifteen hundred men, and another for drafting the militia, when recruits were wanting.

CHAPTER III.

Fresh Hostilities of the Indians—Attempts to Supersede
Washington—Anonymous Libels—Washington wishes
to Resign—Prevented by his Friends—Establishes a Line
of Forts—Harassing Nature of his Duties—Attends a
Convention at Philadelphia—His Sickness and Retirement to Mount Vernon—Progress of the War—Frederick
the Great—Washington's first Acquaintance with Mrs.
Custis—Advance of the Army to Fort Du Quesne—
Washington required to cut a New Road—His Forebodings likely to prove true—Capture of the Fort—Election of Washington to the House of Burgesses—His
Marriage—Life at Mount Vernon—Collision with a
Poacher—Settles the Soldiers' Claims—Expedition to the
Western Wilderness to examine the Wild Lands—Admirable Preparation for his Future Career.

WASHINGTON repaired to head-quarters at Winchester. But few troops, however, were there, the
greater part being stationed in the different forts on
the frontier.

The savages, emboldened by the long inaction of
the whites, began to hover in dark and threatening
war clouds around the settlements. The more remote ones being abandoned, the Indians pushed forward to those beyond the Blue Ridge, and swooped
down around the very head-quarters of the commander-in-chief. Scouting parties were driven in—
forts boldly attacked, and officers killed. The woods
seemed alive with the lurking foe—men were shot
down in the field, and women and children found
massacred on the floors of their own dwellings. From
every direction came tales of horror and thrilling
accounts of suffering and torture. Spreading terror
along the whole frontier, the savages penetrated to
within a few miles of Winchester, killing officers
and men. With but few soldiers under his command, Washington could not be omnipresent, while
it would not answer to withdraw any of the garrisons,
for large numbers of the settlers were gathered in

every fort. Growing bolder by success, the savages seriously threatened the forts themselves, and Washington expected every day to hear of their fall and the massacre of all within. With a heart swelling with indignation and pity, he entreated the assembly to send him help. To add to his anguish, complaints continually reached him of the gross misconduct of some of his officers, and murmurs against him began to rise in various quarters. An anonymous writer published in a newspaper all the floating and exaggerated rumours respecting the officers, and though not daring to charge the blame directly on Washington, he yet plainly hinted that a leader should be held responsible for the irregularities of his subordinates. A faction of Scotchmen had been formed, whose purpose was to get rid of the present commander-in-chief, and place Colonel Innies in his place. Disgusted, and, for the time, depressed, by the apathy of the government, his own fettered condition, the false accusations made by anonymous writers, and above all, by the sufferings of the inhabitants, which he had not the power to relieve, Washington wished to resign his commission. In a letter to the governor, after depicting the deplorable condition of things, he says: "I am too little acquainted, sir, with pathetic language, to attempt a description of the people's distresses, though I have a generous soul, sensible of wrongs and swelling for redress. I see their situation, know their danger, and participate in their sufferings, without having it in my power to give them further relief than uncertain promises." These things, together with the unmerited abuse heaped upon the officers, and thus, indirectly upon himself, made him regret the day he accepted his commission; while the prayers and tears of men and women, begging for that relief he cannot afford, and the increasing reports of Indian murders and cruelty, which will be laid to his charge, as commander-in-chief, fill up the cup of bitterness

which he is compelled to drink, and he exclaims:
"The supplicating tears of the women, and moving
petitions of the men, melt me into such deadly sorrow, that I solemnly declare, if I know my own
mind, I could offer myself a willing sacrifice to the
butchering enemy, provided that would contribute
to the people's ease." It was enough to move a
heart of stone, to see that young man, only twenty-
four years of age, burning to rescue the defenceless
inhabitants, and panting for action; standing with
idle hands and fettered feet, surrounded with gray-
haired fathers and weeping orphans, whom the
Indians had bereft of friends, his ear constantly
stunned with tales of horrid murder, praying in bitterness of spirit, that he might be offered up a sacrifice, to effect that which an inefficient government
will not permit him to do.

His friends in the council and assembly, were
alarmed at the intimation that he wished to resign,
and appealed to his patriotism and pride to dissuade
him from so fatal a purpose. They declared no one
believed the libels that had appeared in print, and
soon the author of them would be detected. A letter
from London, probably had more effect than any
other remonstrance. The sagacious patriot told
Washington that his resignation was probably the
very result his libeler was after, so that he himself
might take his place. He knew this would tell on
the high, sensitive spirit of Washington, and he
wound up with, "No, sir, rather let Braddock's bed
be your aim, than any thing might discolour those
laurels which I promise myself are kept in store for
you."

The plot being discovered, its authors were covered with disgrace, and Washington retained his command. His position, however, continued to be a
most trying one. The officious governor, not content with taking care of matters at home, using his
power to augment, pay, clothe and feed the army,

336 B

was constantly intermeddling with its movements, perplexing and harassing Washington beyond measure with his absurd orders.

The summer and autumn [1756] were passed in building forts and defending the country from Indian encroachments, still every thing was in confusion. Soldiers were wanted, and if furnished, there was no clothing nor provisions prepared for them. Those already enrolled received only sixpence, sterling, per day, two of the eightpence allowed being kept back to buy clothing with, which, some how or other, failed to reach its destination.

Washington wished to hold only a few forts, and have them well garrisoned. Fort Cumberland being out of the state, and too far in advance of the settlements that remained, to be of any service, he proposed to abandon it, or at least withdrew all the troops with the expection of a single company, and build another fort between it and Winchester. But the governor would not listen to the proposal, while instead of lessening the number of forts, the assembly proposed to extend a line of them from the Potomac to North Carolina—running for three hundred miles through the Alleghanies. Washington asked for more men, and the assembly replied by bidding him build more forts. The former declared the garrisons were quite weak enough already, without spreading them over a still larger surface, thus provoking the enemy to cut them off in detail. His remonstrance, however, had no effect; these civilians knew more than the commander-in-chief; and he set about the arduous work forced upon him with all his accustomed energy. The line on which the forts were to be erected was determined by a council of officers at Fort Cumberland, and soon tools and men were despatched to the different localities. These Washington visited in turn, and once made the entire tour of three hundred miles, exposed almost every step of his progress to the rifle shot of the savage. Most of the way he had no escort but a servant and guide, and thus accompanied, passed on one occasion a spot where, an hour afterward, two men were killed by the Indians. He found the militia insubordinate, the officers away, and every thing at loose ends. There was no vigilance—no discipline. In one case he found the militia stubbornly refusing to lift their hands toward erecting the fort, till paid forty pounds of tobacco, which they declared to be their due. The works, however, were slowly carried forward, and the sound of the pickaxe and hammer—the call of the teamster, and the morning and evening gun, awoke the echoes of that vast wilderness, marking the barrier which the white man had reared against the savage, whom from that time on has been crowded back, till the shadows of the Rocky Mountains now fall on his lodges.

Washington's letters to Governor Dinwiddie, during the summer and autumn, are a succession of appeals to put the military of the state on a better footing. Families butchered within twelve miles of his headquarters—insubordination of his troops—the want of clothing, provisions and arms—complaints of being compelled to be in turn his own commissary and engineer—that to-day he is supplied with one batch of orders, to-morrow with others directly contradictory—troubles with Quakers who had been drafted, but would "be whipped to death" rather than fight— short levies of soldiers—court-martials for desertion —empty military chest—skirmishes with the Indians, and often bootless pursuit of them—constant struggle with difficulties, where no glory could be gained, made up the budget of the summer. The encouraging letters of staunch friends—the advice of Col. Fairfax to read Cæsar's Commentaries and Quintius Curtius, in order to learn how to bear trials, were all very well in their way, yet a poor compensation for what he suffered.

At this early stage of his career he commenced that strict discipline which he ever after maintained in an army of the most irregular troops in the world. Hearing that profanity prevailed in his regiment, he issued an order of the day, in which "the officers are desired, if they hear any man swear, or make use of any oath or execration, to order the offender twenty-five lashes immediately, without a court-martial. For the second offence he will be more severely punished." To a captain who had taken advantage of his years to write somewhat haughtily to his young colonel, he replied that he had heard bad reports of him, and concluded by saying, "If I hear any just complaints against you, you may expect to answer them." To another captain, whose lieutenant was refractory, he wrote, "Tell Mr. L—— he is not to *stir from his post at his peril* until he has leave; if he does, I will arrest him for his disobedience of orders, and try him as soon as he arrives here."

Earl Loudon had succeeded Governor Shirley in the chief command in the colonies, and was now on his way to this country. He was expected to land in Virginia, and Washington, in anticipation of his arrival drew up a lucid paper, containing a narrative of events since the beginning of hostilities, pointed out the errors that had been made, and suggested the course that should be adopted in future. Loudon, however, did not go to Virginia, but called a meeting [March, 1757,] of the different governors and chief officers at Philadelphia. Washington was among the number, and was received by the commander-in-chief with marked attention. In that convention it was decided that, in prosecuting the war which had now been openly declared by England against France, the whole force of the army should be directed against the Canada borders. Virginia was to be left to carry out her defensive operations, which doomed Washington to the perplexing, harassing life of the past year. He returned to Winchester, recalled the troops from Fort Cumberland, by order of Loudon, and employed himself in resisting the encroachments of the Indians.

During the summer [1757] he was subject to the orders of Colonel Stanwix, stationed in Pennsylvania, whom London had placed over the middle and southern provinces. In the mean time he urged an expedition against Fort Du Quesne, declaring that the mustering of forces in the north had so exhausted the French garrisons along the Ohio that they would fall an easy conquest. The governor coincided with him in his views, but he was not allowed to carry them out, and the summer wore away in struggling with the old difficulties, and in skirmishes with the Indians, whose presence near the fort was always announced by the murder of white men.

But in the autumn Washington began to decline in health. His magnificent constitution was evidently sinking, and, though he endeavoured for a while to bear up against the pressure of disease, he at length yielded before it, and retired to Mount Vernon. and took to his bed. Although his physical labours had been of the most exhausting kind, it was not so much of these as the harassed and perplexed state of mind he was kept in by others, that finally broke him down. A slow fever settled upon him, and for four months he was kept at home an invalid.

In January, Governor Dinwiddie sailed for England, leaving few regrets behind him. Although zealous and active in the service of the colonies, he was petulant, meddlesome, and a constant marplot to most of the military operations of Washington. In the latter part of his career he seemed to delight in thwarting the plans of the young officer whom he had at first befriended. For defeating one of them he ought to be held in grateful remembrance. It was the earnest desire of Washington to enter the regular army, and he set on foot measures to secure his transfer, and would have succeeded but for the interference of the governor. What effect on his future career his duty and honour as a British officer would have had, it is impossible to determine, but

probably quite enough to prevent his becoming commander-in-chief of the rebel forces.

The great interest of the colonies now gathered
round the northern border, where two strong armies
were assembling to decide the fate of a continent.
But both Loudon and Abercrombie seemed in no
haste to precipitate a crisis, and let the months wear
away in idleness.   All this time the small, rapid,
irritable, yet clear-headed Field-Marshal Montcalm
was improving every hour.   Loading the Indians
with presents, but refusing them rum, singing with
the different tribes their war-songs, he aroused their
enthusiasm and bound them to him by strong affection.   Their activity in his service soon drenched the
frontier in blood.

About two months before Washington retired to
Mount Vernon sick, the capture and massacre of
Fort William Henry took place—the Braddock defeat of the north.   Every movement of the regular
troops proved disastrous, and the provincials effected
all that was done.   The English had now got a
foothold in the basin of the Ohio; they had been
driven away from the St. Lawrence, both sides of
which the French held possession.   The northern
lakes, too, had fallen into the hands of the latter,
and their armies, swelled by vast hordes of Indians,
threatened to sweep downward to Albany.   The
British arms and the provinces were disgraced.   All
this Washington saw and felt, as he lay and tossed
on his feverish bed.   But Pitt once more stood at
the head of the government, and it was expected
that under his energetic administration, affairs would
soon assume a different aspect.   As a relief to the
inertness and imbecility of these distinguished commanders came the war-shout of Frederic of Prussia,
from the heights of Rossbach, as with twenty thousand
men he chased sixty thousand before him—and the
loud chorus of his troops as they stormed over the
batteries of Leuthen.   Standing up in central Europe,

this strong-hearted hero "determined to save his country or perish." With Russia, Sweden, Austria and France closing steadily upon him with their powerful armies, his brave spirit only rose with the increasing danger. "To save the state," said he, "I dare the impossible." "The number and position of the enemy are not questions to be thought of. We must beat them, or all of us find our graves before their batteries." About going into battle, he said—"The regiment of calvalry that shall not instantly charge when ordered, shall be dismounted and sent into garrison—the battation of infantry that shall but falter, shall lose its colours and its swords. Now farewell, friends; soon we shall have vanquished, or see each other no more." With these brave words, though outnumbered three to one, he turned on his powerful adversaries in succession, and with blow after blow, that astounded the civilized world, overwhelmed their pride and redeemed his country. Such tidings ever and anon came to Washington's ears, as he lay an invalid, showing that his views of a true hero were not ideal. Frederic became one of his favourite characters; he watched his struggle with the deepest sympathy, and was no doubt influenced much in after life by his conduct and character. He was the only living man of whom Washington had a bust in his house at Mount Vernon.

As spring opened Washington slowly improved; but he considered his constitution so thoroughly broken down that it would require great care and a long time to recruit, and he seriously contemplated resigning his command and all prospect of preferment. He, however, changed his purpose, and in March set out to join the army. The effort of travel brought on a return of his disease, but he rallied again, and soon after resumed his command at Fort Loudon.

In the mean time Pitt had made some changes in

colonial matters. Francis Fauquier was appointed
to take the place of Dinwiddie, and Forbes of Stanwix. Loudon had been superseded by Jeffrey
Amherst, who was seconded by the gallant Wolf,
while—though Abercrombie retained his command
—Lord Howe had been appointed as the real leader
of the enterprise intrusted to him. Three expeditions
were planned—one under Amherst and Admiral Bos-
cawan against Louisburg—a second under Abercrombie against Ticonderoga, and the third under Forbes
to effect the conquest of the Ohio valley. To insure
the cheerful coöperation of the colonists, Pitt wrote
them a circular letter, calculated to inspire all with
new spirits. Arms, ammunition, tents and provisions
would thereafter be supplied by the king, while the
provincial officers were to hold equal rank with those
of the regular army. The Virginia assembly immediately met and voted to increase the army to two
thousand men. These, divided into two regiments,
and acting in concert with his majesty's troops, were
designated to march against Fort Du Quesne.

It was about this time, while on his way to Williamsburg, that Washington was first made acquainted
with the young widow who was destined to become
his wife. The young colonel, in military undress,
mounted on a splendid charger and attended by a
single tall body servant, both the gift of the dying
Braddock as he fled from the fatal field of Monongahela, had just crossed Williams's Ferry, over the
Pamunkey, a branch of York river, when he was met
by Mr. Chamberlayne, a Virginia gentleman of the
old school, who invited him to his house. Washington excused himself, on the ground of urgent business
with the governor. But the hospitable planter
would take no denial, and at last succeeded in turning the scale by promising to introduce him to a
young and beautiful widow. The colonel finally
consented to stop and dine—nothing more. A short
delay could be made up by hard riding and pressing

further into the night. In dismounting he gave his horse into the charge of his servant Bishop, with explicit instructions to have him at the door at a certain hour. Giving his arm to his guest, the hospitable planter entered the house and introduced him to his family. The young Virginia colonel immediately drew every eye upon him, for a fine commanding appearance heightened rather than lessened the romance that gathered around his chivalrous and adventurous life. The young widow was handsome, fascinating, and possessed a large fortune, and was moreover the widow of a colonel. Colonel Washington was also rich, of high family connections, and, above all, possessed that which ever attracts woman, a valiant, heroic heart, that would beat as calmly amid whistling bullets and death and carnage as in its peaceful slumbers. The lady was only three months younger than he, and from the first did not disguise her admiration of the youthful hero. On the other hand, her society was so agreeable to Washington, that for the first time in his life he forgot his own appointment. His servant Bishop, punctual to his orders, had the two horses saddled and bridled, standing at the gate at the time appointed. Contrary to all military rules, and all former experience, his master did not make his appearance. Lingering under the sweet influence of the beautiful young widow, the time slipped unconsciously away. At length, as the sun stooped behind the western wilderness, the planter stepped forward and declared that it was contrary to the rules of his estate to allow a guest to leave the house after sundown. Washington laughingly acknowledged that he felt bound to submit to such wholesome regulations, and was soon forgetful of every thing but the fascinating woman beside him. Other dreams than those of military glory visited his pillow that night, and other hopes impelled him forward, as next morning he continued his journey to Williamsburg.

On his return he stopped again at the "White House" of his friend, and surrendered at discretion to the blooming widow.

The charms of his betrothed, however, cou'd not detain him from the duties of his command, and he soon was giving his whole soul to the expedition before him. In this campaign he determined, if possible, to have a chaplain. All his solicitations on this point had thus far been disregarded, and he wrote to the president of the council urging the appointment of one, saying, "Common decency, sir, in a camp calls for the services of a divine, which ought not to be dispensed with, although there should be those so uncharitable as to think us void of religion, and incapable of good instructions."

The ardour, however, with which he commenced preparations was soon chilled by the absurd determination of Forbes to cut a new road to Fort Du Quesne from Pennsylvania, instead of using the old one made by Braddock. It was now the latter part of summer, and he knew that by this arrangement the winter would find the army shut up midway in the wilderness. Independent of the necessity of despatch and the importance of saving labour, Braddock's route was known to be the best through the mountains, even though a new road were required. Washington exhausted argument and persuasion to dissuade Forbes and his second in command, Colonel Bouquet, from this insane purpose. He saw another Braddock's defeat in it, and was distressed beyond measure at the prospect before the army. Said he, if it his undertaken, " all is lost ; our enterprise will be ruined, and we shall be stopped at the Laurel Hill this winter— not to gather *laurels*, except of the kind that covers the mountains."

The first of autumn found Washington still at the camp near Fort Cumberland, filled with despondency and forebodings at the fatal determination of his commander. Sickness had entered the army, and the troops, weary and dispirited by their long inactivity, turned with disgust from the prospect before them. "That appearance of glory," said Washington, "which we had once in view, that hope, that laudable ambition of serving our country and meriting its applause, are now no more......In a word, all is lost if the ways of men in power, like certain ways of Providence, are not inscrutable...... The conduct of our leaders, if not actuated by superior orders, is tempered with something I do not care to give a name to. Nothing now but a miracle can bring this campaign to a happy issue."

The general, however, remained immoveable on the route to be taken, but in all other things paid great deference to Washington. The latter, with a thousand men, was sent in advance of the main army, to cut the road for a hundred miles through the wilderness. Guided by blazed trees, he began his long and tedious march. Streams had to be bridged, ravines filled up, and redoubts erected. Working from daylight till dark to gain six or seven miles, the troops saw winter fast approaching, with the almost certain prospect of passing it in the mountains. Washington, however, infused his own spirit into the officers and men, and continued steadily to pierce the wilderness. Filled with memories of the past that clustered around a region with which he had been familiar since boyhood—recalling to mind his first defeat at Fort Necessity, and the fearful rout at Monongahela, he hoped to wipe out the disgrace of both in victory. Major Grant, with eight hundred Highlanders and a company of Virginians, had been sent forward by Bouquet to take Fort Du Quesne, which he had been told was feebly garrisoned. Advancing boldly on the place, he was assailed by the French with such fury that the Highlanders broke and fled, leaving the gallant Virginia company to save the army from utter destruction. The news meeting Washington in the wilderness did not dampen his courage, but increased it, as success would now be a double triumph.

General Forbes, borne on a litter, with the sands of life ebbing slowly away, writing to have a "chimney built" for his use at every camp, followed slowly after, with the main army. He did not reach Loyal Hanna till the 5th of November [1758]. He had made fifty miles in that time, or an average of one mile a day. Fifty miles more of wilderness lay between the army and Fort Du Quesne. What Washington had predicted had now come to pass. The mountain-tops were covered with snow—the frosts of winter had come on, and the soldiers, unaccustomed to such hardships, and scantily clothed, sunk into despondency. It was therefore resolved, in a council of war, to proceed no farther that season. With six thousand men under his command, and the whole summer before him, Forbes had finally succeeded in getting his army into the heart of the Alleghanies. Had he followed Washington's advice, he would at this time have been comfortably quartered in Fort Du Quesne, his object accomplished, and his troubles over. In contrast to this was a long sojourn in that desolate forest, a miserable invalid, or a disgraceful retreat to the settlements.

While things were in this gloomy state, three French prisoners were brought into camp, who reported the fort wholly unable to make any resistance. This unexpected, accidental piece of good fortune alone saved the army from humiliation. It was immediately resolved to push forward. The tents and heavy baggage were left behind, and with a light train of artillery the army again took up its line of march. Washington in advance, cutting the road before him, led on the column. Elate with joy at the favourable turn events had taken, he spoke cheering words to officers and men, and once more the blast of the bugle and roll of the drum were answered with acclamations. "All the men," he wrote back, "are in fine spirits and anxious to go on." He strained every nerve to hasten his progress; but to make a road for the main army toiling in the rear, was slow work, and it took him thirteen days to reach Fort Du Quesne. As he approached the place, the garrison, only five hundred in number, set fire at night to the buildings, and, as the flames lighted up the surrounding gloom, leaped into their boats and disappeared down the river. On the very spot where the heroic stripling had stood when on his way as commissioner to the French, and which he had selected as an excellent locality for a fort, he now again stood, and gazed with kindling eye on the smouldering ruins before him. Du Quesne, so long the goal of his efforts, was at last won. The royal flag was planted amid the ruins, and, as it swayed to the breeze, they named the place Pittsburgh, in honour of Pitt, under whose direction the expedition had been undertaken—a noble monument to the great statesman; and, "long as the Monongahela and the Alleghany shall flow to form the Ohio, long as the English tongue shall be the language of freedom in the boundless valley which their waters traverse, his name shall stand inscribed on the Gateway of the West."

A small garrison was left in the fort, and the army began its retrograde march.

No further interference from the French was at present to be feared, while the Indians, deserted by their allies, no longer threatened the settlements. The state was at peace, and Washington, only twenty-six years of age, laden with honours, resigned his command, and repaired to Mount Vernon [December].

While on the last campaign he had been elected member of the House of Burgesses from Frederic county. There were four other candidates in the field, and his friends wrote him that it was very important he should be on the spot. This his duties prevented; yet, notwithstanding the advantage which his absence gave his competitors, he beat them all. The ill-will that had been engendered against him in some quarters, on account of the stern sway he had often been compelled to exercise over the militia, and even the inhabitants themselves, could not offset the deep and wide spread admiration of his conduct and character. Colonel Wood stood proxy for him in his victory, and was carried round the town amid the deafening acclamations of the people, as "Huzza for Colonel Washington" rent the air. The latter, however, had a nice little bill to pay, which his friends, according to custom, had run up for him. One hogshead and one barrel of punch, thirty-five gallons of wine, forty-three gallons of strong beer, any quantity of cider, wound up with a dinner to his friends, costing in all thirty-nine pounds and six shillings, or nearly two hundred dollars, was the price paid for his election.

Having now returned to private life, he consummated his engagement with Mrs. Custis, and a wedding was given [January 6th, 1759,] on a scale commensurate with the wealth and standing of the parties, and in keeping with the good old customs of the time. From far and near came the laced coats and powdered hair and long cues, till the hospitable mansion overflowed with the wealth and beauty and gaiety of the colony. And a noble couple they were—the young colonel six feet feet three inches in height, towering above all around, and the beautiful bride, radiant with happiness. The rafters of the huge mansion rung that night with mirth and gaiety. The bride brought as a dowry thirty thousand pounds sterling, besides one-third of large landed estates. She had two children; a son, six years old, and a daughter, four. To the former belonged one-third of the estates left by his father, while the latter had the remaining third, together with ten thousand pounds sterling. This swelled

Washington's fortune to an enormous amount for those days.

He did not take his bride immediately to Mount Vernon, but repaired to Williamsburg, and took his seat as member of the assembly. During the session the speaker was directed, by a vote of the House, " to return thanks on behalf of the colony to Colonel Washington, for the distinguished military services he had rendered the country." This the eloquent speaker did in a manner to suit himself, and poured forth a strain of eulogium at once unexpected and embarrassing. Washington, taken wholly by surprise, rose to reply, but could not stammer forth a single word. Out of this painful dilemma the witty speaker helped him as generously as he had helped him into it. "Sit down, Mr. Washington," said he, " your modesty equals your valour, and that surpasses the power of any language that I possess." Nothing could be more elegant and skilful than this double stroke, which at once relieved Washington, while it enhanced the compliment.

In the spring Washington retired to Mount Vernon, and devoted himself to agricultural pursuits. Covered with honour from five years' faithful and arduous service, united to a noble and beautiful woman, surrounded with affluence, and beloved by all, life at this time spread out attractively before him, and its waters promised to bear him smoothly on to the end of his course.

He adorned his library with the busts of distinguished military chieftains of former ages, and, with true Virginia hospitality, kept open house for his friends. He was interested in every improvement in agriculture—entered largely into the cultivation of tobacco, which he shipped directly from his estates to England. He was fond of hunting, and kept a fine pack of hounds, not only for his own amusement, but that of his friends. He was a splendid rider, and when following the hounds in full cry, taking the daring leap as he flew over the fields, he was the admiration of all.　Two or three times a week, with horse and dogs, he was out—his nature finding relief in the excitement and clamour of the chase.

Duck shooting was another favourite pastime, and he spent hours in his boat, stealing stealthily on the coveys of birds, or watching their flight from his place of concealment.　His love of this sport once brought him in collision with a bold, reckless fellow, who lived on the opposite side of the Potomac, but would often cross and shoot near Mount Vernon. Washington had repeatedly forbade his doing so, but without effect.　In some secluded creek or nook the poacher would hide away, and shoot at leisure.　One day the former hearing a shot, sprang on his horse and galloped toward the spot whence the sound came.　The marauder, seeing him approach, ran for his skiff, and had just time to push off from shore and leap in as Washington galloped up.　The latter instantly rode in and seized the boat.　The reckless fellow within immediately levelled his gun at Washington's breast, swearing that he would shoot him dead if he did not let him go.　But the southern blood of the excited young planter was up, and paying no attention to his threats, he drew the desperado ashore.　He then disarmed and dragged him out upon the bank, and gave him a thorough cowhiding, as merely a foretaste of what awaited him if he continued his depredations.　The cure was effectual, and the poacher sought other fields in which to prosecute his calling.　There was something about Washington's demeanour and look, when excited, that would make a bold man hesitate to assail him.

While he was thus passing the first year of married life in the quiet routine of a planter's occupations, the doom of the French empire on this continent was fixed.　Although at the very time the expedition to Fort Du Quesne was drawing to a successful close,

Abercrombie had been beaten by Montcalm, and with the exception of the capture of Louisburg, defeat had attended the English arms all along the Canadian frontier, the struggle still went on, and all eyes were turned northward, where the armies of the two greatest nations on the globe strove for the possession of unoccupied solitudes, and waters undisturbed by commerce.

At length a long, loud shout came rolling from the Heights of Abraham, announcing that the struggle was over. The deaths of the two heroes, Montcalm and Wolfe, were worthy of the great event they helped to bring about.

Washington retained his seat in the House of Burgesses fifteen years, or until the Revolution. His life during this period differed very little from that of most Virginia planters around him. As a member of the assembly he spoke but little. His motto was not to speak except on important subjects, or on those which directly concerned his constituents, and then calmly, and wholly to the point of fact.

Notwithstanding the extensive business on his hands, and the many calls upon his time, he was his own book-keeper. Exact in every thing, he required those with whom he dealt to be the same. He was compelled to import all his wardrobe, farming utensils, harness, etc., from England. Twice a year he made out a list of the things he wanted and sent it to his correspondent in London. An order on his tailor illustrates the ideas of dress in those times. In giving the description of a coat he had requested to be made, he said he did not wish a rich garment, but a plain one, "*with gold or silver buttons.*"

There is another little anecdote showing how he always adhered to *facts.* The church in the parish of which he was vestryman, having become dilapidated, it was resolved to pull it down and build a new one. But a difference of opinion arose respecting the spot where it should be placed, the present site not

336   F

being central.   Washington, taking a practical view
of the matter, wished it located where it would be most
convenient to the parishioners.   George Mason, his
friend and neighbour, on the other hand, was anxious
to retain the old consecrated spot, hallowed by so
many sweet and sacred associations.   After several
meetings had been held without coming to a decision,
a final decisive one was appointed.   When the people assembled, Mason, the leader of the party wishing
to retain the old site, arose and made a long and
eloquent harangue, pouring out rhapsodies over the
spot made sacred by so many joys and tears—by the
worship there rendered and the dead there buried,
till he almost convinced his audience that to remove
it would be sacrilege.   It was evident he had carried
the day, for Washington was no orator like Brutus to
destroy the effect of this impassioned appeal.   But
while Mason was studying his eloquent harangue, the
former, like an old surveyor as he was, had been
cautiously making a map of the whole parish, with
all its dwellings, showing the precise relation which
the old and new site held to them.   Coolly drawing
this from his pocket, at the close of Mason's speech,
and unrolling it before the people, he bade them look
at the matter exactly as it stood, and told them it
was for them to determine whether they would be
carried away by an impulse, or act like men of sense
and reason.   This map acted as a condenser to all
of Mason's vapour—he was deserted in the very moment of victory, and retired discomfited from the
field.

This clear, practical veiw and stubborn adherence
to fact, was one of the most striking characteristics
of Napoleon, and we are reminded of a similar anecdote
of him.   On his way to Egypt, a group of *savans*,
that accompanied the army, discussed one starry
night on the deck of the ship the existence of a God.
It was finally proved to a demonstration that there
was none.   The young Napoleon heard them through,

and then turning his eye upward toward the be-spangled sky, he waved his hand saying, "All very well, gentlemen, but who made all these?"

Peace had returned to the country, and to all human appearance the future history of Washington was to be that of a Virginia farmer. But he carried the same character in his social relations that he had borne in public life. The soul of honour and the incarnation of justice, and he became the depository of sacred trusts, and the umpire between parties throughout the entire region. To a friend he wrote that if his son wished to pass through college, he could draw on him for one hundred and twenty-five dollars a year throughout his course. Deeds of kindness and acts of benevolence came in between his more important business matters, binding his whole life together with golden links. Among other things in which he became deeply interested was the payment of the soldiers and officers under his command. He was one of the commissioners to close up for the colony its military account, and pushed forward the matter so energetically, that he soon had the satisfaction of seeing every claim settled; and where the original holder had died, arranged it so that the heirs would obtain the land. He did not overlook even Vonbraam, the interpreter who had deceived him so grossly at the Great Meadows, and then fled to England. The man had never been condemned legally, and he therefore considered him entitled to his share.

In October, 1770, he once more passed over the route where had transpired the most memorable events of his life. Taking with him his old friend Dr. Craik, who had been with him from the commencement of his military career, he set out on horseback for the Ohio, to see the western lands for himself, in anticipation of having them surveyed and laid off in tracts for the army. As they passed through the wilderness, almost every step recalled some scene of interest. They paused by the grave of Braddock, and mused together on the Great Meadows, where Washington suffered his first defeat. To him it was like living his life over again.

In twelve days he reached Pittsburg. Remaining here three days, dining with the officers of the garrison, and holding a council with some chiefs of the Six Nations, he on the 20th, with a few companions, embarked in a large canoe down the Ohio. They were now beyond the settlements of the whites. An unbroken forest shut in the river, whose bosom, dotted with islands, was disturbed only by the paddle of the red man or the plash of wild fowl. Night coming on they hauled their boat ashore, and kindling a fire on the banks lay down to rest. At daylight they again pushed off. The third day it snowed, and along the white banks, and through the colonnade of trees the solitary boat shot downward—now dancing over the rifts, and again suddenly brought up on a shoal, threatening to upset all in the stream. Toward evening they saw smoke rising from amid the trees below them, and on turning a bend of the river suddenly came upon an Indian village of twenty cabins. Running the boat ashore, they encamped here for the night, and were entertained hospitably by the natives. Hearing that two traders had been killed a little farther on, they hesitated about proceeding, but at length concluded to venture forward, and kept down the river, stopping occasionally to allow Washington to examine the lands along the creeks and streams that put into the Ohio. The call of the wild turkey and the scream of the water-fowl were the only sounds that broke the stillness of the solitude. They scared the wild deer quenching his noonday thirst with the crack of their rifles, and roused the beast of prey from his lair, in solitudes hitherto unvisited by the white man.

On the 28th they came upon the Indian chief Kiashuta, with his hunting-party, by whom they were kindly received, and detained till nine o'clock next morning. Cold autumn rains and snow drenched them by day and chilled them at night, but Washington continued his investigations, now piercing several miles inland, and again accompanying the boat on foot along the bank. At length they reached the Great Kanhawa, the end of their journey. He had now gone two hundred and sixty-five miles from Pittsburg, through a country claimed by Indians, and where the cabin of the white man had never been reared. Passing up this river to observe the land, they proceeded ten miles and encamped. Next morning they pushed on four miles farther, and then encamped to go hunting. The forest soon rung with the report of their pieces, and before night the party had brought in five buffaloes and three deer. Strange wild fowl, with a cry he had never heard before, huge trees, with trunks forty-five feet in circumference, together with every picturesque object of nature, arrested Washington's attention, as well as the rich bottoms which were destined soon to be crowded with an enterprising people.

He was absent nine weeks in all, not reaching Mount Vernon till the first of December. This was his fifth trip to the Ohio, and served to keep up his familiarity with the fatigues of a camp life that he was fast forgetting in the luxuries of home. All this time he was not an indifferent spectator of the strife between the colonies and the mother country respecting their mutual rights, but sympathized deeply with the former.

How strangely Providence shaped the life of this man, to fit him for the high destiny that awaited him. Five years of better training could not have been devised. Stark and Putnam and others, had an experience fitting them only for partisan warfare, while such generals as Artemus Ward were not inured to the hardships and trials through which Washington had triumphantly passed. Besides, as commander-in-chief of the Virginia forces, he was obliged to bear with undisciplined militia and a contradictory and officious governor—left to carry on a campaign without supplies—keep together half-starved and half-clothed troops—compelled to be patient under abuse and neglect—to have courage when others des ponded, and win universal confidence by his integrity and justice. In short, he had been tried beforehand in every difficulty and temptation that was to beset or befall him as the leader of a free people. His five years as colonel was an epitome of the seven years he spent at the head of the national army. God had proved him, and said clearly by his providence, "Thou hast been faithful over a few things; I will make thee ruler over many things."

CHAPTER IV.

Character of the Colonists—First attempt to Tax the Provinces—Its Reception by the People—Taxation discussed in the British Parliament—Speech of Col. Barre—Attitude of Virginia—Speech of Patrick Henry—South Carolina and Gadsden—Attacks on Stamp-Master J. Ingersoll—First Congress at New York—The Stamp Act Repealed—Excitement and Joy of the Colonists—Washington's Views of it—Duties on Tea, Paper, etc.—Tea thrown overboard in Boston Harbour—Port Bill—Virginia Assembly and conduct of Washington—Fast Day—Fairfax Resolutions—Washington's Letter to Mr. Bryant Fairfax—He is elected a Delegate to the First General Congress—Action of Congress—Prayer by Duché—Washington's standing in Congress—Lexington and Concord—Excitement of the People—Stockbridge—The Second Congress—Washington Chairman of every Committee—Appointed Commander-in-Chief—Battle of Bunker Hill—Journey of Washington to Cambridge—Takes command of the Army—Its character—Appearance of the Encampment—Washington's first order—Organization of the Army—Difficulties that beset him—Forced to act contrary to his wishes.

DURING the long interval that Washington passed on his plantation engaged in the quiet routine of his agricultural duties and pleasures, the colonies were shaken from limit to limit with the fierce discussion of the doctrine of civil rights.

In New England, the inhabitants coming directly from the old Puritan stock, were naturally jealous of those rights for which they had abandoned their native land while both they and the other colonists could not but draw in freedom with every breath in the untrammelled life of the wilderness. Besides, cultivators of the soil are always characterized by independence. The fluctuations of trade, the stoppage of commerce, and the derangement of currency may prevent their becoming rich, but these cannot prevent the earth from yielding her fruits, so that the disasters of war do not reach the means of livelihood, and hence do not outweigh all other considerations. Added to all this, a boundless wilderness thronged with savages would naturally attract to it only the more hardy, enterprising, self-reliant, and fearless class of men, restless under restraint and prompt and resolute in the assertion of their rights.

As the colonies increased in strength and wealth England judiciously avoided intermeddling with their internal regulations, and the assemblies of the different provinces were really more independent than the Parliament of England. Such a stock, so educated by external circumstances, and strengthened in their views by long continued concessions on the part of the mother country, would naturally rebel against the first effort to reduce them to bondage. England, however, was not aware to what depth the sentiment of liberty had struck, nor of the sternness and courage with which the colonists would resist the first encroachment on their rights. Regarding the French war as rather the quarrel of the colonies than her own, she resolved they should help to sustain the government which had protected them not only from the rapacity of the French, but from the cruelties of the savages. But at the first suggestion of the British ministry that this should be done by taxation, the colonists were thrown into a high state of excitement, and urgent remonstrances were made to prevent a step so fatal to their liberties.

[1763.] The proposition to lay a stamp-tax was first made under Egremont's administration, but a change in the cabinet prevented it from being immediately carried out. An excise, land-tax, and all other methods for raising a revenue seemed impracticable. But first came the Navigation Act, forbidding America to trade with foreign nations and compelling her to buy only of England. All other trade was declared contraband, and custom-house officers were sent over, and national vessels ordered to cruise along our coasts to make seizure of all goods that had not come through English ports. This aroused a storm of indignation, and the colonists, finding no other mode of revenge, began to do without English manufactures. The loom and the spinning-wheel were soon heard in every part of the land. Boston took the lead, the inhabitants refusing even to wear gloves at funerals. Other towns followed the example, and English manufactures instead of finding a freer market than before met a more stringent one. This, with other burdens imposed on commerce, agitated deeply the public mind. But vexatious and unjust as this policy was, the colonists felt that Parliament had a right to regulate commerce, and no serious resistance was made; but when the next spring a resolution passed the House of Commons [March 10th, 1764] to lay a stamp-tax, the indignation broke over all bounds. What, taxation without representation? this was not only tyranny to the colonists but treason to the British constitution, Franklin, who was in London, wrote home to Thompson, "The sun of liberty is set, the Americans must light the lamp of industry and economy." "Be assured," said Thompson in reply, "we shall light torches of another sort."

The resolution not being acted on this year the

inhabitants had time to consider it. The universal rage, however, with which it was received, breaking down old rivalries, healing bitter feuds, and harmonizing elements hitherto at war, showed clearly what the inevitable result would be of pressing the measure upon them. It was like the "Truce of God," which banded in brotherly love kings and princes who had long been at war, and reconciled ancient foes to hurl them like a single man against the infidel. This odious tax was the topic of common conversation, clubs were formed to discuss it, and the assemblies of the different states despatched agents to England with their firm remonstrances against it.

Notwithstanding all these indications of an approaching storm, the English government fully believed that the colonies were too feeble and timid to offer any effectual resistance, and the next year [March 8th, 1765] the stamp-tax became a law. Its discussion in the House of Commons brought the administration and its enemies into fierce and terrible collision. During it, Colonel Barre, who had stood side by side with General Wolfe on the Plains of Abraham, delivered that short, unpremeditated and thrilling speech, in reply to Charles Townsend's interrogation, "And will these American children, planted by our care, nourished up by our indulgences to a degree of strength and opulence, and protected by our arms, grudge to contribute their mite to relieve us from the heavy burden under which we lie?" Springing to his feet, the fiery soldier replied, "They planted by your care!` No, your oppressions planted them in America...... They *nourished by your indulgence!* They grew by your neglect of them. As soon as you began to care about them, that care was exercised in sending persons to rule them in one department and another, who were perhaps the deputies of deputies to some members of the House, sent to spy out their liberties, to misrepresent their actions, and to prey upon them, whose behaviour on many occasions has caused the blood of these sons of liberty to recoil within them......*They protected by your arms!* They have nobly taken up arms in your defence, have exerted a valour amidst their constant and laborious industry, for the defence of a country whose frontier was drenched in blood, while its interior parts yielded all its little earnings to your emolument."

With a warning to the government to desist from its rash and perilous course, he sat down. A breathless silence followed this sudden and impassioned address, bursting as it did from a soul on fire. J. Ingersoll, of Connecticut, sat in the gallery and listened to it. By the next packet he despatched it to the colonies. "*Sons of Liberty!*" was the baptismal name pronounced in the British Parliament. "Sons of Liberty," echoed the men of Boston, and organized into a band under that name. A large tree stood on the corner of Washington and Essex streets, which they christened "*Liberty Tree*," and beneath its branches assembled from time to time to deliberate on the momentous question of taxation. Southward swept the flame of rebellion. Virginia, whose House of Burgesses had ever been distinguished for stubborn resistance to every assumption of authority by the governor, "rang the alarum bell," and sent her thrilling accents of defiance on. The assembly was in session when the news arrived, and though the denunciations were loud and deep, no one seemed inclined to take the lead in the House till Patrick Henry, who had been a member but a few days, snatching a fly-leaf from old Coke upon Lyttleton, wrote five daring resolutions upon it, and rising read them to the utter astonishment of all. He declared that the colonies alone had power to levy taxes, and defended his resolutions with an eloquence and boldness that electrified the House. Kindling on the glorious theme of Human Liberty, he poured forth withim passioned fervour and vehement energy those sentiments which soon found an echo in every part of the land. Forgetting for a moment every thing but the great subject which engrossed his soul, he suddenly exclaimed, "Cæsar had his Brutus —Charles the First his Cromwell, and George the Third—" "*Treason !*" shouted the defaulting Speaker Robinson. "*Treason ! Treason !*" rang through the House. Pausing till the echo of the damning accusation had died away, he turned his flashing eye full on the speaker and shouted, "*may profit by the example ! If this be treason, make the most of it !*" A fierce and exciting debate followed, but it was only like the occasionl wind guests heard in the pauses of the thunder. Henry's eloquence rolled over and drowned every thing else. His resolutions were carried.

Washington sat there a witness of the scene, and gazed, one may well imagine with what feelings, on the inspired countenance of the young and fearless orator.

The flame spread on every side. British ministers were hung in effigy on Liberty Tree. Associations were formed to reject all British maufactures. People in Philadelphia refused to eat mutton, that they might have more wool for domestic use. Ladies of the first rank dressed in homespun. The stern Puritan clergy cried "To your tents, oh Israel !" When the churchmen preached loyalty to the Lord's anointed, "*The People,*" retorted William Livingston, "are the Lords' anointed." The "Stamp Act" was hawked about the streets of New York, under the title of "Folly of England and Ruin of America."

South Carolina heard the bugle-blast of Virginia and Massachusetts, and snatching up the trumpet, through her Gadsden, blew a call so clear, loud and glorious, that the heart of the nation leaped up at the sound. With the lofty, fearless and eloquent Gadsden at the South, the fiery patriot Patrick Henry in Virginia, and the sanest madman that ever became an Oracle of the Gods, Otis of Boston, at the North, there was no danger of lack of energy or courage.

"*Death to the man who offers a piece of stamped paper to sell!*" shouted the people of Boston. Bonfires, harangues, threats, riots and violence, filled the officers of government with alarm. Hutchinson of Connecticut fled to his castle. The stamp-officer of Rhode Island, trembling for his life, resigned at the clamours of the mob. The house of the stamp-master of Annapolis was levelled to the ground by the infuriated multitude. Ingersoll, stamp-master of Connecticut, fled in terror from New Haven with the governor. In his flight he met first two, then five, and a little after thirty, and finally five hundred men on horseback, armed with clubs cut from the forest and stripped of their bark. Three bugles heralded their approach, and opening to the right and left they received into their midst the trembling stamp-officer. Halting in the main street of Wethersfield, they bade him resign. Ingersoll, having retired to a house, hesitated and delayed. The people grew more and more indignant, and at length their swelling shout for vengeance so alarmed him that he obeyed, saying, "After all, it is not worth dying for."

"Swear to the writing," cried the mob. Ingersoll refused. "Then shout for Liberty and Property three times," they cried. "Liberty and Property!" shouted the crest-fallen stamp-master. Then three loud huzzas rent the air. A thousand men had now assembled, each with his white cudgel, and gathering round Ingersoll, escorted him with the sound of bugles to Hartford, and there, in the presence of the legislature, made him read his resignation. In his journey thither he rode on a white horse, and some one asking him what he thought of the strange cavalcade accompanying him, he replied that he now had a clearer idea, than ever before, of that passage in the Revelations which describes *Death on the pale horse and hell following him.* Thus officer after officer was compelled to resign, until but one, Hughes, the Quaker of Philadelphia, remained. Tossing on his bed of sickness, he at last heard the muffled drums beating their mournful throbs, and the deep toll of the bell of the State House sending its dull echoes over the city, followed by the still more alarming sound, the muffled tread of excited men on their march to his dwelling, and trembling for his life, reluctantly yielded and promised to resign.

In the midst of this excitement, the First Congress of the colonies met at New York [Oct. 7th, 1765,] and laid the foundation of their liberty. The excitement was not confined to this country, but spread to England, and when in the following winter Parliament assembled, the question of the Colonies absorbed all others. A noble attempt was made to repeal the Stamp Act, and during the discussion Pitt uttered those memorable words which so startled the House of Commons, and thrilled every heart on this continent—"*I rejoice that America has resisted!*"

The Stamp Act was re-affirmed. It however again came up, on a motion to repeal it, and Franklin was summoned to the bar of the House, to give information respecting the state of the colonies, and of their ability and willingness to pay the stamp-duty. after a long examination on various points, Grenville asked him if he thought the people would pay the stamp duty if modified. "*No, never,*" he replied—"*they will never submit to it.*"

When the final vote on the repeal was to be taken, the lobbies were crowded with spectators, waiting with breathless interest to hear the decision. At length when, toward morning, the resolution was carried, loud shouts made the roofs of St. Stephen's ring. Around Conway, who had fought nobly for the principles of right from first to last, the multitude gathered with tears of gratitude, while they opened right and left to let the chair of the crippled Pitt pass, and reverently uncovered their heads, many attending him even to his door.

When the news reached America, the country was

thrown into a delirium of excitement. All winter long there had been meetings of excited men, and a black and threatening cloud seemed settling on the colonies. The repeal of the Stamp Act was like the sudden bursting forth of the sun in the midst of darkness. The bell nearest Liberty Tree in Boston, was set ringing. From the tall steeple drooped countless gay banners, and from every window and house-top flaunted flags and streamers, making the bright May morning look still brighter, and promise a far more glorious summer than that of fruits and flowers. The prison-doors were thrown open, and every poor debtor was allowed to go forth once more a free man, and mingle in the general joy. In the evening the town was one blaze of fire. Liberty Tree bent under the weight of lanterns and illuminated figures of the champions of repeal. Bonfires were kindled, fireworks set off, while the town shook to the shouts of the multitude and the roar of cannon. Southward swept the general exultation, till the land echoed with the clamour of bells and the acclamations of men.

The joy, however, was soon damped by the reception of the Military Act quartering soldiers in Boston. Besides, the repeal of the Stamp Act was now understood not to be a concession of principle on the part of Great Britian, or even a permanent act of expediency. The imposition, not long after, of duties on tea, paper, glass, and painters' colours, was the same thing under a different form, and aroused the same spirit of resistance with which the Stamp Act had been met.

The repeal of the Stamp Act was hailed by Washington with delight. He had declared it a " direful attack on the liberties of the colonists." So the imposition of new duties filled him with "indignation." From Boston to Georgia the people were again thoroughly aroused, and catching the notes of preparation which now began to be seriously sounded, he said, " That no man should scruple or hesitate to take up arms in defence of so valuable a blessing (as freedom) is clearly my opinion," though it should be the last resort. The associations formed every where to persecute English manufacturers and trade, met his approval. Mason drew up an agreement for the House of Burgesses, and Washington presented it, in which every signer promised not to buy or use the interdicted articles. They put their names to it in a body, and Washington ever after when he made out orders for England, forbade his correspondent to send any of those included in the agreement.

Thus the affairs of the colony, with now and then a lull in the excitement, were pushed toward the crisis of open rebellion. England, under the pressure, finally took off all duties except the one on tea. The colonists then refused to drink tea, and it accumulated in the English warehouses. No man was found bold enough to be its consignee on these shores. The East India Company endeavoured to get a cargo into Boston harbuor, but the citizens in the garb of Indians threw it overboard. This act of violence was followed by the famous Port Bill, by which Boston was to be shut up, and Salem used as the port of the colony. To carry out this and reduce the rebellious spirit of the colonists, troops were ordered over to be quartered on the people.

When the Assembly of Virginia met, one of their first acts was to pass resolutions of sympathy for Boston, and appoint a day of fasting and prayer. Lord Dunmore, the governor, irritated at this act of disloyalty, dissolved the Assembly. The members immediately re-assembled at a tavern, and, among other acts, recommended the call of a general congress, to deliberate on the course to be pursued. They then dispersed with the exception of twenty-five, of whom Washington was one. These remained to keep the fast which had been appointed. Washington inscribed in his diary, " I went to church, and *fasted all day !"*

He, with the other twenty-four, having in the mean time received a message from the Bostonians requesting the colonies to join them in a non-importation act, issued a call for another convention of the delegates. During the interval the separate counties held meetings to determine on the instructions that should be given their representatives in this convention. In Fairfax county Washington was elected chairman of the meetings, in which the famous Fairfax resolutions were adopted. Those resolves show the firm determination of Washington to resist the encroachments of the mother country. Mr. Bryan Fairfax having withdrawn from the meetings on account of the bold and decided ground taken, Washington addressed him a long letter of explanation. After showing the conduct of Parliament toward the colonies, and proving clearly its designs, he asks, " What hope have we then from petitioning, when they tell us that now or never is the time to fix the matter ? Shall we after this whine and cry for relief, when we have already tried it in vain ? Or shall we supinely sit and see one province after another fall a sacrifice to despotism ?" These sentences have the ring of the true metal, and seem almost to have been embodied in the Declaration of Independence. He was opposed to addressing the throne further. " There *is no relief for us* (said he) *but in their distress,*" (referring to the non-importation scheme,) " and I think, at least I hope, there is public virtue enough left among us to deny ourselves every thing but the bare necessaries of life to accomplish this end." Far-seeing and practical, he no longer puts faith in eloquent appeals and addresses. With the same stubborn adherence to facts which had always characterized him, he says, " *Starvation* is the remedy !"

The convention met on the 1st of August, and adopted, with very little change, the Fairfax resolutions—" No more slaves, British goods, or tea," said they, " shall with our sanction enter the colony."

In answer to the call for a general congress to meet at Philadelphia on the 5th of September, the convention appointed seven delegates, one of whom was Washington.*

The first great united step was now to be taken, and every eye was turned toward that assembly. Lee and Henry stopped on their way for Washington, and the three rode on together to Philadelphia. Washington, with his stately form and calm, self-possessed mind; Henry with his fervid zeal and boi ing courage, and Lee with his rich and flowing language, formed an interesting trio, and grand and glorious must have been the words spoken as they passed through the thriving settlements on whose doom they were about to pronounce.

Congress met, but as the debates were never published, there is no record left of the part taken in them by Washington. Dickinson drafted a petition to the king and to the people of Quebec; Jay an appeal to the inhabitants of Great Britian; Lee a third to the Colonies; and Congress adjourned to wait the response to all these before taking the final step. The feelings, however, which Washington carried into Congress and brought out with him, may be gathered from his reply to a letter written him by Captain Mackenzie, then in Boston. Speaking of the direful issue to which things were tending, he said, "give me leave to add, as my opinion, that more blood will be spilled on this occasion, if the ministry are determined to push matters to extremity, than history has ever yet furnished instances of in the annals of North America." A prediction worth considering, and which shows that he who uttered it had counted the cost, settled his purpose, and stood prepared to move into that scene

* The others were Peyton Randolph, Richard Henry Lee, Patrick Henry, Richard Blond, Benjamin Harrison and Edmund Pendleton.

336   G

of blood and carnage, whether it came sooner or later, a strong defender of the right.

An incident occurred at the opening of this Congress, to which after circumstances gave a peculiar significance. It was proposed to call in a clergyman to invoke the aid of the Divine Being, and Mr. Duché was sent for. Among other portions of the exercises, he read a part of the 35th Psalm. A rumour had reached Philadelphia the morning previous, that Boston had been cannonaded by the British, and every heart was filled with anxious forebodings. The members stood during prayers, all except Washington. He alone knelt—thus by mere accident separating himself from the rest, by an act indicating that he more than they all needed to bow in the dust and plead for help from heaven. As he knelt down—the proudest form there—it seemed as if God had singled him out to be the Joshua of the hosts of Freedom. The house was still as the grave as the earnest accents of the clergyman fell on his ear.

"*Plead my cause, O Lord, with them that strive with me: fight against them that fight against me. Take hold of shield and buckler, and stand up for mine help. Draw out also the spear and stop the way against them that persecute me: say unto my soul I am thy salvation.*"

The reading of this Psalm was wholly unpremeditated, it being a part of the regular service of the day, hence it seemed like the voice of God speaking directly to them. After it was finished Mr. Duché, overwhelmed with the solemnity of the occasion, broke out to the astonishment of all in an extemporaneous prayer, beseeching God to save the land from the evils that overhung it.

Congress adjourned to wait the effect of the several appeals, and Washington returned to his farm. The impression he had made on that assembly of great men may be gathered from a remark of Patrick

Henry. When asked on his return whom he thought the greatest man in Congress, replied—"If you speak of eloquence, Mr. Rutledge of South Carolina is unquestionably the greatest orator; but if you speak of solid information and sound judgment, Colonel Washington is unquestionably the greatest man on that floor." With such a reputation one can imagine what profound silence fell on the House when he rose to speak, and what earnest, respectful attention was given to the opinions he uttered.

In the meantime independent companies were formed in various parts of Virginia, and Washington was solicited to take command of them as field-officer. He accepted, and meeting them at the various places of rendezvous, reviewed the troops and instructed the officers.

While affairs maintained this semi-tranquil state in Virginia, events around Boston were crowding to a crisis. Collisions had taken place between the people and military—blood had been shed, and the cry for vengeance gone over the land. The inhabitants passed the soldiers with a scowl and half-muttered curses, and it was equally apparent to General Gage, the British commander, and to Hancock, Adams, Otis, Ward and other patriotic leaders, that every thing was tending to open war. A provincial Congress was formed, an army of minute-men raised, and the supplies of the British troops cut off. Gage, alarmed at the aspect of affairs, began to fortify the Neck, and sent off detachments to seize gunpowder and cannon in the hands of the rebels. On the 18th of April, Major Pitcairn was despatched with six companies to seize some cannon and stores at Concord. In dead silence, by the dim moonlight, Pitcairn, supposing his movements were unknown, passed quietly out of Boston and pushed on towards Lexington. But news of his advance had preceded him, and towards daylight, as he approached Lexington, his ears were stunned by the loud ringing of bells, the roll of drums, and signal-guns of the Americans. Dimly looming through the gray mist of morning the scarlet uniforms appeared pressing in a compact mass toward the village green, on which a hundred militia were drawn up in confusion. Halting in front, the troops coolly loaded their pieces. Pitcairn then galloped forward and exclaimed— "Disperse, you villains—throw down your arms and disperse!" The summons not being immediately obeyed, he shouted "Fire!" and the signal-gun of American independence was fired, and the knell of the British empire on this continent sounded. Eight patriots, the first holocaust to Freedom, were slain, when the rest dispersed, and the troops pressed forward to Concord, six miles distant. Destroying what stores and arms they could lay hands on there, they were about to retire, when the brave Hosmer led four hundred militia to the attack. The firing had attracted the surrounding farmers, and they now came pouring in from every quarter. The British, alarmed at this sudden uprising of the people, began their retreat. But the woods seemed alive with minute-men. From every barn, fence, and house, sped the unerring ball, as closing darker and fiercer on the flying traces of the enemy, the enraged patriots pressed forward to the attack.

Wearied, mortified and disgraced, the troops at length reached Charlestown, with the loss of two hundred and seventy-three.

The day went out in gloom. Silent terror or burning rage filled every bosom. Adams and Warren and Ward and Otis, and others, rejoiced, for they knew that the clock of Destiny had now struck the hour. Their great, grand hearts, though throbbing with anxiety and sympathy for the people, could not refrain from swelling with triumph and joy, that liberty had at last found defenders, and that the conflict was set. While friends were committing

with more anger than sorrow the dead to the grave,
men on horseback with a drum at their saddle-bow,
were flying over the country, calling the inhabitants
to arms. Past lonely farm-houses, through the thin
settlements, the swift riders speed on, beating the
alarm drum and shouting, "To arms!" As the
clatter of the horse's hoofs and the tap of the drum
came and went, wives gazed with pale faces on their
husbands, mothers with quivering lips, handed down
the trusty firelock to their sons, and sisters weeping
filled the scanty knapsacks of their brothers; yet
one and all said, "Go! in God's name go and strike
for liberty!" And they went pouring forward to
Boston.

Putnam was in the field mending his fence when
the rider, breathless with haste and excitement,
reined up opposite him, and, dismounting, hurried to
where he stood. "The streets of Lexington and
Concord have been soaked in blood, and the country
is in a blaze!" was the fearful message he delivered.
Leaving his oxen where they stood, not stopping to
say good-by to his wife, Putnam leaped on his swift-
est horse, and was soon tearing along the road toward Boston. In ten minutes after the messenger
had delivered the same fearful tidings to Stark, he
was in the saddle and galloping for the same rendezvous. For a long time the New England colonies
had been expecting the resort of the enemy to violence, and minute-men had been chosen and signals
agreed on, by which the fatal news was to be trans-
mitted to the remotest section. A swift rider, with
a drum by his side, was to speed along the great
thoroughfares from colony to colony; but in the
side-settlements other arrangements had been made,
and in an incredible short space of time, it was
known in the obscurest corner of the provinces. It
was as if powder had been laid in trains all over the
land, and a single torch had ignited the whole into
a tracery-work of fire, flashing, leaping heavenward.

The news reached Stockbridge, one of the oldest and most western settlements in Massachusetts, on Sunday morning, and the inhabitants of that peaceful valley were thunderstruck, as they saw their deacon, a Jew of the Jews in his observance of the Sabbath, step out of his door and deliberately discharge his musket. The next moment another pillar in the church emerged from his door and fired his piece. This was the signal agreed upon to inform the inhabitants when blood had been shed. Those musket-shots started the farmer where he knelt at the family altar or sat reading God's word to his family. The young father, at the sound, set down the child he was dandling on his knee, and, with a glance at his pallid wife, seized the gun; the aged sire, preparing to go to the house of God, cast one look on the boy of his love and the prop of his old age, and, as it met the quivering lip and mantling cheek and flashing eye, he said, "Go, and God's blessing go with you!" In a short time men, singly and in groups, were seen walking with rapid strides toward the house of the deacon. It was a cold drizzling morning, and as they arrived they clustered on the stoop of the building, apparently waiting some one. After a little interval, their pastor, Mr. West, was seen coming down the hill with a Bible under his arm. With care and anxiety depicted on his countenance, he walked solemnly into their midst. A few words told the tale. He then opened the Bible, read an appropriate chapter, made a few remarks, and lifted his trembling voice in prayer. "And now may the blessing of God Almighty go with you and nerve your heart and arm in the day of battle," said the afflicted pastor, and turned away. *Before twelve o'clock, from that little settlement twenty sturdy men, with knapsacks on their backs and muskets in their hands, had started on foot for Boston, two hundred miles distant.* There were *men* in those days—*God's men,* worthy to found an empire. Oh, how that question must have taken hold of their souls, when it usurped even the duties of the holy Sabbath. It was more sacred than the worship of the sanctuary, it was one with religion, and, fearlessly appealing to God and the final judgment for the complete vindication of their conduct, they moved resolutely into the strife. All over the land was this marvellous uprising of the people, till the roads leading to Boston were black with men in their homespun garbs, and soon nearly twenty thousand stood on the heights that overlook the city.

While these stirring scenes were passing in Massachusetts, the second Continental Congress was assembling at Philadelphia. Governor Dunmore, of Virginia, had received orders to remove military stores, etc. out of the reach of the colonists. The attempt of General Gage to execute a similar order, had brought on the conflict at Lexington and Concord. Dunmore chose the same hour as Gage to carry out his plan, and at midnight had all the ammunition removed to a vessel in the river. Patrick Henry heard of it at Hanover, and immediately calling together his volunteers, marched to Williamsburg, and compelled the governor to pay the full amount of the powder. He then departed for Congress. The second Congress met [May 10, 1775,] with gloomy forebodings. Their petitions to the king had been treated with contempt, and new outrages perpetrated on the liberties of the colonies. Blood had been shed, and it was evident to every one that "an appeal to arms and the God of battles" was all that was left them. The first thing to be considered was the state of the country, the second to prepare for open hostilities. Several committees were appointed, and it is a little singular that Washington was made chairman of every one. In the debates of the first Congress he must have shown rare ability, and depth and soundness of judgment seldom witnessed, to have been thus selected, as it were, to control every committee appointed by a Congress of men never surpassed in intellect and virtue. Among the most important acts to be done was the appointment of a commander-in-chief. Amid the conflicting feelings of the colonists, and the high claim that Massachusetts had to the honour, this became a very delicate affair. In the mean time, Samuel Adams arose, and moved that the army assembled around Boston should be adopted by Congress as the Continental army. In sustaining his resolution, he remarked that he intended to nominate a member of that house from Virginia as commander-in-chief. His remarks and allusions pointed so directly to Washington, that the latter arose and left the house. When the day for balloting came, he was unanimously elected.

The next morning, immediately after the convening of Congress, the president arose and announced to Washington his appointment. The latter briefly expressed his thanks for the high honour conferred on him, and for the confidence thus expressed in his ability, and then added—"Lest some unlucky event should happen unfavorable to my reputation, I beg it may be remembered by every gentleman in the room, that I this day declare, with the utmost sincerity, I do not think myself equal to the command I am honoured with." Referring to the salary of 6,000 dollars a year, which had been voted him, he said—"I beg leave to assure Congress that, as no pecuniary consideration could have tempted me to accept this arduous employment at the expense of domestic ease and happiness, I do not wish to make any profit from it. I will keep an exact account of my expenses; these, I doubt not, they will discharge, and that is all I desire." No, indeed, it was not worth while to think of money-making in the perilous path he was about to tread. The future was all unknown, even should his life be spared; success as yet was only a vague dream, and, if he failed, his vast fortune would be confiscated and his wife become a beggar. But this, too, was a mere item ; if he failed he would hang as high as Haman, or spend his remaining days in some remote Botany Bay, eating the bread of an exile, and fretting his great soul away in the fetters of a felon. But, like one greater even than he, and speaking of a still nobler cause, he could say, "none of these things move me, neither count I my life dear unto me."

Of Washington's communings that night to himself, after he had retired to his solitary chamber, we have no record. It is strange that one who kept a diary from the time he was sixteen years old, and often of facts trivial in themselves, never alludes to his feelings. We read that diary, extending through years, without ever once penetrating into his inward life. Unlike Cromwell, he discloses none of his inward struggles, secret griefs, misgivings, fears or hopes. His acts are the world's, his thoughts his own, and he moves before us always in light, yet always in shade. If Washington had left us a record of his thoughts, even during the single night after he had cast life and fortune and character in a desperate struggle, what an insight should we get of his character. His family, that he probably would never see again, his honour, his name, above all, the fate of a free people committed to his trust, occupied in turn his thoughts and awakened into painful intensity his sympathies and his solicitude. He was a commander without an available army and without munitions of war, and was required to deliver a nation already bankrupt, and soon to be rent by civil war, from the armies and fleets of the strongest empire on the globe. He was not one of those who build hopes on dreams, and can be cheated into security by the illusions of fancy. The future lay clear before him ; that is, it was darkness unrelieved by scarce a ray of light, into which he was resolved to move with an undaunted heart, trusting in that God who often chooses the gloomiest hour in which to reveal his presence and

extend his aid.   That was not a night for sleep; yet
how little he conjectured, as he lay revolving the
momentous responsibilities he had assumed, and the
fearful issues to his country he was to decide, of
what was then passing around Boston.   All that
night the strokes of the spade and pickaxe were falling quick and strong on Breed's Hill, and column
after column of men was swiftly and silently marching forward to the low redoubt that the morning sun
would reveal to the astonished British.

If Washington's appointment as commander-in-
chief had been borne by viewless messengers to the
army, the latter could not have hailed the news with
more appropriate demonstrations than it did.   The
tremendous cannonading from sea and land—the
flames of burning Charlestown, and the high and
ringing cheers from the intrenched heights, were a
fit acknowledgment of an event destined to be so momentous in its final results.

Four days after he received his commission, and
next day, accompanied by Generals Schuyler and
Lee,* started for Boston.   A committee from the
Provincial Congress of New York met him on the road
and escorted him, amid the acclamations of the poeple,
into the city.   He had heard on the way rumours of
the battle of Bunker Hill, but here he first became acquainted with all the particulars.   The news made him
eager to hasten forward, and escorted by volunteer
companies, he proceeded to Springfield, where he was
met by a committee from the Provincial Congress of
Massachusetts.   He found the country, as he passed
through it, in a blaze of excitement, and the preparations to arm resounding on every side.   The gallant
defence of the militia at Bunker Hill, and the enthu-

* These, together with Artemas Ward and Israel Putnam,
had been appointed major-generals: and Seth Pomeroy,
Richard Montgomery, David Wooster, William Heath,
Joseph Spencer, John Thomas, John Sullivan, and Nathaniel
Greene, brigadiers.

siasm that prevailed, could not but be cheering to the new commander-in-chief; yet he well knew, from past experience, the difference between a single enthusiastic defence of a position, and the harassing disheartening duties of a long campaign.

He reached Cambridge on the 2d of July, and the next morning walked to the great elm-tree standing on the Common, and, drawing his sword, formally took command of the army. Loud acclamations rent the air, and hope and animation pervaded the ranks. The Provincial Congress, then sitting at Watertown, near by, presented an address, in which they pledged him their entire co-operation, and the most flattering testimonials poured in upon him from every quarter. He ascertained that the troops assmebled numbered nearly 15,000 men, while the British force in and around Boston amounted to 11,500. But the troops now christened as the "Continental Army" were as motley a set as ever gathered under one banner. There was no organization, no unity. The militia of the different provinces acknowledged no authority but that of their several commanders, while the excitement and enthusiasm had called together not only true patriots but adventurers of every description. To render matters still worse, this heterogeneous multitude were almost without ammunition. But notwithstanding the disorders that prevailed among them, there was the groundwork of a noble army. Intrenchments had already been thrown up, and a line of defence completed from the Mystic river to Roxbury, twelve miles in extent, entirely hemming in the British army. The encampment of the Americans presented a strange yet picturesque spectacle. Scarcely any but the Rhode Island troops had tents. The extemporaneous shelter thrown up evinced the craft of the frontiersman rather then the knowledge of the soldier. Here stood a collection of rude stone hovels, with an opening that looked like the entrance to a cavern; there a group of board pens, made of slabs and sticks patched with sails ; while farther on were scattered turf mounds, hastily thrown up, and looking more like the home of the prairie wolf than the abodes of men ; yet all showing where the strong-limbed citizen-soldier slept.   The handsome marquees of the officers, here and there relieving the dilapidated fragmentary character of the encampment, completed the singular spectacle.

On the 4th of July, a day made afterward still more memorable by the glorious Declaration of Independence, Washington issured his first general order to the Continental army.   In this, after expressing the hope that all jealousies of the different colonies would be laid aside, and the only contest be who should render the greatest aid to the common cause, and insisting on discipline and subordination, he says—" The general most earnestly requires and expects a due observance of those articles of war established for the government of the army, which forbid profane cursing, swearing, and drunkenness ; and in like manner he requires and expects of all officers and soldiers, not engaged on actual duty, a punctual attendence on divine service, to implore the blessings of Heaven upon the means used for our safety and defence." Such an order read to an European army would have stunned them more than the announcement of treason in their commander.   But Washington wished it understood at the outset, both by his troops and the whole world, that the cause in which he had embarked was a holy one, and must be disfigured by none of those excesses which are considered a necessary part of a camp life.   Reverently fixing his eye on Heaven, he summons his followers to look thither also, ever fervently praying for that help which alone can come from above.

The organization of the army which followed, proved an annoying and a difficult task.   At the very outset murmurs and discontent arose at the appointment of the superior officers by Congress.   Selecting generals, not for their ability and long service, but according to their locality, or to please powerful friends, was one of the first false steps made by Congress, and from which it never receded throughout the war. This pernicious example, thus set at the very commencement of our national existence, the American goverment has ever since adhered to, with a pertinacity that no disgrace or humiliation can weaken. It covered us with defeat for two years in the war of 1812, and, but for the able officers given us by West Point, would have sent the army back discomfited from Mexico.

The excitement that prevailed among the troops, on this account threatened to disrupt the army; but Washington, by promising to lay their complaints before Congress and get justice done, gradually allayed it. By arranging the brigades and regiments in such a manner that the troops from each colony should for the most part be under their own commander, he restored harmony. Still, many of them refused to sign the rules and regulations presented by Congress; they had taken up arms to fight for liberty—not merely provincial, but *personal* liberty, and they were not going to sign it away to Congress any more than to Parliament. Military despotism was a bugbear that constantly stood in the way of thorough organization of a regular army. This constant doubt of the purity of his intentions and practical distrust of his measures and plans, arrested Washington at every step, and would have disgusted, irritated and disheartened any other commander. Even Congress exhibited this jealousy of his power, fettering and baffling him, so that his plans were not the reflex of himself, but rather a compromise of his own wisdom with the fears and demands and follies of those around him. There is no position so trying to a brave commander as this; the most perilous breach is far preferable to it. It is in such circumstances as these that Washington's moral character rises in its grand and beautiful proportions before us. With the hot blood and chivalric daring of a southron, joined to the prudence, forecast and wisdom of the sage, he added the patience, forbearance and meekness of a Christian. Such a combination is the rarest on earth. Thus, while the delays, inaction and incomplete organization of the army around Boston have furnished apparently solid ground for historians to underrate his military ability, they in fact enhance it, by showing him firm and uncomplaining under circumstances far worse to be borne than defeat. Had that army been like a single instrument in Washington's hands, wielded at his will, the siege of Boston would have exhibited a brilliancy of manœuvre, and energy and daring of action, that would have astonished his adversaries; but, chaining his great soul and glowing heart to the wheels of a dilatory Congress and the clogs of prejudice and suspicion, he toiled slowly, patiently, like a bound giant, toward the object of his endeavours. He knew that the great majority of those who had gathered to his standard, however they might err in judgment, were true men and patriots at heart, and example would tell on them in time. His practiced eye also soon discovered there were regiments whose noble devotion would carry them wherever he would lead. Morgan's rifle-men were a splendid body of men, and the words inscribed on their breast, "Liberty or Death," were symbolical of the brave hearts that throbbed beneath.

Pennsylvania and Maryland also responded to the call of Congress for troops, and the constant arrival of reinforcements kept the camp in a glow, and filled the army with confidence and pride.

CHAPTER V.

Washington Remonstrates against the Treatment of American Prisoners—Sends Arnold to Quebec—Want of Powder in the Army—A new Army raised—The National Flag first hoisted—Washington prevented from Assaulting the Enemy's Works—His feelings under the delay—Thinks of the poor at home—"Boston Blockaded," a farce—Washington takes possession of Dorchester Heights—Howe resolves to storm them—Attempt abandoned, and the Evacuation of Boston commenced—Sufferings of the Tories—Washington orders the Army to New York—Lee sent South—His Letter—Washington visits Congress—His Views of a Declaration of Independence—Defeat of the Northern Army—Attempt to spread disaffection in Washington's guard—Congress discusses the Declaration of Independence—Excitement in Philadelphia at the final vote—Its reception by the Army and People—Operations around New York—Howe's Letter to George Washington, Esq.—The assembling of the British force—State of the two Armies.

WHILE Washington was thus cautiously, slowly fusing the discordant elements together, and getting the army into manageable shape, he was told that the American prisoners taken at Bunker Hill were cruelly treated by the British—officers, soldiers and citizens being thrown indiscriminately into prison together. He immediately wrote to his old comrade in arms, General Gage, remonstrating against this treatment. Gage denied the charge, declaring it was an act of clemency on his part that they were not strung up on the gallows; and as to the different rank of those who fell into his hands, he recognized no grade but that bestowed by the king. Washington, in replying to this insolent and dishonourable note, said, "You affect, sir, to despise all rank not derived from the same source as your own. I cannot conceive one more honourable than that which flows from the uncorrupted choice of a brave and free people, the purest source and original fountain of all power."   He immediately, in retaliation for the treatment of Americans, ordered some British prisoners into the country, to be placed in close confinement.   They had not proceeded far, however, before he sent a despatch countermanding the order, and requesting the Committee of Northampton, to whom they had been intrusted, to treat them with all possible leniency.   Just and politic as the measure was, his heart revolted at making the innocent suffer for the guilty.

In the mean time, Congress had ordered General Schuyler to the Northern Department, to take St. John's, Montreal, and other portions of Upper Canada.   Washington, seeing this movement would draw the British troops under Governor Carleton away from Quebec, resolved to send an expedition against it across the wilderness.   Eleven hundred men were put under Arnold, who had just returned from the capture of Ticonderoga.   This extraordinary man entered upon the desperate undertaking with all the energy, daring and high courage that distinguished him.   Notwithstanding the desertion of one of his officers, and the unparalleled difficulties that beset his way, he finally reached Quebec, and affected a junction with Montgomery.   While this expedition was progressing to its disastrous issue, Washington made preparations to fall on the English batteries and storm Boston.   But no powder was to be had, while there remained only a few rounds to each man.   This alarming state of things Washington dare not communicate, except to a few of his own officers, lest it should leak out and get to the ears of the British commander.   To those who were ignorant of this fact, the inactivity that followed seemed unaccountable.

A short time previous to this determination, he had caused six armed schooners to be fitted out, to cruise against the enemy in the neighbourhood of Boston.   Several captures were made, and among them one by Captain Manly, with a quantity of powder aboard.

But now the term of enlistment of a large part of the army was drawing to a close. A new army must therefore be raised, and a committee from Congress came on to consult with him on the best means of doing it. Six months had elapsed since the battle of Bunker Hill, and the excited expectations of the country had met with sad disappointment. But now nothing could be done till the reorganization of the army was effected. This, however, proceeded slowly. Winter set in, and but five thousand recruits had arrived. So few of the old soldiers re-enlisted, and they left in such numbers that Washington at one time feared he would be left without an army. But even for the few that remained no provision had been made, and as the frost and snows of December came on, the troops began to suffer severely, and a feeling of despondency weighed down both officers and men. The latter were scantily clothed and destitute of fuel. Some of the regiments ate their food raw for want of fire, while detached parties were seen in every direction carrying off fences, and cutting down fruit and shade trees, with which to kindle a meagre fire in their dilapidated cabins, through which the winds of winter whistled. Many of those who had joined the army with high spirits, now began to think of their distant friends, and watching the opportunity, stole away from camp, and turned their footsteps homeward. The clouds gathered darker and darker around the head of Washington, and his heart was oppressed with the gravest fears, yet he still stood firm and serene, the pillar of hope to all around. As a last resort he issued a stirring call to the New England militia, which met with a warm response, and the hardy yeomanry came pouring in. Provisions were obtained, and in ten days a wonderful transformation was effected. The camp looked

bright again, and the arrival, at nearly the same
time, of Washington's wife and the wives of several
of the other officers, gave to the holidays a cheerful
aspect, and rekindled hope and confidence in the
commander. The New Year, which threatened to
look on a disbanded army, beheld nearly 17,000 well
ordered men.

On the first day of January the national flag of
thirteen stripes was hoisted for the first time over
the American army, and as it flaunted to the wind,
acclamations and shouts and salvos of artillery
greeted it. As Washington's eye watched it undu-
lating gracefully in the breeze, what thoughts must
have filled his heart. The symbol of liberty, it was
to move in front of his battalions to victory or defeat.
In the fate of that flag was wrapped all that he hoped
for or feared in life. From that moment its destiny
and his own were to be one and the same. He expected to carry it, at the head of his columns, through
smoke and carnage, perhaps be laid upon it in death
after some hard fought field, but how little he dreamed what its marvellous history would be. What
would have been his astonishment had it been whispered in his ear, " before all those who are now looking on that flag shall die, these thirteen colonies
shall be thirty states, the three millions of people,
for whose freedom you are struggling, be more than
thirty."

The king's speech before Parliament, in which he
declared that the most efficient measures would be
taken to put down the rebellion, but at the same
time pardon would be extended to all who sued for
it, arrived on the same day the flag was hoisted in
the American camp. The salvos of the artillery and
rejoicing that signalized the latter event, Howe,
who had succeeded Gage, took as an expression of
joy over the gracious nature of the king's offer.

Washington, who from the first had been very
much embarrassed in prosecuting the siege of Bos-

ton, for want of heavy cannon, at length despatched Knox to the forts on Lake Champlain captured from the British, for them. About this time the latter returned, and the long train of forty-two sleds, laden with thirty-nine cannon, fourteen mortars, two howitzers, over two thousand pounds of lead, and a hundred barrels of flints, as it slowly entered the camp, put a new face on affairs, and Washington resolved to assault the enemy's works at once. Congress was also anxious that the attack should be hurried forward. The regiments, however, were not yet filled, and at the council of officers called, a still further delay was decided upon. Nothing could be more irksome and irritating than the position in which Washington found himself. "I know," said he, "the unhappy predicament in which I stand; I know what is expected of me. I know that I cannot stand justified to the world without exposing my own weakness, and injuring the cause by declaring my wants, and my situation is so irksome to me at times that if I did not consult the public good more than my own tranquillity, I *should, long ere this, put every thing on the cast of a die.*" That is, if it had been a matter of mere personal reputation, he would have ended the suspense that galled him like a fetter, by one desperate onset. He regretted that he had been persuaded into delay on the promise of a larger and better army, and when he saw the disinclination of the soldiers to re-enlist, he said, "could I have known that such backwardness would have been discovered by the old soldiers to the service, *all the generals upon earth would not have convinced me of the propriety of delaying an attack on Boston till this time.*"

In the midst of these trials and embarrassments came the news of Arnold's failure at Quebec, and Schuyler's in Canada, accompanied by a letter from the latter, requesting a reinforcement of three thousand men. But while enveloped in perplexities, and his mind occupied by such vast and varied schemes, he had time to think of the poor on and around his plantation, and early in the winter he wrote home to Lady Washington, "Let the hospitality of the house, with respect to the poor, be kept up. Let no one go hungry away. If any of this kind of people should be in want of corn, supply their necessities, provided it does not encourage them in idleness." Although in the present condition of his affairs, and receiving nothing for his services, the "greatest frugality and economy" are demanded, he wishes two or three hundred dollars to be devoted annually to the poor. Nothing escapes his all-embracing mind, and still more all-embracing heart.

All this time the two armies lay only a mile apart, in full view of each other's operations, while the outposts were almost within speaking distance. Scarcely a day passed in which there was not more or less cannonading by the enemy, to which the Americans, for want of powder, had to submit in silence. What little they had was reserved, as Washington remarked, "for *closer work than cannon distance*, whenever the red-coat gentry please to step out of their intrenchments."

As the winter passed on the British began to feel the want of provisions. Meat of all kinds was ruinously high, while houses were torn down to furnish fuel for the soldiers. The parsonage of the old South Meeting-house, the old North Chapel, and the wooden steeple of the West Church, were one after another pulled to pieces for this purpose, while the glorious old "Libery Tree" furnished fourteen cords of wood. Faneuil Hall was fitted up as a theatre, in which a farce called "Boston Blockaded," was played, to the infinite amusement of the British and Tories. One of the chief characters in it was Washington, who cut a sorry figure on the stage. Shabbily clad, with a long, rusty sword by his side, attended by an ungainly, ragged servant, carrying an ancient gun, he

walked the boards with a gait that drew down the
house, while his speeches were received with immo-
derate laughter. This was all very well in a farce,
but an incident occurred one night that showed how
close fear trod on the heels of laughter.

A detachment had been sent to Charlestown to
destroy some houses either occupied, or used for fuel
by British soldiers. In this they were successful,
making several prisoners. The skirmish that followed was taken by the outposts for a general movement
of the army, and an officer burst into the theatre exclaiming, " the rebels are attacking our works on
Bunker Hill !" The audience, supposing this to be
a part of the play, and intended as a surprise, roared
with laughter, but when, suddenly, high over the
merriment, Lord Howe, who was present, shouted,
" *Officers, to your alarm posts !*" the farce was turned
into a tragedy, and manager, characters, and audience rushed pell-mell from the building.

The winter had been so mild, that but little ice had
formed in the waters around Boston, but at length,
in the middle of February, it froze hard enough to
bear troops, and Washington proposed to take advantage of it at once, and, crossing from Roxbury to
Dorchester Heights, fortify the latter, and at the
same time carry Boston by assault. A council of war,
however, decided that the latter attempt was too
perilous. Mortified and disappointed at this lack of
spirit and daring, Washington, nevertheless, resolved
to take possession of Dorchester Heights, and plant
his batteries above the town, and, if needs be, demo-
lish it, crowded though it was with friends as well
as foes. The noble Hancock had urged him to do
this, and, if necessary, send the first shot against his
own dwelling.

The great difficulty, however, was to cast up intrenchments in a single night, sufficiently strong to
cover the troops from the British fire in the morning.
The manner in which this was done I find thus clearly

related in in the diary of Rufus Putnam, the chief engineer of the army.*

"1776, January and February. During those months the mind of General Washington was deeply engaged in a plan of crossing on the ice, and attacking the British in Boston, and taking possession of Dorchester Neck.

"Now, with respect to taking possession of Dorchester Neck, there were circumstances which fell under my knowledge and sphere of duty, which were so evidently marked by the hand of an overruling Providence, that I think proper to relate them.

"As soon as the ice was thought sufficiently strong for the army to cross over, or perhaps rather before, a council of general officers was convened on the subject. What their particular opinions were I never knew, but the brigadiers were directed to consult the field-officers of their several regiments, and they again to feel the temper of the captains and subalterns.

"While this was doing, I was invited to dine at head-quarters; and while at dinner General Washington desired me to tarry after dinner, and when we were alone he entered into a free conversation on the subject of storming the town of Boston.

"That it was much better to draw the enemy out to Dorchester, than to attack him in Boston, no one doubted; for if we could maintain ourselves on that point or neck of land, our command of the town and harbour of Boston would be such as would probably compel them to leave the place.

"But the cold weather, which had made a bridge

* Judge Putnam of Ohio, the descendant of Rufus Putnam, has kindly furnished me with the manuscript diary of his ancestor, together with other valuable papers. Though not a professed engineer, he had had a good deal of experience in the French war, and the post was almost forced upon him by Washington and the other generals. All the works at Dorchester, Roxbury, and Brookline, were laid out by him.

of ice for our passage into Boston, had also frozen the earth to a great depth, especially in the open country, as was the hills on Dorchester Neck—so that it was impossible to make a lodgment there in the usual way. However, the general directed me to consider the subject, and if I could think of any way in which it could be done, to make report to him immediately.

"And now *mark those singular circumstances* which I call providential. I left head-quarters with another gentleman, and in our way came by General Heath's. I had no thought of calling until I came against his door, and then I says let us call on General Heath; to which he agreed. I had no other motive but to pay my respect to the General. While there, I cast my eye on a book which lay on the table, lettered on the back, '*Muller's Field Engineer.*' I immediately requested the general to lend it to me —he denied me. I repeated my request—he again refused, and told me he never lent his books. I then told him that he must recollect that he was one who at Roxbury in a measure compelled me to undertake a business which, at the time, I confessed I had never read a word about, and that he must let me have the book. After some more excuses on his part, and close pressing on my part I obtained the loan of it. I arrived at my quarters about dark. It was the custom for the overseers of the workmen to report every evening what progress had been made during the day. When I arrived there were some of them already there. I put my book in the chest, and if I had time did not think of looking in it that night.

"The next morning, as soon as an opportunity offered, I took my book from the chest, and looking over the contents found the word '*chandeliers.*' What is that? thought I—it is something I never heard of before; but no sooner did I turn to the page where it was described, with its use, but I was ready to report a plan for making a lodgment on Dorchester Neck, (infidels may laugh if they please.) In a few minutes after I had for myself determined, Col. Gridley (the engineer who had conducted the work at Cambridge) with Col. Knox of the artillery, who had been directed to consult with me on the subject, arrived. They fell in with my plan—our report was approved of by the general, and preparations immediately set on foot to carry it into effect; and, every thing being ready for the enterprise, the plan was put in execution, and a lodgment made on Dorchester Heights in the night of the fourth of March. Such were the circumstances which led to the discovery of a plan which obliged the enemy to leave Boston, viz. a lodgment made of chandelier* fascines, etc."

The better to conceal his purpose, and make it appear that an attack on the line was about to be made, Washington, on Saturday night, the 2d of March, opened a tremendous cannonade, the heavy metal reaching even into the city, and shattering the houses. The British replied, and the two armies thundered on each other all night. The next (Sunday) night Washington again opened his heavy batteries. On Monday night, while the deafening explosions were filling the inhabitants of Boston with terror, he ordered General Thomas with two thousand men to march across the neck and occupy the heights. Bundles of hay had been laid along on the town side to prevent the rumbling of the three hundred carts that followed from reaching the enemy's outposts. This immense train of carts, driven rapidly over the neck, carried the pressed hay and fascines,

* "A chandelier is constructed of one sill ten feet long and six inches square, with two posts five feet long, of the same size, framed into a sill five feet apart, each supported by a brace on the outside. They are placed on the ground at a proper distance from each other—the open space between the posts is then filled with bundles of fascines, strongly picketed together."

etc., for the chandeliers. It was a bright moonlight night as the soldiers wheeled up the heights, unseen by the sentinels below, and commenced their work. The bundles of hay were tumbled out and picketed together in the frames constructed for them, and when the bright sun gleamed down on the frozen waters it revealed to the astonished enemy two dark structures standing on Dorchester Heights. Howe was amazed at the apparition, and after surveying the works long and anxiously through his glass, exclaimed, "I know not what I shall do." The play of "Boston Blockaded" was evidently drawing to a close. These heights commanded the bay, and also Nook's Hill, which overlooked Boston. Something must be done at once. Dorchester Heights had become a second Bunker Hill, and the rebels must be driven from there, or the city abandoned. Washington, not doubting that the enemy would storm his works, had, therefore, planned an assault on the city from the opposite side, when it took place. Two columns of two thousand men each, commanded by Greene and Sullivan, the whole under Putnam, were, at a given signal, to embark in boats near the mouth of Charles river, and pushing rapidly forward effect a landing under the fire of three floating batteries, and fall furiously on the enemy.

Howe prepared at once to storm the American works, and commanded Earl Percy with three thousand men to attack them without delay. Washington anticipating this, galloped to the heights and gazed with kindling eye on the preparations for battle going on in the enemy's camp. He did not doubt for a moment of winning a glorious victory—the soldiers were in high spirits, and their courage was roused to a sterner pitch when he rode along their lines and bade them remember that it was the anniversary of the "Boston Massacre." The firm resolve to avenge that bloody act, mingled with the more exalted purpose to strike for liberty.

The three thousand men, with Percy at their head, were marched to the shore with orders to rendezvous at Castle William, and when night came on mount to the assault.   The hills around were covered with spectators, and thousands of hearts beat anxiously in view of the approaching conflict.   But toward night a heavy wind arose, rendering it impossible for the boats to land, and while the troops stood waiting the orders to advance, the night came on dark and stormy.   The rain fell in torrents, and they returned drenched and chilled to camp.   All next day the storm continued to rage, and a council of war being called, it was resolved to abandon the assault and evacuate the town.   Washington disappointed in not bringing on an engagement returned to camp, and Howe began to make preparations for his departure.   The inhabitants were now filled with alarm lest the latter should destroy the town, and a committee was appointed to wait on him to intercede for the place.   Howe very gladly promised to spare Boston if Washington would spare him and the fleet, and though no agreement was entered into, it was understood on both sides that the evacuation was to be effected quietly and without molestation. Washington, however, was determined not to trust to promises, and commenced planting (March 9th) his batteries on Dorchester Neck, so as to command more completely the enemy's shipping.   The British discerned the movement, and immediately turned their heavy guns upon the Americans.   The latter replied from all their batteries, and all night long it thundered and flamed around Boston, sending terror to the inhabitants, who, thinking it to be the signal for a final battle, expected every moment to see the city in a blaze.   But in the morning Howe ordered the batteries to cease playing, and went on with the preparations for embarking the troops.

At length, on Sunday the 17th, the army numbering, all told, about 11,000 men, together with 1,000 loyalists who fled, leaving all their property behind them, were aboard the transports, whose sails were soon moving down the bay. The American army no sooner saw the enemy in motion, than it paraded at Cambridge, and led by Putnam entered the deserted works of the British. Their loud hurrahs were heard by the retreating enemy, and all was exultation. The next day Washington accompanied by his staff rode into town, and was received with acclamations by the inhabitants.

The English fleet did not at first withdraw entirely, but lay for some time in the Nantucket Road, causing Washington much anxiety respecting its intentions. "What they are doing there," said he, "the Lord only knows." Cramped and confined in the over-crowded ships, the Tories suffered severely. Some enlisted as seamen, and all paid dear for their desertion of the cause of freedom. Washington was far from being pained to hear of their miserable condition, and describing it said, "Two have done what a greater number ought to have done long ago, committed suicide." These misguided men had supposed the British army invincible. "When the order issued therefore for embarking the troops, no electric shock, no explosion of thunder, in a word, not the last trump could have struck them with greater consternation."

The moment Washington got possession of Boston his amazing energies began to develop themselves. Believing that the next demonstration of the enemy would be against New York, he hurried troops off to defend it. Even before the fleet had left he despatched thither a regiment and several companies of riflemen, and wrote to Governor Trumbull of Connecticut, to throw two thousand men without delay into the town, and also to the Committee of Safety of New Jersey to add an additional thousand, that in case of a sudden attack the city might hold out till he could arrive with the army. Officers, in the mean time,

were sent forward to collect vessels at Norwich to
receive the troops the moment they should arrive.
He also despatched artillerists and ammunition to
General Thomas, who had been appointed commander-in-chief of the army in Canada, with a promise of
larger reinforcements soon to follow.   He knew that
the evacuation of Boston would be the signal for
active operations all along the coast, and he ordered
all his necessary camp equipage to be got ready immediately, saying, "after I have once got into a tent
I shall not so soon quit it."   No sooner had the
enemy disappeared entirely than the whole army
was set in motion for New York.   Nearly thirty
thousand troops had assembled around Boston, over
twenty thousand of whom belonged to the army
proper.   Twenty-seven hundred of these were on the
sick list—the remainder, with the exception of five
regiments under Lincoln left for the defence of
Boston, were soon streaming southward.   Division
followed division in rapid succession.   The inhabitants gazed with alarm on the swiftly marching
columns and long trains of artillery and baggage-
waggons as they rolled heavily onward, foretelling
strife and carnage to come.   Washington with his
guard outstripped the slow march of his army, and
passing through Providence, Norwich, and New
London, embarked on board a vessel and reached
New York on the 13th of April.   He immediately
inspected the works erected by Lee, and also by
Putnam, who had succeeded the former in command
of the city, passed from fort to fort directing the different
points to be occupied, and then calmly viewed his
position.   The twilight shadows of the gloomy night
that was so soon to close around the American cause
were already creeping over the land.   The disasters
that had befallen our troops in the north had extinguished the hopes of securing the co-operation of the
Canadians, and at the same time encourage the
Indians to break from their neutrality, so that a dark

and threatening cloud was rising along our unprotected frontiers. The troops were without blankets, and Congress without money, and worse than all without unity of feeling and purpose.

Sending off more troops into Canada, Washington hastened to Philadelphia, and though filled with anguish at the dissensions, timidity, and despondency that reigned in Congress, took courage when he found a large majority with him in insisting on a vigorous prosecution of the war. A resolution was hurried through to raise thirteen thousand eight hundred militia,* and a flying camp of ten thousand more, from Pennsylvania, Maryland, and Delaware.

In the mean time the Virginia Convention passed a bold resolution, recommending Congress to declare the colonies free and independent. "This is a noble vote," said Washington when he heard of it ; "many members of Congress, in short the whole provinces, are feeding themselves with the dainty food of reconciliation, but things have come to such a pass that we have nothing more to expect from the justic of Great Britian. The leaders of the people must not delude themselves and others with pleasing hopes and dreams, but look facts in the face, and prepare for the worst. In no other way can energy f action be secured. One and all," said he, "must enter the contest with the full belief 'that he must conquer or submit to unconditional terms, such as *confiscation, hanging, and the like,'* " *et ceteras,* well to be considered, however disagreeable.

The plan of the campaign on the part of the British had now begun to assume a definite form. Howe was to attack New York, ascend the Hudson, and meet an army from Canada, thus cutting the provinces in two, while Clinton should occupy the southern seaports, driving the Americans back to the interior. It was also known that mercenary troops were on the

* From New York, Massachusetts, Connecticut, and New Jersey

way, and the name of Hessian became a spell-word with which to conjure up shapes of evil.

Washington was absent fifteen days. On his return to New York, he pushed forward the preparations for receiving the enemy with all possible despatch. Gondolas, boats, etc., were built to defend the Narrows, below which the English ships had been driven by the American batteries, and New York soon assumed a formidable appearance. The news, however, from the north and south grew more discouraging. Lee wrote from the south, over which he had been placed, that he was "like a dog in a dancing school," and did not know "where to turn himself, or where to fix himself." The country was so intersected by navigable streams to which the British could fly at any moment on their "canvas wings," that he was left to conjecture alone where the first onset would be made, while the Committees of Safety of Virginia, unlike its convention, was full of hesitation and doubt. "Page, Lee, Mercer, and Payne," said he, "are indeed exceptions, but from Pendleton, Blond, the Treasurer and Company *libera nos Domine.*" From the north came tidings still more disheartening. The army was being driven in disgrace from Canada. The miserable remains of the armament that was to conquer it, lay without tents to cover them on the shores of Lake Champlain, one-half sick with small-pox, fever, and dysentery, over whose bodies myriads of loathsome vermin crawled unmolested; the other half disorganized and desponding, and with scarcely sufficient energy to cast their dead comrades into the two huge pits dug for their reception. Such was the news that ever and anon was brought to Washington, keeping his mind on the stretch from morning till night, and tasking his powers to their utmost limit. In the mean time forty sail [June 30] were reported in sight of the Hook. To add to all these embarrassments and trials, treason and disaffection were in his very midst. Governor Tryon, who remained on board ship down the bay, plotted unceasingly to detach the inhabitants and soldiers from the cause of the colonies. By seductive promises, rewards, and deceptions, he corrupted both, and finally penetrated even into Washington's guard, and set on foot a conspiracy to seize Washington himself. He expected in a short time to have the pleasure of seeing the head rebel on the deck of his ship. The plot, however, was revealed, and one of the guard was arrested, tried by court-martial, and hung—a warning to all who meditated treason.

While events were thus passing around New York, Congress, having assembled in Philadelphia, were engaged in the momentous question of a Declaration of Independence. Many of the separate provinces had already acted on the subject. North Carolina took the first step, and passed a vote instructing her deligate to concur with the other colonies in declaring independence. Massachusetts followed. Virginia next wheeled into the ranks, then Connecticut and New Hampshire. Maryland opposed it; while the delegates from the remaining provinces were instructed to unite with the majority, or left free to act as their judgments might dictate. Thus instructed, the representatives of the people assembled in solemn conclave, and long and anxiously surveyed the perilous ground on which they were treading. To recede was now impossible —to go on seemed fraught with terrible consequences. The struggle had not been for independence, but for the security of rights, in which they had the sympathy and aid of some of the wisest statesmen of England. To declare themselves free would cut them off from all this sympathy, and provoke at once the entire power of England against them. The result of the long and fearful conflict that must follow was more than doubtful. For twenty days Congress was tossed on a sea of perplexity. At length Richard Henry Lee, shaking off the fetters that galled his noble spirit, [June 7th] arose and in a clear, deliberate tone, every accent

of which rung to the farthest extremity of the silent
hall, read, "*Resolved, that these United Colonies are
and ought to be free and independent States, and that
all political connection between us and the State of
Great Britain is and ought to be totally dissolved.*"
John Adams, in whose soul glowed the burning future,
seconded it in a speech so full of impassioned fervour,
thrilling eloquence and prophetic power, that Congress was carried away as by a resistless wave
before it.

The die was cast, and every man was now compelled to meet the dreadful issue. Still weighed down
with fear, Congress directed the secretary to omit in
the journal the names of the bold mover and seconder
of this resolution, lest they should be selected as the
special objects of vengeance by Great Britain. The
resolution was made the special question for next
day, but remained untouched for three days, and was
finally deferred to the 1st of July to allow a committee appointed for that purpose to draft a declaration of
independence. When the day arrived, the declaration was taken up and debated article by article.
The discussion continued for three days, and was
characterized by great excitement; at length the
various sections having been gone through with, the
next day, July the 4th, 1776, was appointed for final
action. It was soon known throughout the city, and
in the morning, before Congress assembled, the streets
were filled with excited men, some gathered in groups
engaged in eager discussion, and others moving toward the State House. All business was forgotten
in the momentous crisis the country had now reached.
No sooner had the members taken their seats, than
the multitude gathered in a dense mass around the
entrance. The old bell-man mounted to the belfry,
to be ready to proclaim the joyful tidings of freedom
so soon as the final vote had passed. A bright-eyed
boy was stationed below to give the signal. Around
that bell, brought from England, had been cast more

than twenty years before the prophetic sentence, "PROCLAIM LIBERTY THROUGHOUT ALL THE LAND UNTO ALL THE INHABITANTS THEREOF." Although its loud clang had often sounded over the city, the proclamation engraved on its iron lip had never yet been spoken aloud. It was expected that the final vote would be taken without any delay, but hour after hour wore on and no report came from that mysterious hall, where the fate of a continent was being settled. The multitude grew impatient—the old bell-man leaned over the railing, straining his eyes downward, till his heart misgave him and hope yielded to fear. But at length, at two o'clock, the door of the hall opened, and a voice exclaimed, "*It has passed!*" The word leaped like lightning from lip to lip, followed by huzzas that shook the building. The boy-sentinel turned to the belfry, clapped his hands, and shouted "*Ring—ring!*" The desponding bell-man, electrified into life by the joyful news, seized the iron tongue and hurled it backward and forward, with a clang that startled every heart in Philadelphia like a bugle blast. "Clang—clang" it resounded on, ever higher and clearer and more joyous, blending its deep and thrilling vibrations, and proclaiming in long and loud accents over all the land the glorious motto that encircled it. Glad messengers caught the tidings as it floated out on the air and sped off in every direction, to bear it onward. When the news reached New York, the bells were set ringing, and the excited multitude surging hither and thither at length gathered around the Bowling Green, and seizing the leaden equestrian statue of George III. which stood there, tore it into fragments.* When the declaration arrived in Boston, the people gathered to old Faneuil Hall to hear it read, and as the last sentence fell from the lips of the reader a loud shout went up, and soon from every fortified

* This was afterward run into bullets, and hurled against his majesty's troops.
336 I

height and every battery the thunder of cannon re-
echoed the joy.

Washington drew up his army, and had the declaration read to each brigade in turn.   The acclamations with which it was received showed how
thoroughly the troops were penetrated with the
principle of Liberty.   In the mean time events were
thickening around New York.   The British fleet
from Halifax had arrived, and while Philadelphia
was yet shaking to the shouts of the multitude, on
the wooden heights of Staten Island the last of the
troops under General Howe were assembling, preparatory to a descent on the city below.   On the
12th July, taking advantage of a strong south wind,
two English ships of war stretched under a press of
canvas up the North river.   The moment they came
within range of the batteries on shore a rapid fire
was opened on them.   But the men, protected by
sand-bags, remained unharmed, while the vessels
being under rapid headway soon passed out of danger, and taking position in Tappan sea, lay beyond
the reach of shot from shore, thus proving what
Washington said he "had long most religiously believed, that a vessel with a brisk wind and strong
tide cannot, unless by chance shot, be stopped by a
battery on shore."

Washington, knowing that the only way the
British could reach the city landward was by Long
Island, along the shores of which they could at any
time disembark their troops, stretched a cordon of
works from Wallabout Bay across Brooklyn Heights,
down to Gowan's Cove, the chief fortifications being
on the Heights.   At each extremity, and where they
touched the water, batteries were placed, to prevent
ships going up the East river.   General Howe in
the mean time remained tranquil in his head quarters
on Staten Island, waiting for reinforcements from
England, before he ventured on an attack.   Washington occupied the long interval that elapsed in

throwing up works at Kinsbridge, and erecting forts Washington and Lee, between which, across the river, were stretched *chevaux de frise* and hulks of vessels, sunk to prevent the British fleet from ascending and outflanking him, and in establishing redoubts along the Hudson and the East rivers.

The two ships that had gone up the Hudson with their tenders, kept cruising below the Highlands, taking soundings, and effectually dividing the northern and southern army.

At length Lord Howe joined his brother, having been sent as royal commissioner, with terms of reconciliation, or, as Washington said, "to dispense pardons to repenting sinners." These, however, were so utterly unsatisfactory that they could not be entertained for a moment. He also sent a letter to Washington with a flag, which the guard-boats detained till the will of the American general could be ascertained. Colonel Reed was immediately sent down to meet the flag, when the officer in charge of it handed him a letter directed to "George Washing, Esq." Reed assured him that there was no such man in the American army, and refused to take charge of it, and the flag was compelled to return. A few days after another letter with the same superscription was sent and met the same reception. General Howe then despatched his adjutant general to Washington's quarters, bearing a letter directed "To George Washington, Esq., etc., etc., etc." The adjutant addressed Washington as his "excellency," which certainly was a great concession to the head rebel of the colonies, and said that General Howe regretted exceedingly that the mode of address was offensive, as no insult had been intended, for both Lord and General Howe "held his person and character in the highest esteem." To meet all objections as to rank or title the *et ceteras* had been affixed, which, like the Italian *Tante grazie*, meant just as much as you chose to imagine. But Wash-

ington declared that he would not receive as a private
person any letter "relating to his public station,"
and that a letter without some indication in its address of its public character must necessarily be considered private.   After much expenditure of courtesy
on both sides, the adjutant, stubbornly refusing to
give any interpretation to the *et ceteras*, returned to
General Howe, who at length, in view of the momentous results at stake, ventured to break through
this punctilio, and address his letters to "General
Washington."   For this extraordinary stretch of his
powers as royal commissioner, he, in his despatches
home, said he hoped his majesty would not be offended.   The change of the mode of the address, however, did not effect a reconciliation with the mother
country, though so great a sacrifice might seem to
merit some reward.

In the mean time various gallant attempts had
been made to capture the two English ships in
Tappan Bay, and though unsuccessful, one tender
had been taken, towed ashore, and burned.   Alarmed at these repeated attacks, they took advantage of
a strong tide and northerly wind to return, running
the gauntlet of the batteries and the riflemen on
shore in gallant style, hurling their grape-shot as
they swept on.   They succeeded in joining the fleet
in safety, though many an ugly rent gave indications of what might be expected should a whole fleet
attempt to pass.

At length, by the middle of August, the British
reinforcements had all arrived, swelling the entire
army to some twenty-five thousand men, supported
by a powerful fleet.   Against this formidable array
Washington could not bring a single ship, and only
eleven thousand one hundred men, a large part of
whom were raw militia.＊   Added to all this tremendous preponderance of force, made still more effective

＊ The army nominally consisted of 25,537—but 3,368
were sick, 97 absent on furlough, and 2,946 on command.

by a covering fleet, the whole army was well supplied with every thing necessary to success, while
the American troops being scattered along from
Kinsbridge to Brooklyn, a space of fifteen miles, was
miserably equipped, without discipline, and at this
very juncture torn asunder by jealousies and bitter
feuds, often breaking out into open animosity.
Washington, expecting an attack daily, strove to
allay this discord, and partially succeeded—still his
position was extremely critical, and it was hoping
against reason to dream of saving New York.

But the news of Moultrie's gallant defence of the
" *slaughter-pen*," as Lee in derision termed it, on
Sullivan's Island, in Charlestown harbour, re-
awakened confidence and kindled fond anticipations
in the hearts of many that a similar fate awaited the
enemy around New York. The salvation of the
city, however, was only a secondary consideration—
with its fall the route to Albany would, in all probability, be opened to the British, and the northern
army, now retreating from Canada, would be
crushed midway, and all the eastern provinces cut
off from their northern brethren. This stroke would
give the finishing blow to the union of the colonies,
leaving each victim to fall alone.

CHAPTER VI.

The British land on Long Island—Sickness of Greene—The Battle—Defeat of Sullivan and Stirling—Masterly Retreat to New York—Causes of Failure—New York abandoned—Retreat of Washington to Harlem Heights—Landing of the British at Kip's Bay—Poltroonery of the Americans and rage of Washington—His severe Order of the Day—Remarks on the Conduct of Washington—Narrow Escape of Putnam with his Division—Skirmish between two Detachments and Death of Knowlton—Manœuvre of Howe and Battle of Chatterton's Hill—Retreat of Washnigton—Fall of Fort Washington.

At length, August 22d, it was announced that the British were landing on Long Island, between the Narrows and Sandy Hook. The plan originally was to bombard the city, but this had been abandoned, and an attack by land resolved upon. General Greene, to whom the works on Long Island had been entrusted, and who was doubtless thoroughly acquainted with every locality, was at this critical moment prostrated by a bilious fever and carried to New York. Putnam succeeded him in the command, but, from some cause or other, did not seem to think his duties extended beyond the lines.

Between the plain on which the British landed and the intrenchments of the Americans, stretched a thickly wooded hill, traversed by only three roads, on each of which redoubts had been thrown up to check the advance of the enemy. But one of these, the Bedford road, which led straight up to the American works, was left wholly unguarded. Sullivan commanded without the lines in this direction, and it seems incomprehensible that any general could commit such a strange oversight in presence of the enemy. Washington had given express orders to have all these passes well guarded, but the fact that Greene was expected to be well enough to resume his command before the attack commenced, prevented the appointment of an officer in his place, in time to allow him to become acquainted with the ground, while Sullivan, Putnam, and Stirling seemed wholly ignorant of the exact duties required of them. Besides, the universal belief that this land demonstration was only a feint to draw off the troops from the city, on which the grand attack, by water, would be made, may have caused the officers in charge to be less soliticous about the defences on the island.

The English, ten thousand strong, with an artillery train of forty pieces, took up their line of march on the warm August evening, (26th,) and slowly approached the wooded heights before them. Howe accompanied the right wing commanded by Clinton, Cornwallis, and Percy, and at two o'clock in the morning stood on the summit, and looked down over the plain stretching to Brooklyn. Grant, commanding the left wing, moved along near the water's edge, toward Gowanus Bay, while the old and veteran De Heister, fully restored from the effects of his three months' voyage by liberal potations of hock, led the centre, composed of Hessians, against the redoubts defended by Sullivan in person. The centre and left of the army were ordered only to skirmish with the enemy till they heard the guns of Clinton on the right, when they were to press to the assault at once, and prevent reinforcements from being concentrated at any single point. With the first sound of artillery, Putnam sent off reinforcements to support both Sullivan and Stirling. The latter having been ordered to defend the coast road, took position at daybreak, in the hills which now form Greenwood Cemetery.

In the mean time Clinton had descended from the hills to the Bedford Plains, and opened his fire on Sullivan's left. This was the signal for De Heister, who immediately ordered Count Donop with his veteran Hessians to storm the redoubt in front, and carry it at the point of the bayonet, while he, with the main body, would advance to his support. The battle was in reality already won by Clinton, who now completely outflanked Sullivan. The latter met the onset in front with his accustomed bravery, and as the Hessians poured, with their wild German war-cry, to the assault, mowed them down with the steady volleys of his handful of resolute men. But the fir-ing on his flank rapidly advancing nearer, threatened momentarily to cut him off from the lines at Brook-lyn, and he reluctantly gave the order to retreat. His small force however had scarcely reached the foot of the slope on which they had been posted, when they were greeted by the blast of bugles, as the Bri-tish dragoons came galloping up the road in rear.

His retreat was now cut off, and he threw himself into a piece of wood for protection. But the loud shouts and gleaming bayonets of the Hessians as they swarmed through the green foliage, showed that this was no place for shelter, and the now surrounded Americans again emerged into the open field, only to be trampled down by the cavalry, and charged by the infantry, which had completely blocked up the way of escape. Driven again to the woods for shelter, they were bayoneted by the Hessians, who, refusing quarter, fought with the ferocity of tigers. Thus backward and forward they were hunted by the hos-tile ranks, until a portion, maddened to desperation, burst with one fierce effort through the barrier of steel that girdled them, and reached the main army in safety. The remainder, with Sullivan, were taken prisoners.

All this time Stirling, ignorant how the battle was going, firmly maintained his position against Grant. But Clinton had no sooner disposed of the American left, than he despatched Cornwallis across the country to take the former in rear, and execute over again the manœuvre that had destroyed Sullivan. This British officer advanced till within a short distance of Stirling, when he fired two cannon shot, the signal before agreed upon for Grant to move to the assault.

The latter then gave the order to advance. Pressed in front and rear by an overwhelming force, Stirling saw at a glance his desperate position. The only chance of saving any part of his force was, with a small band of resolute men to keep Cornwallis employed, while the main body, fording Gowanus creek lower down, could gain the flank of the enemy and escape to Fort Putnam, on Booklyn Heights. The tide was fast rising, and what was done must be done quickly. Calling around him a portion of Smallwood's glorious regiment of Marylanders, composed almost entirely of young men of rank and wealth, he hurled them with such terrible impetuosity on the British grenadiers, that the latter recoiled with amazement from the shock. Flushed however with the previous easy victory, and disdaining to yield to a band of undisciplined rebels, they rallied to the attack, and the conflict became close and murderous. But these gallant young men, each one a hero, pressed so sternly into the fire, that they bore down all oppositon, and for the first time in open combat, rolled back the veterans of England. The steadfast Delawares stood, with their rent colours flying, and let the artillery of Grant plough through them, disdaining to stir till ordered to retire. The fighting here was desperate. Young Callender, who had been cashiered for cowardice at the Battle of Bunker Hill, and afterward entered the service as a volunteer, seeing the captain and lieutenant of the company of artillery to which he belonged fall, took command, and with the determination to wipe out with his life-blood the disgrace that had fallen on him, disdained to surrender, fighting his pieces to the last. Even when the British infantry were charging over his guns he never flinched. A British officer, struck with admiration at his noble, gallant bearing, knocked up the bayonets already pointed at his heart, and spared his life. Though outnumbered more than three to one, Stirling, with his hero-band, steadily pushed back Cornwallis, till the latter was heavily reinforced. The order to wheel off to the left and escape across the marsh was then given. A part succeeded in escaping, and swimming a small creek reached Fort Putnam in safety. The remainder, and among them Lord Stirling, surrendered themselves prisoners of war.

Washington, as the sound of the heavy cannonading broke over the city, hastened to the shore, and leaping into a boat manned by strong rowers, was soon on the Brooklyn side. Galloping up the Heights, he cast a hurried glance over the plains beyond. As he saw Sullivan completely cut off, and that Stirling, though t from the heavy cannonading evidently still maintaining his ground, must soon inevitably share the fate of the former, a cry of anguish burst from his lips. The day was lost beyond redemption, and some of his noblest troops gone forever. All this time Greene lay tossing on his feverish bed, a prey to the most painful anxiety. At length, as the news reached him that Smallwood's—his favourite regiment—was cut to pieces, he groaned aloud, and bursting into tears, exclaimed—"*Gracious God, to be confined at such a time!*"

Thus ended the first battle between the army under Washington and the enemy. Nearly twelve hundred men, or a quarter of the entire force engaged, had been slain or captured, a portion of them the elite of the army. Among the prisoners were Generals Sullivan, Stirling, and Woodhull. It was extraordinary that so many escaped. But the patches of wood and thickly scattered hills furnished concealment to a great many detached parties, that in a more open field or one better known to the enemy, would inevitably have been captured. The manoeuvre of Howe was completely successful, and deserved even a better reward than it received.

The junction of the various divisions of the British army being effected soon after the defeat of the Americans, the whole advanced to within six hundred yards of the works on Brooklyn Heights. Excited by the easy victory, the troops demanded to be led to the assault at once. If it had been permitted there is little doubt but that the overwhelming numbers of the British would have proved too resistless for even the strong works behind which Putnam lay. But Howe, ignorant of the force opposed to him, did not wish to risk all he had gained by an uncertain, desperate onset, and commenced planting his batteries, evidently designing to advance by regular approaches. Washington, who had watched with the keenest anxiety the rapid concentration of the host before him, with its long lines of gleaming bayonets and heavy trains of artillery, saw with inexpressible delight this determination of Howe. Time would now be given to reflect upon his situation and determine his course. If he should resolve to fight it out where he was, he could bring over reinforcements; if to retreat, he might, by great exertions and skilful management, save perhaps the army.

That night the Americans slept but little. Washington had despatched couriers to General Mifflin, at Kinsbridge, to hasten down with a thousand men. These soon after daylight were seen crossing the river to Wallabout, where they took post. The morning dawned dark and gloomy, and as soon as the American works could be distinctly seen, the British opened on them with their heavy guns, and shortly after, the sharp rattle of musketry was heard as the outposts came in collision. The heavens continued to gather blacker and more sombre, and soon after mid-day the rain came down in torrents. In a short time the fields were flooded, and presented a picturesque appearance, dotted with the white tents of the enemy, into which they crept for shelter, but the discouraged, discomfited patriots had no tents or barracks, and stood drenched to the skin. The night brought impenetrable darkness, for a heavy fog slowly settled on sea and land, through which broke only the muffled tread or low call of the sentinel.

Adjutant-General Reed, Mifflin and Colonel Gray-
son had been sent out during the afternoon to reconnoitre, and just before sunset, as they stood looking
seaward, a sudden gust of wind, like a friendly hand,
lifted for a moment the fog that lay over the British
vessels within the Narrows, and revealed to them
boats filled with men, passing from ship to ship, and
all the preparations for some great and combined
movement. The fleet had been directed to act in
concert with the land-force, and attacking the
batteries on shore, pass up the East river, and so
separate the main American army in New York from
that of Brooklyn. But the "stars fought against
Sisera," for a strong east wind surged all day down
the East river, holding back the ships with its unseen
hand.

The movement on board the vessels being reported
to Washington, a council of war was called, and it
was unanimously resolved to retreat to New York.
The fog that covered the island effectually concealed
the movements of the Americans, and at eight o'clock
the soldiers were paraded, and began their silent march
toward the ferry at the foot of Fulton street. But the
strong north-easter which had buffeted back the British
fleet, was now, with an ebb tide, sending such a
furious current seaward that the boats could not be
launched. At length, about eleven o'clock, the wind
changed to the north-west and blew violently. The
troops were then embarked in the fleet of boats prepared for their reception, and passed silently and
swiftly from shore to shore. By five o'clock in the
morning the whole nine thousand, with all their
munitions of war, except the heavy artillery, were
safe in New York. Washington stood the long and
gusty night on the Brooklyn side, watching detachment after detachment disappearing in the gloom, and
as the last boat left the land he also stepped in, and
with a world of care lifted from his heart, crossed over
to the city. For nearly forty-eight hours he had not

closed his eyes, and been a great part of the time in the saddle, superintending and directing every thing, and exhibited a skill, energy and power seldom witnessed in the oldest and most renowned commanders.

The battle of Long Island has given rise to much discussion, and various explanations have been offered and excuses rendered of the sad failure. No doubt there would have been more and severe fighting if Greene had been able to hold his command. No doubt Putnam should have looked out for flank movements, but he was good only for fighting, and knew nothing of strategy. And no doubt Sullivan should have guarded the Jamacia road, or urged Putnam to do it, but he, too, had yet to learn the duties of a general by hard experience. The excuse that he did not command without the lines is not a valid one for his neglect. The simple truth is the battle should never have been fought, for no precautions could have changed the final result. The enemy were in too strong force for the American army on the Brooklyn side to resist under the most favourable circumstances that could have been anticipated. But to abandon New York without a struggle seemed fraught with evil consequences, and it could not be defended by land better than where the stand was made. Washington, like every other general officer, was compelled to leave many of the details on which a battle turns to the efficency and energy of his subordinates, so that he is not responsible for the loose way in which the passes were defended. The great error probably lay in the settled conviction that the land attack would be only partial, and the main assault be on the city itself through the fleet. Of course there could be no comparison between the military knowledge and ability of the British and American officers. The former, many of them had had the advantage, not merely the early training, but of large experience in many a tedious campaign, on the continent of Europe, and it would be a miracle if even Washing-

ton at the outset, could not be outmanœuvred by
them, when the operations were on an extensive
scale.   But he was an apt scholar, and one lesson
was sufficient for a lifetime, and in the unexpected
vicissitudes of war, when tactics had to be made on the
spot to meet the exigencies of the case, he showed
how intellect and genius, and an almost infallible
judgment, could triumph over obstacles that put at
fault the most veteran leaders.

The effect of this defeat on the American army
was most disastrous.   Despondency and despair took
the place of confidence and hope.   The hastily collected yeomanry of the colonies had done good battle on Bunker Hill, and considered themselves in
fact the victors, and when a regular appointed army,
with Washington at its head, should meet the enemy
around New York, a glorious triumph was confidently
predicted.   But in this first battle the superiority of
the enemy was made apparent, and just as high as
the spirits of the troops had been raised previous to
it so low they now sunk.   A sudden paralysis seized
them, and nothing but murmurings and complaints
were heard.   The burning desire to wipe out the
disgrace—the courage rising with increasing danger
—the stern cheerful rally to the side of their afflicted
noble commander, were all wanting.   On the contrary the militia grew insubordinate, and there, right in
front of the enemy, while his strong columns were
gathering closer and darker around the city, began
to disband and march away to their homes.   Nearly
whole regiments at a time, half ones, and by companies, they filed away, heedless of the remonstrances,
appeals, and threats of their officers.   In the very
crisis of affairs the whole army threatened to be disorganized.   Washington looked around him in dismay, and lost all confidence in his troops.   He was
not prepared for this wholesale desertion in the hour
of danger.   Inexperience, want of discipline, jealousies, and rivalries, were evils he anticipated.   He

knew, also, that it would be impossible to keep an efficient army in the field on the short enlistments heretofore practised, but to be left alone when the fate of the largest city in the colonies was depending, was a catastrophe against which no foresight could provide. He wrote to Congress that New York must be abandoned to the enemy, and a council of war was immediately called to decide on the course best to be pursued, which came to the same decision. A bombardment was hourly expected, and Washington issued an order for the inhabitants to leave, and soon the roads leading toward Harlæm were crowded with fugitives, while hundreds more were seen hurrying across the river to the Jersey shore.

In the council of war it was proposed by some to set the city on fire, and thus prevent the British from making it their winter-quarters. General Greene urged this measure, declaring that the Tories would be the chief sufferers, as two-thirds of the property in the town was owned by them.

In the mean time the plans of Lord Howe developed slowly. He had requested Congress to appoint a committee to meet him on Staten Island, and consult on some mode of arranging the difficulties between the colonies and mother country. They met, but the views of the two parties differed so completely that all hopes of adjustment were abandoned. Howe then began to push his advances on New York. The whole fleet moved up into the harbour, and soon after frigate after frigate stood up the East river, and on the 15th September, three men-of-war swept past the batteries along the Hudson, and lay-to off Bloomingdale. It now became apparent that the enemy had no design of bombarding the city, and thus destroy the snug quarters they stood so much in need of, but were about to land above, toward Harlæm, and march down on it from the most unprotected quarter. Washington, penetrating their design, hurried off his baggage and sick, and nine thousand men to Kinsbridge and its vicinity, keeping only five thousand in the city to act as the exigencies of the case might demand. Detachments in the mean time were scattered along between New York and Harlæm, to protect the batteries and resist the attempts of the British to land. On the same day, at eleven o'clock, General Clinton began to land his troops at Kip's Bay, under the heavy fire of three war vessels. The day before he had taken possession of Montressor's Island, and Washington, aware of his intentions, ordered the two brigades under Parsons and Fellows to hasten next morning to the threatened point, while he galloped away to Harlæm, where he spent the night. In the forenoon, while busily superintending the works on the Heights, he was startled by the heavy cannonading from the vessels of war, shaking the very ground on which he stood. Instantly vaulting to his saddle, he rode toward Kip's Bay. As he approached he saw to his utter astonishment the men who had been stationed at the batteries in full flight, leaving their pieces unmanned, although not seventy of the enemy had effected a landing. Before he could recover from the effect of this shameful spectacle, he beheld the two brigades which he had despatched to the support of the batteries also in full retreat, despite the threats and commands of their officers. Such utter poltroonery, coming as it did on the top of all he had undergone from his faithless troops, and placing in such imminent peril Putnam with his five thousand troops, proved too much for his self-command, and that strong soul for once burst the restraints with which he had bound it. Dashing into the midst of the fugitives, he bade them in a voice of thunder halt. But they in their panic did not hear him, or if they did paid no attention to his commands, and dividing around his horse streamed wildly on. Enraged beyond all control, he denounced them with a fearful oath as cowards, and drawing his pistols snapped them in their faces, and cut at the nearest with his sword.

Finding all his efforts vain, and filled with ungovernable rage, he dashed his chapeau to the ground, and
wheeled all alone full on the advancing enemy, apparently determined in that terrible paroxysm of
passion and of scorn not to survive the disgrace of his
army. One of his aids, however, advancing seized
the bridle of his horse and turned him back. The
hurricane had passed, and Washington was himself
again. The stern indignation, however, at such
conduct did not soon subside, and five days after, in
the order of the day, he said, "Any soldier or officer
who upon the approach or attack of the enemy's forces
by land or water, shall presume to *turn his back and
flee, shall be instantly shot down, and all good officers
are hereby authorized and required to see this done,
that the brave and gallant part of the army may not
fall a sacrifice to the base and cowardly part, nor
share their disgrace in a cowardly and unmanly retreat.*'
This terrific outburst sheds a world of light on
Washington's character, and instead of depreciating
it invests it with tenfold interest, and exhibits in a
more striking manner the transcendent qualities he
possessed. This and one or two similar incidents in
his life are avoided by his biographers, or merely
touched upon, as though it were a pity to speak of
them at all, and common charity required them to
be concealed as much as possible. They even feel
indignation toward those who give them prominence,
as though a personal attack were made on the "Father
of his Country." These men are wiser than their
Maker, who does not hesitate to record the single
rash act of Moses, who in his rage dashed the tables
of the law to the earth, or the sinful conduct of David,
the chosen of Heaven, or the quarrel of the Apostles.
They forget that a human character is grand and
exalted only as it overcomes evil, and the more difficult the victory the greater the glory. But for such
terrible outbursts as this we should never have known

what a volcano Washington carried in his bosom, and hence been ignorant of the marvellous strength of character, and the religious principle which kept down its fires. His eulogists seem to think that the more unexcitable and passionless they make him, the more perfect he is, forgetting that moral character is not an endowment, but the result of effort and education, and that a man who is naturally impetuous deserves just as much credit for being *hasty*, as one who is naturally quiet and immobile for being placid and unruffled. It is the man who "*ruleth* his spirit that is greater than he that taketh a city," not one who has no spirit to rule. It is the knowledge of Washington's inflammable, passionate nature, contrasted with his conduct under the severest trials long continued, under injustice, suspicion, neglect, desertion, abuse, discomfiture, and defeat, that makes us regard him with unbounded admiration and astonishment. It is his amazing self-control that fills us ever with fresh wonder, and yet had he been born with a phlegmatic, equable temper, his serenity would have been no proof of this. It is the arm which holds back the torrent that exhibits strength, not that which rests unmoved in the tranquil pool.

The moment Washington saw the British had effected a landing, he despatched an aid to General Putnam in the city, with orders to fall back with his division, as speedily as possible to Harlæm Heights. Putnam immediately put his brigade in motion, followed by a motley multitude of women and children, with loads of baggage and utensils, hurrying on with loud cries after the retiring columns. It was a hot sultry day, and under the burning sun and clouds of dust kicked up by the advance regiments, the soldiers, many of them, sunk exhausted by the road-side, and fell into the hands of the enemy. Not a moment was to be lost. Clinton had already possession of the main road along the East river, so that Putnam was compelled to take the Bloomingdale road, across which the three frigates that had passed up the Hudson could throw their heavy metal. The disgraceful flight at Kip's Bay had allowed the British to gain so much time in landing, that to all human appearance they could stretch a cordon across the island, before Putnam could reach Bloomingdale, and Washington looked upon him and his entire division as lost. Putnam thought so too, but determined not to despair so long as a ray of hope remained, and hurried his flagging columns with all the energy he possessed. Riding from front to rear to encourage, to stimulate, and to threaten, he galloped backward and forward under the burning sun, his horse covered with foam and dust, and every lineament of his bold rough face revealing the intense anxiety under which he laboured. A Quaker lady, named Murray, occupied at that time Murray Hill, and he sent to her to delay by her hospitality as long as possible, Sir Henry Clinton. As the latter, with his staff, passed the house on his way to the Bloomingdale road, this patriotic lady accosted him, and cordially invited him to stop and take a glass of wine. The cool refreshments which followed, were most acceptable to the British officers, and she detained them by her courtesies till her negro servant, who had been stationed on the top of the house to watch the American army, returned and made the sign agreed upon, to indicate it was beyond danger. A portion of the British troops had struck it at right angles, and a severe skirmish followed, in which fifteen Americans were killed, and two or three hundred taken prisoners, but the main body had barely slipped by, the enemy's line closing behind them as they passed. When Clinton emerged from Mrs. Murray's house, he saw, to his utter mortification, the American banners fluttering far in advance, pointing proudly toward the heights on which was drawn up the rebel forces. As darkness shut in the scene, the weary column wound up the slope, and was received with shouts by the whole army, while Washington did not attempt to conceal his delight at the energy and skill with which Putnam had brought off his troops. In the mean time the whole British army advanced, and at night encamped near the American works—their lines stretching from river to river, and supported at each extremity by ships of war. Thus passed the night of the fifteenth of September. When the morning drum, rolling from river to river, awoke the two armies, Lord Howe turned his glass long and anxiously on the American works. Notwithstanding the easy victories he had obtained, he hesitated to attack a position so well chosen, and defended as the one before him. Washington, irritated at the moral effect produced on both armies by the dastardly conduct of his troops, was anxious to remove it, if possible, and resolved to attack any detachments that the enemy might send forward. During the day several parties appeared on the plain between the two armies, and a skirmish followed. This was no sooner reported to Washington, than he hastened to the outposts to ascertain the number and purpose of the enemy. While he was thus examining them, Colonel Knowlton came in and reported their number about three hundred. Washington immediately ordered him with his rangers, aided by Major Leitch, with three companies of Virginians, to attempt to gain their rear and cut them off. At the same time he directed a false attack to be made in front, to distract their attention from the real point of danger. The British detachment seeing the party approaching in front, retired to a cover of bushes and a fence. Knowlton, ignorant of this change of position, instead of gaining their rear as he expected, came suddenly on them in flank. Major Leitch immediately advanced gallantly to the attack, but fell pierced with balls ; Knowlton, hastening to his support, was also shot down. The troops, however, pressed fiercely on, and a reinforcement coming up, charged home so resolutely, that the enemy broke their cover and fled to the open plain. Washington fearing that the British would send out a large reinforcement, ordered the bugles to sound a recall, and the gallant detachment retired to their posts with the loss of sixty killed and wounded. The British acknowledged ninety killed and wounded. The death of Colonel Knowlton, however, made the balance of loss heavy against the Americans. He was one of Putnam's best officers. He had entered service when but sixteen years old, had been with Putnam in some of his hardest battles during the French war, and was among the first to rally to his old leader's side, after the skirmish at Lexington. He fought gallantly at Bunker Hill and Long Island, and was an officer of great promise. He fell at the age of thirty-six, on the threshold of that great struggle to which he would have given a clear head and a fearless heart. In his order the next day, Washington called him "the gallant and brave Knowlton, who would have been an honour to any country."

No one will ever know what he suffered during his retreat from New York up the Island. The embarrassments that overwhelmed him at every turn were enough in themselves to crush a commander, but when to all those was superadded utter want of confidence in his troops, there was nothing left on which to fall back. Disasters he could endure, but with soldiers he dared not trust in battle, no matter how inferior the enemy might be in force, that run away from even the sound of cannon, he was left utterly desolate. In a letter to his brother, speaking of the anguish that weighed him down at this time, he said he would not again undergo what he had suffered during those few days for a quarter of a million of dollars. The troops not only became cowards, but robbers, and under pretence of plundering the Tories, committed violence on the inhabitants indiscriminately. Thirty-nine lashes been the extent of the punishment allowed by the orders of Congress, the culprits treated it with contempt.

Howe was anxious to bring on a general engagement without assaulting the Americans behind their works. Washington, having no confidence in the mass of his troops, was equally determined not to gratify him, and the two armies lay idly looking upon each other for three weeks. Washington, however, improved the time in strengthening his position. At length Howe determined to make another effort to gain the American rear, and sending three vessels of war up the Hudson, which passed the batteries on shore and obstructions in the channel with but little damage, he embarked his troops in flat-bottomed boats, on the East river, and sailing through Hell Gate, landed on Throg's Neck. Remaining here five days, he re-embarked, and landing at Pell's Point, marched to the high grounds near New Rochelle.

The next morning Washington, who had been kept strangely ignorant of the roads and topography of the country to which the movements of the armies had been transferred, sent out Colonel Reed, and Rufus Putnam, engineer in chief, with a foot guard of twenty men, to reconnoitre. Arriving on the heights of East Chester, they saw a small body of British, but could obtain no intelligence—the houses being all deserted. Colonel Reed here said he must return to attend to issuing general orders. Putnam replied that as yet they had made no discovery of consequence, and that if he went back he had better take the guard with him. As for himself, he was determined to proceed, and preferred to go alone. Putnam thus relates what followed, which I transcribe from his manuscript journal, as it throws new light on this portion of the campaign.

"I then disguised my appearance as an officer as far as I could, and set out on the road to White Plains. However, I did not then know where

White Plains was, nor where the road I had taken would carry me. I had gone about a mile and a half when a road turned off to the right; I followed it perhaps half a mile and came to a house where, I learned from a woman that the road led to *New Rochelle, that the British were there,* and that they had a guard at a house in sight. On this information I turned and pursued my route towards White Plains, (the houses on the way all deserted,) until I came within three or four miles of the place. Here I discovered a house a little ahead, with men about it. By my glass I found they were not British soldiers. However, I approached them with caution. I called for some oats for my horse, sat down and heard them chat for some little time, when I found they were friends to the cause of America, and then I began to make the necessary inquiries, and on the whole I found that the main body of the British lay at New Rochelle—from thence to White Plains about nine miles—good roads and in general level open country—that at White Plains was a large quantity of stores, with only about three hundred militia to guard them—that the British had a detachment at Mamaroneck, only six miles from White Plains, and White Plains only five miles from the North river, where lay five or six of the enemy's ships and sloops, tenders, &c.

"Having made these discoveries, I set out on my return—the road across the Bronx was my intended route, unless I found the British there, which haply they were not. But I found Americans on the heights west of Bronx, who had arrived there after I passed up. I found it to be Lord Stirling's division. It was now after sunset. I gave my lord a short account of my discoveries, took some refreshments, and set off for head-quarters, by the way of Philips' at the mouth of Saw-Mill river, a road I had never travelled. Among Tory inhabitants and in the night, I dare not inquire the way—but providence conducted me. I arrived at head-quarters, near Kinsbridge, (a distance of about ten miles,) about nine o'clock at night. I found the General alone, and reported to him the discoveries I had made, with a sketch of the country. He complained very feelingly of the gentlemen from New York, from whom he had never been able to obtain a plan of the country, and said that from their information he had ordered the stores to White Plains as a place of security. The General then sent for General Greene and General George Clinton. As soon as General Clinton came in, my sketch and statement was shown to him, and he was asked if the situation of those places was as I had reported. General Clinton said they were. I had but a short time to refresh myself and horse, when I received a letter from the General with orders to proceed immediately to Lord Stirling's. I arrived at his quarters about two o'clock in the morning, Oct. 21st, 1776. Lord Stirling's division marched before daylight, and we arrived at White Plains, about nine o'clock, A. M., and thus was the American *army saved by an interposing providence from probable total destruction.* I may be asked wherein this particular interposition of providence appears; I answer, first, in the stupidity of the British General, in that he did not early in the morning of the 20th send a detachment and take possession of the post and stores at White Plains, for had he done this, we must then have fought him on his own terms, and such disadvantageous terms on our part as humanly speaking, must have proved our overthrow. Again, when I parted with Colonel Reed on the 20th, as before mentioned, I have always thought I was moved to so hazardous an undertaking by foreign influence. On my route I was liable to meet with some British or Tory parties who probably would have made me a prisoner, (as I had no knowledge of any way of escape across the Bronx except the one I came out.)

Hence I was induced to disguise myself by taking out my cockade, looping my hat, and secreting my sword and pistols under my loose coat. Had I been taken under this disguise, the probability is I should have been hanged for a spy."

In these few words the religious character of the leaders of the revolution appears in a striking light. The cause in which they are embarked is a holy one —it is under God's protection, and to his interference is ascribed every deliverence from threatened destruction. Like Pharaoh of old the heart of the British General was made stupid, so that he should not destroy the chosen of the Lord; while he, the chief engineer of the army, refers to the same divine source the promptings which made him under the circumstances go forward alone, and ascertain the locality of the foe, and the topography of the country.

As a matter of history it certainly possesses great interest. With the British army at White Plains, commanding the roads to New Rochelle and both rivers, and only five miles between him and the North river, it is as clear as noonday that Washington could not have got into the interior. Shut up on the north and south, and shut up by ships of war in both rivers, not a resource would have been left him but to risk all in a pitched battle, and that too not in an open field, but on heights, which gave his enemy a three-fold advantage. The result of such a battle does not admit of a doubt—the American army would have been captured and the struggle ended. No wonder Putnam saw a providence in all this.

Washington, now thoroughly alive to the dangers which threatened him, immediately crossed Kinsbridge, and occupying the heights on the west side of the river Bronx, extended a line of intrenched camps to White Plains, thus rendering it impossible for the British commander to outflank him. The intrenchments ran in parallel lines about four hundred yards apart, and terminated at a small lake.

Howe, at length on the 29th, began to move across the country, evidently determined to make a general assault on the American lines, and carry their intrenchments by storm. From the heights he occupied, Washington could see them in eight massive columns, reddening the yellow wheat fields with their scarlet uniforms, while groups of officers collected here and there betokened earnest consultation as to the best method of attack. Their progress was slow, for the fields were intersected with rough stone walls, which had to be pulled down to make way for the heavy artillery, that could with difficulty be got over the uneven ground. Besides, skirmishing parties took advantage of these walls and clumps of bushes to annoy the advance detachments of the British, and prevent them from clearing a path for the artillery. Slowly, however, and steadily the heavy columns swept on, while Washington, no longer placing any reliance on the militia, awaited with much misgiving and apprehension the final shock.

At this critical juncture, Howe, paused in his march to carry Chatterton's Hill, on which M'Dougall had been placed with fifteen hundred men, assisted by Alexander Hamilton. This hill was separated from the main army by the Bronx, which flowed in front of the American lines. The stream however was fordable here, so that the brigade could easily fall back on the main body. When the artillery got within range, Howe opened at once with twelve or fifteen pieces, whose echoes rolled like thunder along the heights, carrying consternation to the hearts of the militia. A ball having struck a soldier in the thigh, mangling him badly, the whole regiment turned and fled. Colonel Haslet could not induce his troops to drag forward the field pieces, so as to sweep the ascending columns. Only one was manned, and this so poorly that the colonel was compelled to seize the drag-ropes himself. As they were trundling it slowly to the front, one of the enemy's balls struck the carriage, scattering the shot in every direction, and setting fire to a wad of tow. In an instant the piece was abandoned in terror. Only one man had the courage to remain and tread out the fire and collect the shot. By dint of great exertion the colonel was able to fire a couple of shots, when the men ran away, dragging their single cannon after them. Hamilton, however, with two guns in battery, coolly swept the slope, carrying away the whole platoons that attempted to ascend. But the militia most of them soon disappeared, leaving M'Dougall with only six hundred to sustain the unequal conflict. This he did for an hour, and then slowly and in good order, carrying his artillery and baggage with him, retreated across the Bronx and took post within the lines. The whole British force, thirteen thousand strong, now drew up within long cannon shot of the American works, and an immediate assault was expected. All night long the soldiers stood to their arms, awaiting the order to advance. At length the long wished-for October morning dawned, when Howe with his glass examined critically the American intrenchments. They seemed so formidable and the position so admirably chosen, that he concluded to defer the attack till the arrival of Lord Percy, already on his way with reinforcements. Providence here interfered again for the salvation of the American army. Those formidable breastworks, which reminded Lord Howe of Bunker Hill and Dorchester Heights, were the merest sham, being composed of nothing but corn stalks covered with sods and a little loose earth, which his artillery would have scattered like a bank of autumnal foliage. Had he advanced directly on them, instead of stopping to carry the really strong position of Chatterton's Hill, he would without doubt have defeated the American army. Instead of this he had brought on only a partial battle, with the loss of some three or four hundred on either side.

At length, on the evening of the 30th, Lord Percy arrived with four battalions, and Howe resolved to storm the American works early in the morning. Washington, apprised of the arrival of this heavy reinforcement, determined at once to abandon his position and retire farther towards the Highlands. But a heavy storm of wind and rain set in that night, and continued all next day and evening, suspending the operations of both armies. Anticipating the necessity of a further retreat, Washington had cast up intrenchments upon the heights of North Castle, near the Croton river, and on the night of the 31st, while the English host was wrapt in slumber, and the fragmentary clouds were sweeping darkly over the Highlands, through which the north-west wind rushed with the roar of the sea, cautiously led his untrained bands out of the encampment. Some one had set fire to the village of White Plains, and while the flames, fanned by the fierce blast, wrapped the dwellings and church, and shed a lurid light over the landscape, Washington was rapidly defiling over the broken country, and by the morning was snug in his new position, which looked down a hundred feet on the Bronx below.

After a careful examination of the new position occupied by Washington, Howe concluded not to attack him, but return to New York and push his operations in another quarter. During Washington's retreat Fort Washington had been left far in the rear, and was now completely cut off from the main army. Colonel Magaw commanded here, and began to make the best preparations in his power for defence. Washington, considering the fort no longer tenable, urged the necessity of evacuating it at once. But in a full council of war it was decided best to defend the place, and although Washington as commander-in-chief had power to overrule this decision, he was unwilling to incur the responsibility of doing so, especially as future results, whatever they might be, could in no way prove that he had acted discreetly. Had things been reversed, and he been in favour of holding the fort, and when the council opposed it, overruled their decision, then the fate of the fort would have shown whether his judgment was correct or not. Greene, in whom he had great confidence, was placed in command of the troops in that quarter, and he unhesitatingly declared that the fort could and should be held. Washington therefore left the whole matter discretionary with him, though clearly expressing his opinion about it.

In the mean time, while the British army were closing around this place, Washington saw that after its fall the next move would in all probability be against New Jersey, and, if successful, end in an attack on Philadelphia. He therefore ordered five thousand men to assemble at Hackensack, to be under his immediate command, while he separated the other portion of the army into two divisions—one under Heath to occupy both sides of the river in the Highlands and defend its passes—the other, four thousand strong, under Lee, to keep the camp near White Plains, and to act as circumstances might demand. Washington having visited the posts in the Highlands, hastened to Hackensack, where his troops, after a circuitious march of sixty miles, had assembled. Filled with anxiety for the fate of the garrison in Fort Washington, he hurried back to Fort Lee, nearly opposite on the Jersey shore, to ascertain how matters stood. It was late at night when he arrived, but leaping into a boat he ordered the rowers to pull him across to the American works. When part way over he met a boat containing Putnam and Greene returning, who reported the garrison in high spirits and fully able to defend the fort. Washington, though still unconvinced, returned with them. The next morning the British under Knyphausen, Lord Percy, Colonels Rall and Stirling, advanced against the fort on three different sides at once, and though Raulings and Cadwallader fought like lions, yet the overpowering numbers of the enemy broke down all resistance, and their ascending shouts, and the steadily advancing volleys, soon showed that the day was lost to the Americans. Washington, from Fort Lee, surrounded by his officers and with Tom Paine by his side, stood and watched through his glass the swiftly marching columns. To the eager inquiries of how the battle was going he only turned gloomily away, and requesting Greene and Putnam to accompany him, leaped into a boat, and, crossing over, ascended the heights to Morris' house, where with painful apprehension he scanned more narrowly the movements of the enemy. While watching Cadwallader slowly retreating along the road nearest the Hudson, fighting desperately as he retired, he saw Col. Stirling advancing swiftly across where One Hundred and Fifty-Fifth street now is, to assail him in flank. Knowing that the troops would soon be all driven within the ramparts of the fort, and the whole surrounding country in possession of the British, he hastened to his boat and recrossed to Fort Lee. In fifteen minutes after he and Greene and Putnam had left Morris' house the British troops were pouring into it. Arriving at Fort Lee he despatched a messenger to Magaw, promising if he would hold out till night he would bring him and the garrison off. The promise came too late, the British troops were already inundating the outer works, and further resistance could end only in a massacre. To Howe's second summons to surrender, therefore, Magaw hauled down his flag. Washington from morning till noon had gazed with a palpitating heart on that height, and whenever the wind for a moment swept away the smoke that curtained it in, and revealed the flag of freedom still flying, hope would revive in spite of the dark aspect affairs were assuming. But at length, as the firing ceased, he, with an exclamation of anguish, saw that

banner come down, and the British colours go up in
its place. The ince sant volleys and explosions of
artillery had died away, and in their place loud hurras
of the victorious enemy rung over the water. Although
only about fifty had been killed, nearly three thousand had been taken prisoners. This was the severest blow that had yet fallen on the American army,
and crushed for a time the hopes of the country.
Lee, when he heard of it, wrote to Washington—
"Oh general! why *would* you be overpersuaded by
men of inferior judgment to your own? It was a
cursed affair?" It *was* a bad affair enough, and
great blame rested on the shoulders of Putnam and
Greene, especially on those of the latter. He commanded there, and was supposed to know all about
the locality and its capabilities of defence. Greene
was a young officer. and wholly inexperienced in the art
of war. He exfoliated rapidly into an accomplished
officer, and here learned a sad but important lesson—
that by skilful manoeuvres a battle may really be
gained before a shot is fired. The belief that Fort
Washington, under the circumstances, could be held,
was a delusion. Its fall rendered the longer occupation of Fort Lee impossible, and Washington ordered it to immediately evacuated, and the troops that
occupied it to join the army assembled at Hackensack.

CHAPTER VII.

Retreat of Washington through the Jerseys—Disorganization of his army—Finally takes post beyond the Delaware, near Trenton—Unaccountable apathy of the Enemy—Washington takes advantage of it—Reorganization of the Army—Washington resolves to march on Trenton—Passage of the river—The Attack—The Victory—march on Princeton—Astonishment of Cornwallis—Death of Colonel Rahl—The effect of the Victory upon the Country—Poverty of the Army—Robert Morris, the noble Financier.

IN the mean time, Howe pushing up with spirit the advantage he had gained with six thousand men, crossed the Hudson six miles above Fort Lee, and moved rapidly down upon it. Cornwallis, who had command of this division, pressed forward with such vigour that Washington was compelled to leave behind all his heavy cannon, three hundred tents, baggage, provision, and stores of all kinds. The Jersey shore being entirely commanded by the British men-of-war, from which troops could be landed at any time, Washington with his desponding, almost disorganized army, drew off toward the Delaware. The militia, wholly dispirited, deserted in large numbers—even the regulars stole away, so that Washington soon had but little over three thousand men with whom to oppose twenty thousand. He had nothing that could be dignified with the name of cavalry, while the enemy was well supplied, and could overrun the whole flat country through which his course now lay. In the mean time the inhabitants, despairing of the success of the American cause, began to look toward the British for protection. An insurrection was breeding in Monmouth, to quell which Washington was compelled to detach a portion of his troops. The Tories took heart, and fell without fear on those who remained true to the cause of freedom. Encouraged by this state of feeling among the inhabitants the two Howes issued a proclamation, in which pardon was promised to all offenders who would within sixty days submit themselves to the royal authority. Multitudes obeyed, and with an army falling to pieces through its own demoralized state, in the midst of a disaffected population, pressed by an overwhelming victorious army, Washington saw a night closing around him, through the blackness of which not a single ray shot its cheering light. But it was in such circumstances as these that the true grandeur of his character appears. Superior to the contagion of example, he neither doubts nor falters. Rising loftier as others sink in despair, moving serener the greater the agitation becomes around him, he exhibits a reserve power equal to any emergency—a steadfastness of soul that nothing earthly can shake.

He immediately ordered Lee, by forced marches, to join him; sent to General Schuyler to forward him troops from the frontiers of Canada; called on Pennsylvania to assemble her militia if she would save Philadelphia, and on the governor of New Jersey, to furnish him with troops, if he would not see the entire province swept by the enemy. But the country was paralyzed, and with his feeble band he continued to retire before the enemy. Lee, intent on delivering some bold stroke of his own, and thus eclipse Washington, whom the provinces began to suspect of inefficiency, refused to obey the orders of his commander, and finally, a victim to his own folly, fell into the hands of the enemy, thus adding another to the list of calamities, for the country had placed great reliance in his skill and experience as a general.

Driven from the Hackensack, Washington took post behind the Aqukannunk. Pressed hotly by Cornwallis, he was compelled to abandon this position also, and retiring along the Raritan halted at New Brunswick. Here the Maryland and New Jersey troops declared the time of their enlistment

336   L

had expired, and shouldering their muskets, left the
camp in a body.   Their departure shook the rest of
the army, and it required all of Washington's efforts
to prevent it from disbanding wholly.   Unable
to offer any resistance, he retreated to Trenton.
Here, receiving a reinforcement of two thousand
men from Philadelphia, he began to assume the offensive; but finding Cornwallis advancing in several
columns, so as to cut off his retreat, he crossed, on
the 8th of December, 1776, to the right bank of the
Delaware, destroying all the bridges and boats after
him.   Here he sat down, knowing it was the last
stand that could be made between the enemy and
Philadelphia.

The English general taking up his head-quarters
at Trenton extended his army up and down the
river, but made no serious demonstrations to cross.
He neither collected boats, nor materials for bridges,
nor attempted to pass by means of rafts.   A sudden
and unaccountable apathy seemed to have seized
him, and the energy with which, since the taking of
Fort Washington, he had pressed the American
army, and which threatened to crush the rebellion
at once, deserted him.   Nothing was easier than to
ford the river, and seize Philadelphia, and compel
Washington to carry out his sublime purpose, "retreat, if *necessary, beyond the Alleghanies.*"

The delay of the British here enabled Washington
to strengthen his army.   He sent Mifflin and Armstrong through Pennsylvania, rousing the patriotic
citizens to arms.   Sullivan joined him with Lee's
division, and Gates arrived with four regiments from
Ticonderoga.   Still the prospect was inexpressibly
gloomy.   Rhode Island, Long Island, New York,
nearly all the Jerseys, had one after another fallen
into the hands of the enemy, and nothing seemed
able to resist his victorious march.

The reinforcements, however, that had come in
encouraged Washington in the hope that he might

yet strike a blow which, if it did not seriously embarrass his adversaries, would nevertheless rekindle hope throughout the country. Although the force under him was inadequate to any great movement, something must be done before the winter shut in, or spring would find Congress without an army, and the American cause without defenders. The British were waiting only for cold weather to bridge the Delaware with ice, when they would cross; and, crushing all opposition by their superior force, march down on Philadelphia. Though the heavens grew dark around Washington, and fear and despondency weighed down the firmest hearts, his sublime faith in God and the right never shook, and even in this hour of trial and of gloom, he lifted his voice of encouragement, declaring he saw the morning beyond it all. He sent Putnam to Philadelphia to erect defences, behind which the army might, if driven back from the Delaware, make a desperate stand for the city.

In the mean time the reorganization of the army on the plan adopted by a Committee of Congress and Washington at Harlæm Heights, was carried forward.* Congress, however, at this time retired in affright to Baltimore, and the Tories of Philadelphia, embracing nearly all the Quakers, taking courage, rendered Putnam's situation precarious.

While trouble and uncertainty pervaded both Congress and the army, Lord Howe, having resigned the command to Cornwallis, retired to New York, where he remained tranquil, in the full belief that an

---

* By this plan all the continental troops were to constitute one grand army of eighty battalions, in all sixty thousand men. To induce enlistments during the war a bounty of twenty dollars was offered, together with a section of land to be given at the close to the survivors, or to the family of him who had fallen. The amount was in proportion to the grade, advancing from one hundred acres, the share of a common soldier, to five hundred, that of a colonel.

easy victory awaited him. The latter officer having lost all fear of the American troops, stretched his army in a chain of cantonments, from Trenton to Burlington, and also retired to the snugger quarters of New York. Colonel Rahl, with fifteen hundred men, was stationed at Trenton; Count Donop occupied Bordentown with a brigade of Hessians, while still lower down, and within twenty miles of Philadelphia, lay another corps. Other portions were quartered at Amboy, Brunswick, and Princeton. This was the position of affairs as the cold blasts and heavy frosts of the latter part of December began to gather the ice on the Delaware, promising soon to construct a solid bridge, over which the victorious enemy could march without resistance. The American army, thinly clad, poorly fed, and worse housed, presented a sorry spectacle as it paraded on the frozen ground, amid the drifting snow-storm. The bands of music, failed to stir into enthusiasm the blood of those who could see no morning beyond the night that enveloped them. The Tories were in high spirits, and the patriots correspondingly downcast and depressed.

Washington, firmly resolved to smite his over-confident adversary, if fortune would give but the faintest promise of success, carefully scrutanized every position, and pondered well every plan suggested to his mind. The fiery Stark remarked to him one day , "You have depended a long time on spades and pickaxes, but if you ever wish to establish the independence of the country, you must rely on fire-arms." "That," replied Washington, "is what I am going to do To-morrow we march on Trenton, and I have appointed you to command the advance-guard of the left wing." He had resolved to cross the Delaware at night, and surprise the Hessians at Trenton. Christmas Eve was fixed upon for the expedition, because he knew this to be a time of carnival among the German troops, and hoped to fall upon them overcome with wine and sleep. The Pennsylvania militia, under Cadwallader and Ewing, the former stationed at Bristol, opposite the corps at Bordentown, and the latter just below Trenton, were ordered to cross at the same time, and by a simultaneous attack, confuse and distract the enemy. Washington with two thousand four hundred men, marched to McKonkey's Ferry, nine miles above Trenton, and at dusk began to cross. It was an hour big with results to the cause of his country, and he felt the heavy responsibility he had assumed. He was calm but solemn, and as he stood dismounted beside his horse and gazed on the turbulent river, adown whose bosom the ice, which the sudden cold had formed, was angrily drifting, and listened to its crushing, grinding sound against the frozen shores, blending in its monotonous roar with the confused tramp of the marching columns, and heavy roll of the artillery waggons, and hoarse orders of the officers, his aspect and air were those of one who felt that the crisis of his fate had come. He was about to put a large and impassable river across the only way of retreat, and the morning dawn would see his little army victorious, or annihilated, and his country lifted from the gloom that oppressed it, or plunged still deeper into the abyss of despair. As he thus stood absorbed in thought and pressed with anxious care, Wilkinson approached with a letter from Gates. Roused from his contemplation, he fixed a stern look on the officer, and exclaimed, *"What a time is this to hand me letters!"*

The night closed in dark and cold—the wind swept in gusts down the river, while the rapidly increasing ice threatened to prevent entirely the crossing of the troops in time for a night attack. A few boats reached the opposite shore, when a blinding snow storm set in, casting such utter darkness on the river, that those which followed became lost, and drifted about in the gloom. General Knox, who had a voice like a trumpet, stood on the farther shore, and kept hallooing to those in the middle of the stream, and thus indicated the point toward which they should steer. It was a long and inconceivably distressing night to Washington. He had calculated on a surprise, but as hour after hour wore away, and the boats entangled in the ice delayed their arrival, he saw that this on which he had placed his chief reliance, must be abandoned. His position grew more and more critical every moment, Cadwallader and Ewing might have crossed, and relying on his co-operation attacked the enemy alone and been defeated, or unable to cross at all, left him unsupported to meet in open daylight a prepared enemy, whose heavy artillery could effectually sweep every street up which his untrained troops might attempt to advance. For nearly twelve hours he watched on the banks of the Delaware, listening to the shouts and uproar of his scattered army, floundering in the gloom, and though an eternity seemed to intervene between the arrival of the boats, he showed no irritation, but stood like a column of marble amid the storm, his great heart almost bursting with anxiety, and yet not an indication of it in his voice and bearing. This at length arrived, and at four o'clock in the morning the army took up its line of march. He was still nine miles from Trenton, and the whole distance to be made against a storm of sleet beating full in the soldiers' faces. The army was divided into two columns— one under Sullivan, taking the road along the bank, while Washington, in person, accompanied by Greene, led the other by the Pennington road nearly parallel and a little farther inland. As day broke dimly over the dreary landscape, Washington saw that his troops were suffering severely from the fatiguing work of the night, and ordered a halt that they might take a few moments' rest. No one, however, was permitted to leave the ranks. The order had scarcely passed down the line before every man was leaning heavily on his musket, and the whole column standing as if suddenly frozen in its place, while the storm silently sifted its white covering over all. Many were but half-clad, and without shoes or stockings stood shivering on the frozen ground. Only a short respite, however, could be given, and soon the order, "FORWARD," passed down the ranks. As the column put itself in motion, Washington, to his surprise, saw one portion quietly slip away from the other, leaving it standing motionless and fast asleep in its place. It was with difficulty the poor fellows could be roused, but when, not long after, the guns of the advanced guard broke on their ears, there was no lack of wakefulness and energy.

Under the driving sleet many of the muskets of Sullivan's troops became wet and unfit for use. On making the descovery, he despatched his aid, Colonel Smith, to Washington, stating the fact, and saying that he could depend on nothing but the bayonet. Turning suddenly on the astonished officer, Washington thundered in his ears : "*Go back, sir, immediately, and tell General Sullivan to* MOVE ON." In relating the occurrence afterward, Colonel Smith said that he "*never saw a face so awfully sublime*" as Washington's when he gave that stern command. All the lion in his nature was roused, every strong faculty had been summoned from its repose, and the marble calmness of his demeanour was like that strange hush of nature which betokens the approaching storm. Captain Forest moved in advance with the artillery, and Washington rode beside him. Passing a countryman chopping wood before his door, the latter pointed to Trenton, now dimly looming in the distance, and asked him if he knew where the Hessian picket lay. The man replied he did not. Said Forest, "You may tell, for it is Washington who addresses you." Overcome with sudden joy, the poor man lifted up his hands and exclaimed, "God bless and prosper you." He then pointed to a house in which the picket lay, and to a tree near it, where the sentry stood. The guns were then unlimbered, and the whole column pressed rapidly forward. Washington still rode in advance amid the artillery, and some of his officers becoming alarmed for his safety, urged him to retire. But he paid no heed to their remonstrances—it was not a time to think of himself, and he still led the column, and was just entering King street, when he heard the thunder of Sullivan's guns in another direction, as Stark broke into the town, and with his strong battle-cry roused the Hessians from their drunken slumbers. Forest then opened with his artillery, and Washington, watching anxiously the effect of each shot, pointed out the different objects at which he wished him to direct his aim. All now was confusion and terror in the enemy's quarters. The roll of drums, the shrill blast of bug'es, and discordant cries of "to arms, to arms," rang out on every side. Detached companies of dragoons careering through the street—officers galloping almost alone, and wildly about—men hurrying to and fro in the uncertain light—irregular volleys of musketry mingling with the heavier explosions of cannon, combined to create a scene of confusion and disorder in the Hessian camp, that no effort could allay. A few soldiers succeeded in wheeling two cannon into the street along which Washington was advancing. Young Monroe, afterward President of the United States, and Captain Washington sprang forward with their men, and though the matches were about to descend on the pieces, charged up to the very muzzles. A volley of musketry met them, and when the smoke cleared away, those two gallant officers were seen reclining in the arms of their followers, wounded, though not mortally. A shout, however, told that the guns were captured. Washington then ordered the column to advance rapidly, when one of his officers exclaimed—

" *Their flags are struck!*"   Looking up in surprise,
he replied, " *So they are,*" and spurring into a gallop,
dashed forward.   He was victorious—the burden
was suddenly rolled from his heart, and turning to
one of his officers, he grasped his hand, exclaiming—
" *This is a glorious day for our country.*" His " country" was his only thought. The suddenness of the victory surprised every one.   But the Hessians finding
themselves hemmed in by the Assanpink, Sullivan, and
Washington, and their leader gone, saw that resistance
would be in vain.   About six hundred light-horse
and infantry made their escape to Bordentown.
Ewing had not been able to effect a passage, or his
division would have crossed the track of these fugitives, and captured them.   Cadwallader had also
found it impossible to get his army over, so that the
troops in Bordentown, Burlington Block House, and
Mount Holly, escaped.   The victory, though incomplete through the inability of those two commanders
to co-operate with Washington, as anticipated, was
nevertheless great.   A thousand prisoners, six brass
field-pieces, a thousand stand of arms, and four
colours, were the glorious results, while the Americans lost only four privates, two of whom were froz-
en to death.   Among those of the enemy killed was
Colonel Rahl, the commander.   He had been spend-
ing the evening, by invitation, at the house of a Tory,
and while Washington stood on the bleak shores of
the Delaware, watching his army struggling in the
icy stream, was pleasantly engaged in a game of
cards, to which he gave greater zest, by frequent and
heavy potations, to the merry Christmas.   A Tory
had discovered the approach of the American army
toward morning, and hurried off to find Colonel
Rahl.   Being directed to the house where he was, he
knocked at the door and gave a letter to a negro
waiter, with the request that it should be handed to
his master immediately.   The servant at first refused to disturb him, but on being told it was of great

importance, delivered it. It being Rahl's turn to deal, he thrust the note into his pocket and continued the game. Half-an-hour had scarcely elapsed when a heavy explosion of cannon shook the house where he sat. He started bewildered to his feet, when another and another followed in quick succession. He called for his horse, but before he could be saddled and bridled, the pealing bugle and rapid roll of drums told him that the enemy was already in his camp. Dashing forward, he rallied a few troops in an orchard, and was leading them up the street against the advancing column, when he fell mortally wounded.

Before leaving Trenton, Washington snatched a moment to visit the dying officer, and expressed the deepest sympathy for his misfortune.

The enemy being in great force in the vicinity, Washington resolved to recross the Delaware to his old encampment, and at evening the weary but elated soldiers were in the boats, pulling to the same shore they had left the night before with such sad misgivings. At midnight they entered their old quarters again, so utterly exhausted by their thirty-two hours toil, they could hardly stand. But for once they were forgetful of their cold bivouac and scanty clothing, and slept the slumber of the brave.

The effect of this victory on the country was like sudden life to the dead. It was a bright Aurora fringing with light and glory the hitherto dark and wintry heavens. The enthusiasm and joy were the greater, springing as they did out of sorrow and despair, and wherever over the land the name of Washington was uttered, tears fell like rain-drops, and blessings innumerable were invoked on his head.

Washington scarcely heard the long shout that went rolling over the land as the news of the victory of Trenton spread on every side, and paid but slight attention to the numerous congratulations that came pouring in from Congress and the distinguished men

of the colonies, so intent was he on taking advantage
of the enthusiasm of his troops, and the panic of the
enemy, and follow up the unexpected blow he had
given with another still more terrible and disastrous.
It was now mid-winter, and his troops were without
tents and clothing, yet he hoped, by great energy and
daring, to press so hard on the cantonments of the
British that they would be compelled to break them
up and evacuate the Jerseys.   But this little band
presented a sorry spectacle as it lay, half clad, scattered around on the frozen ground, while to add to
his calamities he knew that the term of service of
several of the regiments was drawing to a close.   One
cheering feature, however, presented itself.   Congress
having got over its fears of a military despotism, or
oppressed with the still greater fear of ultimate failure,
conferred at this time [Dec. 27] on Washington powers
making him practically military dictator.   He was
authorized to raise sixteen battalions of infantry, three
thousand light-horse, three regiments of artillery,
together with a corps of engineers, and appoint the
officers himself.   He had also full power when he
deemed it necessary to call on the several States for
the militia—to appoint throughout the army all the
officers under brigadiers—fill up all vacancies—to
take whatever he wanted for the use of his troops,
wherever he could find it, with no other restriction
than that he must pay its value—finally, seize and
lock up every man who refused to receive continental
money.   This was a tremendous stride from the doubtful and suspicious course Congress had hitherto adopted.
Such power was never before placed in the hands of a
single man without being abused.   But Washington
was as destitute of mere ambition and self-love as he
was of vain glory; one object alone filled the whole
field of his vision—his country; and one thought
only engrossed all his heart—her good.   The council
of safety of New York wrote him an apology for having, unintentionally, as they afterwards found,

encroached on his authority, while endeavouring to
aid him. His letter shows how irksome the power
he wielded was to him. "Heaven knows," said he,
"that I greatly want the aid of every good man, and
that there are not such enviable pleasures attending
my situation as to make me too jealous of its prerogatives." The very day after the battle of Trenten,
while he stood musing on the banks of the Delaware,
amid his excited but suffering soldiers, the vote investing him with these extraordinary powers passed
Congress. The following day he recrossed the river
and marched to Princeton. But at this critical juncture the terms of service of several of the regiments
expired, and the troops worn down with fatigue and
exposure, were determined to go home. Washington, in this emergency, promised them ten
dollars bounty if they would remain six weeks longer,
though he did not know where the money was to
come from. He also made a strong appeal to officers
and men. He praised their fidelity and gallantry,
acknowledged they were entitled to an honourable
discharge, but begged them to think of the sad condition of their country should they take it at the
present juncture. He bade them remember they were
standing on the very spot they had rendered immortal,
and where they had covered themselves with glory.
He spoke of the gratitude of their country and the
mortification of the enemy, and then told them all they
had achieved would be vain if they disbanded and
left him without an army. The enemy would immediately re-occupy his posts and march without
obstruction to Philadelphia. The officers were moved
by this noble appeal, and in turn pleaded with the men,
and by these means more than half were persuaded
to remain. Washington, with an empty military
chest, then wrote to that noble patriot, Robert Morris,
who was to his country in its financial troubles what
the former was to her in the field, for immediate help.
Morris borrowed on his own personal credit fifty thou-

sand dollars, and despatched the amount without delay to head-quarters, and in the note announcing its departure, bade Washington call on him again when in trouble and he should have more.

In the mean time Cadwallader and Mifflin had succeeded in crossing the Delaware, each with some eighteen hundred men, and formed a junction with Washington at Trenton.

While the latter was thus concentrating his troops at Trenton, Howe, on whom this sudden and bold irruption had fallen like a thunder-clap, immediately ordered off reinforcements to New Jersey. Cornwallis, who, supposing the campaign was closed, had taken passage for England, was directed to repair with all haste to his post, and soon a formidable army assembled at Princeton. On the 2d of January, 1777, Cornwallis put his columns in motion, and before daylight in the morning was in front of Trenton. Washington, who had ascertained from scouts in what overwhelming numbers the enemy was moving against him, withdrew his forces over the Assanpink, and planted batteries so as to command the bridge and the different fords in the vicinity. His position now became one of extreme peril. To make a successful stand there on the banks of the Assanpink was impossible, for so soon as Cornwallis should discern how small was the force opposed to him, he would by the mere weight of numbers crush it at once. To deliver battle, under the circumstances, would insure the utter overthrow of the army. Victory could not be dreamed of, while retreat was impossible, for the ice-filled Delaware was surging in the rear, and before the enemy's cavalry the half-disciplined militia would become a herd of fugitives. One can hardly imagine what great object Washington had in view to compensate for the hazardous position he had voluntarily taken, for he now stood with his hands tied. Nothing was to be done except meet his fate manfully, unless fortune or Heaven interfered in some unlooked for way in his behalf. One thing, however, was evident : he must gain time or be lost hopelessly. The night might bring relief, and he therefore sent forward detachments to harass the enemy's march and detain him as long as possible from reaching the Assanpink. Colonels Reed and Howard, and Captain Forest with the artillery, aided as they closed fiercer and sterner with the foe by Morgan and Miller, caused the vanguard to halt and the massive columns to close up in order of battle. Waiting for the artillery to scour a wood in which the two latter officers lay concealed, and kept up an incessant, galling fire, the British were delayed two hours. This in all probability saved the American army. Washington stood on the shores of the narrow Assanpink and watched with the most painful anxiety the steadily approaching fire. The gallant regiments that had thrown themselves so resolutely in the path of the enemy were being gradually forced back, and as they approached the banks of the stream Washington rode across and thanked them for their heroic conduct. He called on them to dispute every inch of ground, and retire only when necessary to save their pieces. A loud and cheering shout ran along their ranks, and the next moment their volleys were again telling on the enemy. But at length, being driven to the river, the order was given to defile over the bridge to the main army. The advance columns of the British followed eagerly after, and as they reached the shore attempted to force a passage, both at the fords and the bridge. But the well planted batteries of the Americans swept the heads of the advancing columns with such a deadly fire that they recoiled before it, leaving the stream filled with the dead. Between every discharge the whole army cheered.

At length Cornwallis arrived with the remaining artillery, when a terrific canonade was opened on the American lines. Battery answered battery, and the deep thunder rolled away over the plains, carrying consternation to the inhabitants. It was now sunset, and Washington expected every moment to see the heavy columns under the protection of their artillery move to the assault. Had this been done, there is but little doubt that the American army would have been annihilated. Cornwallis, however, being ignorant of the force opposed to him, and not liking to make a decisive effort in the dark, resolved to wait till morning and renew the attack. The stubborn resistance he had met with during the day, and the bold attitude of his antagonist, misled him, and he supposed Washington designed to offer him battle on the spot where he had drawn up his army. Erskine, who was with Cornwallis, remonstrated against this fatal resolution, declaring that in the morning Washington would not be there. The former, however, was firm, and soon the loud explosions of artillery gave way to the confused hum of the two armies as they sunk to their bivouacs, within sight of each other's camp-fires. Washington immediately called a council of war at the tent of St. Clair, to determine what course to adopt in this extremity. Judging from the large force opposed to him that many regiments had not been left behind at Princeton and Brunswick, he proposed by a circuitous vigorous night-march to get into the enemy's rear, and threatening at the same time his stores at Brunswick and his communication with New York, frighten him back from Philadelphia. If Howe kept on, the city must inevitably fall, as the only obstacle between it and him would be removed, still the preservation of the army was now the great question, and not that of Philadelphia.

This daring resolution to march back into the heart of New Jersey, and resume a furious offensive, at the very moment when all defence seemed hopeless, was one of those inspirations of genius by which Bonaparte so often saved his army and empire. He wished to execute a similar movement and march on

Berlin, when pressed so heavily by the allies after the disastrous retreat from Russia, but he was overruled by his officers—took post at Leipsic, and was overthrown. He adopted the same bold resolution in his last struggle on the soil of France, and gaining the rear of the allies attempted to draw them back from Paris, but the latter would not be diverted from their purpose, and so reached the capital before him.

There was, however, one apparently insuperable obstacle in the way of carrying out this daring plan. There had been a thaw, and the roads were so soft that it would be impossible to get forward the artillery, composed of forty pieces, rapidly enough to reach Princeton by morning. To the infinite delight of Washington this objection was most unexpectedly and suddenly removed—the wind changed into the north while the council was deliberating, and in two hours the roads were frozen as hard as iron. This settled the question, and preparations for marching were immediately set on foot. The baggage was sent down to Burlington, while fires were ordered to be kindled in front of the lines. The soldiers, scattered and in groups, roamed the fields, tearing down fences for fuel, and in a short time a bright fire blazed around the American camp. Guards were placed at the fords and bridge, and working parties were detailed as if to throw up trenches, the sound of whose heavy toil lulled into great security the sentinels on watch. Washington kept up also his patrols, who were so near to those of the enemy that the countersigns of each could be distinctly heard by the other.

At one o'clock in the morning the army began its stealthy march, and silently and swiftly defiled away from its intrenchments. But the road chosen was unfortunately a new incomplete one, filled with stumps. Against these the wheels of the artillery, as they were driven rapidly along, thumped heavily, and many of them were broken, thus seriously retarding the march. But for this the army would have reached Princeton before daylight, and Washington had time to have advanced on Brunswick, where large stores and £70,000 were collected. It was a cold, blustering night, and the scantily supplied troops, who had now been twenty-four hours without sleep, and mostly without food, suffered severely. As it grew toward morning, Washington kept exclusively with the advance column, watching eagerly for the daylight. At length the cold, gray dawn appeared, when the troops were hurried forward with greater speed. They were now close on Princeton, and as the bright sun rose over the hills, the white columns of smoke arising from the chimney-tops through the frosty air were a grateful spectacle to the hungry, weary and benumbed soldiers. But the next moment there flashed forth in the wintry beams a long line of bayonets, and the whole road before the Americans was reddened with scarlet uniforms. Three British regiments had been quartered over night at Princeton, whose arrival at the head-quarters of Cornwallis in the morning was to be the signal of a general assault on the American lines. Two of these were already on the march, and did not at first observe the main American army, which, concealed behind a piece of wood, was swiftly passing along a by-road over a low piece of ground, straight for Princeton. General Mercer, with about three hundred and fifty soldiers, many of them young men of wealth from Philadelphia, was sent by Washington to take possession of the travelled highway to Trenton, and seize the bridge over which it passed and cut off any fugitives who might attempt to escape to Cornwallis. He had scarcely commenced his march when he became revealed to the astonished British. Mawhood, the commander, had just crossed the bridge on his way to Trenton, when this apparition burst upon him. Instantly seeing the danger he was in of being cut off from Princeton, and attacked in the open country, he suddenly wheel-

336 M

ed and recrossed the stream—reaching the opposite
bank just as Mercer's column arrived. The two
commanders then made a desperate effort to gain the
high ground nearer Princeton, ascending the slope
on opposite sides. Mercer was first up, and pressing
through an orchard saw the British line rapidly approaching. A rail-fence lay between them, behind
which the Americans took shelter and poured in a
deadly volley. The British, who were advancing at
the charge step, halted and delivered their fire at the
same moment. The lines were so near to each other
that the smoke of the two volleys met and curled
gracefully upward together in the morning sunlight.
The moment the enemy had delivered their fire the
order to charge was given, and they rushed forward
with the bayonet. The Americans, many of them
being armed only with rifles, soon broke and fled
down the hill. Mercer, his horse being wounded,
rushed on foot amid his men, endeavouring by word
and example to rally them. With a portion of them
he was in a hand to hand fight with the British,
when a soldier levelled him to the ground with his
musket. A half a dozen bayonets immediately
gleamed over his breast, and the soldiers cried out
" call for quarters, you d—d rebel." Mercer indignantly refused, and cut at the nearest with his sword,
when he was transfixed to the earth and left for
dead.* As Mawhood pushed across the hill in pur-

* Hugh Mercer was a Scotchman by birth, and came to
this country as a physician. He early entered the military
service, and served with Washington when the latter was a
Virginia colonel. He was wounded at the battle of Mo-
nongahelia, and unable to keep up with Braddock's army
in its wild retreat, lay down behind a log to die. The
savages were all around him, tomahawking the wounded
and scalping the dead, yet he remained concealed, listening
to the groans and diabolical yells that marked their infer-
nal labour. At length as night drew on he was left alone
with the forest and ghastly dead. Faint with the loss of
blood, and parched with fever, he crawled forth, and reach-

suit of the flying detachment, he came to the brow
that looked down on the army under Washington,
moving rapidly up to the aid of Mercer. He saw the
latter, who was in advance of the main body with a
select corps, ride forward to arrest the fugitives, and
with his hat swinging above his head, gallop swiftly
from point to point to steady his troops, who had already begun to feel the effects of the first panic. His
quick eye detached at a glance the desperate odds
against him, but taking advantage of the confusion
the defeated detachments had created, he gallantly
resolved to charge, and with loud shouts the troops
rushed forward. Before the threatened shock the
Americans began to recoil. Washington, knowing
that defeat would be annihilation, no sooner saw his
ranks begin to shake than he spurred forward, shouting to his astonished troops to follow him, and rode
to within thirty yards of the enemy, and halted,
while his staff gazed on him with astonishment. The
hitherto wavering militia wheeled instantly into line.
The enemy then halted and dressed their line also,
and the order to fire passed simultaneously along the
ranks of both. Washington still sat midway between

ing a little rivulet quenched his raging thirst. Refreshed
by the cooling draught, he endeavoured to follow in the
track of the army. But he was a hundred miles from any
settlement, and unable with his shattered shoulder to obtain any food. Faint and exhausted, he was compelled to
halt at short intervals for rest. Slow death by famine
now stared him in the face, but as he stumbled along he
saw a rattle snake in his path. By great exertion he succeeded in killing the viper. He then with his unwounded
arm and hand skinned him and devoured part of the flesh
raw. The remainder he flung over his unwounded shoulder
and pressed on. When the pangs of hunger could be no
longer endured, or nature became exhausted, he would
chew a piece of the reptile, and thus succeeded in reaching
Fort Cumberland, though a mere walking skeleton. He
survived the battle of Princeton but a few days, and died
in great pain. He was a gallant officer, and his death was
universally lamented.

the two, his eye turned full on the foe.   One of his
aids, horror-struck at the sight, dropped the reins
upon his horse's neck and covered his face with his
chapeau, so as not to see his commander fall.   A
crash of musketry followed, and when the smoke
lifted there sat Washington, to the amazement of
all, unharmed.   The next moment his loud shout
rose over the din of battle, and swinging his hat over
his head for a banner to those who pressed after, he
spurred against the flying enemy.   His favourite aid
wept like a child at the spectacle, while Fitzgerald,
another, and the finest horseman in the army, dashed up to him, and in the suddenness of his joy exclaimed, *"Thank God, your excellency is safe."*
Washington gave one grasp of the hand to his weeping aid, and turning to Fitzgerald, exclaimed —
*"Away, my dear colonel—bring up the troops, the
day is our own."*   *"Long live Washington!"* rolled
back over the field, and went up like a morning anthem to heaven.   The second regiment advancing to
sustain the first, was also routed.   All now was excitement and exultation in the American army, and
patriots forgetting the exhaustion of the last night's
march streamed after the fugitives.

The first heavy explosions of cannon at Princeton
roused up Cornwallis, who thought it thundered.
But Erskine knew too well what the sound betokened,
and exclaimed, *"To arms, general! the enemy is at
Princeton!"*   A single glance at the empty intrenchments of the Americans revealed the whole terrible
plot that had been sprung upon him, and the cry of "to
arms," "to arms," and rapid roll of drums, and blast
of the bugle sounded wildly through the camp, and
in a few minutes artillery, infantry, and cavalry were
thundering along the road toward Princeton, which
lay only ten miles distant.   Washington, knowing
that the first sound of his guns would bring the enemy
upon him, pressed the regiments he encountered
with all the energy and vehemence in his power.   He

also sent a detachment to destroy the bridge that Mercer had been directed to occupy, in order to arrest their progress and delay the pursuit. Major Kelley, who commanded it, had just begun to tear up the planks when the van of the British rose over the hill in the distance, coming on a run. The latter immediately threw a discharge of round shot into the detachment, which drove it away from the river. The Americans succeeded, however, in tumbling all the planks into the stream, leaving only the skeleton of timbers standing. This stopped the progress of the artillery, but Cornwallis, hearing the roar of Washington's cannon beyond Princeton, and fearing for his stores at Brunswick, ordered the soldiers into the stream where it was fordable. Breast deep they plunged in, and struggled bravely through the ice-filled channel. But they had scarcely mounted the opposite bank before the cold January morning froze their uniforms stiff upon them. Still the urgent order of the officers was "forward," " forward," and the benumbed troops pressed on to Princeton. As the advance-guard approached the town an iron thirty-two pounder, left on a breast-work, was fired by some one, which brought them to a sudden pause. Cornwallis riding up, surveyed a moment the battery, and concluding that Washington had made a stand there to offer him battle, ordered a halt. A sharp reconnoisance was immediately made by parties on horseback, and the whole hour was wasted in consulting on the best mode of taking this formidable battery. At length the steady columns moved forward to the assault, but meeting no resistance quietly entered the half-finished works when' to their amazement they found not a soul within. Washington all this time was chasing up the two regiments fleeing towards Brunswick.

Having pursued the enemy as far as Kingston, he halted, and collecting his officers hastily around him on horseback, asked whether it was best to continue on to Brunswick. The prize was tempting, but Cornwallis was in close pursuit with a large army of fresh troops, supported by cavalry, while many of the Americans, having marched two whole nights without shoes and stockings, measuring the frozen highway and charging in battle barefoot, and that too without breakfast or dinner, were completely exhausted. It was resolved, therefore, to abandon the pursuit; and turning off into a narrow road, the army reached Pluckemin that evening in safety, with three hundred prisoners, while between one and two hundred of the enemy had been left stark and stiff on the slopes before Princeton. Halting at the battle place only long enough to give his tired gallant little army food and rest, he pushed on to Morristown, where he soon after took up his winter-quarters. Here, girdled in by mountains from whose bases a country rich in supplies extended on every side, he gathered his victorious troops, but not to rest. Scarcely a morning passed without the bugle call resounding through the camp announced that a detachment was on the march to intercept or attack the foraging parties of the enemy. These were cut off or driven in so constantly that the British commander found it impossible to sustain his army except at those places which had open water communication with New York. Soon all New Jersey, Brunswick and Amboy, were cleared of the enemy, and Philadelphia relieved from immediate danger.

Thus in less than a single fortnight Washington, by a succession of the most brilliant and daring manœuvres on record, had lifted the nation out of the depths of despondency, gave confidence to the government, turned the tide of misfortune, and covered his tattered troops with glory. The shout of exultation that followed rung round the civilized world till even kings learned to reverence the name of Washington, and baptized him the "American Fabius." Such unexpected, sudden results, took friends and foes equally by surprise. The British commander was stunned. He had been chasing Washington all the autumn, endeavouring by every means in his power to provoke him to battle. He had taken more then four thousand prisoners—divided and reduced his army, till, without shelter and almost without clothing, it lay shivering on the banks of the Delaware. To this downward point he had forced it in mid-winter, when he thought it could not possibly resume successful operations. But just at this moment, when Washington was never so little able even to defend himself, the British commander saw him suddenly wheel about and breaking into one of the most furious offensives on record, fall like successive thunder-claps on his strong battalions, and roll them back at every point. He found that Washington, with all the wariness of the fox, had the terrible spring of the lion.

The amount of suffering Washington endured in this long and tedious retreat, the noble struggles he had passed through to bear up against the want of supplies, or arms, and even of ammunition—against a murmuring, rebellious, and, worse than all, cowardly army—against the suspicion of his own officers and neglect of the very States he was striving to defend—against the jealousy of Congress—against poverty, destitution and wholesale desertion, will never be known. It remained locked up in his great heart, and even in after years was never spoken of. Neither shall we know what dreadful anxiety weighed him down after he had taken the desperate resolution he did, until success crowned his efforts. With his almost infallible judgment he had evidently measured in its length and breadth the cause of the colonies, and knew that if he should continue to retreat, and Philadelphia fall into the hands of the enemy, his demoralized army would disband, and spring find the current setting so strongly back toward the mother country that it would be impossible to offer any effectual resistance to the enemy.

The moral effect of a victory he must have, or be lost, and be determined to risk all to gain it.   It is evident he had made up his mind never to survive defeat.   He felt he had reached the turning point in the struggle—beyond lay both hope and despair.   In this crisis of his country's destiny, he resolved to occupy the post of greatest danger himself, and if the decree had gone out against his own country, receive the first blow on his own breast.   He was too noble, too great, to peril so fearfully his army and the cause of freedom, and wish to survive their overthrow. Hence, although commander-in-chief, he became in fact leader of the advance guard, both in the march on Trenton and Princeton.   To the remonstrance of his officers in the first battle, not to expose his person so recklessly, he scarcely deigned a reply.   At Princeton he planted himself where his death must inevitably follow the desertion of his troops, and where it was almost certain to happen whatever the issue might be.   He had reached a crisis demanding a sacrifice, and he cast himself and his little band on the altar, and by that sacrifice, great as it was glorious, redeemed his country.   The triumph was complete, but the officers trembled when they reflected at what peril to Washington it had been achieved, and besought him in future to be more prudent, for too great interests were bound up in his life to have it so lavishly exposed.

CHAPTER VIII.

Washington's Fame in Europe—Barbarity of the Hessians
—Depredations of the Troops—General Heath summons
Fort Independence to surrender—Washington issues a
counter Proclamation to that of Howe, which is poorly
received in New Jersey—Five additional Major Generals
and ten Brigadiers appointed—Inhuman treatment of
American Prisioners by the British—Arnold and Wooster
drive Governor Tryon back to his ships—Meigs' Expedition to Sag Harbour—The British Evacuate New Jersey
—Arrival of Lafayette—His interview with Washington
The British land at Elk and march on Philadelphia—
Washington advances to meet them—Skirmishing—
Washington re-crosses the Brandywine and takes position near Chad's Ford—Position of the Northern army,
etc.

An officer, writing from Morristown, after the battle
of Princeton, said, "Our army love their general
very much, but they have one thing against him:
which is the little care he takes of himself in any action. His personal bravery and the desire he has of
animating his troops by his example make him fearless of danger. This occasions us much uneasiness.
But Heaven, which has hitherto been his shield,
will, I hope, still continue to guard his valuable
life."*

As one traces Washington through this campaign,
and learns to appreciate all the difficulties that beset him, and looks into his secret heart and sees how
pure, how noble, how unselfish and full of devotion
to his country all his feelings are, he exclaims at
every step, "INCOMPARABLE MAN!" No suspicion
and distrust can excite his hostility, no reproaches
or unjust insinuations drive him in hasty action—
no accumulation of disaster or oppression or want
shake his purpose or unsettle for a moment his judgment.

*Vide Sparks' Letters and Speeches of Washington.

The nations of Europe had watched the progress of the struggle with great interest, and the news of these sudden victories at Trenton and Princeton, and of the first great check of the enemy, filled them with admiration. Says Botta, " Achievements so astonishing gained for the American commander a very great reputation, and were regarded with wonder by all nations, as well as by the Americans. Every one applauded the prudence, the firmness, and the daring of General Washington. All declared him the saviour of his country ; all proclaimed him equal to the most renowned commanders of antiquity, and especially distinguished him by the name of the *American Fabius.* His name was in the mouths of all men, and celebrated by the pens of the most eminent writers. The greatest personage in Europe bestowed upon him praise and congratulations. Thus the American general wanted neither a noble cause to defend, nor an opportunity for acquiring glory, nor the genius to avail himself of it, nor a whole generation of men competent and well disposed to render him homage."

Washington had no sooner got his army well housed in log huts, than he began, as before remarked, to send out detachments to cut off English foraging parties. In this he received great assistance from the inhabitants, who, aroused by the atrocities committed by the Hessian and the English troops, thirsted for vengeance. The pardon granted by Howe to those who took the oath of allegiance had been of no avail. The Hessian soldiers, looking upon the Americans as barbarians and outlaws, denied to friend and foe alike the protection usually extended to peaceful inhabitants by an invading army. The wintry heavens were made lurid with the flames of burning dwellings, and the shrieks of murdered men, and of women outraged and ravished in the presence of their own families, were borne on every breeze over the land.

Oppressed with a powerful army, the inhabitants had been compelled to remain passive under these aggravated acts of violence, and those who had taken the oath of allegiance saw that their cowardice or lukewarmness in the cause of their country, had only brought on them contempt and ruin. New Jersey had become a scene of horror and desolation, and the atrocities committed by the enemy were bruited over Europe, and awakened in the French people the deepest indignation, who compared the English to the Goths and Vandals in their incursions against the civilized nations of Europe. This wholesale pillage of the inhabitants was not confined to the invaders, the American troops themselves sacked the dwellings of the wealthy, declaring they were partisans of the king, and hence their property should be confiscated.

But this sudden success of Washington put a different aspect on affairs. The outraged patriots flew to arms—many a wronged and robbed inhabitant became at once a spy, a scout, and a soldier, and did good service in scourging these marauders back.

In the mean time Washington strung cantonments from Princeton to the Highlands, connecting his army with that of Heath, whom he had urged to make a demonstration against New York, for the purpose of compelling Howe to withdraw his troops from New Jersey and concentrate them in that city. This commander after much delay at length put his troops in motion, and appearing before Fort Independence, summoned it in a pompous manner to surrender. The whole expedition, however, proved a failure, and General Heath retired without any laurels to the Highlands.

Washington, having witnessed the effect of Howe's proclamation on the people of New Jersey, and finding that many, though wholly estranged from the British cause by the barbarities under which they had suffered, still regarded their oath as binding them at least to a strict neutrality, issued a counter-proclamation, [January 25th,] in which he commanded all persons who had received protections from British commissioners to deliver them up at once, and take in place an oath of allegiance to the United States. Thirty days were allowed them in which to do it—after that time all who refused would be treated as enemies. This was the first palpable use Washington made of his dictatorial power, and the manner in which it was received by the state authorities of New Jersey argued poorly for its working in the country at large. It was asserted that, there being no confederation of the states formed, Congress had not the power to exact such an oath, and hence could not delegate it to another—that its assumption by Washington was a direct encroachment upon the prerogatives of the separate states to which alone this power belonged. The complaints extended even to Congress, and members were found technical and unpatriotic enough to take sides with New Jersey. Mr. Abraham Clark, a delegate from this very State, and one of the signers of the Declaration of Independence, opposed it in Congress, and, in a letter to Colonel Dayton, placed his objections on the ground already mentioned, and added, "*I believe the General honest, but fallible.*"

Previous to this, Washington had addressed an earnest, pressing letter to the Governor of the state, remonstrating against the raising of several battalions, as he had done, for the defence of the State alone, and not as a part of the continental army. That letter, though courteous and guarded, is couched in language that could not be mistaken, and gave the Governor to understand most emphatically that the extraordinary powers with which it had been invested were not an idle ceremony, but would be wielded when the exigencies of his condition required it. After speaking of the superior advantages of having the drafts made for the service of the country at large instead of the single state of New Jersey, he adds,

" I am sure that the necessity of having the continental regiments immediately completed is too obvious to need any further arguments. *I hope the powers of government are such as to complete the new levies by draft if they cannot be filled reasonably by voluntary enlistments. Necessity obliges me to call upon you, as I shall upon every other state, in the most pressing terms to complete, without delay, your proportion of the eighty-eight batalions.*" A call for the several quotas was also made from the other states, and Washington employed the power given him, to collect and organize an army for a spring campaign. He also wrote to Congress, but this body seemed to have been suddenly exorcised of all its greatness, and much of its patriotism, and regarded his appeals apparently like petitions, which it had resolved beforehand to lay on the table. In the mode of appointing five additional major-generals, and ten brigadiers, in obedience to the long and urgent request of Washington, they showed how small a portion they possessed of the self-denying patriotism and noble devotion to the interests of their country which characterized the commander-in-chief, about whose abuse of power they had been so solicitous. When the fate of the country was involved, and the salvation of the army depended, in a great measure, upon the ability and character of the commanding officers, their appointment was brought about by political shuffling, and used to gratify personal friendship or personal ambition. Each state had its favourite candidates, and each candidate had his supporters. There were exceptions to this conduct, it is true, but, in the main, Washington was not consulted, and officers were forced on him he never would have chosen. In order to apportion them properly to the different states and thus gratify local jealousies, incompitent men were appointed, and in some instances made to outrank officers who had served from the outset of the war. The latter were indignant at this injustice, and it required all Washington's influence to pacify them. The miserable and low view Congress took of its duties in this respect, resulting as it did in sowing dissensions in the army and increasing the embarrasment of Washington, laid the foundation, doubtless, of Arnold's after treason.

The pernicious precedent set at this time has ever since been followed, and probably will be to the end of the chapter. Congress, always ignorant of military matters, will thrust civilian generals on the army, just as the President dispenses offices, and political favour will carry a man to a higher grade than honourable scars.

While the two armies lay in winter-quarters, negotiations were opened for an exchange of prisoners. Various offers had previously been made to effect the release of Lee, and both Washington and Congress were very anxious about his fate. Although Lee had resigned the commission which he held in the English army before he joined that of the colonies, Howe chose to regard him as a deserter, and treated him as such, and threatened to try him by court-martial. Congress immediately retaliated by placing Col. Campbell, a British prisoner, in a common jail, and refusing to five Hessian field-officers, taken at Trenton the usual privileges of prisoners of war. The English government fearing the effect of this treatment would be to disgust their mercenary troops with the service, relented, and allowed Lee to be regarded as a prisoner of war; and finally consented to his exchange. Washington opposed these retaliatory measures as both inhuman and impolitic. "Why," he asked, "should an ineffectual attempt to relieve the distresses of one brave, unfortunate man involve many more in the same calamities?" It was bad policy, because the balance of prisoners was heavy against us, and hence, if the British commander followed our example, Americans would be by far the heaviest sufferers. Howe, to his credit be it said,

did not retaliate, though it might be asserted with
some show of truth that he *could* not, for to what
more loathsome dungeons, or dreadful want and suffering, the American prisoners confined in New York
could be doomed, it would be difficult to conceive.
More unprovoked, useless barbarity, more cold-blood-
ed, damning cruelty was never witnessed amid savages.   The loathsome dens into which the victims
were crowded were filled with stench and vermin;
and unclad, unfed, uncared for, they died by hundreds, while those who survived till spring, came forth
from their dismal abodes looking more like skeletons
emerging from their graves, than strong-limbed soldiers whose only offence had been that of fighting for
their fire-sides and their homes.   Of the five thousand
who had been locked up in the prisons, churches and
sugar-houses of New York, but few sound, healthy
men ever came out.   An Irish cut-throat by the
name of Cunningham had charge of the "New Jail,"
in which most of the American officers and eminent
Whigs were confined.   This miscreant jailer kept
these officers of rank and gentlemen of wealth in miserable cells, or confined in an upper chamber, and
crowded so close together that when stretched at night
on the plank floor, they could not turn over except
all at once, at the word "RIGHT—LEFT."   He had
a gallows erected, apparently for his own amusement,
on which he almost every night hung some poor
wretch.   His hour for these occasional recreations
was just after midnight.   Howe was too lazy and too
indifferent to the fate of a few rebels to make any inquiries about the condition of his prisoners; and, although he does not stand charged with personal cruelty, he is guilty of a crime closely akin to it—utter
indifference to whether it was practised or not under
his authority.   He indignantly denied the charge
which Washington made against him, but the facts,
as afterward proved, and his statements are as wide
apart as heaven and earth.

So reduced had these prisoners become, that they were wholly unfit for duty, and when Howe proposed to exchange them, Washington refused to give the same number of healthy British and Hessian soldiers. Howe then accused him of violating the agreement made between them. Washington retorted in a withering letter, in which, after declaring that an exchange of strong, healthy soldiers for sick and helpless ones would be putting a premium on inhumanity, and that an agreement to exchange prisoners was based on the principle of equality, in not recognizing which *he* was really the one guilty of violating the compact, he adds, "It may, perhaps, be fairly doubted whether an apprehension of their death, or that of a great part of them, did not contribute somewhat to their being sent out when they were. *Such an event whilst they remained with you would have been truly interesting*; because it would have destroyed every shadow of claim for a return of the prisoners in our hands; and therefore policy concurring with humanity dictated that the measure should be adopted. Happy had it been if the expedient had been thought of before these ill-fated men were reduced to such extremity." He also accuses him directly of treating the prisoners in his hands cruelly, and thus causing the death of large numbers.

The measures proposed for an exchange of prisoners thus became embarrassed, and were not carried out until some time afterwards. The balance of prisoners against the Americans after the battle of Princeton was about one thousand. The British having taken in all a little less than five thousand, and the Americans about four thousand.

Spring opened without any general movement on the part of Howe. This was fortunate for Washington, as the enlistments for the war or for three years went on slowly, and the new levies arrived tardily, and at long intervals, leaving the army weak and unable to offer any effectual resistance to Howe if he

had taken the field vigorously. But he too was waiting
for reinforcements, and tents and field equipments.
In April, however, he sent Governor Tryon with ten
thousand men to destroy the stores at Danbury. But
this officer was chased back to his ships by Arnold
and Wooster; the latter, though nearly three score
and ten, gallantly leading on his men till shot down
by the enemy. Another expedition was sent against
Peekskill. These, however, were mere by-plays, to
occupy the troops till the time for a grand and decided
movement should arrive.

Meanwhile Washington waited the further development of the plans of the enemy. The troops assembling from the East he ordered to concentrate at Peekskill, while those from the Middle States and Virginia
were directed to join him at Morristown. It was
evident that an enterprise was on foot, designed to
crush the colonies at once, but in which direction the
blow was about to fall remained in obscurity. A storm
was brewing on the Canadian frontier, whether Howe
was preparing to co-operate with any movement in
that direction, or push his way on to Philadelphia,
could only be conjectured.

In the mean time, internal troubles continued to vex
and embarrass the commander-in-chief even more
than the conduct of the enemy. The constant reports
of men deserting—letters from officers all over the
country, complaining of the neglect and injustice of
Congress, and offering their resignation—the want
of money and a commissary-general furnished daily
and almost hourly annoyances which he had no power
to escape. To some, like Arnold, he replied in the
language of friendship and sympathy, to others he
wrote sternly and rebukingly. Sullivan received a
severe reprimand for his childish complaints about
not being entrusted with a separate command. Gates
a lighter one, for asserting that an equal distribution
of tents, etc. was not made to the different sections of
the army. While the different military departments

were thus exhibiting only weakness, Lieut. Col. Meigs, a companion of Arnold in his bold march through the wilderness, showed what a single enterprising officer could do.   Embarking on the 21st of May from New Haven, he sailed for Guilford, and there taking with him a hundred and seventy men, in whale-boats, crossed over to Southold, and dragging his boats over land to the bay between the north and south branches of the island, pushed on to Sag Harbour, where he arrived at two o'clock in the morning, and immediately with fixed bayonets charged the outposts of the British stationed there.   The alarm was instantly given, and an armed schooner with twelve guns and seventy men opened its fire upon the Americans within less than thirty rods.   The gallant detachment, however, pressed forward, driving the enemy before them, and having killed and captured nearly a hundred men, and destroyed twelve brigs and sloops and a large quantity of merchandise, retired without the loss of a man.   Col. Meigs reached Guilford at two o'clock in the afternoon, having marched and rowed ninety miles in twenty-five hours, besides fighting the enemy and destroying his ships and stores.

At length Washington moved his army, [May 21,] fourteen thousand strong, to Middlebrook, and intrenched himself in a strong position, resolved to give battle if the enemy advanced.   Howe, who had collected a large force at Brunswick, only nine miles distant, [June 21,] pushed his lines into the country until his left rested on Millstone.   Here he remained a week, hoping to tempt Washington from his stronghold to battle.   But the latter having long before discovered what his raw troops were worth in an open field fight, refused to stir from his position.   Howe then returned to Brunswick, evacuated it, and retreated to Amboy, pursued and harassed by General Greene, with three regiments.   Washington followed with the main army to Quibbletown.   The moment

Howe saw that he had decoyed Washington out into
the open country, wheeled, and marched swiftly to
the American left, hoping to turn it and gain the high
ground beyond. Had he succeeded, a battle would
have been inevitable. Washington, however, was
too quick for him. The roar of cannon, and heavy
explosions of small arms in that direction, as the enemy came in collision with a detachment of seven hundred Americans, revealed the well-laid scheme.
Though severely pressed, he fell back, and reached
his strong position at Middlebrook in safety. As soon
as Howe saw Washington quietly in his den again,
he gave up all attempts to bring on an engagement,
and, abruptly leaving the Jerseys, passed over to
Staten Island. Washington, who from boyhood had
shown a peculiar love of agricultural pursuits, indeed
seems to have had a positive attachment to the soil, saw
with pleasure the withdrawal of the troops. It pained him deeply to behold the green fields ready for the
mower, filled with the marching columns, and the
ripening grain trampled down by the ruthless hoof of
war, or wrapt in conflagration. In a letter to Armstrong, he says, "The evacuation of Jersey at this
time seems to be a peculiar mark of Providence, as
the inhabitants have an opportunity of securing
their harvests of hay and grain." The farmer was
never forgotten in the warrior, and the husbandman
always received his peculiar attention.

The relief which this apparent abandonment of all
immediate attempts against Philadelphia gave, was
only momentary, for on the very next day a courier
arrived in camp, bringing the astounding intelligence
that Burgoyne, with ten thousand men, an artillery
train of forty pieces, the whole commanded by officers
of experience and renown, had crossed the St. Lawrence from Canada, and was moving against Ticonderoga. Whether Howe, under these circumstances,
would renew his attempts against Philadelphia, or
endeavour to form a junction with Burgoyne, and

thus separate the New England provinces from their
brethren, was the important problem which Washington endeavoured to solve. If the former course
was adopted he must hover around Philadelphia, if
the latter, his army could not be too soon in the strong
passes of the Highlands. Howe was certainly collecting a large fleet, and evidently either for the purpose
of ascending the Hudson, or of going by sea to Philadelphia. At length news was brought that the British army was embarked. Washington immediately
despatched Lord Stirling to Peekskill, while he himself, still uncertain of the enemy's purpose, slowly
followed by way of Ramapo, and finally encamped in
the pass of the Clove. In the mean time he ordered
the two brigades of Parsons and Varnum from the
east to Peekskill—wrote to Governor Clinton to call
out the militia, and hastened off a courier to Schuyler,
who commanded in the northern department, to hold
on to Ticonderoga. All eyes were suddenly turned
to the northward, where the great and decisive conflict seemed about to take place. Roused by the impending danger, the settlers along the rich banks of
the Mohawk, and the hardy yeomanry of Vermont
and Massachusetts, and Connecticut and New York,
left their fields burdened with the rich promise of a
coming harvest, and hastened to strike hands and
move shoulder to shoulder with the battle-cry of freedom on their lips, against the common invader.

But while Burgoyne was slowly pushing the heads
of his massive columns through the northern wilderness, the fleet of Howe hoisted sail and moved slowly
down toward the Hook. The news no sooner reached
Washington than he despatched messengers to Sullivan and Stirling, at Peekskill, ordering them instantly to recross the Hudson, and hasten by the most
direct routes to the banks of the Delaware, where he
would wait their arrival. But though the vessels
were moving seaward, he was still doubtful of Howe's
designs, and resolved to remain where he was till he

could ascertain them more fully. At length it was reported that the ships had been seen off the Capes of the Delaware. The army was then marched rapidly to Germantown, and Washington hurried forward to Chester, to gather more accurate intelligence. Here he was told that the fleet had again stood to the eastward and disappeared. Baffled by this strange conduct—without the least data to act on, Washington was compelled to base his movemets entirely on conjecture. It was plain that nothing could be done till the enemy's plans developed themselves more fully. He, therefore, ordered Sullivan to take post in New Jersey, ready to move in either direction, while the main army was quarterd at Germantown, prepared to march at a moment's warning.

While things were in this harassing and trying state of suspense, Washington rode over to Philadelphia, to confer a day or two with committees of Congress. He here, for the first time, met the young Marquis of Lafayette, whose ardent and noble espousal of our cause eventually wrought such a change in our prospects. A mere stripling, eighteen years of age, rolling in wealth, and basking in the sunshine of court favour, he tore himself away from all the luxuries that surrounded him—from the arms of a young and affectionate wife, whose expostulations and reproaches were harder to be borne than the threats of his friends and frowns of his king, to struggle in an almost hopeless cause, in a foreign land. Purchasing a vessel, and clothing and arms for soldiers at his own expense, he, with the brave De Kalb and eleven other officers set sail for America. After a voyage of nearly two months, he reached Charleston, and, distributing arms and clothing to a hundred and fifty of the gallant defenders of Sullivan's Island, mounted his horse and rode nine hundred miles to Philadelphia.

Silas Deane had been for some time our minister at Paris, and with Franklin and Arthur Lee, who were afterward added to the embassy, was endeavouring to enlist France in our struggle. With the former young Lafayette had made an agreement respecting the rank he was to hold in the rebel army. But Congress received the latters which he presented coldly, for it had been much embarrassed of late with applications of foreign officers for appointments, which, if made, would deeply offend our own officers. Only a few weeks before, Knox, Greene, and Sullivan, hearing that a Frenchman by the name of Decoudray, had been appointed major-general, his appointment to be antedated, so as to outrank them, abruptly sent in their resignations. Besides all other considerations Lafayette was a mere boy, only nineteen years of age, and could not be considered fit for a position of responsibility. Being told that his request would probably be denied, he sat down and wrote a note to Congress, saying—"After the sacrifices I have made, *I have the right to exact two favours ; one is to serve at my own expense, the other to serve at first as a volunteer.*" This magnanimity was too much for Congress, and it immediately made out his commission. The next day he was introduced to Washington at a dinner party. As it was about breaking up, the latter took him aside and spoke to him long and tenderly. The tall, commanding general of nearly fifty, and that youth of nineteen presented a most interesting contrast as the one spoke of freedom, and the other stood and reverently listened, every feature beaming with excitement. There was something in the enthusiastic love for liberty of this young stranger—the revelation of an exalted purpose, not to be shaken by neglect or suffering—a noble, unselfish devotion, so unlike the petty rivalries, groundless jealousies, and selfish behaviour of some of his own officers, that touched the tenderest chord of Washington's nature. His great, grand heart opened to him at once like a father, and from that hour Lafayette became a son, returning the wealth of affection lavished on him with all the devotion of his impulsive, impassioned, generous nature. Washington told him to consider himself at all times as one of his own family, but he must not expect to find in the republican army, the luxuries of a court, or the comforts even of an ordinary camp. Both the one and the other were indifferent to Lafayette, who had already triumphed over infinitely greater difficulties, and endured more suffering than could be meted out to him in the American army. That night he sent his horses and equipage to camp, and became an American soldier. His after career in connection with our cause, and with Washington, furnishes some of the most interesting incidents in American history. That apparently boyish enthusiasm proved to be the solid judgment and inherent principles of the man, and as he stood in all the fiery ardour of youth before Washington, so he afterward stood with white locks amid the infuriated mobs of Paris and Versailles. The impression Washington made on him may be inferred from the letter describing his first interview. In it he says—" Although he was surrounded by officers and citizens, it was impossible to mistake for a moment his majestic figure and deportment." His surprise, however, at the army was equal to his admiration of Washington. On the very day he arrived in camp there was a grand review of the whole eleven thousand men, and the young marquis never before even in imagination beheld such a spectacle. Many were in their shirt sleeves—many without any shirts to their backs, their whole uniform consisting of a pair of pantaloons, while the majority of those who were clad wore simply long linen hunting-shirts. These were drawn up in two long lines—the smaller soldiers occupying the first line—presenting a most striking contrast to the military bearing and manner of their commander. " *As to their military tactics,*" he wrote home, " *it will be sufficient to say that for a regiment ranged in order of battle, to move forward on the right of its line it was necessary for the left to make a continued countermarch.*" The next day Washing-

ton took Lafayette with him to inspect the fortifications
of the Delaware. As they rode along together, the
former soon discovered that his young protegé possessed a knowledge of military matters by which the
oldest generals in the service might profit.

Though Congress continued its sessions in apparent
tranquillity, the greatest excitement prevailed throughout the city and country. Sentinels were on every
high peak that overlooked the ocean, sweeping the
water in every direction with glasses to detect the first
appearance of the fleet, whose approach was so much
dreaded. But day after day passed by, and still no
tidings of it came from the seaboard. At last the
lookouts caught a glimpse of it, leagues away to the
south of the capes of Delaware. Washington immediately inferred that its destination was south, probably
Charleston. Ten days more passed by, and as nothing
further was seen of it, a council of war was called, in
which it was resolved to march back toward the
Hudson, either to operate against Burgoyne, or, if
circumstances proved favourable, to attack New York.
Every thing was got ready to march, when on that
very morning the exciting report was brought that
the fleet was already two hundred miles up the
Chesapeake Bay, and standing steadily on. It was
now evident that Philadelphia was the object of attack,
though, as Washington said, the enemy had taken
a strange route to reach it. This at once relieved him
from all indecision respecting the northern army.
Previous to this, not only was he annoyed beyond
measure by the surrender of Ticonderoga, the defence
of which had been entrusted to St. Clair, but at the
apparently resistless manner in which Burgoyne moved
southward. He had sent the gallant Morgan with his
five hundred riflemen north, and in announcing it to
Governor Clinton said he thought it would be a good
plan to let the fact be pretty well circulated, as well
as to exaggerate their numbers, for these troops were
the terror of the Indians. In this, which is dated on

the very day of the battle of Bennington, he speaks of Stark's intention to close on Burgoyne's rear as a most excellent plan. As things grew worse and worse, Congress recalled both Schuyler and St. Clair, and put Gates over the northern army. Washington had also sent Arnold north, a host in himself. Still, so long as Howe's movements remained undeveloped he could not call on the New England states to hasten to New York state to resist the invasion of Burgoyne. But now all immediate danger to the eastern board was removed, and he wrote to Putnam to press on Governor Trumbull the urgent necessity of getting the whole force of New England *" to turn out, and by following the great stroke struck by general Stark near Bennington, entirely crush General Burgoyne."*

In the mean time the militia from Delaware, Maryland and Pennsylvania turned out, and the country was alive with armed citizens, hastening to the defence of Philadelphia. Sullivan, who had just been rudely repulsed in an attack on Staten Island, was also ordered from the Jerseys, and the army soon assumed a formidable appearance, at least in magnitude.

At length the reconnoitering parties came in and announced that the enemy were landing near the head of Elk river. [Aug. 25th.] Washington advanced to meet them, and taking Philadelphia in his route, marched through the city with flying banners and martial music, cheered by the multitude. This was done to encourage the patriots and check the movements of the disaffected and disloyal. The next day, after the British effected a landing, a heavy rain storm set in, which deluged both friends and foes, and injured the arms and ammunition of each. Washington at the outset sent forward skirmishing parties to harass the enemy, while he pressed on with the main army. Between these and the advance detachments of the British severe conflicts took place, ending, of course, in the retreat of the Americans, as the heavy columns of their adversaries closed upon them. On

the 28th the Americans took some forty prisoners.
Twenty deserters also arrived in camp, who stated
that the infantry of the enemy was in good condition,
but that the horses were knocked up by their long
voyage. This was fortunate, as Washington's cavalry,
under Pulaski,* was too feeble to cope with any considerable force, while the country presented an
admirable field for the movements of horse.

The next day Captain Lee took twenty-four more prisoners.   Five days after, Cornwallis, while advancing
with his column, was suddenly assailed by Maxwell's
regiment, the riflemen of which, having formed a
sort of ambuscade, poured in a deadly fire upon him.
But swept by the artillery and pressed by the
formidable masses of the enemy, this brave regiment
was compelled to retire with the loss of forty killed and
wounded.   The British reported their loss to be
twenty-two, though a woman from their camp next
day said she saw nine waggon loads of wounded brough;
in.   They doubtless suffered more severely than they
acknowledged ; in fact, as a rule, it was always safe
to multiply the current account given by the enemy
of their loss by three.   The two armies had continued
to draw closer together, and now stood front to front,
and a battle was daily expected.   Philadelphia was
the prize to be struggled for, and Howe and Washington both determined that the conflict should be
a decisive one.   The latter took position behind Red
Clay Creek, directly across the route leading to the
city.   Howe then advanced, and being joined by
General Grant, made a feint to attack the Americans,
but instead of concentrating his forces at the assailing
point, extended his lines far away to the American
right.   The two armies were now only two miles
apart, and threatened momentarily to come in collision,

* Previous to this there had been no officer in the cavalry
of higher rank than colonel.   Reed, after being made
brigadier, was offered the command, but declined.   It was
then given to Count Pulaski, a Polish officer of great distinction and bravery.

when Howe ordered a halt. Washington, whose experience during the last campaign had taught him to distrust every movement of Howe, soon discovered that a flank movement was being made to cut him off from Philadelphia, and hem him in on a narrow tongue of land from which escape would be impossible, and where he would be compelled under disadvantageous circumstances to fight a decisive battle. He, therefore, after carefully reconnoitering the enemy, passed the order quietly through the camp to march, and at two o'clock in the morning of the 9th of September withdrew his army toward the Brandywine, and crossing the river, took prossession of the high grounds on the opposite side, near Chad's Ford.

While Pennsylvania, New Jersey, Delaware and Maryland were gazing with mingled expectations and fears on the two armies under Washington and Howe, as they slowly closed on each other, and the whole country was filled with conflicting rumours, agitating and cheering by turns, the works were rapidly going up at Saratoga, from which was to recoil the veteran army of Burgoyne. Stark had dealt him a staggering blow by his victory over Baum at Bennington, while Gansevoort's gallant defence of Fort Stanwix, had frustrated his plans in that direction. From every valley and mountain slope the sturdy yeomanry went pouring in to Gates, their patriotism kindled into brighter glow by the shouts of victory that came rolling from Vermont, and down the Mohawk from Fort Stanwix and the bloody field of Oriskany; and their rage redoubled to see the enemy with his ruthless savage allies in the very midst of their autumnal fields, and ravaging the firesides of the innocent and the helpless. Washington's anxiety for the fate of the northern army was equal to that for his own, and he listened with as deep a solicitude for the reports that might reach him thence, as he did to the thunder of the enemy's cannon in his front. In the meantime, Burgoyne finding him-

self cut off from the assistance of St. Leger by way
of the Mohawk, and a dark storm-cloud gathering in
his rear, extinguished the last hope that illumined
the weary wilderness he had traversed, and seeing a
mighty army rising as it were from the very earth
before him, surveyed with a stern and gloomy eye
the prospect that surrounded him.   The second crisis
in the American revolution had come.   With the
simultaneous defeat of the northern and southern
armies the nation would be prostrated, and the last
hope of securing the alliance of France extinguished.
Two such calamities would darken the land with
despair, and fill the friends of freedom with despondency and gloom.

——.——

CHAPTER IX.

Battle of Brandywine—A new account of the loss of the
   British, found among General Clinton's papers—Wash-
   ington again offers Howe battle—Defeat of Wayne at
   Paoli—Philadelphia taken—Fortifications erected at Mud
   Bank and Red Bank—Tenacity of Washington—Battle
   of Germantown—Cause of the Defeat of the Americans.

ON the morning of the 11th of September the
American army, eleven thousand strong, lay stretched
along the Brandywine, whose shallow bed at that time,
the stream being very low, furnished frequent fording-
places.   Washington concentrated his main force
against the most important of these, called Chads'
Ford.   The right wing, composed of the three brigades of Sullivan, Stirling, and Stephens, extended
up the river, to look out for the fords in that direction,
while Armstrong with a thousand militia guarded
Pyles' Ford, the only one below.   At daybreak Howe
put half of his force under Cornwallis, and accompanying it in person, took a road running nearly
parallel with the Brandywine, a few miles inland,

for the purpose of ascending the stream beyond the
farthest outposts of the American army, and crossing
it unperceived, come down on Washington's flank.
This extraordinary movement, by which an army
was separated seventeen miles, a movement similar
to one which, but from mere accident or treachery,
would have overthrown the allies at Waterloo, here
also, by a strange fatuity, was destined to be completely successful. It was a foggy morning, and a
dense forest darkened the bank of the stream, on the
side where the British lay, almost the entire distance.
About nine o'clock Knyphausen, with the other
division of the army, took up his line of march directly
for Chads' Ford, where Wayne commanded. The
fog soon lifted and rolled away, and the long lines of
gleaming bayonets looked like streams of light
through the forest, as in beautiful order, and to the
sound of fife and drum the columns pushed their
way to the river. But the woods as they proceeded
seemed alive with Americans, who, concealed by the
thick foliage, kept up an incessant attack upon the
advance parties and strewed the green uniforms
thickly under the greener arcades. Maxwell, who
commanded them, made such havoc with his sharp-
shooters that a strong corps was sent against him,
which forced him back upon the Brandywine. Here,
met by reinforcements, he turned furiously on his
pursuers, driving them before him till they closed
in with the main column. Knyphausen then sent
a large detachment to take Maxwell in flank, but the
latter detecting the movement, ordered a retreat and
recrossed to Wayne. Having cleared the woods of
the enemy, Knyphausen moved forward and drew up
his division on the bank, and began to plant his
cannon. The Americans were in high spirits, and
several detachments boldly dashed into the stream,
and securing a footing on the farther side, fell with
loud shouts on the working parties and those detailed
to guard them. Knyphausen, enraged at these con-

stant and bold attacks, ordered forward a large force,
which advancing to the charge forced the Americans
to a rapid retreat.   They came on a run through the
water which was dashed into spray by the shower of
bullets that fell around them.   In the meantime
Knyphausen opened a heavy cannonade on Wayne,
who returned it with spirit, and to all appearance the
main effort was to be made at this ford.   The former
manœuvered his troops so as to convey the impression
of a much larger force than he possessed, while at
the same time he was apparently making extensive
preparations for an immediate assault on Wayne's
battery.   While Washington was watching the
effect of this heavy cannonade, Sullivan, who had
been ordered to take care of the fords above him,
received the following note from Lieutenant-Colonel
Ross:

"*Great Valley Road*, 11 *o'clock*, A.M.

DEAR GENERAL,—A large body of the enemy,
from every account five thousand, with sixteen or
eighteen field-pieces, marched along this road just
now.   This road leads to Taylor's Ferry, and Jeffrey's Ferry on the Brandywine, and to the Great
Valley at the sign of the Ship, on the Lancaster
Road to Philadelphia.   There is also a road from
the Brandywine to Chester, by Dilworthstown.   We
are close in their rear with about seventy men.
Captain Simpson lay in ambush with twenty men,
and gave them three rounds within a small distance,
in which two of his men were wounded, one mortally, I believe.   General Howe is with this party, as
Joseph Galloway is here known by the inhabitants,
with whom he spoke and told them that General
Howe was with him.

Yours,   JAMES ROSS,
Lieutenant-Colonel.

Here was accurate information from a responsible
officer, and every road designated by him should
have been secured beyond the Brandywine.   Ross

had seen the army, nay, fired into it, and was steadily following it in its rapid march up the river.   Its destination was apparent to the most casual observer, and how, after such information, Sullivan could allow himself to be surprised by an army of five thousand men, dragging a heavy train of artillery after them, baffles all explanation.

Washington immediately penetrated Howe's design, and resolved to defeat it by sending Sullivan to occupy him, while he, with the rest of the army, would cross over, and falling on Knyphausen in rear and front at the same time, crush him before the other division could arrive.   This daring resolution was the inspiration of true genius, and had it been carried into effect, Brandywine would doubtless have been another Saratoga to the British.   He issued his orders at once, and riding along the lines to animate the troops, was received with loud huzzas; and "long live Washington," rolled over the field. General Greene was ordered to lead the advance, and crossing above Knyphausen assail him in flank and rear.   In a few minutes the field was alive with the marching columns.   At this critical moment another aid came galloping in from Sullivan, who reported no enemy around the forks of Brandywine. This was a fatal mistake, and Washington immediately reversed his orders, and the army again took up its former position.   It was now high noon, and Knyphausen having received despatches from Cornwallis announcing that the river was won, opened on the Americans with a tremendous discharge of artillery and musketry, so as still more to confirm the delusion under which he saw Washington was evidently labouring.

In the mean time Cornwallis had formed his troops on the banks of the stream, and was coming rapidly down on Sullivan's flank.

A Squire Cheney, reconnoitering on his own responsibility the movements of the enemy, suddenly

came upon the advance as he was ascending a hill.
He immediately wheeled his horse, a fleet, high-
spirited animal, and dashed away toward head-
quarters.   Shots were fired at him, but he escaped
and reached the American army in safety. To his
startling declaration that the main body of the enemy
was on his own side of the stream, and coming rapidly down upon him, Washington replied that it was
impossible, for he had just received contrary information.   "*You are mistaken, General, my life for
it you are mistaken,*" exclaimed Cheney, and carried away by the great peril that threatened the Americans, added, " By h—ll it is so; put me under guard
until you find my story true," and, stooping down,
he drew a rough draft of the road in the sand.   In a
few moments a hurried note from Sullivan confirmed the disastrous tidings.   The enemy were only
two miles from the Birmingham Meeting-House,
which was but three miles from Chads' Ford.
Washington saw at once the fatal error into which
he had been beguiled by the false information of
Sullivan, and saw, too, that in all human probability
the day was lost.   Suddenly calling to his side his
aids, he asked if there was any one near acquainted
with the country, who could guide him by the shortest
route to Birmingham Meeting-House.   An elderly
man named Brown, living in the vicinity, was instantly seized and asked to act as guide.   He began
to make excuses, when one of Washington's aids,
mounted on a splendid charger, leaped to the ground
and told the old man to mount at once, and conduct
the General by the shortest, quickest route to the
meeting-house, or he would run him through with
his sword.   Alarmed by this threat, Brown mounted
and pused straight across the country, his high-bred
animal taking the fences in his course like a hunter.
Washington with his suite pressed after, and though
the old man seemed to fly over the fields and fences,
the head of Washington's horse constantly lapped

the flank of the animal he rode, and there rung continually in his ears from the excited, anxious chieftain by his side, " *Push along, old man ; push along, old man.*" The fate of his army was trembling in the balance, and no fleetness could equal his burning impatience to be at the point where it was so soon to be decided, for already the loud roar of the cannon and the rattle of musketry ahead, told him that the shock had come. The tremendous cannonading at Chads' Ford, blending in with that around Birmingham Meeting-House, needed no additional confirmation of the deep disaster that had overtaken him. As he approached the scene of conflict the balls fell so thick around him that the old man stole away. His absence was unnoticed, for his services were no longer needed ; the roar of battle and shouts of men were a sufficient guide. When Washington first set out he had ordered Greene to advance with his division, as fast as possible, to the support of Sullivan. The latter with two brigades immediately pushed forward. The brigade under Weadon led off, and starting on a trot, with trailed arms, made the four miles that intervened between them and the enemy in the astonishingly *short time of forty minutes.* Not a sound was heard from this noble brigade save the clatter of their arms and panting of the men as shoulder to shoulder they swept like cavalry to the rescue of their companions.

Sullivan had been completely taken by surprise, but with his accustomed bravery strove to remedy the error that had been committed. Rapidly advancing to a gentle slope near the meeting-house, he formed his line in an open space, each extremity resting on thick woods. But in executing a manœuvre designed to thwart a French General Deborre, who insisted on occupying the right of the line contrary to his orders, his brigade did not arrive on the field in time to get fully into a position before the action commenced. Howe on his huge raw-

336   o

boned horse, Cornwallis glittering in scarlet and
gold, together with other officers, sat grouped on
Osborne Hill, and watched with unfeigned surprise
the beautiful, regular formation of the American
line.

The battle was commenced by an advance company of Hessians, who crossed the road, and resting
their pieces on the fence fired at a small body of
Americans in an adjoining orchard.   Soon the field
was piled with baggage, blankets, etc., thrown aside
under the oppressive heat, and the troops went
pouring forth to the conflict.   The artillery opened,
and the contest became close and murderous.   The
American troops, though most of them were undisciplined militia, behaved with astonishing coolness.
From their steady deliberate volleys the disciplined
ranks of the enemy recoiled in amazement.   The
chasseurs came charging down the slope with clat-
tering armour and to the sound of trumpets, but
could not break the firm formation.   Grenadiers and
guards were each all hurled back, but the overwhelming numbers continued to pour forward, bearing down by mere weight alone the American ranks,
till at last they began to shake and undulate over
the field.   Sullivan, who had seen two of his aids
fall by his side, galloped along the disordered line,
and strove by word and gesture to animate the soldiers to another effort.   But his example and appeals
were alike in vain.   First the right and then the left
wing broke and fled towards Chads' Ford.   Finding
his troops could not be rallied, he then separated
from them, and threw himself into a part of Stirling's division, in the centre, which still heroically
maintained its ground.   Here was also the youthful
Lafayette, kindling by voice and gesture the enthusiasm of the men.   Dismounting from his horse,
he passed through the ranks exposing himself like a
common soldier, when a musket ball pierced his leg.
Cornwallis seeing with what stubborn resolution

this band of eight hundred men maintained their ground, ordered his artillery to be concentrated upon them. The effect was instantaneous, and the troops, scourged into madness by the close, deadly fire, fled to the woods for protection. Washington, in the mean time, had ordered Greene to take possesssion of Dilworth's Pass, and hold it against the enemy. He did so, and as the fugitive Americans came on he would open his ranks and let them flow to the rear, then close again and present a firm front to the enemy.

The heavy conflict at Birmingham Meeting-House, and the sudden departure of Greene's division, was the signal for Knyphausen to advance. The head of his column entered the stream under the protection of the heavy batteries, and though severely shaken by Wayne's artillery, pressed firmly forward. The American force was too small to re-sist half the whole British army for any length of time, and though Wayne bore up nobly against the unequal numbers for awhile, he saw, after Sullivan's defeat, that a retreat was inevitable. This, how-ever, was hastened, in fact became a flight, at the appearance of a large body of the enemy emerging from the woods above him, and hastening along the banks of the Brandywine, to take him in flank and rear. Leaving behind all their stores and artillery, the broken and disordered columns helped to swell still more the tumultuous torrent that rolled on. Greene, however, firmly maintainted his position amid the turbulence and uproar of the pursuit and the flight, and unshaken alike by the wreck that tossed around him, and the assaults of the victorious and confident enemy, saved the army from destruc-tion. Behind him, as an impregnable rampart, the defeated but not disheartened troops rallied and de-manded to be led again to the attack. Muhlenburg and Weadon with their two brigades fought nobly to defend this pass. The latter was formerly an innkeeper in Virginia—the former a clergyman of the established church in the same state. The martial spirit of the divine kindling at the wrongs heaped upon his country, he preached his farewell sermon to his people, saying, at the close, that there was a time to fight as well as to pray, and that time had come. He had been previously elected colonel, and now taking off his gown and putting on his regimentals, he walked amid his congregation, and ordered the drum to beat for recruits at the church-door, and before night he had three hundred men at his back. He did good service in the south, and here at the Pass of Dilworth, covered his brigade with glory. During the battle and the flight, Washington had been everywhere present, directing and guiding all things. Night was now drawing on, and many of the officers enraged at the result of the day's action, demanded to be led against the enemy. "You must obey my orders," said Washington. "Our only resource is to retreat." Greene, whose blood was up from the conflict and defeat, asked how far they must retreat. "*Over every hill and across every river in America if I order you*," was the stern reply.

As night came on the firing ceased, and the American army retreated in confusion toward Chester. The roads leading thither were crowded with men, some marching with the order and discipline becoming troops, others rushing blindly on through the gloom, haunted by the fear of pursuit. The British encamped on the field of victory, which was thickly strewn with friends and foes. But along the slope where Stirling fought the dead lay thickest.

There is no battle recorded in our history respecting which there has been such diversity of opinion as that of Brandywine. Washington made no report of it to Congress, and without any data but the verbal statements of those who could give only conjectures, the historian has been unable to come to any definite results. The British force has been variously estimated at from eleven to seventeen thousand. Their loss, as stated by Howe, and universally conceded by Sparks and others, was only some six or seven hundred, while that of the Americans ranged from one thousand to fourteen hundred men. These figures have always appeared to me incorrect, for several reasons. In the first place, it was evident that the two main divisions of the enemy averaged but from four to five thousand each, so that eleven instead of seventeen or eighteen thousand composed their actual force in the field. In the second place, their loss seemed wholly at variance with the accounts of the battle itself. It is generally conceded that Maxwell's skirmishing parties killed and wounded three hundred out of Knyphausen's division alone, before it reached the Brandywine. That Stirling, who fought like a lion, and Greene, with his two gallant brigades, and Wayne, who kept up a heavy cannonade for five or six hours, should all together have killed and wounded only three hundred more, is evidently absurd. Still, following our best authorities, I have heretofore adopted their statements. But lately I have fallen on a document which shows these statements to be wholly erroneous, and makes the facts more consistent with reason. It was found among General James Clinton's papers, carefully filed away and endorsed by himself. On the back, in his own hand writing, is inscribed— *" Taken from the enemy's Ledgers, which fell into the hands of General Washington's army at the action of Germantown."*

Within is the following statement:

State of the British troops and position they were in when they made the attack at Brandywine, the 11th September, 1777.

The Upper Ford under the command of Lt. Lord Cornwallis.

2d Regiment British Guards, ⎫	1740	612 killed and wounded.*
2d " Light Infantry, ⎭		
2d Brigade British Foot,	2240	360 " "
1st Division Hessians,	800	70 " "
Ferguson's Riflemen,	80	46 " "
Total,	4860	1088 " "

Middle Ford, under the command of Major-General Gray.

2d Battalion Guards,	500
2d " 2d Highlanders,	700
2d " 70th "	700
Total,	1900

Lower Ford, under the command of Lt. General Knyphausen.

2d Brigade consisting of the ⎫ 4th, 5th, 10th, 15th, 23th, 27th, ⎬ 28th, 40th, 44th, 55th Regts. ⎭	2240	580 killed and wounded.
Hessians to the amount of	800	28 " "
Queen's Rangers,	480	290 " "
Total	3520	898
	1900	
	4860	1088
The whole British force,	10,280	1986 killed and wounded.
	1,986	
	8,294	

    The estimate of the total force which the British had on the field, makes the two armies actually engaged about equal. The heavy loss here given seems at first sight almost incredible, and puts an entirely different aspect on the battle. Of the authenticity and accuracy of this document I think there can be no doubt. In the first place, General Clinton is known to have been one of the most

    * Where Lord Stirling's division fought.

careful and accurate men with his papers in the army, and he would not have endorsed and filed away a document, the statements of which were not well authenticated. In the second place, the document itself bears the strongest *prima facie* evidence of its truth. Mere tables of figures without note or comment are not apt to be fabrications. The registry as given above could be nothing but a plain business paper. In the third place, the loss corresponds more with the length and severity of the battle, while all the details are complete, even to the numbers of the regiments, battalions, etc. The division under Gray was not in the battle, and hence suffered no loss. The terrible manner in which the Queen's Rangers were cut up, losing nearly three hundred out of four hundred and eighty, is explained by the fact that they were the troops sent against Maxwell in the woods, where they received that severe drubbing mentioned in the former part of the chapter. It is a little singular that the loss of Knyphausen in the woods before reaching the Brandwine should correspond so completely with the account of Maxwell. So of Ferguson's riflemen, more than half, according to this statement, were killed or wounded, showing what we all know to be true, that whenever it came to specific warfare, the picking off men in detail, the enemy always suffered severely. In the last place, it explains Howe's caution after the battle. He was evidently afraid to meet Washington in open conflict, and refused again and again to accept the battle which the latter endeavoured to force upon him. The fierce and desperate manner with which the Americans fought after they had been completely outmanœuvred – especially the firmness shown by the militia against the heavy onsets of the British infantry, made him afraid to risk another engagement, unless he had clearly the advantage of position. The French officers in Stirling's division, with the exception of Deborre, by their bravery and exhortations did noble service, and the untrained troops were held to the fire with a steadiness that had not before been exhibited in the open field. The difference between a loss of six hundred and two thousand is certainly very great, but it must be remembered that Howe was in the heart of the enemy's country, and it was clearly his policy, nay, it was necessary to his safety, to make that loss appear as inconsiderable as possible.

Washington has been criticised for fighting this battle, but the result instead of proving that he erred in judgment, seems to me to show that his plans were sound and judicious. It certainly never could have entered into any one's calculations that an army of five thousand men could march some twenty or more miles, and in broad daylight approach within two miles of Sullivan, and coolly halt and eat their dinner, without being discovered.

How Sullivan could have allowed the story of a major, as is stated, who declared he had been along the upper fords and could see no enemy, to overbalance the official declaration of lieutenant-colonel Ross, that he was actually following them toward the upper fords of the Brandywine, is utterly incomprehensible. I know that he was deficient in lighthorse with which to scour the county, but after the despatch of Ross, the few roads that led to his flank should have been constantly traversed for at least ten miles, even if his own staff were compelled to perform the service. Encamped in the open field, with a report in his hand stating that Cornwallis was far above him, he allowed himself to be surprised by a large army with a heavy train of artillery, and attacked before he could fairly get in position. Whether Sullivan be blameworthy or not, one thing is clear, such errors on the part of commanders of divisions will baffle the wisest laid plans of a commander-in-chief, and make every battle a defeat.

Had the troops fought on a fair field as they did on

this ruinous one, Washington would have stopped Howe's advance; and had he acted on the first information and crossed the Brandywine and attacked Knyphausen, he would, in all probability, have completely ruined him. As it was, the gallant manner in which the greater part of the army behaved, elated him almost as much as a victory would have done. Congress also, instead of being disheartened, took courage, and immediately despatched an order to General Putnam, in the Highlands, to send on with all possible despatch fifteen hundred continentals, while the militia from the surrounding states were summoned to the field. Foreseeing that in all probability Philadelphia would fall into the hands of the enemy, it invested Washington with extraordinary powers, to be used in case of its absence. He was authorized to suspend officers for ill-conduct and appoint new ones, to forage the country for seventy miles around for provisions and other articles necessary to the army, and remove and secure all goods which might benefit the enemy.

Undaunted by the repulse he had met with at Brandywine, Washington, who the day after the battle had retreated to Germantown, allowed his troops but a single day to rest, when he recrossed the Schuylkill, and marched back to meet Howe, and give him battle. His troops, though suffering from long exposure, without sufficient clothing, a thousand of them being barefooted, pressed cheerfully forward. The latter had scarcely left Brandywine, when he was told that the enemy was seeking him on the very field of victory. Grant and Cornwallis pushed forward in the direction of Chester, while Howe, with the main body, advanced toward the Lancaster Road leading to Philadelphia. On arriving at Goshen, twenty miles from the city, the latter was told that Washington was only five miles distant, marching up to give him battle. He immediately took position on a hill, and in a short time the heads of Washington's columns appeared in view. The latter continued steadily to

advance, directing his course against the left wing of
the enemy, and soon the sharp firing of the skirmishing parties began to ring over the field. It was a
dark sombre afternoon, and the overcast heavens
every moment grew more threatening. Washington
knowing what ruinous work heavy rain would make
with the ammunition of his troops, cast an anxious
look at the clouds, but still pressed forward. Officers
were seen hurrying over the field, the artillery was
brought forward, and the attacking columns were
already in motion, when the long pent-up clouds
opened, and a deluge of rain descended, flooding the
field and drenching both armies. It was one of
those blinding, pelting rains, to which both animals
and man succumb, and its effect on the army was like
the sudden order to halt. The weary troops, soaked
to their skins, endeavoured in vain to protect their ammunition. The water penetrated everywhere. The
powder was soon wet, and the fire-locks rendered
useless. The British army was in no better condition,
for, without a tent to cover them, they had been
exposed to the same storm. The rain continued all
night, and a sorry night it was to the shivering
army, as it crouched in the open field, supperless and
weary. In the morning Washington ordered a retreat.
He first retired to Yellow Springs, and finally recrossed the Schuylkill, resolved as soon as he could get
his arms and ammunition in order, again to cross
Howe's path, and fall on him with his suffering but
valorous little army.

In the mean time, however, he ordered Wayne, with
fifteen hundred men, to hang on the British, and, if
possible, cut off their baggage. This officer, making
a circuitous march, took, on the night of the 20th, an
excellent position, two miles from the Paoli Tavern,
and three miles from the British encampment. Howe,
informed by spies of Wayne's proximity, resolved to
surprise him. The latter, however, received information of the design, and though hardly believing the

report, doubled his pickets and patrols, and ordered
his men to sleep on their arms with their ammunition
beneath their coats.   It was a dark and rainy night,
and every thing remained quiet till about eleven
o'clock, when the rapid firing of the pickets announced the enemy close at hand.   Wayne immediately
ordered a retreat, but, before it could be effected, the
British rushed with loud shouts upon him, crying,
"No quarter." They swept the encampment like a
whirlwind, chasing Wayne into the darkness, and
strewing the ground with a hundred and fifty men.
As the attack was expected, its complete success caused
many to blame Wayne severely.   But he declared
that the disaster was owing to the delay of Colonel
Hampton to obey his orders to wheel the line and move
off, while he covered the retreat.   Another explanation, and a very probable one is, that Wayne thought-
lessly encamped amid his fires, instead of away from
them, thus lighting the enemy to the assault, and
showing them exactly where to strike.   At all events
it was a bad affair, and rendered still worse by the
preceding misfortunes.

Howe, instead of pushing on to Philadelphia, wheeled off toward Reading, apparently to gain Washington's flank, and at the same time destroy the military
stores deposited in the latter place.   Washington
immediately moved in the same direction.   But the
whole country so swarmed with Tories that he could
gain no reliable information of Howe's movements
till next morning, when he discovered that his enemy
had turned back again and crossed the fords below.
A forced march to overtake him was quite impossible,
especially with a barefoot army, and Philadelphia fell.
Congress, in anticipation of the catastrophe, had
adjourned to Lancaster, whence it removed to Yorktown.   The public archives and magazines had been
previously secured, and the ships at the wharves carried up the Delaware.   On the 26th of September,
Lord Cornwallis, in brilliant uniform, rode into the

city at the head of a detatchment of British and
Hessian grenadiers, welcomed with loud greetings
by the Tories, and received with congratulations by
the disloyal Quakers, who remained behind to receive
him.

Three days after this triumphal entry the first battle
of Stillwater was fought.

The main part of the British army did not advance
into the place, but encamped at Germantown, eight
miles distant. Washington, chafing like a foiled lion,
slowly followed after, and pitched his camp at Skip-
pack Creek, only fourteen miles distant, where he
narrowly watched every movememt of the enemy.
In the mean time the British fleet came up Delaware
Bay with the intention of communicating with the
land forces around Philadelphia. Anticipating this
movement, Washington had directed fortifications to
be built, and obstructions sunk in the channel, the
whole defended by forty galleys, five rafts, fourteen
fire-ships, and other vessels. The chief batteries
were at Mud Bank, a low island, and at Red Bank
on the Jersey shore, opposite. In order to assist his
brother in the attempt to break through these formidable barriers, Howe sent off two regiments to attack
a fort at Billing's Point. Washington, finding the
British army thus weakened, while his own had been
reinforced by the arrival of troops from the north,
and the Maryland militia, resolved to fall upon Germantown, and, if possible, carry it by assault.

The marvellous tenacity with which Washington
clung to an object that he had set his heart upon,
and the energy, almost fierceness, with which he
pressed toward it, were never more strikingly exhibited than in these repeated attacks on the British
army. Chased from the Jerseys, he took post behind the Brandywine, and though defeated by a
blunder which no foresight of his could have guarded against, left nearly two thousand of the enemy on
the field. Giving his tattered, unshod army but one

day's rest, he boldly turned on his heel, and marched back to assail his victorious enemy. Again disappointed and thwarted by the interposition of
heaven, he was compelled reluctantly to retreat.
Still unyielding, he turned hither and thither to
meet his antagonist and dispute with him for Philadelphia. Deceived and misled by the Tory inhabitants, he was compelled to see the object of so much
solicitude and toil fall into the hands of the enemy,
while the fugitive Congress and crowds of men and
women escaping over the country, gave additional
keenness to the mortification and disappointment
under which he suffered. Notwithstanding all this,
and the impoverished state of his army, he now determined with his undisciplined troops to attack the
enemy in his camp, and sweep him with one terrible
blow into the Schuylkill. The British encampment
at Germantown lay along the Schuylkill, passing
directly through the place. The left wing, between
the town and the river, was covered in front by the
mounted and dismounted chasseurs—the centre, in
the town, by a regiment and battalion of infantry
stationed three-quarters of a mile in advance, while
the right, extending beyond the town into the country, was protected by the Queen's American Rangers,
and a battalion of light infantry. This was the position
of the British army on the night of the 3d of October,
and the watch-fires burned cheerfully along the
lines, and the sentinels walked their weary rounds,
little dreaming of the storm that was about to burst
upon them. Washington's plan was a complicated
one for a night attack, but if successful at all would
be completely so, and result not merely in the defeat but utter overthrow, and probable capture of
the British army. He resolved to divide his army
into four portions, and entering the town at four
different points, attack the enemy in front, flank and
rear, at the same time, and thus throw them into
disorder, and force them back on the Schuylkill.

Greene and Stephens, with their brigades were selected to attack the British right wing, while the Maryland and Jersey militia, under Smallwood and Foreman, were to take a road nearly parallel to the left, so as to fall on the wing in flank. Armstrong, with the Pennsylvania militia, was to keep along the river shore, attack the British left, and, forcing it back, get to the rear; while Sullivan and Wayne, flanked by Conway's brigade, and accompanied by Washington in person, should move straight on the centre. The plan of attack being thus arranged, the columns took up their line of march at seven o'clock in the evening, and moved rapidly forward. It was a clear autumnal night, and the dark mass went hurrying along the highway, now passing open fields, and again lost in the deep shadows of the forest, their heavy tread and roll of artillery carriages being the only sounds that disturbed the stillness of the scene. The inmates of the farm-houses along the road, roused from their slumbers by the continuous and muffled tread of the heavy columns, gazed forth with alarm as the long array swept past. Germantown lay fourteen miles distant, and Washington hoped to make his attack by daylight. But as the head of the division rose over Chestnut Hill, that looked down on Germantown, day was already broadening in the east. Here the columns appointed to attack the centre broke off, and began to move to their respective destinations. As Washington with his staff rode down the hill the sun rose over the eastern horizon, lighting up into momentary beauty the quiet valley beneath, while the morning gun of the British broke dull and heavy on the ear. In a few minutes a thick fog rising from the Schuylkill shut everything from view, and almost at the same moment was heard the firing of Sullivan's advance as it came upon the enemy's picket at Mount Airey. The sudden cry of "to arms," the shrill blast of the bugle and roll of drums showed that Washington had pounced upon them unawares. The pickets being reinforced, made a stand, till Sullivan, with the main body, advancing, drove them back. He then left the road and began to cross the fields. But being compelled to fling down every fence as he advanced, which also furnished a rallying point to the enemy, his progress was slow.

He, however, kept steadily on, and at length came up with the left wing of the enemy, drawn up in order of battle, and a close murderous conflict commenced. Washington all this time was moving along the main road with the rear of the army. Hearing the heavy firing in advance, he knew that Sullivan was warmly engaged. As it continued without any cessation, he became anxious, for he knew that the troops had only about fifty rounds of ammunition, and turning to Colonel Pickering, he exclaimed, "I am afraid General Sullivan is throwing away his ammunition; ride forward and tell him to preserve it." Pickering dashed off on a gallop, and delivered his message. "*Shoulder arms*," passed along the American line—"*Forward, march,*" followed, and the whole line, with shouldered pieces, moved steadily up to the enemy, who, struck with astonishment, recoiled. Wayne, with his division, kept on his terrible way, bearing down all opposition. The fog was so thick that the opposing lines could not see each other till within a few rods, and hence fired at each other's volleys, and charged where the last blaze was seen. Wayne, carried away by his eagerness and daring, was riding gallantly at the head of his column when he was struck in the foot by a ball—a second grazed his hand, a third and fourth pierced his horse, and he sunk to the earth. Springing to his feet, he shouted, "*Forward,*" and sweeping the field before him, carried confusion into the whole British army, so that it threatened momentarily to break and fly. But Colonel Musgrave, commanding the British centre, threw himself with a body of men into a stone building, called Chew's house, and having barricaded the lower story, opened a destructive fire of musketry from the upper windows. Here, while the battle was roaring further and further away in the gloom, Washington, with several of his officers, halted to consult on the best course to be pursued.

Grouped together in front of an old stone building that looked dimly through the mist, they let the precious moments pass, while they discussed the propriety of pushing on without first reducing Chew's house. Knox loudly insisted on halting the army, till the house could be summoned to surrender. The younger officers opposed this course as ruinous. "It is unmilitary," exclaimed Knox, "to leave a castle in our rear" "What," replied Hamilton and Reed, "call this a castle, and lose the happy moment!" Hamilton and Lee and Pickering earnestly, almost fiercely, insisted on pushing rapidly forward. "Leave a regiment here," said they, "to take care of them, this will be all-sufficient." Knox, however, whose opinion had great weight with Washington, prevailed, and Lieutenant Smith, of Virginia, was sent forward with a flag. The enemy paid no attention to it, but continued to fire, and Smith, struck down by a musket-ball, was borne, mortally wounded, to the rear. A brisk cannonade was then opened on the building, but the pieces being only six-pounders, they could produce no effect. Wayne's division, which till this moment had carried everything before it, hearing the heavy firing in the rear, supposed very naturally that they had been cut off by the enemy, and immediately fell back. This uncovered Sullivan's left, that was pressing on nearly abreast. The British, who had begun to look about for a safe retreat, no sooner saw themselves relieved from the presence of Wayne's division, than they wheeled on the flank of Sullivan's. About this time also, the distant firing of Greene, which had been very heavy and constant, suddenly ceased, for want of ammunition. Being compelled to countermarch his division, as he found the enemy so differently posted from what he had been told, he was unable to commence his attack till long after the appointed time. Armstrong had come in sight of the enemy and halted, apparently engrossed in listening to the tremendous explosions that burst on every side from the dense fog. Still a portion of Sullivan's left wing kept on through the forsaken encampments, and passed the deserted tents, driving the enemy for two miles before them, and finally drew up within some six hundred yards of a large body rapidly forming in a lane, though scarcely visible from the dense fog. Colonel Matthews, from Green's division, here got entangled amid the houses, and before he could escape was attacked on three sides at once, by three times his number. Thus encompassed, he stood and fought like a lion, charging at the head of his troops with a desperation and valour that astonished friends and foes, till nearly his whole command was killed and wounded, when he and a hundred men surrendered themselves prisoners. This, together with the failure of ammunition, completed the disaster—the cry arose on all sides that the enemy was surrounding them, and the whole army recoiled in disorder to Chew's house, and past it. The assailed at once became the assailants, and charging on the broken ranks with loud shouts, drove them back over the dead and the dying. The scene now became one of indescribable confusion. Officers galloped around the broken squads, in the vain effort to rally them, while Washington, fully aroused to the extent of the danger which threatened him, spurred among the fugitives, and by his personal daring, and apparently reckless exposure of life, held a portion of the troops to the shock. His voice sounded over the din of battle, and his form glanced like a meteor through the smoke and fog that enveloped the field. Catching a glimpse of him

336   P

sitting in the very blaze of the enemy's volleys, Sullivan, who had just seen two aids fall by his side,
forgetful of his own danger, rode up to him and begged him not to remain in such an exposed position,
for the salvation of the army and country depended
on his life.   Washington wheeled away for a moment, but Sullivan, on looking back again, saw him
riding as before, where the shots fell thickest.   But
the day was irrevocably lost—defeat had come in the
very hour of victory, and the shout of triumph died
away in the cry of fear.   Such a sudden reverse, so
unexpected an overthrow from the very height of
success, was almost too much for Washington's
firmness, and he expressed more chagrin and disappointment than at the result of any battle he ever
fought.   Discomfited, weary, though not dispirited,
the army, weakened in killed, wounded and missing,
by nearly a thousand men, retreated for twenty miles
into the country, and finally reached their old camp
in safety.   When the separate divisions compared
notes, all felt that they had lost a battle already
gained—been beaten after they had conquered, and
were now compelled to report a defeat instead of a
glorious victory.   Several valuable officers were
slain, and among them General Nash.   Most of the
officers behaved nobly—there were, however, some
few exceptions, and among them General Stephens,
who reeled in his saddle from drunkenness as he led
his men into action.   He was consequently struck
from the army, and his command given to Lafayette.
Cornwallis, in Philadelphia, eight miles distant, was
startled at an early hour by the arrival of an officer,
announcing the attack on the camp at Germantown.
Summoning a corps of cavalry and the grenadiers,
he hastened thither.   But the battle was over, and
the day of his humiliation postponed.
    There has been a vast deal written about this
battle, and the contradictory accounts growing out
of the state of the atmosphere, the utter impossibility

of one division to judge what another was doing, and the various causes that in different localities conspired to produce the same result will always involve it in more or less uncertainty. Washington ascribes his failure principally to the fog; another to the failure of the ammunition; a third to the neglect of Armstrong, and the delay of the militia under Smallwood and Foreman on the left, which never came into action at all, thus breaking up the unity and efficiency of the combined movement. All these, doubtless, had their effect. Night attacks are always subject to many contingencies, especially if they are crippled by complicated movements. Different points cannot be reached at the specified and desirable moment. Unexpected obstacles will arise; delays not anticipated become unavoidable, and mistakes not only as to positions, but also as to the friendly or hostile character of troops concentrated in the darkness, very probable, and the firing in different quarters wrongly interpreted. The dense fog made this in reality a night attack, and hence subject to all the casualties of one. As a primary cause, therefore, not anticipated by Washington, he very naturally, and might very truly, regard it the true one. Had the morning been clear the result would, doubtless, have been different. But it must be remembered the very fog which confused the Americans, confused still more the enemy. The former knew perfectly well what they were about, while the latter were wholly ignorant of the number of their assailants, or where the weight of the attack was to fall. After going over all the different authorities, the great mistake, it seems to me, lay in halting at Chew's house. Had the advice of Pickering, Lee, Hamilton, and others been taken, and a regiment left to occupy those in the building, should they attempt to make a sally, all the other casualties would have effected nothing in the general result. Howe's army would have been destroyed, and this calamity, followed so rapidly by the capture of Burgoyne at Saratoga, finished the war with a clap of thunder.

An unexpected heavy firing in the rear of an army, while the commander-in-chief is absent, will always prove disastrous. It was as clear as noonday that the inmates of Chew's house, finding themselves watched by a regiment with artillery, would never have dared to sally forth on the rear of a victorious army, and the Battle of Germantown was lost by the very conduct which constitutes a *martinet*. Knox was the only *general* officer in the consultation held upon the building, and it was natural that Washington, who had, and justly, a high opinion of his military skill, should place more confidence in his judgment than in that of his young aids. But in battle, rules should never arrest fortune, or be used to stem the current of events, when setting favourably. Impulse in the heat and excitement of close conflict is often wiser than the sagest experience. At all events in this case it was applying a general rule where it did not belong, and arresting the whole practical action of a battle by a mere technicality; and although Washington attributes the failure to Providence, Providence will always be found against such bad management as that halt at Chew's house most indubitably. Knox and Providence are by no means one and the same, and had the opinion of the general been less scientific and more practical, the course of Providence would have taken a far different, and more satisfactory direction. Not that I would intimate that Providence does not overrule all our actions and bring about the best results in the end. I mean simply to say what no man doubts, that blunders, bad management, and unwise conduct, Providence generally allows to work mischief to those who are guilty of them. It is not a difficult matter now, when everything is understood, to fix the turning point of the battle, or to locate the blame, but it is quite another thing to say how great, under all the circumstances, that blame was. Finding his entire army enshrouded in a dense fog ; knowing by the heavy and constant firing that the troops were nearly out of ammunition, and fearing to get entangled in a net-work of just such houses as that of Chew's, Washington may have well hesitated about advancing, unless he could make a clean sweep as he went. But so far as the regarding of this single house as a fort or castle, it is palpable as noon-day that the junior officers were right, and Knox totally, fatally wrong. The whole upper part of the building would scarcely hold a regiment, while not a hundred men could fire to advantage from it at a time. After the field in front had been swept, a flag sent to it would not have been fired on, and a valuable officer lost his life. Still, though chagrined, the troops were not dispirited. They had attacked the veterans of England, and enjoyed the pleasure of chasing them in affright from their own encampment. Neither did Congress mourn over the defeat. Almost a victory was rather a subject of congratulation, for it gave confidence to the troops and lessened their fear of the enemy. The British confessed it was the severest handling they had yet received, and although Howe, as usual, made his loss but trifling, it evidently amounted to about eight hundred men. Mr. Sparks thinks that this battle had nearly as much to do in fixing the wavering determination of France, respecting the recognition of our independence, as the capture of Burgoyne, remarking that Count De Vergennes said to one of our commissioners in Paris, "that nothing struck him as much as General Washington attacking and giving battle to General Howe's army; that to bring an army raised within a year to this, promised everything." This may have had its weight in the French Councils, but such a remark was doubtless more complimentary than serious, for one cannot imagine what an army is raised for, except to attack the enemy, and that, too, within less than a year.

CHAPTER X.

Fall of Burgoyne—Sermon of Timothy Dwight—Letter
from Washington to Howe—Attack on Fort Mercer, and
Death of Count Donop—Gallant Defence and Fall of
Fort Mifflin—Fall of Fort Mercer—March of Howe against
Washington, and Address of the latter to his Troops—
The Conway Cabal and Fate of the head Conspirators—
Valley Forge—Sufferings of the Soldiers—Washington at
Prayer—Labours of Washington, and Inefficiency of
Congress—The Half-Pay Establishment—Washington's
Answer to the Complaint that he did not make a Winter
Campaign—News of the Alliance of France—Celebration
of it in Valley Forge—Baron Steuben and the Effects of
his Discipline on the Army—Howe resolves to Evacuate
Philadelphia—Council of War in the American Camp on
the best course to adopt.

FOUR days after the failure at Germantown, the
second battle of Saratoga was fought, and Burgoyne,
now completely hemmed in, turned, as a last resource, to Sir Henry Clinton, who was endeavouring to force his way up the Hudson to his rescue.
The latter had succeeded in taking both forts Montgomery and Clinton, though bravely defended by
Generals James, and George Clinton.   His effort,
however, came too late.   For six days Burgoyne
gloomily bore up against the decree which he knew
was written against him.   But his unrelenting foes
day by day gathered closer and darker around him.
They pitched their balls into his uncovered camp,
and from every height played with their artillery on
his dispirited columns.   Through the hall of council,
where his officers were moodily assembled, through
the very apartment where he sat at dinner, cannon
balls would crash, while all around his camp the
steadily increasing storm gave fearful indications of
his overthrow.   For awhile he turned and turned,
like a scorpion girt with fire, but his proud, ambitious heart was at last compelled to yield, and that

splendid army, on which he had fondly hoped to build his fame and secure rank and glory, laid down its arms.   Forty-two brass cannon, five thousand stand of arms, and all the camp equipage fell into the hands of the Americans, and one long, loud shout of triumph and of joy rolled through the northern colonies.   Gates, inflated by success, for which he had Arnold to thank, refused to report his victory to Washington, but sent his despatch to Putnam, at Fishkill, with the request to deliver it to Congress.   Putnam, overjoyed at the news, spread it through the army, and shouts, and the firing of cannon signalized the glorious event.   The Rev. Tim. Dwight, a chaplain in the army, preached a sermon at head-quarters, next day from the text, "I will remove far off from you the northern army."   Never was a sermon so listened to before by the officers and troops.   Putnam could not refrain from nodding and smiling during the discourse at the happy hits with which it was filled, and at the close was loud in his praises of Mr. Dwight and the sermon, though, to be sure, he said there was no such text in the Bible —the chaplain having coined it to suit the occasion. When shown the passage, he exclaimed, "Well, there is every thing in that book, and Dwight knows just where to lay his finger on it."

Washington, distressed for want of men, had written Gates, after the first battle, to send him Morgan's corps, if the enemy was retreating.   Gates declined, on the ground that Burgoyne was still in front. Two days after, the decisive battle was fought, and yet he retained the troops until the terms of the capitulation were settled, and its formalities gone through with.

About this time Washington received a letter from Howe, in which the latter remonstrated warmly against the destruction of several mills, by the American troops, on the ground that it inflicted distress on the inhabitants.   Washington defended his conduct as perfectly consistent with the usages of war, and added, " I am happy to find that you express so much sensibility to the sufferings of the inhabitants, as it gives room to hope that those wanton and unnecessary depredations which have heretofore, in many instances, marked the conduct of your army, will be discontinued. The instances I allude to need not be enumerated; your own memory will suggest them to your own imagination, from the destruction of Charlestown, in Massachusetts, down to the more recent burning of mills, barns, and houses, at the head of Elk and in the vicinity of the Schuylkill." No man knew better how to deal these severe home thrusts than Washington. They were given, however, as a just punishment, and did not spring from a revengeful temper, for on the very day the flag bore this caustic note, another accompanied the following civil card : " General Washington's compliments to General Howe, and does himself the pleasure to return to him a dog which accidently fell into his hands, and by the inscription on the collar appears to belong to General Howe."

The two armies lying so near each other, constant skirmishes took place between detached parties, in which great skill and bravery were frequently exhibited. It became very difficult for Howe to collect forage, and in the partisan warfare which the attempt created the British were sure to be losers

In the mean time, Howe pushed his efforts to clear the Delaware below the city, so that the fleet could come up. Washington, on the other hand, determined at all hazards to prevent it; for he knew that unless Howe could open his communication with the ships he would be compelled to evacuate Philadelphia. Forts Mercer and Mifflin, on Red and Mud Banks, protected by a fleet of galleys and other vessels, under the command of Com. Hazlewood, were the only barriers between the British army and their ships, and against these Howe immediately directed a large force. Col. Christopher Green, with four hundred men from the two Rhode Island regiments, garrisoned Fort Mercer, while Colonel Smith, with about the same number of Maryland troops, defended Fort Mifflin. Count Donop, with twelve hundred Hessians, was sent against the former, and early in the morning of the 22d of October, suddenly emerged from the wood within cannon shot of the fort. The little garrison was taken by surprise, but not unprepared. In a few minutes a Hessian officer rode up with a flag, and ordered them to lay down their arms, declaring that if they refused no quarter would be given. Enraged at this insolent demand, Colonel Green replied, "*We ask no quarter, nor will we give any.*" With this murderous understanding, the two armies prepared for action. Donop immediately ordered a battery to be erected, within half a gun shot of the fort, and notwithstanding the cannonading of the Americans, completed it, and at four o'clock opened his fire. He played furiously on the American works for three-quarters of an hour, and then gave orders to move forward to the assault. In two columns, one against the north and the other against the south side, they moved swiftly and steadily over the intervening space. The little band within gazed sternly on the overwhelming numbers, bearing down in such beautiful array, resolved to die where they stood rather than surrender. The first division, finding the advanced post and outworks abandoned, imagined the Americans had left them in affright. A loud cheer ran through the ranks, a lively march was struck up, and the column moved swiftly forward toward the silent redoubt itself, in which not a man could be seen. The soldiers were already ascending the ramparts to plant upon them the flag of victory, when suddenly every embrasure vomited forth fire, while a shower of grape-shot from a partially masked battery swept them away with frightful rapidity. Stunned and overwhelmed, they broke and fled out of the reach of the fire. The troops comprising the other column approached the south side of the fort, and pressing gallantly on, passed the abattis, crossed the ditch, and were pouring over the pickets, and mounting even the parapets, when the same deadly fire smote them so terribly that they recoiled and fled, leaving their commander mortally wounded on the field. The next day he died. He was only thirty-seven years of age, and just before his death exclaimed, " It is finishing a noble career early, but I die the victim of my ambition and the avarice of my sovereign."* The loss of the enemy was about four hundred, while that of the Americans was but thirty-eight. The first cannon shot aimed at Fort Mercer was the signal for the British fleet to advance against Fort Mifflin. It was, however, kept at bay by the American galleys and floating batteries, and did not make its attack on the fort till next day, when the Agusta, of sixty-four guns, the Roebuck, of forty-four, two frigates, the Merlin, of eighteen guns, and a galley opened a heavy fire on the fort and flotilla. The Americans replied with a terrific cannonade, the echoes rolling up the Delaware, filling friends and foes with the deepest anxiety. But the balls of the Americans crashed so incessantly through the ships that the commander at length gave the orders to fall down the river out of the reach of the fire. A shot had set the Agusta on fire, and at noon she blew up with a tremendous explosion. Soon after, the Merlin was seen to be in a blaze, and she too blew up, when the enemy withdrew. The officers commanding both forts were highly complimented by Washington, and swords were voted them and Commodore Hazlewood by Congress. Though repulsed, Howe did not abandon the attempt to force the passage of the river, and thirty vessels arriving, not long after, from New York, bringing reinforcements, he set on

* Referring to the fact that the troops were hired to Eng. land solely to obtain money.

foot more extensive preparations. Province Island, in rear of Mud Island, was taken possession of, and batteries were erected, while a large fleet, the vessels of which, drawing but little water, assembled near the forts. Washington, from his camp at White-marsh, saw these preparations with the extremest anxiety. With the fall of these forts would be ex-tinguished his last hope of compelling the British to evacuate Philadelphia that season. He wished to dislodge the enemy on Province Island, but in the attempt he would expose himself to an attack in the rear by Howe, who had thrown a bridge across the Schuylkill, and could easily reach him and cut off his retreat with a vastly superior force. Thus fetter-ed, he saw the works go up day by day, and the vessels and floating batteries slowly swing to their places, and a circle of fire gathering around Fort Mifflin, from which nothing but a miracle could de-liver it. In the mean time, a heavy rain-storm set in, and the fatigued soldiers were compelled, in re-lieving guard, often to wade breast-deep in the water. By the 10th, [Nov.,] a floating battery of twenty heavy cannons had been brought, through a new channel, to within forty yards of an angle of the fort, and four sixty-four, and two forty gun ships to within nine hundred yards, while fourteen strong redoubts, protected by heavy artillery, covered Province Island.

Against this formidable array Colonel Smith could muster but three hundred men, protected by com-paratively few batteries. At noon, on the 10th, the cannonading commenced from all the ships and land batteries, at once, and it rained shot and shells upon that little fort. But its guns, trained by skilful artillerists, spoke sharp and quick amid the deafening echoes, and it flamed and thundered over that low island, as though a volcano were upheaving it from the sea. Before night the commander of the artillery was killed by the bursting of a bomb, and the pallisades began to suffer. One cannon was also damaged. All night long the heavens and the waters were illuminated by the blaze of the guns, whose sullen reverberations rolled with a boding sound over the American camp. The cannonading continued all next day, slowly grinding the fort to powder. Col. Smith, struck senseless by a brick which a cannon ball hurled against him in its passage through a chimney, was, with Capt. George, also wounded, carried over to Red Bank. The enemy played night and day, without cessation, on the works, to prevent the garrison from repairing damages, and on the 12th dismounted two eighteen-pounders. The next day the ruin of the block-house was complete.· Lieutenant Russel succeeded Colonel Smith in command, but overcome with fatigue, withdrew, and Major Thayer volunteered to take his place. A more gallant officer was never inclosed by the walls of a fort. Against the hopeless odds that pressed him so sorely, with his cannon dismounted one after another, all his outworks demolished, and his garrison thinned off, he bore up to the last, refusing to yield while a gun could carry shot. The scene around that low fort at night was indescribably grand and fearful. Girdled with fire, and the target for so many cannon, canopied with shells bursting over and within, it still spoke forth its stern defiance, and answered thunder with thunder. On the 13th, the heavy floating battery of twenty cannon, anchored within pistol shot of the fort, opened with frightful effect, but before noon it was knocked to pieces and silenced by the well-directed fire of Thayer's artillery. Thus day after day wore on, while the garrison, though sick and exhausted, stood bravely to their guns. All this time Major Fleury sent daily despatches to Washington. A mere line or two detailed the progress of the enemy. Compelled to sit listless while this brave defence was going on, his indignation was aroused against Gates and Putnam, for their refusal to send the reinforcements he had demanded, and which might have prevented the terrible calamities that nothing now seemed able to avert. At length a deserter to the British informed the commanders, to their astonishment, of the breaking up of the garrison. The attack was about to be abandoned, but encouraged by the report of this deserter, they, at daylight on the 15th, brought up two frigates to cannonade the fort in front, while the Vigilant, cut down so as to draw little water, was carried so close to the works that her guns overlooked those within. At ten o'clock a signal bugle rung out over the water, and the next moment a terrific cannonade opened. The effect was appalling. The already half-destroyed batteries were soon completely demolished, the ditches filled with ruins, while the top-men in the rigging of the Vigilant picked off the artillerists on the platforms, and cast hand-grenades into their midst. With only two mounted guns, whose echoes could scarcely be heard in the surrounding uproar, Thayer still kept up a brave defence. In a short time these shared the fate of the others, and before night every embrasure was in ruins, the parapets all knocked away, the artillery company almost to a man killed or disabled, and the whole fort presenting only a painful wreck. As darkness approached, Thayer sent over to Red Bank all the garrison but forty men. With these he remained till midnight, when, seeing that every defence was swept away, and the enemy making preparations for storming the place in the morning, he set fire to the ruins, and by the light of the flames crossed over to Red Bank. Scarcely fifty unwounded men were left of the whole garrison. It was one of the most obstinate battles that had yet been fought, and stood side by side with Arnold's naval action on Lake Champlain, and covered the heroes of it with honour.

Fort Mercer, at Red Bank, was still in possession of the Americans, and Washington strained every nerve to save it. But Green, the commander, and Morgan, whom he sent to his relief, were too weak to oppose Cornwallis, rapidly approaching it with a heavy force. Colonel Green, despairing of succour, at length abandoned it, leaving all the artillery and stores in possession of the enemy. The American fleet, no longer protected by the forts, was now inevitably lost. Taking advantage of a dark night, some of the galleys, and two or three small vessels crept past the batteries at Philadelphia, and escaped up the river. The remaining portion, seventeen ships in all, were completely hemmed in by the enemy. The crews, seeing that escape was impossible, set them on fire at Gloucester, and fled. In their blazing timbers was consumed the last hope of rescuing Philadelphia from the British. The Delaware was now swept clear of every battery and vessel, and the enemy could sit down in safety in their snug winter quarters. The reinforcements, so culpably withheld, at length arrived, but too late to render aid, and only in time to increase the suffering and starvation of the army.

Howe, elated by his success, and strengthened by reinforcements, resolved to advance against Washington, and marched his army within two or three miles of the American camp. The latter, not doubting that a great and decisive battle was at hand, reviewed his troops with care, told them that the enemy was about to attack them, and expressed his confidence that victory would remain with the Americans. He praised the patience and valour of those who had combated with him at Brandywine and Germantown, and rousing their ambition and pride, told them that now was the time to show the conquerors from Saratoga, who were to stand by their sides in the approaching conflict, that they were their equals in heroism and love of country. He addressed the northern troops in a language of praise, saying that they were about to have another opportunity to add fresh laurels to those which they had so gloriously gained. He spoke of their common country, and by his impassioned manner, earnest appeals, and noble self-devotion, kindled every heart with enthusiasm and love till even the half-clad, half-famished, and worn-out soldiers panted equally with the strongest and freshest for the conflict. But Howe, after manœuvering for three days in front of the American lines, concluded not to venture an attack. Having lost more than a hundred men in the skirmishes* of the detached parties with Morgan's riflemen, he at length retired to Philadelphia, while Washington, weighed down with care and disappointment, led his suffering, starving army through the snow to the gloomy encampment of Valley Forge, there to make up the most sad and touching chapter in our history.

It seemed at this time as if Heaven was determined to try the American commander, in the sevenfold heated furnace of affliction, for while struggling against the mortification and disappointment of his continued failures, and against the gloomy prospect before him, and actual suffering of his destitute army, and compelled to bear the reproaches of men in high places for his want of success, he saw a conspiracy forming to disgrace him from his command as unequal to its duties. What Washington suffered during this autumn and winter no one will ever know. It was all black around him and before him, while, to crown his accumulated afflictions, his own officers, with members of Congress, were plotting his overthrow. Yet his serenity did not forsake him. Conscious of his own integrity, caring only for his country, the injurious comparisons drawn between him and Gates, the falling off of his friends, the disloyalty of the inhabitants, and the dreadful trials he knew to be in store for him, could not move him to jealousy, or angry expression, or force him to despair. All the shafts which misfortune hurled at him fell powerless at his feet. Still he felt for his country. Here was his vulnerable point. Her danger and sufferings aroused all the terrible and the tender in his nature.

* Major Morris, fresh from Saratoga, was killed in one of these skirmishes.

Much has been said of the Conway cabal, and various accounts of its origin and progress given. The whole affair, however, admits of an easy and natural explanation. A man rising, like Washington, to power in troublous times, will always make rivals and enemies. There will be one class of officers who, having a high opinion of their own merit, will resent any refusal to their claims, and become secretly embittered. Such were Gates and Mifflin, who never forgave Washington for not granting their requests at Boston, the former to have command of a brigade to which he considered himself entitled, and the latter that of a regiment. There are others, mere ambitious adventurers, who, if foiled in their efforts in one quarter, will endeavour to succeed in another, and placing their personal aggrandizement before every thing else, are ripe for conspiracies, revolutions, or any thing that promises to advance their own interests. Such was Conway. There is still a third class who measure excellence by success, and whose feelings grow cold toward a defeated commander. Such were some in the army, and some in Congress, and many in the higher walks of social life. Then each of these has personal friends more or less impressible. Added to all these, there were, in the case of Washington, men of influence who, while they had the reputation of being patriots, secretly inclined to the loyalists, and would gladly seize the first opportunity to overthrow the only man that stood in the way of the submission of the colonies. All these classes and characters remain quiet so long as they see that the man that they assail is too strong in popular affection or in power to be attacked with safety. But the moment his own misfortunes, or the successes of others, weaken that popularity, and sap that strength, they combine against him, and what was before mere private complaints and abuse, becomes organized action. By this natural process the Conway cabal, doubtless, was formed. Conway was an unscrupulous, dangerous man, and had joined the army as a mere adventurer. Although an Englishman by birth, he had lived in France since he was six years of age, and seen much service in the French army. He came to this country with high recommendations, and was appointed by Congress brigadier-general. Arrogant, boastful, and selfish, he was especially repugnant to Washington, who, with his deep insight, penetrated the hollow character of the man at once, and would never trust him. He therefore stood in Conway's way, and the latter would naturally seize the first opportunity to help to remove him. The constant defeats in Pennsylvania, during the summer of 1777, gave great weight to his opinion against Washington's military capacity, and it was not difficult to win over many members of a Congress so contemptible as the one which then ruled our affairs. Still there was a great difficulty in taking the initiatory steps. If Washington could be displaced, there was no leader sufficiently popular to secure the confidence and co-operation of the people and the army. If successful, therefore, in its first attempt, the plot would afterward fall to the ground through its own weakness. But the great and decided victory of Gates over Burgoyne, linking his name with plaudits and honours all over the land, contrasting as it did with Washington's successive defeats and helpless condition, gave to the former the very prominence, the want of which had hitherto brought every thing to a dead lock. From this moment the malcontents grew bold, and, the conspiracy strengthened with wonderful rapidity. Gates, an essentially weak, vain man, was just the tool to be used in this nefarious scheme. He entertained no more doubt of his superiority to Washington as a military man, than his friends appeared to have, and would have had no hesitation in accepting the chief command. The first thing to be secured was the co-operation of a sufficient number of the superior officers. Congress was already corrupted to an extent

that promised success, and the army alone was wanting to take a decided step at once.   The officers were
cautiously sounded, but here the conspirators made
poor progress.   The remark which Wilkinson dropped to Stirling, and which exploded the whole scheme,
was evidently thrown out as a feeler.   As if in casual
conversation, he remarked that Conway had written
to Gates, saying—" Heaven has been determined to
save your country, or a weak general and bad coun-
sellors would have ruined it."   This brought on a
correspondence between different parties, and developed, at once, the feelings of both the army and the
people.
   Patrick Henry, Governor of Virginia, received
an anonymous letter, which Washington ascribed to
Dr. Rush, in which, after some flattery, the latter says
—" A dreary wilderness is still before us, and unless
a Moses or a Joshua are raised up in our behalf, we
must perish before we reach the promised land ;"
and again, " The spirit of the southern army is no
way inferior to the northern.   A Gates, a Lee, or a
Conway, would, in a few weeks, render them an irre-
sistible body of men."   This letter Patrick Henry
inclosed to Washington, accompanying it with his
severe condemnation.   Said he, " I am sorry there
should be one who counts himself my friend, who is
not yours."   Another anonymous paper was sent to
Laurens, President of Congress, filled with accusations against Washington and his course.   This,
Laurens refused to lay before Congress, and sent it
to Washington, with his condemnation of the writer.
The latter replied, saying he hoped that the paper
would be submitted to Congress, that the charges it
contained might be investigated, and added, " My
enemies take ungenerous advantage of me.   They
know the delicacy of my situation, and that motives of
policy deprive me of the defence that I might otherwise make against their insidious attacks.   They
know I cannot combat their insinuations, however

injurious, without disclosing secrets which it is of the utmost moment to conceal. My heart tells me that it has been my unremitted aim, to do the best that circumstances would permit, yet I may have been very often mistaken in my judgment of the means, and may in many instances deserve the imputation of error." Patrick Henry, hearing of the part General Mifflin was taking in the conspiracy, wrote again to Washington, to comfort and strengthen him. Said he, "While you face the armed enemies of your country in the field, and, by the favour of God, have been kept unhurt, I trust your country will never harbour in her bosom the miscreant who would ruin her best supporter." Letters from others came pouring in, showing what a stern rally his friends would make when action became necessary. Conway endeavoured to make friends with Lafayette by flattery and falsehood, but the young patriot penetrated at once, and denounced the villainous faction which sought to make him its tool. He wrote Washington a long letter, stating that the conspiracy had involved many in the army, but closed by saying, "*I am bound to your fate, and I shall follow it, and sustain it as well by my sword as by all the means in my power.* You will pardon my importunity. Youth and friendship make me too warm, but I feel the greatest concern at recent events." Washington replied to this free and full offer of his sword and his efforts, in terms of warm affection. He had, from the outset, taken him like a son to his bosom, and loved him with parental affection to the last. Notwithstanding these ominous exhibitions of popular feeling, and directly in the teeth of Washington's most earnest, solemn, and even prophetic remonstrances, Congress raised Conway to the rank of major-general, and made him inspector-general of the army. It also created a Board of War, invested with large powers, and placed Conway, Mifflin and Gates at the head of it. This board immediately planned an ex-

pedition to Canada, the command of which was
offered, as a bribe, to Lafayette. The latter carried
the offer directly to Washington, telling him ho
should decline. Washington advised him not to do
so, as the appointment was an honourable one, and
would advance his reputation. He, therefore, accepted, and went to Yorktown to meet the Board of War.
On his arrival, he found General Gates at dinner,
surrounded by his friends, all of whom received him
with the warmest expression of friendship. He sat
down to the table, and the wine passed rapidly around
as complimentary toasts were given in turn by the
guests. Just as the company was about to break up,
Lafayette remarked that, with their permission, he
would propose a toast. The glasses were filled, when,
looking steadily at those around him, he said, "*The
Commander-in-chief of the American Armies.*" They,
by a great effort, succeeded in swallowing the toast,
but Lafayetta never went to Canada. The strength
of the conspiracy lay in Congress, where it had reached to an alarming extent. But of the plots then
hatched, and the men who then showed themselves to
be enemies of Washington, we yet remain in ignorance, and perhaps ever shall. The record of their
deeds is destroyed. In a letter to me, a gentleman
thoroughly informed on matters of American history,
says—"It has been said over and over again, and by
those best able to speak, that the history of our Revolution could not be written for many years to
come—some say never—and, as to some parts of it,
I subscribe to the latter. The diary of Charles
Thompson, Secretary to Congress, was destroyed.
It was more than full, and something of its character
was known. Colonel North, too, kept a full diary,
of such a character that not even his own son was
permitted to see certain parts of it. It too was destroyed. When success crowned the patriotic struggle
those who had faltered and wavered, gladly destroyed
the evidence of their weakness, while the generosity

which filled the brave men who never despaired, led them to cover the shortcomings of their weaker brethren." There is food for much thought in the above paragraph. If Dr. Rush's papers could be obtained for publication, they would, doubtless, fling some light on this transaction. But all efforts to get them have thus far proved abortive. After agitating the army and the country for a while, the conspiracy at length fell through. Conway, one of the leaders, was afterward shot in a duel, and, supposing himself to be dying, wrote to Washington, " I find myself just able to hold the pen during a few minutes, and take this opportunity of expressing my sincere grief for having done, written, or said anything disagreeable to your excellency. My career will soon be over; therefore, justice and truth prompt me to declare my last sentiments. You are, in my eyes, the great and good man. May you long enjoy the love, veneration and esteem of those States whose liberties you have asserted by your virtues." Gates, the chief leader, shorn of all his stolen plumes by his disastrous defeat at Camden—recalled in disgrace by the very Congress which had lauded him—mortified, humbled and depressed, was compelled at last to receive the condolence and sympathy of the man whose overthrow he had plotted. Mifflin, the other leading officer, did not receive the punishment he deserved, but, on the contrary, was rewarded with honour by his State. Washington had remained unmoved amid it all. Calm in the consciousness of his integrity, indifferent to the power and place he occupied, only as he could use them to serve his country, upheld by that serene trust in Heaven which he believed had ordained the triumph of liberty, he moved steadily forward in the path of duty and of trial. Like the mountain summit, around which the mists of morning gather, only to dissolve before the uprisen sun, so he, under the light of truth, emerged from the partial obscuration with undimmed splendour, and with a cloudless heaven bending above him. But the deed deserved a deep reprobation from its cruelty, and from the peril in which it brought the country. To add to the suffering which Washington already endured, and weave a plot designed to effect his ruin around the gloomy encampment at Valley Forge, revealed hearts hard as iron to all generous and honourable appeals.

I have not mentioned as a part of the Conway conspiracy, as it is called, the publication of some forged private letters, said to have been found in Washington's valise when he fled over the Hudson into Jersey, and which contained opinions adverse to the independence of the colonies. Writers have dwelt with more or less severity on this matter. But the attempt was so absurd that I cannot conceive that it could have formed a part of the scheme itself. It must have been the private enterprise of some very weak-headed or ignorant man. That an anonymous publication could weigh a feather against Washington's public acts and sacrifices, was an expectation too preposterous to be entertained by any sensible persons. Washington, at that time, did not even take the trouble to deny it.

Valley Forge! What thoughts and emotions are awakened at the mention of that name. Sympathy and admiration, pity and love, tears and smiles chase each other in rapid succession, as one in imagination goes over the history of that wintry encampment. Never before was there such an exhibition of the triumph of patriotism over neglect and want; of principle over physicial sufferings; of virtue over the pangs of starvation. Those tattered, half-clad, and bare-foot soldiers, wan with want, taking up their slow march for the wintry forest, leaving their bloody testimonials on every foot of the frozen ground they traversed, furnish one of the sublimest scenes in history. A cloud, black as sackcloth, seems to hang over their fortunes, but through it shoots rays of dazzling brightness. A murmur, like the first cadences of a death-song, heralds their march, but there is an under tone of strange meaning and sublime power, for no outward darkness can quench the light of a great soul, no moans of suffering drown the language of a lofty purpose.

The encampment at Valley Forge was chosen after much deliberation, and frequent consultations among the officers. Various propositions were made, but to each and all there were many and grave objections. Of course, the first and natural wish was to keep the army in the field ; but with such naked troops this would be impossible, and every feeling of humanity in Washington revolted from making the attempt. But how and where to quarter them seemed equally difficult. It was proposed to retire to the towns in the interior of the state ; but to this there was the two-fold objection— that of inflicting the same destitution and suffering on the inhabitants, and of leaving a large extent of country unprotected, with forage and stores in prossession of the enemy. To distribute the troops in different sections would render them liable to be cut off in detail. Washington, therefore, determined to take to the woods, near his enemy, and there hut, so that he could both protect the country and his stores, and also be in striking distance in case of need.

The army commenced its march on the 11th of December, but did not reach the place selected for the encampment till the 19th. In his order of the day, dated December 17th, Washington informed the troops of his decision, and the reasons which urged him to it. He also praised their good conduct during the tedious campaign now closed, declared that it furnished evidence that their cause would finally triumph, even if the colonies were left alone in the struggle, but added that there was every reason to believe that France would soon ally herself openly against England. He promised to share in the hardships, and partake of every inconvenience. The next day had been appointed by Congress as a day of thanksgiving and praise. The army, therefore, remained quiet in their quarters, and divine service was held in the "several corps and brigades," by the chaplains, and hymns of praise and the voice of prayer arose there on the confines of the bleak forest, from men who, to all human appearance, had little to be thankful for, except nakedness, famine, and frost. The next day the work of hutting commenced. Each regiment was divided into parties of twelve, each party to make its own hut, which was to be of logs, fourteen by sixteen feet on the ground, and six feet and a half high. The sides were to be made tight with clay, and the roof with split slabs, or such material as could be obtained. To stimulate the parties to greater exertion, Washington offered a reward of one dollar to each man of that party which finished its hut in the shortest time and most workman-like manner. Fearing that there would not be slabs or boards sufficient for roofing, he offered a reward, also, of a hundred dollars to any one who should "substitute some other covering," that might be more cheaply and quickly made. In a short time the arms were all stacked, and with their axes and other tools in their hands, this army of eleven thousand men, with the exception of about three thousand who were unfit for duty, were scattered through the woods. The scene they presented was strange and picturesque. There was not a murmur or complaint, and with laugh, and song, and loud hallo, they went about their allotted toil. The forest soon rung with the strokes of the axe, and the rapid and incessant crash of falling trees resounded along the shores of the Schuylkill. Little clearings were rapidly made, the foundations of huts laid, and a vast settlement began to spring up along the valley and slopes of the hills. But here and there were scattered groups of fifties and hundreds, sitting around huge fires, some of them with scarcely a rag to cover their nakedness, crouching closely to the cracking logs to escape the piercing December blast; others sick and emaciated, gazing listlessly on the flames, their sunken and sallow visages clearly foretelling what would be their fate before the winter now setting in was over. In another direction were seen men harnessed together like beasts of burden, and drawing logs to the place of destination. Washington's tent was pitched on the brow of a hill overlooking this strange spectacle. One after another the rude structures went up, till a log city, containing between one and two thousand dwellings, stood in the clearings that had been made. Over the ground floor straw was scattered, and into these the "*Sons of Liberty*," as Colonel Barre had christened them, in the English Parliament, crept to starve and to die. The officer's huts were ranged in lines in the rear of those of the soldiers, one being allowed to each of all those who bore commissions, the whole being surrounded with intrenchments. But scarcely had the troops got into these comfortless houses, when there began to be a want of food in camp. Congress, with the infallible certainty of doing the wrong thing, had recently, against Washington's advice, made a change in the quarter-master's and commissary's department, by which, in this critical juncture, the army was left without provisions. In the mean time, news came that a large party of the enemy was advancing in the country to forage. Washington immediately ordered the troops to be in readiness to march, when, to his surprise, he found that they were wholly unable to stir, for want of food, and that a dangerous mutiny had broken out. The soldiers were willing to suffer or die, if necessary, but they would not submit to the neglect and indifference of Congress, which they knew could easily relieve their wants. The statements made by the different officers were of the most alarming kind. General Huntingdon wrote a note to Washington, saying that his brigade was out of provisions, but he held it in readiness to march, as "*fighting was far preferable to starving.*" General Varnum wrote, also, saying that his division had been two days without meat and three days without bread, and that the men must be supplied, or they could not be commanded; still they were ready to march, as any change was better than slow starvation. On inquiry there was found only one purchasing commissary in camp, and he made the frightful report of not a "*single hoof of any kind to slaughter, and not more than twenty-five barrels of flour*" to the whole army. Only small detachments, therefore, could be sent out. These hovered about the enemy, now bursting on a small party from some forest, and again surrounding the dwelling where they were reposing. The weather came on intensely cold, and the soldiers could hardly handle their muskets with their stiffened fingers. They rarely entered a house, and dared not kindle a fire at night, lest it should reveal their position to the enemy.

Thus, for a week, they kept marching and skirmishing, till the enemy withdrew to Philadelphia, when they returned to camp, having collected but little forage. Here suffering and want were fast bringing things to a crisis. The soldiers were at first satisfied with the excuse given for the delay of provisions, viz. that the rains had made the roads almost impassable. But day after day passing without relief, they began to complain, and soon their murmurs swelled to loud clamours and threats. First the different regiments began to assemble, and the excitement increasing, whole brigades and divisions gathered together without order, and against the commands of their officers. The latter did not attempt to enforce obedience, but spoke kindly to them, saying that Washington was aware of their suffering condition, that it grieved him to the heart, and he was straining every nerve to obtain relief. Washington himself exhorted them to be obedient, saying that provisions would soon be in the camp, and insubordination could result only in evil. The soldiers, in return, were calm and respectful. They told him they knew their conduct was mutinous, but their condition justified it. They were actually starving, and relief must be had. They then respectfully communicated to him their fixed determination, which was to march in an orderly manner into the country, seize provisions wherever they could lay hands on them, giving in return certificates as to the amount and value of the articles taken, and then return to camp, and to their duty. Never before was there a mutiny so devoid of crime, and which, in fact, partook of the moral sublime. Their language was, "We are starving here, and shall soon be of no service to you or our country. We love you, and the cause in which we are embarked. We will stand by you at all hazards, and defend with our last drop of blood our common country, but food we must and will have." Washington was overcome by the condition and conduct of these men. So self-sustained in their sufferings—so constant to him in their destitution—so firm for their country, though abandoned by Congress, their language and attitude moved him deeply. There was something inexpressibly touching in the noble regret they manifested for appearing to be disobedient, and the high, manly grounds in which they defended their conduct. Washington, in reply, told them that he was well aware of the sufferings of his faithful soldiers. He had long admired their patience and resignation, and devotion to their country, under the most trying circumstances, and if the provisions did not arrive by a specified hour, he would place himself at their head, and march into the country till they were found. To this they consented, but the promised supplies arriving before the time fixed had expired, quietness and subordination were restored, and a movement, the results of which could not be foreseen, prevented.

This supply, however, was soon exhausted, and then the same scenes of suffering were repeated. Nearly all the inhabitants in the vicinity of Valley Forge were Tories, and hence withheld the food they could have furnished. Finding that neither offers of pay nor threats could wring it from them, Washington, acting under a resolution of Congress, issued a proclamation in which he ordered all the farmers within seventy miles of Valley Forge, to thresh out half their grains by the first of February, and the other half by the first of March, under penalty of having the whole seized as straw. The Tories refused to comply, and many of them defended their barns and stacks with fire-arms. Some, unable to do this, set fire to their grain, to prevent its falling into the hands of the Americans. The soldiers turned themselves into pack-horses, yoked themselves to waggons, and shrunk from no labour required to bring in provisions. But all the efforts and ingenuity of Washington could not prevent the gaunt figure of famine from stalking through his camp. Horses died for want of forage, and the men became so reduced that scarcely enough could be found fit " to discharge the military camp duties from day to day :" and even these few were compelled to borrow clothes to cover their nakedness while performing them.

A week passed without a pound of flesh being brought into camp, and at last the bread gave out, and for several days the starving soldiers had not a morsel to eat. Heavy snow-storms, followed by excessive frosts, swelled the sufferings that before seemed unbearable. So few blankets had been supplied that the benumbed soldiers were compelled to sleep sitting around their fires, to prevent freezing. Many were so naked that they could not show themselves outside of their huts, but hid shivering away in the scanty straw. Others would flit from hut to hut, with only a loose blanket to cover their otherwise naked forms. These huts, half closed up with snow, and the men wading around in their rags to beat paths, presented a singular spectacle on a bright wintry morning. In the midst of this accumulation of woes, the small-pox broke out, and Washington was compelled to resort to inoculation to prevent the severer ravages of the disease. The sick, in consequence, were everywhere, and without blankets or provisions and hospital stores, and stretched on the earth wet and frosty, by turns, presented a scene of woe and wretchedness that beggars description. Starvation and despair will in the end demoralize the noblest army that ever defended a holy cause, and they at length began to tell on this band of patriots. A foreign officer, in walking through the encampment one day with Washington, heard through the crevices of the huts as he passed, half-naked men muttering, "*no pay, no clothes, no rum.*" Then he said he despaired of American Liberty. Had Howe been made aware of this deplorable state of the army, he could have with a single blow crushed it to atoms. Amid this woe and suffering, Washington moved with a calm mien but a breaking heart. The piteous looks and haggard appearance of his poor soldiers—the consciousness that his army was powerless to resent any attack of the enemy, nay, on the point of dissolution, never probably to be re-united, all combined to press him so heavily with care, that even he must have sunk under it had he not put his trust in a higher power than man. One day a Quaker, by the name of Potts, was strolling up a creek, when he heard, in a secluded spot, the solemn voice of some one apparently engaged in prayer. Stealing quietly forward, he saw Washington's horse tied to a sapling, and a little farther on, in a thicket, the chief himself, on his knees, and with tears streaming down his cheeks, beseeching Heaven for his country and his army. Before God alone that strong heart gave way, and poured forth the full tide of its griefs and anxieties. Though the heavens grew dark around him, and disaster after disaster wrecked his brightest hopes, and despair settled down on officers and men, he showed the same unalterable presence—moved the same tower of strength. But to his God he could safely go with his troubles, and on that securely lean. How sublime does he appear, and how good and holy the cause he was engaged in seems, as he thus carries it to the throne of a just God, feeling that it has his sanction and can claim his protection.

The poor man who had witnessed this spectacle hurried home, and on opening the door of his house burst into tears. His wife, amazed, inquired what was the matter with him. He told her what he had seen, and added, "If there is any one on this earth whom the Lord will listen to, it is George Washington, and I feel a presentiment that under such a commander, there can be no doubt of our eventually establishing our independence, and that God in his providence has willed it so."

No wonder peace sat enthroned on that brow when despair clouded all others.

In February his wife joined him, and as the two walked through the wretched camp, even the half-starved and mutinous soldier raised his head to bless them, and from many a pallid lip fell "long live Washington," as his tall form darkened the door of the hovel. She was worthy of him, and cheerfully shared his discomforts and anxieties. Having at length got a little addition, built of logs, attached to their quarters, as a dinner-room, she writes that their straitened quarters were much more tolerable.

But the sick, powerless, and famished army that lay around him did not wholly occupy Washington's attention. He wrote to the various officers to the east and north, took measures to have West Point fortified, and pressed on Congress the necessity of a complete change in the organization and discipline of the army, and mode of obtaining supplies. This body at length yielded to his solicitations, and a committee of five was appointed to wait on him at Valley Forge, to decide on some feasible plan. Washington laid before them a project, which, after receiving the various opinions of the officers, he had, with great labour and care, drawn up. The committee remained three months in camp, and then returned to Congress with a report, which, with a very few amendments was adopted. On one point he and Congress differed widely. Hitherto, the officers received pay only while in the service, and no provision was made for them in the future. Washington wished to have the half-pay system for life adopted, and finding Congress averse to it, he wrote a strong and urgent request, in which he declared that he " most religiously believed the salvation of the cause depended upon it, and without it, officers would moulder to nothing, or be composed of low and illiterate men, void of capacity, and unfit for their business." He said he had no interest in the decision, personally, as he had fully resolved never to receive the smallest benefit from the half-pay establishment ; but he added, " *As a man who fights under the weight of proscription, and as a citizen who wishes to see the liberty of his country established on a permanent basis, and whose property depends on the success of our arms, I am deeply interested.*" Still Congress hesitated, doubtful whether this matter did not belong to the separate States. Some saw in it the basis of a standing army; others the elements of a privileged class; indeed, saw every thing but the simple truth, that officers will not sacrifice all their interests, and run the hazards of war for a country which will not even promise after her independence is secured, to provide for their support. Deeply impressed with the necessity and importance of this measure, Washington wrote again to a member of Congress, declaring " that if it was not adopted he believed the army would disband, and even if it should not, it would be without discipline, without energy, incapable of acting with vigour, and destitute of those cements necessary to promise success on the one hand, or to withstand the shocks of adversity on the other." He said, "Men may speculate as much as they will; they may talk of patriotism, they may draw a few examples, from ancient story, of great achievements performed by its influence, but whoever builds upon them as a sufficient basis for conducting a long and bloody war, will find himself deceived in the end........I do not mean to exclude altogether the idea of patriotism. I know it exists, and I know it has done much in the present contest. But I will venture to assert that a great and lasting war can never be supported on this principle alone." He might have added that officers and men felt that if they owed the State obedience, the State in turn owed them protection; or that if they risked life and fortune in the defence of their country, she, when delivered, owed them some provision against want. It is hard to fight for a country that degrades our efforts to the mere duties of a hireling. Patriotism, like love for a fellow being, must have regard in return or it will soon die out. Urged by Washington's appeals, Congress at length passed the half-pay bill, but shortly after reconsidered it, and finally compromised the matter by allowing the officers half-pay for seven years, and granting a gratuity of eighty dollars to each non-commissioned officer and soldier, who should serve to the end of the war. Thus, while struggling with the difficulties that beset him in camp, he was compelled to plead with a suspicious feeble Congress, and submit to its implied imputations. The course it was taking he saw clearly would lead to mischief. Its openly avowed suspicions of the army, he declared, was just the way to make it dangerous. "The most certain way (said he) to make a man your enemy, is to tell him you esteem him much." Besides, the conduct of the army did not warrant this jealousy. From first to last, it had shown an example of obedience to the civil authorities, worthy of the highest commendation, not of distrust. Washington boldly asserted that history could not furnish another instance of an army " suffering such uncommon hardships, and bearing them with the same patience and fortitude. To see men (said he) without clothes to cover their nakedness, without blankets to lie on, without shoes, for the want of which their marches might be traced by the blood from their feet—and almost as often without provisions as with them, marching through the frost and snow, and at Christmas taking up their winter-quarters within a day's march of the enemy, without a house or hut to cover them till they could be built, and submitting without a murmur, is a proof of patience and obedience which, in my opinion, can scarce be paralleled." No, it could not be paralleled, and yet the greater the devotion and sufferings of the army, the more neglectful, suspicious and hostile Congress became. Its noble conduct demanded gratitude and confidence, but received instead distrust and injury. Thus, while exerting all his powers to protect and keep together the army, he had to devise and propose every important military measure, and then, at last, see many of his plans fail through party spirit, and others so altered as to lose half their value. It was under these accumulations of evils the Conway cabal came to a head, and Washington saw his own officers conspiring together to effect his overthrow. This was the darkest hour of his life, for not only misfortunes, but things far more wounding to him than any misfortune, were crowding him to the furthest limit of endurance.

Thus passed the long, severe and gloomy winter, but spring at last with its balmy breath arrived, and was hailed with delight by the suffering troops.

Unjust and inconsistent as it may seem, there were
many in Congress and out of it who blamed Washington for not carrying on a winter campaign. Of
these members of Congress he spoke in bitter sarcasm,
declaring that they at first denied the soldiers clothes,
and then wanted them to keep the field in winter.
"I can assure these gentlemen," sad she, "that it
is a much easier and less distressing thing to draw
remonstrances in a comfortable room, by a good fire-
side, than to occupy a cold, bleak hill, and sleep under frost and snow, without clothes or blankets.
However, although they seem to have little feeling
for the naked, distressed soldiers, I feel superabun-
dantly for them, and from my soul I pity those miseries which it is neither in my power to relieve nor
prevent." His indignation and scorn are moved at
the inhumanity of such complaints, but they both
yield to pity as he contemplates the condition of his
soldiers. But notwithstanding the conspiracies surrounding him, the disaffection of some of his best
officers, and the conduct of Congress, and the state
of his troops, he did not waver a moment in his course.
And when, in the middle of April, he received a
draft of Lord North's conciliatory bills, as they were
called, containing a new project for settling the difficulties between the two countries, all his solicitude
was aroused at once, lest the favourable terms offered
might be accepted, or at least urged by men tired of
the war, and despairing of success. He immediately
wrote to a member of Congress, saying, "Nothing
short of Independence, it appears to me, can possibly
do. A peace on any other terms would be, if I may
be allowed the expression, a peace of war." He expressed his views in full, in which, fortunately, Congress coincided, and the three commissioners sent
over by the British government, Lord Carlisle, Governor Johnstone, and William Eden, after vainly
striving for three months to make arrangements with
Congress, returned. Previous to their departure,

however, they attempted to send circulars to each of the States, showing the terms of reconcilation which had been rejected, and threatening those who continued their rebellious attitudes with the vengeance of the king.

Another event soon after occurred, which shed sudden sunshine on the gloomy encampment of Valley Forge, and made its rude hovels ring with acclamations of joy. The overthrow of Burgoyne had fixed the wavering attitude of France, and on the 6th of February a treaty of defensive alliance, as well as of amity and commerce, was signed on her part, by Geraud, and on ours by the American commissioners, Franklin, Duane, and Lee. The bearer of these glad tidings arrived the last of April, and bonfires, illuminations, the firing of cannon and ringing of bells, announced the joy with which it was received by the people. The army was wild with excitement, and the bright May morning that dawned over the huts at Valley Forge did not more certainly promise a coming summer than did this alliance with one of the strongest powers on the globe assure our success. Washington set apart the 7th of May to celebrate this important event in form. At nine in the morning, the troops were assembled to hear divine service, and offer up their thanksgiving. A signal-gun, fired at half-past ten, summoned the men to the field. At half-past eleven, another signal-gun was fired, and the columns began their march. At a third signal, a running fire of musketry went down the first line and back the second. A moment's silence followed, when at a given signal a loud shout went up, and *Long live the King of France,* " rolled like thunder over the field. Before the echo had died away, the artillery broke in, shaking the earth with its deep reverberations, and sending its sullen roar of joy far over the spring-clad hills and valleys. After thirteen rounds, it ceased, and the loud rattle of musketry succeeded, and then the deepening shout of " Long

live the friendly European powers," again arose from
the whole army. As a finale, thirteen cannons were
fired, followed by a discharge of musketry and a
loud huzza to "*The American States.*" All the
officers of the army then assembled to partake of a
collation provided by Washington, and for once,
plenty reigned in the camp. When he took his leave,
the officers arose and began to huzza and shout "*Long
live Washington.*" They kept it up till he and his
suite had gone a quarter of a mile. The latter, his
heart swelling with joy and gratitude at the bright
prospect so suddenly opened before his country, and
his face lit up at the enthusiasm manifested on every
side, would often turn, and swinging his hat above
his head, echo back the wild huzza. The uproar
would then be redoubled—hats flew into the air,
and "Washington, long live Washington," was
echoed and re-echoed over the field, and taken up by
the army, till the whole atmosphere seemed an ele-
ment of joy.

The troops at this time presented a very different
appearance than when they went into winter-quarters.
Better clad, they had with the opening of spring
been subject to constant and severe discipline, by
Baron Steuben, who had joined the army during the
winter. This generous stranger had been aid to
Frederic the Great, and was afterward made grand-
marshal of the court of Prince Hohenzollern-Hechin-
gen. The King of Sardinia, anxious to obtain his
services, had made him flattering offers to enter his
army, but the baron was well settled, with ample
means, and refused to accept them. In 1777, he
passed through France, on his way to England, to
visit some English noblemen. Count Germain, the
French minister of war, was an old companion-
in-arms of Stuben, and he immediately began to
press the latter to enter the American service. The
wary French minister knew that our weakness lay
in our want of discipline, and ignorance of our mili-

tary tactics, and there could be no one found better
fitted to render us aid in this department than he.
For a long time Steuben steadily refused, but the
indefatigable Germain finally overcame all his scruples, and he embarked for this country, where he
arrived on the 1st of December [1777]. Congress
received him with distinction, and at his own request,
he joined the army at Valley Forge, as a volunteer.
His astonishment at its aspect was unbounded.
Such a famished, half-naked, miserable collection of
human beings he never before saw dignified with the
title of soldiers, and he declared that no European army
could be kept together a week under such privations
and sufferings. His amazement at the condition of
the army gave way to pity and respect for men who,
for a principle, would endure so much. As soon as
spring opened he commenced, as inspector-general,
to which office he had been appointed by Congress,
to drill the men. Ignorance of our language crippled
him sadly at first, but undiscouraged, he threw his
whole soul into his work, determined that such noble
patriots should also become good soldiers. Though
choleric and impetuous, he was generous as the day,
and possessed a heart full of the tenderest sympathy.
The men, notwithstanding his tempestuous moods,
soon learned to love him. The good effects of his
instructions were quickly apparent, and now, when
Washington was about to open the summer campaign,
he saw with pride an army before him that could be
wielded, and that had confidence in its own skill.
Still it was small, and recruits came in slowly. The
committee sent by Congress to Valley Forge, to confer with Washington, agreed that the whole force in
the field should be forty thousand men exclusive of
artillery and cavalry; but when the next day after
the grand celebration of the alliance with France, a
council of war was called, it appeared that there were,
including the detachments in the Highlands, only
fifteen thousand troops, and no prospect of increasing

the total number to more than twenty thousand. At Valley Forge were eleven thousand eight hundred, while nineteen thousand five hundred British occupied Philadelphia, and ten thousand four hundred more occupied New York, not to mention between three and four thousand in Rhode Island. Over thirty-three thousand British soldiers were on American soil; a force which Congress had nothing adequate to oppose. In this council it was resolved almost unanimously that it would be unwise, under the circumstances, to commence offensive operations. The army, therefore, remained quiet. Meanwhile, Howe began to make preparations for evacuating Philadelphia.

CHAPTER XI.

Lafayette at Barren Hill—The Oath of Allegiance taken by the Officers—Strange Conduct of Lee—Evacuation of Philadelphia—Determination of Washington—Battle of Monmouth and Conduct of Lee—Arrival of the French Fleet —Attack on New York planned—Failure of the Attempt against Newport, and displeasure of the French Commander—Massacre of Baylor's Dragoons and American Troops at Egg Harbour—Destitute Condition of the Army, and Opinions of Washington as to the Result of it—The Army in Winter-quarters—Miserable Condition of Congress—Sickness of Lafayette—Washington Consults with Congress on the Plan of the Summer Campaign—Resolves to act solely against the Indians—Sullivan's Expedition —Taking of Stony and Verplanck's Points—Governor Tryon's Foray—Successful Attack of Wayne on Stony Point—Wretched state of the Currency—Washington's Indignation against Speculators—Count Vergennes' Views of Washington—Suffering of the Troops in Winterquarters at Morristown—The Life Guard—Death of the Spanish Agent—Washington partakes of the Communion in a Presbyterian Church—National Bankruptcy threatened—Arrival of Lafayette with the News of a large French Force having Sailed—Noble Conduct of the Ladies of Philadelphia, and of Robert Morris, in Supplying the Soldiers with Clothing.

THERE was much truth in the reply of Dr. Franklin, when told in London that Howe had taken Philadelphia, "Say, rather, that Philadelpia has taken General Howe." He had lost more than three thousand men in the attempt to reach the city, and having accomplished nothing toward the real conquest of the country, was now to march back again. He had, in fact, been to this amazing expense, loss of soldiers, and labour, to get into quarters which he could have obtained quite as well in New York.

In the mean time, Washington, in order to restrain the depredations of the British foraging parties. which were of almost daily occurrence, and to watch more narrowly the movements of Howe, sent forward Lafayette, with about two thousand men, who took post on Barren Hill, nine or ten miles from Valley Forge. This hill was across the Schuylkill, and furnished an advantageous position. A Tory Quaker, however, at whose house Lafayette had at first taken up his head-quarters, informed Howe of the state of affairs, who immediately sent out five thousand troops to seize him. The plan was to pass along the banks of the Schuylkill, between Lafayette and the river, and while two detachments held the only two fords he could cross in his retreat to camp, a third, constituting the main body, should advance to the attack. This plan was well laid, and promised complete success. Lafayette was taken by surprise, and nearly surrounded before he was aware of the presence of the enemy. Only one ford lay open to him, and the column advancing to occupy it was nearer to it than he. Yet it was his last desperate resource. The road he took ran behind a forest, and was invisible to the enemy. Along this he hurried his troops, while, at the same time, he sent across the interval between him and the enemy heads of columns, which, showing themselves through the woods, deceived Grant, the British commander, and he ordered a halt and prepared for an attack. This produced a delay which enabled Lafayette to reach the ford first, and cross it in safety, while his baffled pursuers returned chagrined and mortified, to Philadelphia. Washington, who had been informed in some way of this movement, hurried forward, but as he rose a hill, he saw that he was too late. The wood and shores between him and Lafayette seemed alive with the red-coats, and the long line of gleaming bayonets that almost surrounded the American detachment, left scarcely a hope for its deliverance. Washington was exceedingly agitated. It was Lafayette's first essay at a separate command, and he would feel the failure of his favourite boy-general more than of his own. Besides, he could ill afford to lose two thousand men in his present condition. He watched every movement with his glass, and, at last, to his inexpressible joy and astonishment, saw Lafayette lead his swiftly-marching columns up to the ford and across it, in safety. The intensest excitement prevailed in camp. The danger, indeed the almost certain overthrow, of Lafayette had been communicated to the army, and Washington had ordered it to stand to arms, and when the former again entered Valley Forge in safety, those occupying it made it shake with their exultant shouts.

A short time before the breaking up of the camp at Valley Forge, Washington, by the direction of Congress, administered the oath of allegiance to the officers of the army. The form of this oath was printed on a slip of paper, with blanks to be filled with the name and rank of the officer, to which he affixed his signature. Washington administered it to the chief officers, and Stirling, Greene and Knox to the others. To expedite the ceremony, several took the oath together. As Washington was reading it to the leading generals at the same time, Lee, who had been exchanged for Prescot, taken at Newport, suddenly withdrew his hand; as quickly replacing it, he again withdrew it. Washington paused, and inquired what he meant by his hesitation. Lee replied, "As to King George, I am ready enough to absolve myself from all allegiance to him, but I have some scruples about the Prince of Wales." A roar of laughter, in which Washington himself could not help joining, followed this extraordinary exhibition of conscience.

Howe, having completed his preparations for evacuating Philadelphia, secretly and silently stole out of the city before daylight, on the 18th of June, and commenced his inland march for New York. Washington, anticipating this movement, had despatched Maxwell's brigade to New Jersey, to co-operate with General Dickinson commanding the militia of the state, in retarding the enemy. The news at length

arriving of the actual departure of the British, he
immediately ordered Arnold, still lame from the wound
received at Saratoga, to occupy the city with a small
detachment, while Wayne and Lee, at the head of
two divisions, were directed to push rapidly across the
Delaware and seize the first strong position found on
the further bank.   Washington, with the remainder
of the troops, followed, and in six days the the whole
army encamped at Hopewell, five miles from Princeton.   He had previously, however, sent off Morgan
to hang with his six hundred riflemen on the enemy's
right flank.   General Scott, with fifteen hundred
picked men, and Cadwallader, in command of the
Jersey militia and Pennsylvania volunteers, were
afterward added, and directed to concentrate rapidly
on the left flank and rear.

In the mean time the motley host composing the
British army, was pressing slowly forward.   With
its long train of baggage-waggons, horses and artillery, it stretched twelve miles along the road.   The
apparently interminable line was nearly half the day
in passing a giving point, and presented a singular
spectacle, with its mixture of regulars and loyalists,
the whole terminating in a disorderly, boisterous,
immense crowd of camp-followers.

Washington had previously called a council of
war, to determine whether it was best to hazard a
general engagement.   The decision was against it,
which embarrassed him much, for it was clearly his
wish to bring on a decisive battle.   In this he was
seconded strongly by Greene, Lafayette, Steuben,
Wayne, Duportail, and Patterson.   There is but
little doubt that from the first he had determinded to
attack Lord Howe, for after this council he asked no
one's advice, but proceeded on his own responsibility
to take such measures as would make an engagement inevitable.   Wayne was directed to join the
divisions already pressing the enemy, while all the
advance parties, numbering nearly four thousand

men, were put under Lafayette, and ordered to gain
the left flank.   Howe had designed to march directly to Brunswick, and there embark for New York,
but finding Washington in front, and not wishing,
encumbered as he was, to give battle, he turned off
at Allentown, and took the road leading to Monmouth Court-House and Sandy Hook.   At the latter
place he expected to get his troops and baggage
aboard of the ships.   But finding, as he approached
the court-house, that the American army was steadily closing on him, he ordered the whole baggage-
train to move to the front, and selecting a strong
position, flanked by woods and swamps,   halted.
Knowing that the gallant young Lafayette, in executing the orders given him, would inevitably bring
on a battle, Washington took measures to sustain
him with the entire army, left under his own immediate command.   At this juncture Lee, whose rank
entitled him to the command of the advance, but
who had yielded it to Lafayette in disgust, because
Washington paid no attention to his advice, now
asked to be reinstated.   Embarrassed by this inconsistent conduct, Washington, however, concluded to
send him forward with two additional brigades to
the aid of Lafayette, the whole to be under his own
command, but with orders not to interfere with any
plans which the latter had already set on foot.   He,
at the same time, wrote to Lafayette, explaining the
unpleasant position into which this eccentric conduct of Lee had thrown him, and expressed the confidence that he would waive his right, and thus relieve him from it.   It was well that the American
commander had such a noble, self-sacrificing heart
to appeal to, or there would have been a serious
quarrel here, on the very eve of an engagement.
The next morning, at five o'clock, Washington,
some six miles distant, was aroused by the news that
the British army had recommenced its march.   He
immediately despatched an aid to Lee, with the

orders to attack the enemy, *"unless there should be very powerful reasons to the contrary."* With any other commander but Lee, this would have brought on an immediate battle. Washington expected this to be the result, and immediately ordered the troops to march to his support. The 28th of June was one of the hottest, sultriest days of the year. It was also the Sabbath day, but the fierce mustering was not to the sanctuary, nor the sounds that broke over the fields the sweet call of the church-bell to quiet worshipers.

At early dawn Lee, in carrying out his orders, began to close on the enemy. Soon after, word was brought him that the whole British army was preparing to attack his division. Spurring with his staff along a causeway across a swamp, he galloped up a height beyond, on which Dickinson had drawn up his troops, and surveyed the field before him. He could not ascertain, from the conflicting reports, whether the rumour was true or false. In the mean time, Lafayette, observing a false movement of a portion of the British army, hastened to Lee and asked if a successful attack could not be made there at once. "Sir," replied the latter, "you do not know British soldiers. We cannot stand against them. We shall certainly be driven back at first, and must be cautious." The fiery Frenchman did not hold British valour in such high estimation, and replied that they *had* been beaten, and presumed could be beaten again. At all events *he* would like to make the trial. It was now perfectly evident to him that Lee did not intend to carry out Washington's orders, and seeing at that moment an aid from the latter gallop up, to obtain information, he told him aside, to say to the general that his *immediate presence on the spot was of the utmost importance.* In the mean time, Scott and Maxwell were moving forward in beautiful order toward the right of the enemy. Lafayette had wheeled his column, and was pressing steadily toward the left, while Wayne was descending like a torrent from the heights. Lee was apparently about to second this movement, when he saw the whole British army wheel about and march back on the Middletown road, as if to fall on him in one overwhelming attack. The whole sandy plain, which, like that of Marengo, seemed made on purpose for a battle-field, was filled with marching columns, and echoed to the sound of stirring music and shouts of men. In the distance streamed the long line of baggage-waggons, while nearer by, the glittering columns fell one after another into the order of battle, the rattling cavalry hurried forward to the blast of the trumpets, and to Lee's distempered vision, he was about to be overwhelmed, while a deep morass in his rear cut off all retreat. He, therefore, immediately despatched his aids to the different corps, with orders to fall back over the causeway, to the heights of Freehold beyond. Lafayette, stung with rage, slowly and reluctantly obeyed, while Wayne, astounded at the sudden order, could with difficulty extricate himself from the position in which this unexpected movement left him. The whole army at length repassed the morass, but Lee neglected to occupy the advantageous heights of Freehold, and continued to retreat, followed by the shouting, taunting enemy. He did not even announce his retreat to Washington, and thus prepare him for an event so disastrous as the collison of one-half of the army in disorderly flight with the other half, must inevitably prove. Early in the morning, when about commencing the attack, he had despatched a message to the commander-in-chief, briefly explaining his plans, and promising success. On the reception of this, Washington ordered Greene to march to the right of Lee, and support his flank, while he himself pressed on directly in rear. Although it was early in the morning, the heat was intense. Not a breath of air stirred the foliage, and the round, fiery orb of day seemed to roll up a brazen sky. Washington, foreseeing how severely the troops would suffer from the heat, ordered them to throw away their knapsacks and blankets. Many went still further, and stripped off their coats also, and marched in their shirt-sleeves. It was a terrible day, the thermometer stood at ninety-six in the shade, while the deep sand through which the panting soldiers struggled, gave still greater intensity to the heat, and hence increased immensely the pangs of thirst. But the scattered firing in front had been heard, and the army pressed forward with shouts. Washington, ignorant of Lee's retreat, had dismounted where two roads met, and stood watching his marching columns, when a countryman dashed into his presence and announced that Lee was in full and disorderly retreat. His countenance instantly grew dark as wrath, and with a burst of indignation he sprang into the saddle, and burying the rowels in his steed, parted from the spot like a bolt from heaven. A cloud of dust alone told the course of the fiery and indignant chieftain. Meeting the head of the first retreating column, he flung a hasty inquiry to Osgood, the commander, as to the cause of this retreat, who replied with an oath, " Sir, we are *fleeing from a shadow*," and then dashed on to the rear, and reined up with a sudden jerk beside Lee. Leaning over his saddle-bow, his face fairly blazing with concentrated passion, he demanded, in a voice of thunder, the meaning of this disorderly retreat. Stung by the overwhelming rebuke, Lee retorted angrily.* But it was no time to settle differences, and wheeling his horse, Washington spurred up to Oswald's and Stewart's regiments, and ex-

* Mr. Sparks informed me that he once asked Lafayette, at Lagrange, what the language of Lee really was. Lafayette replied, that although standing near to both at the time, he could not tell. It was not the words but the manner that struck so deeply. No one had ever seen Washington so terribly excited—his countenance was frightful !

claimed—"*On you I depend to check this pursuit.*" He then galloped along the ranks, and roused the enthusiasm of the soldiers to the highest pitch, till the glorious shout of "*Long live Washington,*" rose over the din of battle, and drowned the loud huzzas of the enemy. Never, even while heading a charge, did Washington's personal appearance and conduct inspire his troops with such wild enthusiasm. Under the sudden excitement into which he had been thrown, and the extreme heat combined, the colourless face which so rarely gave any indication of the fires within, was now suffused, and two bright red spots burned on either cheek, while his blue eyes fairly gleamed, and seemed to emit fire. His reeking horse was flecked with foam as he dashed hither and thither, and wherever his voice reached, men stood still. The troops gazed on him with astonishment, and even Lafayette forgot for an instant the peril of the army, in admiration of his appearance, declaring afterward that he thought him at that moment the handsomest man he had ever beheld. In a few minutes the whole appearance of the field was changed—the disorderly flying mass halted—order sprung out of confusion, and right under the galling fire of the enemy's guns, the ranks wheeled and formed in perfect order. Having thus established a firm front to the enemy, Washington rode back to Lee, and exclaimed—"Will you, sir, command in that place?" "Yes," replied the latter. "*Well, then, I expect you to check the enemy immediately.*" "*Your orders shall be obeyed,*" retorted the enraged commander; "*and I will not be the first to leave the field.*" The conflict then became close and severe, and Washington, trusting to the steadiness of the troops, hurried back to bring up his own division.

Lee had now the main army on his hands, which pressed against him with resistless power. The artillery played on his exposed ranks, while to the

sound of bugles the English light-horse charged
furiously on his left. Young Hamilton watched
with beating heart the bursting storm, and fearing
that Lee would again retreat, crossed the field on a
furious gallop, and with his hat off, his hair streaming in the wind, pressed straight for the spot where
he stood, and reining up beside him, exclaimed in
that noble enthusiasm which that day pervading all
hearts saved the army, "*I will stay with you, my
dear general, and die with you. Let us all die here
rather than retreat.*" Grand and glorious words,
spoken there in the din of battle, amid the whistling
balls, and worthy of the hero who uttered them.
Lee struggled nobly against the overwhelming numbers that pressed on him, but was at length forced
back.* So stubbornly, however, did the Americans
dispute every inch of ground, that when they retired
from the woods, the opposing ranks were inter-
mingled. Half that gallantry two hours before
would have given a glorious victory. As it was,
Lee succeeded in effecting a safe retreat.

At this critical moment Washington arrived with
the other division, which came up on almost a trot,
and panting with thirst and heat. Hastily ordering
up Greene on the right, and Stirling on the left, he
himself led the centre full on the enemy. Stirling
brought up Lieutenant Carrington's artillery on a

* It was during this part of the battle that an Irishman,
while serving his gun, was shot down. His wife, named
Molly, only twenty-two years of age, employed herself,
while he loaded and fired his piece, in bringing water from
a spring near by. While returning with her supply, she
saw him fall, and heard the officer in command, order the
gun to be taken to the rear. She immediately ran forward,
seized the rammer, declaring she would avenge his death.
She fought her piece like a hero to the last. The next
morning, Greene, who had been struck with her bravery,
presented her to Washington, who immediately promoted
her to a sergeant, and afterwards had her name put on the
half-pay list for life. Previous to this she fired the last gun
when the Americans were driven from Fort Montgomery.

full gallop, and unlimbering them with astonishing rapidity, opened a terrible fire on the advancing columns. Lee rode up to Washington, saying coldly, "Sir, here are my troops; how is it your pleasure I should dispose of them?" Between the exhausting heat and their fierce conflict, they were completely beaten out, and Washington ordered them to the rear of Englishtown, while he led on the battle with fresh troops. The victorious enemy, pressing eagerly after Lee, came suddenly on the second line, now formed, and, flushed with success, bore steadily down on the centre. But here was Washington, around whom the troops gathered with invincible resolution and dauntless hearts, while Wayne, from a hill crowned with an orchard, rained a tempest of balls on the advancing columns. Hurled back by the steady volleys, the latter then moved almost simultaneously against the right and left flanks of the Americans, but were immediately scourged back by Knox's heavy guns and the fierce firing of Stirling's battery. All this time Wayne kept firing with such deadly precision on the British centre that every attempt to charge proved abortive. Again and again the royal grenadiers moved forward in splendid order, and with a resolute aspect, but were as often compelled to retire from the close range of the American fire. Col. Monckton, their leader, saw at once that no progress could be made till Wayne was driven from that orchard, and riding along the ranks of his brave grenadiers, aroused their courage by his stirring appeals. He then formed them in a solid column, and shouted *"forward!"* Moving swiftly forward at the charge step, but with the regularity and steadiness of a single wave, they swept up the slope. Wayne, the moment he detected the movement, ordered his men to reserve their fire till the column came within close range, and then aim at the officers. The grenadiers kept steadily on till they arrived within a few rods of the

336   8

silent Americans, when Monckton waving his sword over his head shouted, "CHARGE!" At the same moment the order "*Fire*" ran along the ranks of Wayne. A deadly volley followed, and nearly every British officer bit the dust, and among them the gallant Monckton. A close, fierce struggle ensued over his dead body, but the Americans finally bore it off in triumph. Wayne now bore steadily down on the centre, while the shouts of his excited troops, were heard in the intervals of the heavy explosions of artillery, as they bore the strong battalions fiercely back. Their march was like the step of fate, and they crowded the astonished enemy to the head of the causeway, and across it into the woods beyond.

All this time Morgan with his brave riflemen lay at Richmond Mills, only three miles from Monmouth Court-House, waiting for orders. This iron-hearted commander, a host in himself, had his men drawn up in marching order, and as the heavy and constant explosions of cannon rolled by, followed by the sharp rattle of musketry, he paced backward and forward in the road, a prey to most intense excitement. His eager eye sought in vain to catch the form of a swift rider, bearing the order to move on. All day long he chafed like an imprisoned lion, yet, strange to say, his existence seemed to have been forgotten in the sudden excitement and danger that followed Lee's mad retreat. Had he been allowed to fall on the British rear, he would have broken them to pieces.

The scorching Sabbath day was now drawing to a close, and as the blood-red sun sunk in the west, the whole British army retreated, and took up a strong position on the spot occupied by Lee in the morning. Woods and swamps were on either side, while the only causeway over which troops could approach, was swept by heavy batteries. Washington rode up and scrutinized the position long and anxiously.

His strong frame had been tasked to the utmost, and as he sat on his exhausted steed and cast his eye over his gallant army, he saw that heat and thirst had waged a more terrible conflict with them, than the balls of the enemy. On every side arose the most piteous cries for water, and the well were hardly able to carry the wounded to the rear, while scores lay dead amid the sand, untouched by the foe. The battle seemed over for the night, but Washington, stung and mortified at the unpardoned errors and consequent misfortunes of the day, determined to rest with nothing short of a complete victory. He, therefore, brought up the two brigades of Poor and Woodford, and ordered them to force their way through the woods to the right and left flanks of the enemy, while he hurried the heavy cannon of Knox to the front. In a few minutes the heavy batteries on both sides opened. But the two brigades found so many obstacles obstructing the way, and delaying their progress, that night came on before they could reach their posts. The attack was then abandoned; the bugles sounded the recall of the advance parties, the heavy firing ceased, and nothing but the moans of wounded, and the heavy tread of the battalions taking up their position for the night, broke the stillness of the Sabbath evening. The fainting army laid down to rest on the heated plain, in the full expectation of another battle in the morning. Washington stretched himself in his mantle, and the young Lafayette, feeling deeply for the disappointment under which he knew him to be suffering, stole quietly to his side. Washington wrapped him affectionately in his mantle, and the two tired heroes slept together under the open sky.

The British commander, however, had no intention of risking another battle, and so, at midnight, quietly aroused his slumbering army, and hurried away from the spot that had so nearly witnessed his overthrow. The morning drum roused up the

American army at dawn, but no answering sound came from the enemy's camp.   The moment Washington was informed that they had fled, he sent on officers to ascertain what distance the army had reached.   He found, to his great disappointment, that it had gained a march of nearly nine miles, and with its long train of baggage-waggons and artillery, was streaming swiftly along the road toward Sandy Hook.   Feeling that his troops were too exhausted to overtake them, he gave up the pursuit.

The American loss in this battle was in all, killed, wounded and missing, three hundred and fifty-eight; some of the latter, however, afterward rejoined the army.   The British left two hundred and fifty on the field.   Many they had buried during the night, and a large number of those not badly wounded accompanied the army in its flight, so that their loss was never ascertained.   Fifty-nine lay dead without a wound upon their persons.   Several hundred took occasion, during this battle and the march, to desert, and returned to Philadelphia and to the sweethearts they loved, better than their country's service, and others remained in New Jersey, so that the enemy was weakened in all, probably not less than two thousand men.

This though a less bloody one, was one of the most remarkable battles in the Revolution, and fixed the turning point in the history of the army.   The rally of the troops while in full retreat, the steady formation of the lines under the blaze of the enemy's guns, and after victorious assaults, were achievements worthy of the most veteran troops, and reflected honour on their teacher Steuben.   Hamilton, who had been accustomed only to the movements of militia, was filled with admiration at the spectacle, and said he never before knew the value of discipline.   From that time on, the regulars relied much on the bayonet, and the British grenadiers saw with amazement themselves beaten with their favourite weapon.

Though justly indignant with Lee for thus robbing him of victory, Washington immediately reinstated him in his old command. Lee, however, was not content with this, and wrote the latter an impertinent letter, to which a cold and curt reply was made. Enraged at this second attack, as he deemed it, on his honour and character, he wrote a still more insolent letter, which brought down the charge from his commander of being "guilty of a breach of orders, and of misbehaviour before the enemy, and in *making an unnecessary, disorderly and shameful retreat.*" Lee's answer to this severe accusation was so insulting that he was immediately placed under arrest. His after trial and suspension from the army are well known.

The army being recruited, Washington moved by easy marches to the Hudson, and crossing at King's Ferry, encamped near White Plains. In the mean time he had heard of the arrival on the coast of the French fleet, composed of twelve ships of the line and four frigates under Count D'Estaing. He immediately despatched a letter of congratulation by his aid, Colonel Laurens, to the count. Soon after, on being informed that the fleet had reached Sandy Hook, he sent Colonel Hamilton to consult with him on the best course to pursue. It was at first hoped that a combined attack, by sea and land, could be made on New York, but the pilots reporting that it would be impossible to take the heavy ships over the bar, the enterprise was abandoned. Philadelphia being evacuated, there seemed now no direction in which the fleet and the army could co-operate except Rhode Island. There was a garrison of six or seven thousand British at Newport, and it was therefore resolved that Sullivan should proceed thither with five thousand men, followed by Lafayette with two brigades, while the vessels would proceed by sea. But the delay caused by the want of troops proved disastrous to the expedition. Sullivan, however, succeeded at length in gathering an army of ten thousand men, and proceeded to besiege the place, while the French fleet came steadily up the channel, past the English batteries. Every thing now promised an easy victory, when the fleet of Lord Howe was seen hovering in the distance. D'Estaing immediately put to sea to engage it. But a violent storm suddenly arose, disabling both fleets, and compelling the vessels to return to New York for repairs, while those of the French came limping back to Newport. Sullivan's hopes again revived, but the French admiral, deaf to appeals, would not co-operate with him, declaring his orders were in case of any damage to repair to Boston and refit. Sullivan, enraged at what he considered pusillanimous conduct sent the count a fierce remonstrance. This only made matters worse, and the fleet took its departure for Boston, and the enterprise was abandoned. The ill will caused by this protest of Sullivan annoyed Washington exceedingly, and he took unwearied pains to heal the breach that had been made. He wrote to Lafayette to act as mediator, saying, "Let me beseech you to afford a healing hand to the wound that has been unintentionally made. America esteems your virtues and your services, and admires the principles on which you act. Your countrymen in our army look up to you as their pattern. The count and his officers consider you as a man high in rank, and high in estimation here, and also in France, and I, your friend, have no doubt but you will use your utmost endeavours to restore harmony, that the honour, glory, and mutual interest of the two nations may be promoted and cemented in the firmest manner." Lafayette needed no greater stimulus to action than the wishes of Washington, and he put forth unwearied efforts till harmony was restored.

There being a suspicion that the British might plan an expedition to the east, for the purpose of attacking the French fleet, and perhaps Boston,

Washington took post at Fredericksburg, near the Connecticut line, and commenced repairing the roads as far as Hartford, so that the army could march without impediment. Gates was sent, also, to take command at Boston, in place of Heath. This almost entire withdrawal of the troops east of the Hudson, left the smaller detachments which remained on the other side, much exposed, and provoked the attacks of the British. One part fell on Major Baylor's dragoons, located near Tappan, surprising and massacreing them without mercy. A similar attempt was made on Pulaski's legion, stationed at Egg Harbour, where privateers were being fitted out, and, through the villainy of a deserter, met with like success.

For four months the army lay comparatively idle, waiting the further movements of the British. In the mean time Washington became very solicitous about the future. The want of funds in the treasury, together with the high price of food and clothing, seemed to threaten greater evils than mere physical exposure and suffering. The officers could not live on their pay, and Congress was without means to raise it, while discontent and loud complaints pervaded the army. In a letter to Gouverneur Morris, replying to certain inquiries, he says—"Can we carry on the war much longer? Certainly not, unless some measures can be devised, and speedily, to restore the credit of our currency, restrain extortion, and punish forestallers. Unless these can be effected, what funds can stand the present expenses of the army? And what officer can bear the weight of prices that every necessary article is now got to? A rat in the shape of a horse is not to be bought at this time for less than two hundred pounds, nor a saddle under thirty or forty; boots twenty, and shoes, and other articles in proportion. How is it possible, therefore, for officers to stand this without an increase of pay? And how is it possible to advance their pay when flour is selling at different places from five to fifteen pounds per hundred weight; hay from ten to thirty pounds per ton, and beef and other essentials in this proportion." It was plain that this state of things could not last. The officers, wholly unable to meet their necessary expenses, would inevitably become bankrupt.

During this summer a project was set on foot for the invasion of Canada by the allied armies, assisted by the fleet, but it met with Washington's decided opposition, and was finally abandoned.

Autumn closed without any expedition of importance being undertaken, and the army retired to winter-quarters. The artillery was taken to Pluckemin, while the troops stretched in a line of cantonments from Long Island Sound to the Delaware. Head-quarters were at Middlebrook, where were stationed, also, seven brigades. One brigade was at Elizabethtown, another near Smith's Close, to act as a reinforcement in case of need to West Point; and one at West Point. There were, also, two brigades at the Continental village, situated between West Point and Fishkill, and three near Danbury, Connecticut. Thus the enemy in New York were confined to a small space for action, while our troops, by reaching over so large a territory, could more easily obtain forage. Putnam was at Danbury, and McDougall in the Highlands, while Lincoln was sent to take command at Charlestown, to repel any attack the British might make on that city during the winter. Of the four regiments of cavalry, one was in each of the States of Virginia, Maryland, Pennsylvania, and Connecticut.

The vexed question of exchange of prisoners again came up, and Wahington was much annoyed at the difficulties thrown in the way of its final adjustment. But the greatest cause of distress and anxiety was the contemptible condition to which Congress was reduced. During the whole year it averaged not more than thirty members. Says Sparks: "Whole States were frequently unrepresented; and, indeed, it was seldom that every State was so fully represented as to entitle it to a vote." But although so feeble in numbers, it was still feebler in intellect. There were but few even second-rate men among the members. Still its feebleness both in numbers and intellect, was not the worst features it exhibited. It had descended to a mere political arena, where private jealousies, and party feuds fought their battles, reckless alike of the great struggle without, or the welfare of the country, except so far as they effected their selfish ends. Perhaps it is not to be regretted that its journals were destroyed, and the history of our country saved from so great a blemish as the records of its acts would have been. The views and feelings of Washington on the subject are exhibited in a letter to Benjamin Harrison, of Virginia. In that he declared without hesitation, that he thought the separate States should "*compel their ablest men to attend Congress.*" He said they were too busy with their individual concerns, but if the whole government should be continued to be mismanaged, they, too, would "sink in the general wreck, which will carry with it the remorse of thinking that we are lost by our own folly and negligence." "The public," he said, "believe that the States at this time are badly represented, and that the great and important concerns of the nation are horridly conducted, for want either of abilities or application in the members, or through the discord and party views of some individuals." It was plain that without somechange in the adminstration of the national affairs the Revolution, with all its momentous interests, must end in utter failure.

While Washington remained at head-quarters, Lafayette arrived at Fishkill, on his way to Boston, previous to embarking for France. Here he fell sick. His journey from Philadelphia, in the midst of severe storms, had brought on an inflammatory fever, which carried him to the verge of the grave. His life was despaired of, and the whole army was in mourning. Washington immediately repaired to his bedside, and watched over him with the solicitude and fondness of a father. The young marquis was deeply affected by this attention, and carried the remembrance of it with gratitude and affection to his grave.

The army being well hutted, and things comparatively quiet, Washington proceeded to Philadelphia, to consult with Congress on the best means to be adopted. He proposed three plans. First, to operate against the enemy on the sea-coast. The second to attack Niagara, and the British forces in that region, and the third, to remain entirely on the defensive against the British, and act only against the Indians, who had grown bold by their impunity. The latter was resolved upon as giving repose to the country, and at the same time permitting a retrenchment in the expenses of the war, and restoring the currency, which was now in a shocking condition. The evils growing out of an army unemployed, and also of such a tacit confession of weakness, Washington thought would be overbalanced by the relief from military exaction, and by the fact that the alliance with France, and the threatened war of Spain with England, would tend more to secure the acknowledgment of our independence, than victories. If he had consulted personal ambition, he would not have consented to idleness, which is always dangerous to a commander's reputation.

Having completed his arrangement with Congress, he returned to Middlebrook. The army was consequently reduced, and more attention paid to its discipline, which was entrusted to Steuben. In the mean time the expedition resolved upon against the Indians, was set on foot. The Six Nations, with the exception of the Oneidas, and a few of the Mohawks, had joined the English, and, assisted by the Tories,

LIFE OF WASHINGTON. 283

kept the New York frontiers drenched in blood. The tragedies which were enacted at Cherry Valley and Wyoming, with all their heart-sickening details and bloody passages, were fresh in the recollection of every one. The Six Nations were spread along the Susquehanna, and around our inland lakes, extending as far as the Genesee Flats. The plan adopted by Washington was, to have Sullivan, with three thousand men, start from Wyoming, and advance up the Susquehanna, while General James Clinton, with one brigade, should ascend the Mohawk, and form a junction with the former wherever he should direct. Sullivan left Wyoming the last day of July, and did not return till the middle of October. He traversed the solitudes as far as Genesee river, burning and laying waste the towns and villages, and rich fields of grain ; moving like a devastating scourge over the land, and inflicting a punishment on the Indian tribes, which they never forgot.

While Sullivan's army was thus feeling its way through the wilderness, Sir Henry Clinton, with a large body of troops ascended the Hudson, for the purpose of attacking Verplanck's Point and Stony Point, standing opposite each other, and, if possible, force his way through the Highlands. But Washington, being apprised of his designs, hurried off couriers to the different brigades in New Jersey, and soon their tread along the banks of the Hudson convinced Clinton that it would be a desperate undertaking to attempt to force the strong passes above, while so well guarded. He, however, took possession of the two points, which were feebly manned, and leaving strong garrisons in each, returned to New York. Washington then removed his head-quarters to New Windsor, a few miles above the gorge of the Highlands, and looking directly on West Point, while his army swarmed the forest-clad shores on either side, watching with anxious care this gateway of the State.

Having thus drawn the forces under Washington into the Highlands, Clinton made a sudden incursion into Connecticut, hoping to tempt him thither also, where a more open country would make a battle less hazardous. Governor Tryon, with two thousand men, sailed up Long Island Sound, and plundered New Haven. He then returned to Fairfield and Norwalk, and burnt them to the ground. No public stores were at either of these places, and the whole expedition was simply to pillage and to burn the dwellings of peaceful citizens. It was the unexpected irruption of a band of robbers, and the atrocities committed inflicted a lasting disgrace on the name of Tryon, and covered Sir Henry Clinton with infamy. This attempt to entice Washington away from his stronghold proved abortive. It, however, broke up his plan of not acting on the offensive, and he determined to strike a blow which, while it inflicted a severe chastisement on the enemy, should at the same time hush the complaints against his inaction. This blow was no less than the recapture of Stony and Verplanck's Points, with all their stores and armaments. It was his purpose at first to assail them both the same night, but this he afterward abandoned, and concluded only to make a feint on the garrison at the latter place, to distract it from the attack on the former. To prevent miscarriage, through want of information, he carefully reconnoitered the place himself, and directed Major Henry Lee, who commanded a body of cavalry in the neighborhood, to ascertain accurately the condition of the fortress, and strength of the garrison. This being done, he called no council of war, consulted none of his officers, but having fixed on Wayne as the proper person to take charge of the hazardous enterprise, sent for him, and explained to him his plans. Wayne at first seemed doubtful of success, but was ready to attempt any thing on Washington's request. To prevent any information of the project reaching the enemy, Washington communicated it to no one but Wayne, and one member of his family. The night before the attack, however, he sent for Colonel Rufus Putnam, and took him into the secret, because he wished him to make the false attack on Verplanck's Point.

Stony Point was considered almost impregnable to any storming party, it being washed on two sides by the Hudson, while on the other lay a morass, which was overflowed at high water. Besides these natural defences, a double row of abattis surrounded the hill, the whole surmounted by the fortress, itself garrisoned by six hundred men, and bristling with cannon. Washington, fully aware of the peril of the undertaking, drafted every officer and soldier himself, and a more splendid body of men never moved unflinchingly up to the cannon's mouth.

On the night of the 15th July, Wayne set out with his command, and at eleven o'clock reached the morass, which he found covered with two feet of water. The word "halt" then passed in a whisper down the line, and the whole stood to their arms while he and some of the officers reconnoitered. It was resolved to make the attack in two columns, and on both sides at once. Every musket of the advance parties was unloaded, and at the word forward, they, with shouldered pieces, plunged into the water, and pushed swiftly toward the heights. The sentinels on watch immediately gave the alarm, the shout of "*to arms !*" "*to arms !*" and roll of drums rang along the hill, and in a moment that lofty rock was in a blaze, and raining a fiery deluge on Wayne's columns. But nothing could shake their steady courage. Through the iron sleet, over their own dead, over the abattis and up the steep acclivity, they pressed sternly on, the only sound heard in their otherwise silent ranks, being the high and ringing order "*forward*," "*forward*," of the officers. Their tread was like the march of destiny, and bearing down every obstacle, both columns entered the fort together, and as they met, the shout of victory rose wildly to the midnight heavens. It was gallantly, gloriously done. Wayne had a narrow escape. A musket-ball grazed the top of his head, and brought him to his knees. "*March on*," he shouted, "*carry me into the fort. I will die at the head of my column.*" Next sunrise the morning-gun was fired by an American hand, and carried consternation to the English ships below. The land rung with acclamations. Wayne was overwhelmed with compliments, and his name was in every one's mouth. It was the most brilliant exploit during the war, and would have covered the veterans of a hundred battles with glory.

Washington went up to the fortress after the capture and examined it. Finding that it would require too many men to hold it against the force which the enemy could bring against it, by means of their fleet, he ordered the works to be destroyed. Lee's subsequent daring and successful attack at Paulus Hook, with his dismounted dragoons, was a repetition of the affair at Stoney Point, and added fresh laurels to those which already adorned that noble officer's head. With these brilliant exceptions, the army under Washington remained for the most part quiet. He employed this season of comparative inaction in corresponding with Congress, and other distinguished men, on the afiairs of the country, especially on the state of the currency. Congress continued to issue its worthless paper to such an extent, that by the following spring two hundred million dollars were found to be afloat, and not one dollar redeemable. So low had this paper depreciated, that forty dollars of it, at that time, was equivalent to only one dollar in coin. This state of the currency was ruinous to every class of inhabitants, but on none did it fall so heavily as the soldiers and officers. As money sunk prices rose, and the officers were compelled to pay double for every thing, so that many resigned to escape beggary. "It was no uncommon thing to give a month's pay for a breakfast," said Colonel, afterwards General, William Hull. He himself gave eleven thousand two hundred and fifty dollars for a chaise with a double harness. Added to this, speculators who had funds would buy up any article which they ascertained would soon be in demand, and thus exhaust the market, and then lay their own prices. These things aroused the indignation of Washington, and troubled him exceedingly. He declared that he was not afraid of the enemy's arms, but of this prostrate currency, and utter want of patriotism. He reasoned, he expostulated, he appealed. He pleaded not only for the living, but for the "unborn millions," whose fate this struggle was to affect. "Shall," he exclaimed, "a few designing men, for their own aggrandizement, and to gratify their own avarice, overset the goodly fabric we have been rearing at the expense of so much time, blood and treasure? And shall we at last become the victims of our own lust of gain? Forbid it—Heaven!" He found, also, cause of great annoyance in the unceasing assassin-like attacks of Gates, and the more bold, open and malevolent assaults of Lee, who pursued him with such relentless fury, that the name of Washington became the "moon of his madness."

The French minister, Gerard, who accompanied Count D'Estaing, came to camp this summer, and had long consultations with Washington, and formed various plans for the future. His letter to Count Vergennes at this time, shows that he was as much impressed by Washington's presence and greatness of intellect as others. That impalpable influence and grandeur, which it has been found impossible to convey an idea of through language, affected all alike, from the most accomplished noblemen of Europe, to the wild Indian of our own forests.

As winter approached, the head-quarters were

established at Morristown, and the army, pitching its tents on the southern slope of Kimble's Mountain, commenced building huts.　The cavalry was sent to Connecticut, while strong detachments guarded the passes of the Hudson.　Clinton finding himself closely watched, and constantly thwarted in any movements around New York, resolved on an expedition to the South, and at the latter end of December set sail for Charleston, with seven thousand troops.

Washington, during the winter, occupied the house of Widow Ford, to which he in February added two log buildings.　In a meadow at a short distance from the dwelling, between forty and fifty huts were erected for the Life Guard, numbering at this time two hundred and fifty.　It was in this meadow Pulaski drilled his legion, and performed those daring and extraordinary feats of horsemanship, for which he was celebrated.　The winter set in excessively cold—nothing like it had ever been experienced in this country.　The ice in New York Bay was frozen so solid, that heavy artillery and troops crossed from the city to Staten Island.　The sufferings of the troops were consequently severe.　The snow averaged from four to six feet deep on a level, obstructing the roads and keeping back provisions from camp, so that the half frozen soldiers would sometimes go a week without meat of any kind, and then again without bread.　All through January this half-starved army was protected only by tents, and with nothing but straw between them and the frozen ground, and a single blanket to cover them. Human nature could not bear up against such protracted sufferings, and desertions and plunder of private property became frequent.

Washington, all this time, had not a kitchen to cook his dinner in, although his guards had put up the logs of one for him.　His family consisted of eighteen, which, with that of Mrs. Ford, were "all crowded together in her kitchen, and scarce one of them able to speak for the colds they caught." Washington crowded into a kitchen with more than twenty others, for two months, without salary, without reward of any kind, and struggling with a selfish Congress, and compelled to defend the purity of his motives, from the asperations of those for whose benefit he is labouring, is a study for a patriot.

During this extreme cold weather, Lord Stirling took fifteen hundred men in sleds, and crossed the ice at midnight, from Elizabethtown to Staten Island, to surprise the British. The latter had, however, got wind of the expedition, and the troops returned with only a few prisoners, some blankets and stores as trophies. One third of this detachment had some parts of their persons frozen, and were more or less seriously injured. A sort of partisan warfare was maintained all winter, keeping the camp in a constant state of watchfulness. As an illustration of the duties of the Life Guard, it was their habit during the winter, at the first discharge of guns along the line of sentinels, to rush into Washington's house, barricade the doors, throw up the windows, and stand five to a window, with muskets cocked and brought to a charge. On some mere foolish alarm, Washington's wife and Mrs. Ford would often be compelled to lie shivering within their bed-curtains, till the cause of it could be ascertained.

The Chevalier de Luzerne, who had succeeded Gerard as minister, visited Washington in camp, as he had previously done at West Point. The cheerful manner with which he, from the first, accepted the poor fare and miserable accommodations offered him, had won the good-will and respect of both officers and men. Spain having also at last declared war against England, our prospect grew still brighter, and a Spanish agent, though not an accredited one, named Miralles, accompanied Luzerne to look after the interests of his government in the south. He died this winter at Morristown, and was buried with distinguished honours, Washington and the principal officers appearing as chief mourners. To prevent any one from re-opening the grave, to obtain possession of the diamonds and jewels that were buried with him, a guard was placed over it till the body could be taken to Philadelphia for interment.

It was while encamped here that the following incident occurred, illustrating Washington's religious character. On hearing that the sacrament of the Lord's Supper was to be administered in the Presbyterian church, the following Sunday, he called on the pastor, Dr. Jones, and inquired if they allowed the communicants of other churches to unite with them in the service. "Most certainly," replied the doctor, "ours is not a Presbyterian table, but the Lord's table, general, and hence we give the Lord's invitation to all his followers of whatever name." Washington replied that he was glad of it —that so it should be, and next Sunday was seen seated among the communicants. Unsullied by his camp life, with not a stain on his blade, he could go from the battle-field to the communion-table, as well as to his closet in the wintry forest.

The subject of the exchange of prisoners being again presented by the British commander, the French minister was very solicitous that Washington should not consent to any but the most favourable terms ; urging the double motive that the British government now found it hard to replenish the army from Germany, and needed men badly, and, also, that it was of the utmost importance to insist on a perfect equality in all things, not only for our own sake at home, but from the effect of such a position abroad.

During this winter the finances of the country reached their lowest ebb, and national bankruptcy seemed inevitable. Lotteries for loans, laws making

paper a legal tender, and every substitute only plunged the nation into deeper difficulties. Every measure calculated to bring relief was seized on by
speculators, to advance their own interests, and thus
added to the embarrassment already existing. Washington became so indignant at this villainy of "*forestallers*," as he called them, or mere speculators,
that in a letter to Read, he said—"I would to God
that some of the more atrocious in each State were
hung in gibbets, upon a gallows four times as high as
the one prepared for Haman." The British loyalists
saw the dilemma into which the government had
fallen, and increased it by issuing large quantities of
forged paper. They felt and said that unless we
could obtain a foreign loan, which they did not believe possible, "unless all the moneyed nations had
turned fools," we must inevitably go to the wall.
No more battles were needed; bankruptcy would
finish the rebellion. Washington had all along predicted such a crisis, and now, with other patriots,
looked gloomily into that gloomiest of all gulfs in
time of war, a bankrupt treasury.

At the beginning of April the army consisted of
only ten thousand four hundred men. This number
was soon after still more reduced, by sending off
reinforcements to the South, where now was the chief
theatre of the war.

To enliven a little the gloom that at this time encompassed the struggle for liberty, Lafayette, the
untiring friend and resistless pleader for the American
cause, arrived with the cheerful intelligence that the
French government had sent six ships-of-the-line,
and six thousand troops, which would soon be on our
coast. He landed at Boston amid public rejoicing,
but locked up the glad tidings he bore, till he could
pour them forth to the man he loved better than his
life. The meeting of Washington and Lafayette
was like that of a son and father. The eager delight
with which the one recounted what he had done, and

told of the aid that was approaching, and the deep and affectionate interest with which the other listened, would form a subject for a noble picture. The marquis had obtained the promise of large supplies of clothing, while he had purchased on his own account, a quantity of swords and military equipage for the light-infantry he commanded. In speaking in council one day, of the enthusiasm and impetuosity of Lafayette, the Prime Minister of France, old Count de Maurepas, remarked—"It is fortunate for the king that Lafayette did not take it into his head to strip Versailles of its furniture, to send to his dear Americans, as his majesty would be unable to refuse it." How little the governments of France and Spain dreamed what a train they were laying under their own thrones, when they came to our relief in the struggle for independence. There never has been a more striking illustration of the folly of human scheming, and of the ease with which Heaven works out its grand designs, over all earthly mutations, as the ultimate result of our success on the destiny of Europe.

As the summer advanced, the destitution of the troops in the article of clothing became an object of the deepest solicitude. Many of the officers looked like beggars, while the tattered soldiers, most of them, had not a shirt to their backs. Congress being apparently unable to do any thing, private sympathy was invoked. The ladies of Philadelphia, from the highest to the lowest, met together to make garments for the soldiers. Lafayette gave a hundred guineas in the name of his wife. The wife of the French minister six hundred dollars of continental paper. Like the heroines of old, the women sacrificed their jewelry, and laboured as common seamstresses in the noble work. Twenty-two hundred shirts were thus made, each bearing the name of the maker. A ship load of military stores and clothing, belonging to Robert Morris arriving about this time, this noble

financier immediately made a present of the whole
to the army. Such flashes of light shot through the
gloom, keeping alive the faith, and love, and courage
of those on whose shoulders the Revolution rested.

CHAPTER XII.

Fall of Charleston—Arrival of the French Fleet—Defeat
of Gates—Washington visits Rochambeau—Treason of
Arnold—Arrest of Andre—His Execution—Cornwallis in
the South—Project of an Attack on New York—Suffer-
ing of the Troops—Mutiny in Wayne's Command—Mu-
tiny of the New Jersey Troops, and prompt action of
Washington—Inefficiency of Congress, and Jealousies of
the States—Arnold's Expedition into Virginia—Action
between the English and French Fleets—Lafayette sent
South to co-operate with Steuben—Operations in Virginia
—Washington's Letter to the Manager of his Estates—
State of the Army—Letter to Paul Jones—Patriotism of
Robert Morris—Washington prepares to Attack New
York—Cornwallis Retreats before Lafayette to Yorktown
—The Allied Army marches rapidly South—Washington
visits Mount Vernon—Arrival of the French Fleet in the
Chesapeake—Anxiety of Washington—Yorktown Invest-
ed—Progress and Incidents of the Siege—Capitulation of
the Army—Excitement and Joy of the American People—
Effect of the News on the British Ministry.

WASHINGTON remained comparatively inactive during the summer, waiting the arrival of the French fleet
and army. Nothing could be done with his feeble
force, unsustained by a fleet, except to hold the
country around New York. In the mean time his
heart was filled with the deepest solicitude for the
fate of Charleston and the army under Lincoln,
which occupied it. Hemmed in by the enemy,
whose shot and shell fell with an incessant crash
into the dwellings of the inhabitants, this intrepid
commander, who had held out long after hope had
abandoned every heart, was at last compelled, with

his three thousand troops, to surrender.   A dark cloud was resting on the South; and that portion of the country which had hitherto escaped the ravages of an army, seemed now marked out for general devastation.

In the mean time, the French fleet arrived (July 10) at Newport.   Rochambeau, the commander of the land forces, was required by his government to act in all cases under the direction of Washington, while American officers were to command French officers of equal rank.   This wise arrangement produced harmony between the two armies, and gave universal satisfaction.   Washington immediately drew up a plan for a combined attack on New York by sea and land.   But the British fleet having received a reinforcement which gave it a decided superiority, the French squadron dared not put to sea, and remained blockaded in Newport.   There also the French army remained for its protection, waiting the arrival of the other division of the fleet* and land forces, and the summer passed away without any thing being accomplished.

In the place of success, there came the news of successive defeats at the South.   The fall of Charleston in May, was followed in August by the complete overthrow of Gates, at Camden—the loss of many noble troops and the death of Baron de Kalb.

While in this state of inaction Rochambeau wrote to Washington, requesting an interview.   This was granted, and the latter passing through Peekskill, met the former on 21st, at Hartford.   Before starting he had written to Arnold, commanding at West Point, to send a guard of fifty men to meet him at Peekskill, and collect forage for about forty horses.

Arnold came down the river in his barge, and crossed the river with him at King's Ferry.   The English vessel Vulture was in sight, and Washington scanned it long and carefully with his glass, and

* This was blockaded in Brest, and never arrived.

spoke at the same time, in a low tone, to one of his officers. This made Arnold very uneasy. Soon after, Lafayette, turning to Arnold, said, "General, as you have secret correspondence with the enemy, you must learn what has become of Guichen."* For a moment the traitor thought himself discovered, and demanded, sharply, what the marquis meant. The next minute, however, the boat touched the shore and nothing more was said.

Washington's visit to Rochambeau resulted in no plan of action, as every thing depended on the arrival of the expected fleet and forces.

After two days of pleasant intercourse, he started on his return, taking the upper route by way of Fishkill, so as to visit West Point. In the mean time, Arnold had completed his scheme, by which a blow was to be struck, against the colonies, so momentous in all the circumstances attending it, and in the results designed to be accomplished, that even its failure fell like a thunderbolt at noon-day on the nation. This intrepid commander, who had won such laurels before Quebec, on Lake Champlain, and at Saratoga, sought and obtained the important command at West Point, solely to deliver it into the hands of the enemy. Incensed at the injustice of Congress, in promoting juniors over him, maddened by the accusations of his enemies, and mortified by the reprimand ordered to be administered by a court-martial; he, with a baseness almost unparalleled in history, resolved to quench his rage in the ruin of his country. Down the abyss of infamy into which he was about to plunge, he gazed without flinching, hurried forward by the single intense, burning passion for revenge. He had long been in correspondence with Sir Henry Clinton, for the delivery of West Point, and the absence of Washington to the

* Guichen was the commander of the other portion of the French fleet, which had for a long time been expected, but which at this time was blockaded at Brest.

east, was thought to be a favourable time to effect his object.

Major Andre, under the name of Anderson, had been the medium through which the corrrespondence was carried on, and he was, therefore, selected to consummate and close the bargain. He proceeded up the river with the intention of having an interview with Arnold, on board the British vessel Vulture.

But difficulties being thrown in the way of this arrangement, he was finally induced to consent to go ashore. After midnight, on the morning of the 22d of September, he stepped into a boat sent by Arnold to receive him, and over the unruffled, placid bosom of the Hudson, glittering with reflected stars, was rowed silently and swiftly to the shore. Arnold met him on the bank, and the two retired to a thick wood, and there, amid the darkness and silence, discussed in low tones the treason and the reward. It was Andre's intention to retire on board the Vulture, but not being able to conclude the business by daylight, he was persuaded by Arnold to go with him to his quarters at Smith's house. He had been directed by Sir Henry Clinton not to enter our lines or assume any disguise. He, however, now under the change of circumstances, did both, and thus at once became a spy, and exposed to the doom of one. During the day, Colonel Livingston opened a sharp fire on the Vulture, which compelled her to drop down the river. Andre listened to the cannonading with visible emotion, but on its cessation resumed his composure. By ten o'clock the arrangement was completed, and Arnold returned in his barge to West Point. Andre passed the day alone, gloomily. Although he had at great peril consummated an arrangement which would secure a vast advantage to his king, and promotion and glory to himself, yet he could not but reflect that he was surrounded by enemies, and held concealed about his person the evidences of his character as a spy. He had been supplied by Arnold with two passports, one to the ship and another for the land route, should he be compelled to take the latter. Smith, who had brought him ashore, remained with him to take him back. Late in the afternoon, however, Andre ascertained, to his dismay, that Smith would not row him aboard the Vulture. He stubbornly resisting all appeals, Andre was compelled to choose the land route. Accompanied by Smith and a negro boy, he set out soon after sunset for King's Ferry. As they passed leisurely along the country, Smith would often stop to converse with acquaintances by the way, but Andre, taciturn and gloomy, kept slowly on. The hostile tone of the conversation, and the many eager inquiries put to Smith, naturally kept him in a state of intense anxiety. About nine o'clock they were hailed by the sentinel of a patrolling party commanded by Captain Boyd. The latter was unusually pressing in his inquiries of Smith, and urged him with great importunity to stay over-night. The latter declining, Boyd requested to see his passport. This was too positive and peremptory to be disobeyed, but the captain still pressed his inquiries and entreaties to stay over-night. He at length so worked upon Smith's fears, by representing the dangers in advance, that the latter concluded to stop, and, notwithstanding Andre's expostulations, remained all night near the patrol. The two occupied the same bed, but it was a long and restless night to the British officer. Across the bright prospect which the successful issue of his expedition spread out before him, would sweep the black clouds of anxiety and fear. In the morning they proceeded on their journey, and at length, having got beyond the reach of the patrolling party, and, as Andre thought, beyond all imminent danger, his naturally joyous spirit resumed its wonted cheerfulness, and his companion saw with amazement the sudden change from taciturnity and despondency to unusual hilarity and pleasant conversation. Poetry, art, and literature, one after another, became the theme of discourse, and he already seemed to see the end of the war and the reduction of the colonies, to the consummation of which his sagacity and personal daring would so largely have contributed. Near Pine's Bridge, Smith parted with him and returned to Peekskill. Andre kept on alone till within a half mile of Tarrytown, when he was suddenly stopped by three men lying in wait for suspicious persons and cattle going toward New York. Andre inquired to which party they belonged, and understanding from their answer that they were adherents of the English, immediately announced himself as a British officer. In a moment he saw his mistake, and pulled out his passport. This would have been sufficient but for the fatal confession that he had already made. The men then took him into the bushes and began to examine him. They stripped off his clothes, but could discover nothing. At length, in drawing off his stockings, they detected the papers containing the drawings of West Point, together with a full and accurate description of every part of the entire works, and estimates of the forces; also a plan of the future campaign which had been sent to Arnold by Washington a few days before. Andre then offered heavy rewards if they would let him go; but true to their country, these three patriots refused the bribe, and took him to Col. Jameson, commanding at North Castle.* This officer, bewildered and almost bereft

* Much has been said respecting the character of these three men—John Paulding, David Williams, and Isaac Van Wart—many maintaining that they were nothing but common plunderers, and were governed solely by the hope of reward in retaining Andre. I must confess that from the most careful investigation of the matter, Paulding seems to me to have been the only one in whom the thought of a bargain, after the discovery of Andre's true character, ever entered. Their occupation, was, doubtless, very equivocal—but it must be remembered that the times were dreadfully out of joint, and love of country could be strong under circumstances that at this day seem strange. It

of his senses, or else possessed of stupidity that rendered him unfit to command, resolved, with all this damning proof before him, to send Andre to Arnold. Major Talmadge, second in command, was absent when Andre was brought in, and did not return till evening. When Jameson told him what had occurred, he was filled with amazement, and declared openly that Arnold was a traitor, and offered to take on himself the responsibility of acting on that conviction. To this Jameson would not listen. Talmadge then insisted vehemently on bringing the prisoner back. Jameson finally consented to do so, but, in spite of all remonstrance, would send a letter to Arnold, informing him of the arrest of John Anderson, (as he was called.) The papers he had already despatched to meet Washington, now on his return from Hartford.

The messenger being well mounted overtook the party having charge of the prisoner, and they returned to North Castle. Andre now saw that, in all probabilty, his fate was sealed. Exposure was unavoidable; the proofs of his and Arnold's crime he knew were more than ample. The prospect grew black as midnight around, and he was absorbed in gloomy reflections. Pondering solemnly on his condition, he paced up and down his apartment with a

showed itself in MUTINY. The utter want of honesty on the part of government to pay its troops, rendered many of them not very scrupulous about the method of reimbursing themselves. To the curious in such matters I would say, that the following complaint is among General Rufus Putnam's papers, now in possession of Judge Putnam of Ohio : —"Mrs. Hannah Sniffen says, that Gabriel, Joseph, and Abraham Riquard, David Hunt, *Isaac Van Wart*, and Pardon Burlingham, did, on the night of the 27th ult. take from James Sniffen, an inhabitant of White Plains, without civil or military authority, *three milch cows*, which they have converted to their own private use.

"HANNAH SNIFFEN, in behalf of her father.
"*Crane Pond, July 9th*, 1780."

slow and measured stride. Talmadge sat watching him, and as he observed the manner in which he turned on his heel, and his military tread, as he paced the floor, he was convinced that the indifferently dressed prisoner before him had been bred to the profession of arms.   The next morning Andre wrote a letter to Washington, in which he frankly confessed his name and rank, and the manner in which he came within the American lines.   Previous to sending it he showed it to Talmadge, who was confounded at the startling developments it contained.

The papers sent to Washington missed him, as he did not return by the road he went, but took the northern route to Fishkill, where, Sept. 24, he arrived late in the afternoon, the very day after Andre's capture.   Stopping here only a short time, he pushed on for Arnold's head-quarters, eighteen miles distant. He had gone, however but a mile or two, before he met the French minister, Chevalier Luzerne, on his way to Newport, to visit Rochambeau.   The latter prevailed on him to return to Fishkill for the night, as he had matters of importance to communicate.

The next morning Washington was early in the saddle, having sent word beforehand to Arnold that he would breakfast with him.   It was a bright autumnal morning, and the whole party in high spirits pushed rapidly forward through the gorges of the Highlands.   As they came opposite West Point, Washington, instead of continuing on to Arnold's quarters, which were on the same side, turned his horse down a narrow road toward the river.   Lafayette observing it, exclaimed " General, you are going in the wrong direction; you know Mrs. Arnold is waiting breakfast for us, and that road will take us out of our way."   " Ah!" replied Washington, laughingly, " I know you young men are all in love with Mrs. Arnold, and wish to get where she is as soon as possible.   You may go and take breakfast with her, and tell her not to wait for me.   I must ride down and examine the redoubts on this side of the river, and will be there in a short time." The officers preferring not to proceed without him, two aids were despatched to tell Arnold not to wait breakfast. The latter, therefore, with his family and the two aids sat down to the table. While they were conversing on different topics, a messenger entered and handed a letter to Arnold, who opened and read it in presence of the company. It was the one from Jameson, announcing the capture of Andre. Although the thunderbolt fell sudden and unexpectedly at his feet, it did not startle him from his self-command. Merely remarking that his presence at West Point was necessary, he requested the aids to say to Washington on his arrival that he was unexpectedly called over the river, and would be back soon. Repairing to his wife's chamber, he sent for her at the breakfast table, and told her he must instantly leave her and his country for ever, for death was his certain doom if he did not reach the enemy before he was detected. Paralyzed by the sudden blow, she fell senseless at his feet. Not daring to call for help, Arnold left her in that state, and rapidly descending to the door, mounted one of the horses belonging to Washington's aids, and taking a byway pushed for the river, where his barge was moored. Jumping in, he ordered his six oarsmen to pull for Teller's Point. Stimulating them to greater efforts by the promise of two gallons of rum, he swept rapidly past Verplanck's Point, and as he approached the Vulture waved a white handkerchief, and was soon safe on board. In the mean time Washington having finished his survey, rode on to Arnold's house. Taking a hasty breakfast, he said he would not wait for Arnold to return, but cross over to West Point and meet him there. As the boat swept over the water, he remarked, "Well, gentlemen, I am glad on the whole that General Arnold has gone before us, for we shall now have a salute, and the roaring of the cannon will have a fine effect among these mountains." At this moment an officer was seen coming down the rocky hill-side, to meet the barge. It was Colonel Lamb, who looked confounded on seeing the commander-in chief. He commenced an apology, declaring that he was wholly ignorant of his Excellency's intention to visit West Point. "How is this, sir," broke in Washington, "is not General Arnold here?" "No, sir," replied the colonel, "he has not been here these two days, nor have I heard from him in that time." "This is extraordinary," replied Washington, "he left word that he had crossed the river. However, our visit must not be in vain. Since we have come we must look around and see in what state things are with you." After passing through the garrison and inspecting the various redoubts he returned to the landing-place and recrossed to Arnold's house. As the boat touched the opposite shore, Hamilton, who had remained behind, was seen coming rapidly down to the shore. Approaching Washington, he spoke in a low and anxious tone, when the two immediately hastened to the house. Here Hamilton gave him the papers found on Andre, together with the letter of the latter to Washington. Had an earthquake suddenly opened at the feet of the commander-in-chief he could not have been more astounded. Himself, the army, West Point, and all, were standing above a mine that might explode at any moment. How far did this treason extend? Whom did it embrace? When was the hour of its consummation? were questions that came home, like the stroke of a serpent's fang, to his heart. Ordering Hamilton to mount a horse and ride as for life to Verplanck's Point, and stop Arnold, if possible, he called in Lafayette and Knox, and told them what had occurred, merely remarking at the close, "Whom can we trust now?" His countenance was calm as ever, and being informed that Arnold's wife was in a state bordering on insanity, he went up to her room to soothe her. "In her frenzy" she upbraided him with being in a plot to murder her child. "One moment she raved, another she melted into tears. Sometimes she pressed her infant to her bosom and lamented its fate occasioned by the imprudence of its father, in a manner that would have pierced insensibility itself."* It was four o'clock in the afternoon when these disclosures were made to Washington, and an hour later, dinner being announced, he said, "Come, gentlemen, since Mrs. Arnold is unwell and the general is absent, let us sit down without ceremony."

No one at the table but Knox and Lafayette knew what had transpired, nor did Washington exhibit any change of demeanour, except that he was more than usually stern in voice and manner. But his mind, oppressed with nameless fears, wandered far away from the dinner-table, and no sooner was the repast over than he addressed himself to the task before him. He wrote rapidly, and couriers were soon seen galloping in every direction. He announced the treason to Colonel Wade, commanding at West Point, in the absence of Colonel Lamb, in the single sentence, "*General Arnold is gone to the enemy*," and directed him to put every thing in instant preparation for a night attack. He sent a messenger to Colonel Gray, ordering him to march at once to West Point with his regiment; a third to General Greene at Tappan, with directions to leave his heavy baggage behind, and press swiftly as possible for King's Ferry, where, or on the way, other orders would meet him. To Colonel Livingston, at Verplanck's Point, he sent the laconic letter, "*I wish to see you immediately, and request that you will come without delay.*" To Major Low, at Fishkill, and an officer with a party at Stratsburg, he sent couriers "directing them to march for West Point without delay." He also wrote to Colonel Jameson, to guard Andre closely and send him immediately to West Point. The latter messenger

* Vide Letter from Hamilton.

arrived at midnight in a pouring rain, and summoned Andre from his bed, to face the pitiless storm. The guard marched the whole dark and dismal night, and arrived at Robinson's house, Arnold's head-quarters, early in the morning.

Washington having done all he could to arrest the enormous evil that threatened to overwhelm him, retired late at night to his bed, fearful that the sound of the enemy's cannon would awake him before daylight.

Not knowing how many officers might have been corrupted by Arnold, and finding a major-general's name mentioned in the papers taken from Andre, he next morning sent Major Lee with his dragoons to hover near New York, and obtain all the information in his power from the secret agents that he always kept in the city, and who advised him of every movement of the enemy. These spies were unacquainted with each other, and their communications came through different channels, so that by comparing the several accounts, Washington at any time was able to come to pretty accurate conclusions respecting any project of Sir Henry Clinton. They usually wrote with an invisible ink which a particular chemical fluid alone could bring out. A few lines on an indifferent subject would be written in common ink and the rest of the letter filled up with important news. Through these spies Washington soon ascertained that Arnold was alone in his treason.*

A court-martial was now called to judge Andre, and he was condemned as a spy. When Sir Henry Clinton heard of it, he put forth every effort to avert the dreadful fate of his officer. He sent three commissioners to reason and remonstrate with the officers of the court. He appealed to Washington, while Arnold wrote him a threatening letter, declaring if Andre was hung he would revenge his death on every American prisoner that fell into his hands.

* Vide Sparks' Life of Washington.

Washington, though his heart was filled with the keenest sorrow for the fate of one so universally beloved, and possessed of such noble qualities of heart and mind, refused to arrest the course of justice. As in all cases where great trouble came upon him, so in this, he said but little, but silently and sternly wrestled with it alone. The vastness of the plot, and the rank of those engaged in it, only rendered the example still more imperative—besides, stern justice to the nation required it. Just after the battle of Long Island, Captain Nathan Hale, a graduate of Yale College, a young man of rare purity and elevation of character, went over to Brooklyn, at the request of Washington, to ascertain the plans and movements of the enemy, and just as he was passing the outposts on his return, was taken, tried, and hung as a spy. His nobleness of heart did not shield him even from the brutality of his enemies. Washington, therefore, in looking at the matter from every point of view, could see no way of sparing Andre except by exchanging him for Arnold. Although he did not make this formal proposition, he caused Clinton to be aware of his views. The latter, however, could not give up the traitor, richly as he merited death, and justice had to take its course. When Andre found that all hope was at an end, he addressed the following letter to Washington, which doubtless shook his resolution more, and inflicted a keener pang than all which had gone before.

"*Tappan*, *Oct.* 1*st*, 1780.

"SIR,—Buoyed above the terror of death by the consciousness of a life devoted to honourable pursuits, and stained with no action that can give me remorse, I trust that the request I make to your excellency at this serious period, and which is to soften my last moments, will not be rejected. Sympathy toward a soldier will surely induce your excellency and a military tribunal to adapt the mode of my death to the feelings of a man of honour. Let me hope, sir, that if aught in my character impresses you with esteem toward me, if aught in my misfortunes marks me as the victim of policy and not of resentment, I shall experience the operation of those feelings in your breast by being informed that I am not to die on a gibbet.''

He waited anxiously but in vain for an answer. Still he could not believe his request would be denied, and never ceased to hope till the scaffold rose before his vision. It required a severe struggle on the part of Washington to refuse this touching request. The soul of honour himself, and keenly alive to the feelings of an officer and a gentlemen, he felt in his own bosom how great the boon asked by Andre was; but the sense of duty to his country forbade the granting of it. It was necessary to have it understood that nothing could avert the fate or death of shame of a convicted spy, and on the 2d of October, with the courage and composure of a truly heroic man, Andre expiated his crime on the scaffold.

In the mean time the prospects of the colonies in the South assumed a still more gloomy aspect. Cornwallis was sweeping the Carolinas with his troops, while a strong expedition was being fitted out to overrun Virginia. The complicated and disheartening state of things, however, produced one happy effect—it imparted some humility to Congress, so that it was glad to turn to Washington for help. Gates, its favourite general, whom it had sent South, was now completely disgraced, and it was compelled at this late day to request the commander-in-chief to appoint a successor. He selected Greene, who soon showed the wisdom of the choice, and commenced that career which covered him and his tattered army with glory. Congress also passed the measures which Washington for years had urged in vain—established the half-pay system, and decreed that all future enlistments should be for the war.

The summer having passed in comparative idleness,

Washington resolved, if possible, to strike a blow before winter set in. This was no less than a combined attack on New York. The position of the enemy was thoroughly reconnoitered—boats were kept mounted on wheels—and the whole plan of attack fully developed. Washington had spent a whole campaign in maturing this scheme, which promised the most brilliant success. Every thing was nearly ready for the attempt, when several British vessels of war entered the river, and put a stop to the preparations. Not long after, the army went into winter-quarters near Morristown, at Pompton, and in the Highlands, and nothing further was done. Washington established his head-quarters at New Windsor, which looked directly down on West Point.

As cold weather came on the troops began to suffer severely for want of clothing and stores, and to save and feed a portion of them he was compelled to send back the new levies. He had predicted this state of things in the latter part of November, in a letter to General Sullivan, a member of Congress at that time. After discussing the subject at length, he says—

"Another question may here arise. Where are the means? Means must be found or the soldiers must go naked. But I will take the liberty in this place to give it as my opinion that a foreign loan is indispensably necessary to the continuance of the war. Congress will deceive themselves if they imagine that the army, or a state, that is the theatre of war, can rub through a second campaign as the last. It would be as unreasonable as to suppose that because a man had rolled a snow-ball till it had acquired the size of a horse, he might do so till it was as large as a house. Matters may be pushed to a certain point, beyond which we cannot move them."

Greene wrote from the South that his troops were "literally naked"—and they did march naked by hundreds into battle, presenting an exhibition of patriotism and valour never before surpassed in the annals of war. Not only was clothing withheld, but the pay of the troops also, and the evils which Congress could not anticipate, though constantly thundered in their ears by Washington, now began to fall on the army. On the 1st of January, 1781, a mutiny broke out in the Pennsylvania line, stationed at Morristown, and thirteen hundred men drew up on parade preparatory to a march on Philadelphia, to force Congress at the point of bayonet to give them redress. The officers rushed among them and unable by commands to restore obedience, resorted to force. The mutineers fired in turn, killing one officer and mortally wounding another, and for two hours there was an indescribable scene of horror and confusion. At length the mutineers got into marching order, and scouring the grand parade with four pieces of cannon, marched off. The inhabitants fired alarm-guns on the route to Elizabethtown, and beacon-fires blazed on the hights, announcing some great and imminent peril. Sir Henry Clinton hearing of the revolt, sent commissioners to them, offering them high rewards to join the British service. They rejected with scorn the infamous propositions, saying, "What! does he take us for Arnolds?" and immediately sent these proposals in an envelop to Wayne, declaring, that if the enemy made any hostile demonstration they would march at once against him. The emissaries were seized and given up, and afterward tried by court-martial and shot. Congress, which could turn a deaf ear to the counsels and prophetic appeals of Washington, was now thoroughly alarmed. Although it had stubbornly resisted his advice, resolutions would not put down bayonets, and a committee was appointed to confer with the mutineers. They met at Trenton, and the claims of the latter to their pay and to be discharged at the end of three years, instead of at the close of the war, being granted, nearly the whole line disbanded for the winter. Washington clearly foresaw that this success of the revolters would stimulate other portions of the army to a similar attempt. The result would be the self-destruction of the entire army, and he resolved that a second mutiny should be put down by the strong arm of force, whatever might be the loss of life that accompanied it. He therefore ordered a thousand men, who could be trusted, to be picked from the different regiments in the Highlands, with four days' provision constantly on hand, and ready to march on a moment's notice. His anticipations proved true, for encouraged by the success of the Pennsylvania troops, those of New Jersey, stationed at Pompton and Chatham, revolted also—determined to march to Trenton, where Congress was then sitting, and demand their rights by force of arms. Washington immediately despatched six hundred men, under Howe, with orders to march rapidly and secretly to the camp of the mutineers. The snow was deep and the cold intense, but this band of resolute men pushed swiftly forward, bivouacking where night overtook them, and on the fourth day arrived near the camp of the revolted troops, Jan. 27th, 1781. Halting till midnight, Howe resumed his march, and taking positions, and planting his artillery so as to command every approach, he waited for daylight to appear. When light broke over the encampment, the mutineers to their amazement saw ranks of armed men on every side, and cannon sweeping the entire field. Howe ordered them to parade at once, and without arms, in front of their huts, saying that he would allow but five minutes in which to do it. "What," said they, "and no conditions?"

"No conditions!" was the stern reponse.

"Then, if we are to die, we might as well die where we are as any where else."

The regiment of Colonel Sprout was immediately ordered to advance, when the promise of submission was reluctantly given. They then paraded without arms and gave up three of the ringleaders, who were tried and condemned on the spot. Two were shot, twelve of their own companions being compelled to act as executioners. The report of those twelve muskets, and the lifeless bodies of their leaders stretched on the snow, carried consternation into the hearts of the others, and they made concession to their officers, and promised obedience in future. The blow had been sudden and terrible, and needed no repetition. Washington and Congress were not unlike only in preventing evil, but in arresting and curing it. But just, as well as severe, the former immediately appointed commissioners to inquire into the grievances of the soldiers, which he knew were not imaginary, and have them redressed. This one example was sufficient, and the whisper of revolt was heard no more in the army.

While these painful events were transpiring, Laurens, who had been appointed by Congress a commissioner to visit France, to negotiate a loan of money and obtain supplies, was in communication with Washington to receive the advice and instructions which Congress had appointed the latter to give him.

The jealousies of the different States, and the fear of Congress to assert its authority, and *command* troops to be raised, taxes levied, and clothing supplied, kept the army in a pitiable condition. The resolutions it had passed, in accordance with Washington's views, were all well in their way, but worthless unless enforced. Right in the face of its decrees that troops should be enlisted for the war, the States continued on the old system of engaging them only for a specified time. The bugbear of dictatorial power which they feared that Washington, with an army entirely under his control, might assume, wore a more horrid aspect than the evils under which the nation suffered, and while they allowed Congress to make alliances, vote away the money of the nation, and do all other acts of the highest executive authority, it must not draft soldiers and lay personal taxes, lest it should infringe individual liberty.

During the winter, Clinton planned an expedition South, composed of fifteen hundred men, and placed it under Arnold, who was directed to ascend the Chesapeake and reduce the country. The traitor, zealous for his new master, passed up the James River to Richmond, which he burned to the ground, and by his depredations seemed determined to carry out the threat he had made to Washington, if he should allow Andre to be executed. Washington despatched forces to the South to meet this new inroad, and was exceedingly anxious that a portion of the French fleet should co-operate with them, and blockade Arnold in James River. Such a movement, he was confident, would secure the destruction of the corps. But the fleet was blockaded in Newport by the British, and could not with safety put to sea. In the middle of January, however, a severe storm swept the eastern coast, and when it broke, a British sixty-four was seen off Montauk Point, under jury-masts, the Culloden, a seventy-four, aground on a reef near Gardiner's Island, while the Bedford, another seventy-four, was adrift in the Sound, swept of every spar, and her whole upper tier of guns thrown overboard. Destouches, who had succeeded Chevalier de Ternay, after his death, reconnoitered the shattered fleet for the purpose of engaging it, but found it still too strong to be attacked. He, however, took advantage of its scattered condition to send three vessels of war, in accordance with Washington's request, to blockade Arnold. These, under M. de Tilly, arrived in the Chesapeake; but Arnold, who had been advised of the movement, withdrew his ships so far up the Elizabeth River that the heavier vessels of the French could not reach him. Thus the expedition, which, if it could have sailed sooner, as Washington expected, would have been successful, was rendered abortive, and the vessels returned to Newport.

M. Destouches now resolved, at the earnest recommendation of Washington, to proceed to sea with his whole fleet, and sailed for the Chesapeake. He departed on the 16th of March, followed by the British admiral with the whole of his fleet. An action took place off the capes of Virginia, which terminated without any decisive result, and the French squadron returned to Newport. Previous to this, when Washington was informed of the departure of the three vessels to blockade Arnold, he despatched Lafayette with twelve hundred men, by land, to co-operate with him and aid Baron Steuben, who with a mere handful of militia had been left to resist the invasion.

In the mean time, (March 2d,) Washington made a visit to Newport, to consult with Rochambeau on a plan for the summer campaign. He was received with great honour, and after an absence of three weeks returned to head-quarters. The movements of the enemy, however, were so uncertain, that nothing definite could be decided upon except in any case to act in concert. Whatever shape affairs might ultimately assume, one thing was evident, the British were directing their attention more exclusively to the South. Notwithstanding the defeat of Tarleton by Morgan, and the consummate generalship exhibited by Greene, Cornwallis had obtained a strong foothold in the Carolinas, and it was clearly the opinion of the latter that the theatre of the war should be transferred in that direction, even if it were necessary to abandon New York. Clinton, in consequence, sent off heavy detachments to co-operate with him, and it became evident that the forces accumulating there would soon be able to trample under foot all the opposition that could be offered. Light armed vessels pushed up the various rivers of Virginia, plundering and desolating as they advanced. One ascended the Potomac as far as Mount Vernon, and Lund Washington, the manager of the estate, wishing to save the building from conflagration, sent on board and offered the enemy refreshments. Washington when he heard of it expressed his regret, saying, in that lofty patriotism which like the fire never ceased to burn. " I am very sorry to hear of your loss ; I am a little sorry to hear of my own ; but that which gives me most concern is, that you should go on board the enemy's vessels and furnish them with refreshments. It would have been a less painful circumstance to me to have heard, that, in consequence of your non-compliance with their request, they had burned my house and laid my plantation in ruins. You ought to have considered yourself as my representative, and should have reflected on the bad example of communicating with the enemy, and making a voluntary offer of refreshments to them with a view to prevent a conflagration." This is not a public letter, designed to meet the public eye, but a private, confidential one, revealing the feelings of a heart in which love of country absorbed every other interest and emotion. It furnished, also, directions for future conduct. It was saying to his manager, rather than ever again hold any intercourse with the enemy, or make any terms with them, let them burn down my dwellings and lay waste my possessions. Indeed, in this very letter he says he expects such a result. What perfect harmony there is between his secret thoughts and public acts in every thing respecting the welfare of his country.

With what prospects he was about to enter on the summer campaign may be gathered from the following entry made in his diary on the first of May: "Instead of having magazines filled with provisions, we have a scanty pittance scattered here and there in the different States; instead of having our arsenals well supplied with military stores, they are poorly provided, and the workmen all leaving them; instead of having the various articles of field equipage in readiness to be delivered, the quarter-master general, as the dernier resort, according to his account, is now applying to the several States to provide those things for their troops respectively; instead of having a regular system of transportation established upon credit, or funds in the quarter-master's hands to defray the expenses of it, we have neither the one nor the other, and all the business being done by military impress, we are daily and hourly oppressing the people, souring their tempers, and alienating their affections; instead of having the regiments completed to the new establishment, which ought to have been done agreeably to the requisitions of Congress, scarce any State in the Union has at this hour an eighth part of its quota in the field, and little prospect that I can see of ever getting more than half; in a word, instead of having every thing in readiness to take the field, we have nothing; and instead of having a glorious offensive campaign before us, we have a bewildered and gloomy defensive one, unless we should receive a powerful aid of ships, land troops, and money, from our generous allies, and those at present are too contingent to build upon."* It required more than a prophet's ken to see light beyond this darkness, more than the spirit of man to breathe on such a chaos to bring error and form out of it. But, "our generous allies" did fortunately come to our relief. A French frigate, with Count de Barras on board, arrived at Boston, bringing the cheering intelligence that troops and vessels of war were on the way, while a fleet, under Count de Grasse, designed to leave the West Indies for the American coast in July or August.

About this time Washington wrote to Paul Jones, who had arrived at Philadelphia in February in the Ariel, with stores and clothing, which had long been expected, congratulating him on his glorious victory over the Serapis, and the highly complimentary report of the Board of Admiralty, that had been directed to inquire into the cause of the delay. His daring cruise along the coast of England, the con-

* Vide Sparks' Letters and Speeches of Washington, vol. viii. page 81.

sternation he had spread throughout the kingdom, and the gallant deeds by which he had "made the flag of America respected among the flags of other nations," were mentioned with the warmest approbation, and declared worthy of particular regard from Congress.

The news of the arrival of fresh troops and additional vessels, and of more soon to be on our coast, spread new life through the American camp, and Washington resolved at once to open a vigorous campaign. The commanders of the allied armies met at Weathersfield, Connecticut, to determine on the best plan to pursue. The French proposed to make a Southern campaign in Virginia, but Washington was of the firm opinion that a combined attack, by sea and land, should be made on New York. To the strong reasons which he gave, the former yielded, and immense preparations were set on foot. In the mean time, Washington watched with the deepest anxiety the operations of Lafayette and Greene in the South, fondly hoping that their successes would draw off large reinforcements from the army at New York, and thus materially weaken the garrison. Robert Morris, who had been appointed superintendent of finance, animated with the same spirit of self-devotion as Washington, sent forward voluntarily, two thousand barrels of flour to the army, which he had purchased on his own credit, promising to follow it with a large sum of money, to be raised in the same way.

In the mean time orders had been issued to the different sections of the army, and they closed rapidly in upon the Hudson, forming a junction at Peekskill. Washington, on the 2d of July, left his tents standing and his baggage behind, and rapidly descended the river, hoping to take the enemy's garrison at Kingsbridge, and posts in the vicinity, by surprise. The night before, Lincoln, with a strong detachment, passed down the stream with muffled oars,

and landing a mile below Yonkers, pushed rapidly
and silently over the hills in the darkness, unob-
served by the British light-horse, and before daylight drew up near Kingsbridge.   But the enemy's
pickets, hearing the tread of the advancing columns,
and beholding through the gloom the advance parties, opened a brisk fire.   Washington, who had
marched with the main army all night, was already
on the slope of Valentine's Hill, when the sharp
rattle of musketry was borne by on the night air.
The order to march was instantly given, and the
troops hastened forward to the support of Lincoln.
The enemy retired behind their works, and De
Lancey, stationed on Harlem River, also aroused
by the firing, hastily retreated before the Duke de
Lauzun, approaching by way of Hartford, could cut
him off.   Baffled in this attempt, Washington withdrew, and on the 4th of July, pitched his camp near
Dobbs' Ferry.   Two days after, the heads of the
French columns appeared in view, with drums beating and colours flying, and were received with enthusiasm by the whole army.

Rochambeau had rapidly marched them from
Newport, in four divisions, by way of Hartford;
one regiment, that of Saintonge, never halting for
a single day's rest the entire distance.   As Washington's army lay in two lines, resting on the Hudson, the French took position on the left, extending
in a single line to the Bronx.   As the national colours of the two armies swayed away in the breeze,
joy and enthusiasm animated every heart, and a
glorious issue to the summer campaign was confidently expected.

But just in proportion as foreign aid was received, the colonies, especially those of New England,
New York, Pennsylvania, and New Jersey, grew
more listless, and the recruits came in slowly.

The mission of Laurens had been partially successful.   France promised six millions of livres, and

the king had pledged himself to negotiate a loan for the United States for ten millions, so that at the close of the year he would have furnished in all twenty-five millions.

The two armies remained inactive in their encampment for a fortnight, but Washington kept in constant communication with the Southern armies, through a chain of expresses. On the 18th, he, and three French generals, crossed the river at Dobbs' Ferry, and escorted by a hundred and fifty men, ascended the hills that terminate the Pallisades, and spent the entire day in surveying through their glasses the portion of the enemy on the northern part of the island. Three days after, with five thousand men, he advanced to reconnoitre the works at Kingsbridge, and cut off such of Delancey's light troops as might be found without the lines. The next day the army displayed on the heights opposite the enemy. The latter was wholly unaware of their approach, till their sudden apparition on the neighbouring hills announced it. Washington and Rochambeau then took with them the engineers and reconnoitred the enemy's works. They afterward went over to Throg's Neck, and measured the distance across to Long Island. The enemy discovered the party, and levelled some cannon shot at them, which, however, passed harmlessly by. Having finished the reconnoisance, the whole division retired, reaching the camp at midnight.

It was impossible, of course, while the French fleet at Newport was blockaded, to effect any thing against New York. Washington, therefore, waited with the deepest anxiety the arrival of Count de Grasse. He despatched to General Forman, at Monmouth, a letter to the Count, written in Rochambeau's cypher, with directions to keep ceaseless watch on the heights, and the moment the fleet hove in sight to proceed on board and deliver it.

In the mean time affairs in the South were assum-

ing a more favourable aspect.   Greene had handed
Cornwallis over to Lafayette, and this gallant young
commander,* on the very day that the French army,
under Rochambeau, marched with flying colours
into the camp of Washington at Dobbs' Ferry,
fought the battle of Green Spring, in which he and
Wayne showed themselves worthy of each other,
and the trust committed to them.   The next night
Cornwallis retreated before "*the boy*," whom he
contemptuously declared could not "*escape*" him,
passed James River, and afterward proceeded to
Portsmouth.   Here he received orders to take a position on the Chesapeake which could serve as the
basis of future operations.   Selecting Yorktown as
the most secure and favourable, he moved his forces
thither and began to entrench himself.   By the 23d
of August his army was concentrated and well secured.

The constant success of his favourite and friend,
gratified Washington exceedingly, who was afraid,
in case of any disaster, that he would be blamed for
putting so young and inexperienced a commander
into the field, against one of the best tacticians, and
most accomplished generals of the age.

While Cornwallis was employed in erecting fortifications (Aug. 14th,) Washington received a letter
from Count de Grasse, in St. Domingo, stating that
he was about to sail with his entire fleet, and some
three thousand troops, for the Chesapeake, but could
not remain later than the middle of October.

After a brief consultation with Rochambeau, it
was decided to be very doubtful whether New York

* This noble stranger, when he arrived at Baltimore,
found the troops badly clothed, discontented, and averse to
return South.   Immediately borrowing ten thousand dollars on his credit, he expended them in shirts, shoes, etc.,
for the soldiers, which so touched their hearts, that their
murmurings and complaints gave place to enthusiasm and
love, and they closed around him like veterans.

could be reduced within that period, and that Virginia furnished the only field promising immediate success. They resolved therefore to march thither without delay. Every effort, however, was made to deceive Sir Henry Clinton respecting the change of plan. Boats were gathered in the neighbourhood of New York—ovens built and forage collected, as if in preparation for a thorough investment of the city—false communications, sent for the purpose of falling into the hands of the enemy, corroborated this external evidence, and Clinton had no doubt that he was to be the object of attack. Washington took great pains to deceive his own troops also, knowing, as he said, "where the imposition does not completely take place at home, it would never sufficiently succeed abroad." He informed Barras at Newport of his intention, and requested him to sail immediately for the Chesapeake, but the latter had an enterprise of his own on foot against Newfoundland, besides, being senior in rank to the Count de Grasse, he did not wish to serve under him. At the earnest remonstrance, however, of both Washington and Rochambeau, he at last consented to go, though grumblingly, saying it was the last expedition he would ever undertake.

Every thing being ready, the combined armies struck their camps and turned the heads of their columns southward. Twenty regiments, under Heath, were left to guard the Highlands. The American army crossed the Hudson on the 21st—the French commenced next day, completing the passage on the 25th. They proceeded by different routes to Trenton, where they formed a junction and moved rapidly southward. Washington and Rochambeau here left the armies, and rode on to Philadelphia, to provide vessels in which to transport the troops from Trenton to the head of the Elk. The city received the commander-in-chief with acclamations, and as he passed slowly through the streets, the enthusiasm broke over all bounds, and the clamour of the multitude drowned even the clang of bells and thunder of artillery.

But only boats enough could be procured to carry a single regiment, and the main army, under Lincoln, continued its march by land. Passing through Philadelphia, it was followed by almost the entire population, who hailed them with exultant shouts, and invoked blessings on their heads. Heavy rains came on, and through the wet and mire the weary suffering troops were kept to the top of their endurance. The French, well clad and well fed, suffered but little, while the destitute Americans presented a most pitiable spectacle.

Washington had written to Lafayette announcing his departure, and requesting him to watch Cornwallis narrowly and not let him escape into the Carolinas. But the 2d of September arriving without hearing any thing from Count de Grasse, who was to have sailed on the 3d of August, or from Barras, who had notified him he should leave Newport on the 23d, Washington was "*distressed beyond measure.*" The English fleet might occupy the Chesapeake first, and then the whole plan would fall through, while if even Barras, who had much of the heavy siege artillery on board, was taken, the entire aspect of affairs might be changed. But three days after, the joyful intelligence was received of the safe arrival of the French admiral, with twenty-six ships-of-the-line and several frigates. The army was electrified, while the French officers were almost delirious with joy. The prospect now brightened, and the threads of fate were evidently weaving a net for Cornwallis.

The two armies had passed the Delaware before Clinton was aware of their destination. He then despatched Arnold to make an irruption into Connecticut, and threatened an invasion of New Jersey and an attack on the Highlands to induce Washing-

ton to halt.   But the latter could not be turned aside
from the great object on which he had set his heart,
and pressed resolutely and swiftly toward its accom-
plishment.

Cornwallis saw with alarm this sudden and tremendous combination designed to crush him, and
gazed anxiously around for an avenue of escape.   If
he had been left to his own resources he probably
would have made a desperate attempt to cleave his
way through the defences of Lafayette and escape to
the Carolinas.   From his known energy and skill the
success of such an effort might not have been so hopeless, but he received a despatch from Sir Henry Clinton promising reinforcements both of troops and
ships.   Thus, the second time, did this commander
lull into fatal security one of his lieutenants, and
first in the case of Burgoyne, and now in that of
Cornwallis, make certain an impending calamity.

While the two armies were pressing southward,
Washington turned aside, and, for the first time in
six years, visited his home at Mount Vernon.

In the mean time Count de Grasse was told that
the British fleet, under Admiral Graves, who had
been reinforced from the West Indies, was in pursuit
of him off the Chesapeake.   He immediately put to
sea and offered battle.   An engagement followed,
but without any decisive result.   The next day the
English admiral, who had the weather-guage, declining to renew the action, De Grasse put back into the
Chesapeake, where to his great joy he found Barras
safely arrived.

Washington, as soon as Rochambeau joined him,
continued his journey, and on arriving at Williamsburg heard of the return of the French fleet and the
junction of De Barras with it.   Every thing now
rested on the despatch of troops, and Washington's
energies were now roused to the utmost.   A single
day's delay might ruin a great enterprise and defer
indefinitely the independence of his country.   He
336   x

wanted an army that could fly, and wrote to General
Lincoln to hurry forward the "*troops on the wings
of speed.*" "*Every day we now lose,*" said he, "*is
comparatively an age.*" He sent a messenger to the
Count de Grasse for boats to transport the troops by
water from Annapolis and the head of the Elk, but
the French admiral had anticipated his wants, and
he soon had the satisfaction of seeing the fleet of
transports move away to the scene of operation. He
then requested an interview with De Grasse. Accompanied by Rochambeau, Knox, De Chastellux
and Du Portail, he embarked in a small vessel and
was received by the admiral with distinguished honours. The plan of attack was soon arranged, and
Washington returned to land. In the mean time
Admiral Digby arrived at Sandy Hook with a reinforcement of vessels. De Grasse was no sooner informed of this than he resolved to put to sea and give
the enemy battle. When this astounding intelligence
was communicated to Washington he could not conceal his anxiety. He immediately wrote a letter to
the count, which he despatched by Lafayette, who he
knew would second its contents with all the influence
he possessed. In it he depicted in the strongest
language the fatal consequences that would follow
such an abandonment of the land forces, declaring
that it might result in no less a calamity than the
total disbanding of the army. At all events, if he
was afraid to be attacked in a stationary position, he
must at least cruise in sight of the capes. But the
true reason with De Grasse was, not that he feared
to be attacked at anchor—he wished to perform a
brilliant action in which the glory would belong to
himself alone—in short, to capture or disperse the
entire English fleet, and thus secure, by one *grand
coup*, the overthrow of both the British armies, and
put an end to the war. But for fear of the consequences that might result from disregarding the firm
remonstrance of both Washington and the French

commanders, there is but little doubt that he would
have insisted on executing his brilliant object, and
thus overthrown the whole campaign, and put far off
the day of peace.   He, however, consented to remain;
though, it is said, that Washington, afraid to trust
to his steadiness of purpose, sent Hamilton to him
during the siege, who, passing in an open boat by
night, had an interview with him to strengthen his
determination.
    Cornwallis at this time was at the head of more
than 7000 troops, which were concentrated mostly in
Yorktown, containing at that time about sixty houses.
A few occupied Gloucester, on the opposite side of
York river.
    The allied armies, nearly sixteen thousand strong,
took up their line of march from Williamsburg on
the 28th of September, at five o'clock in the morning,
and advancing by different routes toward Yorktown,
arrived in view of the enemy's lines at four o'clock in
the afternoon.   Cornwallis watched their approach
through his glass with feelings of the most painful
anxiety.   At the first departure of De Grasse to give
Admiral Graves battle, and afterwards as the distant
cannonade of the hostile fleets broke over the sea,
hope reanimated his heart.   But how as he saw the
French fleet quietly riding at anchor in rear of his
works, while this overwhelming force slowly and
steadily took up its position in front, his heart sunk
within him.   Washington, on the other hand, as the
declining sunbeams streamed over the long lines of
glittering bayonets, and polished pieces of the French
artillery, as, with strains of martial music, the steady
columns one after another deployed on the field, and
saw far away the peaks of the French ships of war,
tipped with light, felt that the hour of triumph had
come, and a glorious victory was in reserve for his
country.
    The next day the morning reveille beat cheerily
through the allied camp, and soon the field presented

a brilliant spectacle, as the French on the left and the Americans on the right advanced, and extending in a semicircle entirely round the enemy's works to the river on either side, completed the investment. The British then retired from their advanced works, leaving two redoubts undamaged within cannon shot of their fortifications. The succeeding day the allied troops took possession of the neglected works, the French occupying the two redoubts, while the Americans broke ground for two new ones on the right. In the mean time the heavy siege guns were hurried forward. On the morning of the 1st of October, the British seeing the redoubts begun by the Americans, directed their artillery upon them, and a heavy cannonade was kept up all day and night. For three days and nights the deep reverberations of their guns shook the field, and swept far out over the deep, but not a shot replied. The stroke of the spade and pickaxe, as the earth was thrown up to form the redoubts—the confused hum of workmen erecting tents, and shops, and ovens, and unloading baggage and provisions—the heavy rumbling of artillery waggons as the long line of teams stretched over the uneven ground—and the stern orders of officers, were the only sounds that rose from the allied armies. In the centre, where they met as they swept up in a semicircle from the river, Rochambeau and Washington stationed themselves, and here, too, was drawn up the artillery.

By the 6th of October, every thing was ready to commence the approaches, and, as an omen of good, Washington that very day received the cheering intelligence of Greene's victory at Eutaw Springs. The night came on dark and stormy, and amid the driving rain, unheard in the roar of the blast by the British sentinels, six regiments under the command of Lincoln, Clinton, and Wayne, opened the first parallel within five hundred and fifty yards of the British works on the right. The men were pushed

vigorously all night, and by morning were well covered from the guns of the fortifications. Up to
this time the French and Americans had lost in all
but one officer, and sixteen privates, killed and
wounded. The next two days the enemy fired but
little, and the parallel was completed. On the afternoon of the 9th, the French had established one battery of four twelve pounders, and six mortars and
howitzers, and the Americans another of six, eighteen
and twenty-four pounders, and four mortars and
howitzers. Washington then rode up an eminence,
and through his glass took a long and careful survey
of the enemy's works, and his own batteries. Apparently satisfied he closed his glass, and waved his
hand as a signal. The next moment the French
battery opened, and two hours after the American
blended in its thunder on the right, and the first act
of the tragedy commenced. All night long thunder
answered thunder, echoing over land and sea.

The next day two more French batteries, mounting in all twenty heavy cannon and mortars, and
two American, of six guns, making twenty-six
pieces, were put in operation. Forty-six guns had
now concentrated their destructive fire on the limited
works of the British, and it rained a horrible tempest of shot and shells upon Cornwallis. It was impossible to withstand such a tremendous fire, and
the enemy were soon compelled to withdraw their
guns from the embrasures behind the merlins—and
for the remainder of the day, without firing scarcely
a single shot, they sat silent and sullen within their
works, and took with calm sternness the terrible
pelting.

As night drew on, and darkness slowly settled
over the landscape, the scene became terrifically
grand. The heavens were illuminated with red
shot and blazing bombs, as they stooped on their
fiery track into the doomed garrison, while the deep
silence out of which the explosions came, added to

the solemn terror of the spectacle. These messengers of destruction passed over the town, and dropping amid the shipping beyond, kindled into conflagration four large transports, and a forty-four gun ship.* "The ships were enwrapped in a torrent of fire, which spreading with vivid brightness among the combustible rigging, and running with amazing rapidity to the tops of the several masts, while all around was thunder and lightning from our numerous cannon and mortars, and in the darkness of night presented one of the most sublime and magnificent spectacles which can be imagined. Some of our shells overreaching the town, were seen to fall into the river, and bursting, threw up columns of water, like the spouting monsters of the deep."†

The firing continued all the next day, (the 11th) and at night a second parallel was commenced, within three hundred yards of the enemy's works, and in two days was nearly completed.

Cornwallis still held two redoubts which stood in advance of his works on the left, and from which he could enfilade this second parallel. After a brief consultation it was resolved, therefore, to storm them. To incite the rivalry of the troops, the storming of one was intrusted to the French, under Baron de Viomenil, and the other to the Americans, under Lafayette. The French baron, while preparing for the assault, hinted to Lafayette that he was rather unfortunate in his command, as the American troops were not so reliable as the French in a work of this kind. Lafayette, who had come to look on the Americans as peculiarly belonging to him, was stung by the remark, but quietly replied, "*we shall see.*" Toward evening the storming columns were drawn up, and marched to their respective positions. Two shells were to be the signal to advance. The shell from the American battery rose first, but it had scarcely reached the zenith in

* The Oberon.   † Vide Thatcher's Military Journal.

ts blazing track, before, in another direction, that
of the French mounted the heavens. The next moment the loud shout "FORWARD" rang along the
ranks. Colonel Hamilton led the van of the Americans, and carried away by his boiling courage, strode
in advance of his men, and scorning to wait till the
abatis was removed, mounted over it, and on the
parapet beyond, with but three men at his side.
Waving his sword to his brave followers, crowding
fiercely after him, with levelled bayonets, he shouted
"*On! on!*" and leaped into the ditch. A thrilling
"*huzza!*" replied, and soon the enemy were flying
in every direction. Not a shot had been fired—the
cold steel had finished the work, and in nine minutes'
time. As the loud ringing cheer rose on the evening air, the delighted Lafayette turned to the other
redoubt, and knowing by the sharp firing that it was
not carried, and remembering the sneer of Viomenil,
despatched a messenger to that officer, saying that
his own redoubt was carried, and asking if he needed any help. "Tell Lafayette," proudly replied the
Baron, "that my redoubt will be carried in five
minutes." He made good his word, and soon cheer
answered cheer, and the French and the American
flags waved a salutation to each other, across the intervening space. The loss of the Americans was
only sixty-five killed and wounded, while that of the
French was over a hundred. The *latter* stopped to
remove the *abatis.*

The possession of these redoubts was of the utmost importance, for, besides being relieved from
their flank fire, Washington with batteries erected
there, could enfilade the whole English line.

The girdle of fire was now narrowing to a fatal
interval, and even desperate measures must be resorted to, or the tragedy would close. Cornwallis
therefore determined, it is said, to leave his sick and
baggage behind, and crossing over to Gloucester, cut
up by an unexpected, impetuous assault, the French

and American troops stationed there—mount what he could of his infantry, on the horses of the Duke's Legion, and others which he might be able to seize, and fleeing through Portland, Pennsylvania, and New Jersey, gain New York. This absurd attempt, if ever really intended, was cut short by a sudden storm of wind and rain, which rendered the passage of the river impracticable.

Toward morning of this same night, Cornwallis made a sortie with 800 men on the incomplete French batteries, and carried them, but the Duc de Chastellux advancing to their support, drove the assailants back. The latter succeeded in spiking four cannon, but having time to do it only by ramming the points of their bayonets into the touch-holes, and then breaking them off, the pieces were soon rendered serviceable again. At daylight new batteries in the second parallel were opened, when there was not a spot within the town, unexposed to the desolating fire of the besiegers. The buildings were pierced like a honey-comb—the earth rose in furrows and mounds on every side, as the heavy shot and shells ploughed through, while carcases of men and horses were strewn amid the broken artillery carriages, and wrecks of the works. In short, the camp was completely uncovered, and cannon balls searched every part of it. The English troops stood still in despair, and let the iron storm beat on them. Cornwallis had hoped for succour to the last, but this useless sacrifice of his men, was too dreadful to be long endured, and at ten o'clock the loud beat of the *chamade* was heard in the intervals of the explosions of cannon, and the firing ceased. Cornwallis then sent a flag of truce, requesting a cessation of hostilities for twenty-four hours, to arrange the terms of capitulalation. To this Washington would not consent, fearing that the arrival of the English fleet in the mean time, might alter the aspect of affairs, and allowed him but two hours in which to transmit his proposals.   A rough draft was sent, and the next day the terms of capitulation were agreed upon.   On the 18th, the garrison, with colours cased and playing a melancholy march, moved slowly out of their dilapidated works.   The French and American armies were drawn up on opposite sides of the road with Rochambeau and Washington, splendidly mounted, at the respective heads of the columns, while the fields around were black with thousands of spectators, who had heard of the victory, and flocked hither to see the army and the man who had so long been the terror of the country.   Not a sound broke the deep silence that had settled on the field, save the measured tread of the slowly advancing thousands, and the mournful air of their bands. Cornwallis, wishing to be spared the mortification of the scene, feigned sickness, and was allowed to remain in his quarters.   In his absence, General O'Harra advanced and offered the sword of his commander to Washington.   The latter directed him to Lincoln, who so recently had been compelled to surrender his own at Charleston.   The latter received and immediately returned it to the officer.   Twenty-eight British captains then advanced, with sad countenaces, and surrendered the twenty-eight flags of the army.   Ensign Wilson, only eighteen years of age, was appointed to receive them.   The whole army then laid down their arms, and the humiliating ceremony was over.   Over seven thousand men, with their arms, seventy-five brass, and one hundred and sixty iron cannon, twenty-eight standards, with all the ammunition and stores, and the entire shipping, were the fruits of this victory.

The next day was the Sabbath, and Washington ordered divine service in each of the brigades of the American army.

The news of this glorious victory flew like lightning over the land.   Washington despatched at once one of his aids* to Congress, then sitting in Phila-

* Colonel Tilghman.

delphia.   The swift rider dashed on at a gallop into
the city at midnight—the clatter of his horse's hoofs,
the only sound that broke the silence of the deserted
streets, as he passed straight to the house of McKean,
then president of Congress.   Thundering at the door
as though he would force an entrance, he roused the
sleeping president, saying, "*Cornwallis is taken!*"
The watchmen caught the words, and when they
called "*one o'clock*," they, added, "*and Cornwallis
is taken!*" And as they moved slowly on their
nightly rounds, windows were flung open and eager
countenances were seen scanning the streets.   A
hum, like that of an awakening hive, immediately
pervaded the city.   The inhabitants went pouring
into the streets, while shout after shout rose on the
midnight air.   The old bellman was roused from his
slumbers, and soon the iron tongue of the bell at the
state-house rung out as of old, "PROCLAIM LIBERTY
THROUGHOUT ALL THE LAND TO ALL THE INHABI-
TANTS THEREOF."   The dawn was greeted with the
booming of cannon ; and salvos of artillery, and
shouts of joy, and tears of thanksgiving, accompanied the glad news as it travelled exultingly over the
land.   It is impossible, at this day, to conceive the
wild, ecstatic joy with which it was received.

Not so in England.   It had been sent by a French
frigate, and as if the winds and waves were anxious
to waft it on, the vessel reached France in eighteen
days.   Lord Germain, Secretary of the American
department, received it in London, on Sunday the
25th of November, just two days before Parliament
was to meet. Lord Walsingham, who had been selected to second the address in the house of Peers on the
following Tuesday, happened to be present when the
official intelligence arrived.   Lord Germain immediately called a hackney coach, and taking Lord Walsingham with him, proceeded to Lord Stormount's
in Portland Place.   The three then hastened to the
Lord Chancellor's, when, after a brief consultation,

hey decided to go at once and present the intelligence
to Lord North in person. They reached his house
between one and two o'clock. The dreadful tidings
completely unmanned the stern prime minister.
When asked, afterward, how he took it, Lord Germain
replied, "*As he would a ball in his breast*. For he
opened his arms, exclaiming wildly, as he paced up
and down the apartment during a few minutes, ' *Oh,
God, it is all over !*' As the full extent of the catas·
trophe continued to press on him, he could only repeat,
' *Oh, God, it is all over—it is all over !*'" In it he
saw the hand-writing on the wall, and knew that the
hour of his overthrow had come. At length he became
more composed, and the four ministers began to discuss the matter seriously. They concluded it would
be impossible to prorogue Parliament for a few days,
and the first thing to be attended to, therefore, was
the alteration of the King's speech, which had already
been prepared. Lord Germain then sent a despatch
to the king, George III., at Kew. Sir N. W. Wraxall,
who dined with Lord Germain that day, says that
the first news was publicly communicated at the table.
All were anxious to hear how the king bore it, when
Lord Germain read aloud his reply. It was calm
and composed, bearing no marks of agitation, except,
as Lord Germain remarked, " I observe that the king
has omitted to mark the hour and minute of his writing
with his usual precision."

The opening of Parliament was the signal for the
onslaught of the opposition. This humiliation of the
British arms furnished them the occasion and material for the most terrible invective. Fox, and Burke,
and the younger Pitt, came down with the swoop of
an eagle on Lord North. The stern minister, however, bore proudly up for awhile against the storm,
but was at last compelled to bow before its force.

CHAPTER XIII.

Sickness and Death of young Custis—Departure of the
French Fleet—Destitution of the Troops—Circular Letter
to the States—Lincoln Secretary of War—Greene around
Charleston—Head-quarters at Newburgh—The Temple—
Case of Captain Huddy and Captain Asgill—Defeat of the
English Ministry—Proposal to make Washington King—
Settlement of the Case of young Asgill—Meeting of French
and American Troops at King's Ferry—Destitution of the
Officers—Washington's Views on the Subject—"Newburgh
Addresses"—Proclamation of Peace—Washington ad-
dresses a Circular Letter to the States—Visits Northern
Battle Fields—Disbanding of the Army—Evacuation of
New York—Farewell to the Officers—Washington Surren-
ders his Commission to Congress—His Feelings on laying
down Power—Visits his Land West—Improves his Farm
—Interview with Lafayette, and Letter to him after his
Departure—His Habits of Life—Inefficiency of Congress—
Washington's Views and Feelings respecting it—Society
of the Cincinnati—Convention called to form a Constitu-
tion—Washington elected First President of the United
States.

WHILE Yorktown was yet ringing to the acclamations of the allied armies, Washington received a
blow which made him for a time forget even the
glorious victory which he had achieved. The only
child of his wife, and beloved by him like an own
son, had been from the commencement of the war his
aid-de-camp. The mother's heart was wrapped up
in that youth, and often in battle his safety lay nearer
the father's heart than his own. He rode by the
chieftain's side during the siege of Yorktown, and
saw with pride and exultation the British army march
forth and lay down its arms. But this victory cost
him his life. While the balls of the allied troops
were demolishing the enemy's intrenchments without
the camp, fever was desolating frightfully within.
To this disease young Custis fell a victim. Immediately after he was attacked by it, Washington

directed him to be removed to Eltham in New Kent, whither he was accompanied by his mother and Dr. Craik, the old family physician. The disease made frightful progress, and it was soon apparent that nothing could save him. A messenger was immediately despatched to Yorktown with the melancholy tidings. He arrived in the night. Instantly mounting his horse, taking with him but one officer, Washington started for the sick-bed of the sufferer. The two solitary horsemen galloped silently and swiftly forward, and just as day was breaking, reached the house where the young aid lay dying. Summoning Dr. Craik, Washington eagerly asked, *"Is there any hope?"* The doctor shook his head. He immediately retired into a private room where his wife joined him, and the two remained for a long time closeted together. Washington, with the tears of grief still depicted on his countenance, then remounted his horse and rode back to camp.

He had been exceedingly anxious to enlist the Count de Grasse in an expedition against Charleston, but the orders of the latter forbade his compliance. An attempt to obtain the use of the troops for nearer service was equally unsuccessful. Finding the fleet was about to set sail, Washington went on board the admiral's vessel to pay his respects and express his thanks to the Count, to whom also he presented two superb horses.

The latter having at length re-embarked that portion of the troops commanded by the Marquis St. Simon, sailed for the West Indies. Two thousand Continentals under St. Clair were despatched to the aid of Greene in the South, while the remainder, under Lincoln, embracing those north of Pennsylvania, marched to their winter quarters of New Jersey—the light troops of New York joining their respective regiments in the Highlands. The French under Rochambeau remained in Virginia, the head-quarters of the latter being at Williamsburg. The prisoners being marched to Winchester, Virginia and Fredericktown, Maryland, Lord Cornwallis and the principal officers went on parole to New York. Washington repaired to Philadelphia to consult with Congress on the measures necessary to be adopted for the next campaign. Lafayette in the mean time and many other French officers, had obtained leave to return to France, carrying back with them the warmest feelings of love and admiration for Washington.

Notwithstanding the disasters that had befallen the British army, there were no indications that the government intended to relax its efforts to reduce the colonies. But fearing such would be the impression of the different States, causing them to put forth less energy, Washington, in consultation with Congress, issued two circular letters to them—one asking for supplies, and the other stating the condition and prospects of the army. Said he, "The broken and perplexed state of the army's affairs, and the successes of the last campaign on our part, ought to be a powerful incitement to vigourous preparation for the next. Unless we strenuously exert ourselves to profit by these successes, we shall not only lose all the solid advantages that might be derived from them, but we shall become contemptible in our own eyes, in the eyes of our enemy, in the opinion of posterity, and even in the estimation of the whole world, which will consider us a nation unworthy of prosperity, because we know not how to make a right use of it." Notwithstanding all his efforts, however, there was a general belief that the war was virtually over. Still the government did not act on this basis. Money was sought from France, General Lincoln was appointed Secretary of War to give greater energy and efficiency to that department, and every effort made to put the nation in a posture to renew hostilities the coming spring.

While these events were transpiring at Philadelphia, Greene, with his suffering, half-clad army, was gathering closer and closer around the enemy in

Charleston. The British general, however, maintained his position till the next autumn, when, despairing of help, he at length agreed to evacuate the place, and on the 14th of December marched his troops to the ships, pursued close by the column of Wayne. A short time previous to this, the gallant Laurens was killed in resisting a foraging party.

Washington having spent the winter in constant and arduous correspondence, repaired in the middle of April to the camp at Morristown, and a few days after continued his jurney, and took up his quarters at Newburgh.*

An event happened at this time which exasperated the inhabitants of the colonies greatly, and filled Washington with the deepest indignation. Captain Huddy, commanding a small detachment in Monmouth county, New Jersey, was seized by a party of refugees and taken to New York. A few days after, he was dragged from prison, and carried by Captain Lippincott, at the head of a band of refugees, to Middletown, and there hung. This gallant officer, unmoved by the brutality and ribaldry of his enemies, met his fate with perfect composure. Washington, acting under the decision of a Council of war, immediately wrote to Sir Henry Clinton, demanding that Lippincott should be given up. The British general refusing to comply with the demand, it was determined to execute an English prisoner of equal rank. Lots being drawn by the officers, a young man, only nineteen years of age, named Capt. Asgill, was designated as the victim. The extreme youth of this officer rendered it still more painful for Washington to adhere to his original determination. Previous to his ascertaining who was to be the sufferer he had said, *" Keenly wounded as my feelings will be, at the deplorable destiny of the unhappy victim, no gleam of hope*

* The building he occupied has been retained in its original state, and is now owned by the State of New York, and made the depository of relics of the Revolution.

can arise to him but from the conduct of the enemy themselves." And again, "I will receive no application, nor answer any letter on the subject, which does not inform me that ample satisfaction is made for the death of Captain Huddy on the perpetrators of that horrid deed."

In the mean time Sir Guy Carleton arrived in New York to assume the command in place of Clinton. Previous to his departure great changes had taken place in the aspect of affairs in Parliament. On the 2d of March, General Conway introduced a resolution, declaring that a further prosecution of the war in America, for the purpose of subduing the colonies, was impracticable. The Ministerial party endeavoured to dispose of this by a motion to adjourn. The House divided, when the ministry was found to be in a minority of nineteen. Conway then moved that an address, based on that resolution, be presented to his Majesty. The die was cast. The news spread like the wind, and in a short time the city was in a state of intense excitement. Lord Stormount, anticipating some public demonstration, "wrote to the lord mayor and aldermen to prevent, if possible, illuminations in the city." They were accordingly prevented; but in the gallery on the top of the Monument, there blazed more than a hundred lamps.* Long and loud acclamations rent the air, announcing to Lord North, that the hour of his overthrow had come. The different ambassadors from the various courts of Europe, immediately hurried off expresses to announce the momentous news. The king's reply to the address was equivocal, but to every one acquainted with the state of affairs, it was evident that the opposition had gained a permanent ascendancy. On the 20th, Lord Surrey made a formal motion respecting the removal of the ministers. Lord North interrupted him, saying that the

* Vide Journal and Letters of Curwen, by George Atkinson Ward, page 336.

ministry was about to resign their duties.* As a
last desperate expedient to retain their places, the
Cabinet proposed a dissolution of Parliament. This
was defeated by Thurlowe, the Lord High Chancellor, who, with a virtue that honoured him more
than his office, refused to affix the seals to such an
order.

But as the prospect of peace brightened, the discontent and murmurs of the troops increased. A
long season of idleness had given them time to brood
over and discuss their grievances, while they saw
that the termination of the war would be the signal
of their dispersion, and the end of their power.
Moreover, the independence of the country naturally
begat questions and discussions, respecting the form
of government to be adopted. They had not originally taken up arms against a monarchy, but against
its oppressive acts. The English government was
considered by many of the wisest men of the day to be
a model one, and they wished only to see its like
adopted by their country, when its liberty was once
secured. Besides, the most thorough republicans
had seen quite enough of the government of a Congress. It had lost the respect of both civilians and
officers. It was clear, therefore, that a head was
needed. But this head must be invested with power
sufficient to control and overrule Congress to a great
extent, or it would not possess the efficiency required to coerce obedience. Circumstances, of course,
indicated Washington as that head, and the next
question naturally arose—under what title should he

* It was on "this occasion Lord Surrey happened to espy
Arnold in the House, and sent him a message to depart,
threatening, in case of refusal, to move for breaking up the
gallery; to which the general answered, that he was introduced there by a member; to which Lord Surrey replied,
he might, under that condition, remain, if *he would promise never to enter it again*—with which General Arnold
complied."—*Vide Curwen's Journal and Letters, by Mr.
Ward.*

govern? The officers around Newburgh called meeting after meeting, and warm and eager discussions evinced the deep interest the army took in the form of government that should be adopted. At length an old and respected officer, Colonel Nicola, was empowered to sound Washington on this delicate point. He, therefore, addressed him a letter, in which, after going over the points referred to above, he, in a circuitous manner, at length succeeded in communicating the plain fact, that the army wished him to be "KING." This letter took Washington by surprise. An unexpected danger had arisen before him—an abyss suddenly opened at his very feet. The army was actually assuming the control of the government—the military power appointed the civil. And, more than this, disgusted with the working of republican institutions, it was thinking seriously of setting up a king. Washington seemed doomed ever to wrestle with evils. No sooner did one disappear before his wisdom or strength, than from an unexpected quarter another rose, to fill him with grief, and oppress him with anxiety. But he never seemed to despond, and nothing exhibits the grandeur of his character, more than the promptness and courage, with which he met and overcame every new form of danger. But not in the darkest hour of his country—not in the midst of his starving, naked, dying troops—not when overborne and scattered by the enemy—under no blow with which fate had yet smitten him, did his heart so sink as under the revelation made in this letter. What! become a king over a free people, who had struggled so nobly for their freedom—dash to earth the hopes which had borne them up in the midst of such trials and sufferings, and wrong so deeply human faith, and confidence, and rights, as turn traitor at last? To hint that HE was capable of such turpitude, was striking at the very soul of honour. Pride, grief, resentment, anxiety, commingled and intense, swelled his bosom. "Sir," said he, in reply, "with a mixture of great surprise and astonishment, I have read with attention the sentiments you have submitted to my perusal. Be assured, sir, no occurrence in the course of the war has given me more painful sensations, than your information of there being such ideas existing in the army, as you have expressed, and as I must view with abhorrence and reprehend with severity. For the present the communication of them will rest in my own bosom, unless some further agitation of the matter shall make a disclosure necessary.

"I am much at a loss to conceive what part of my conduct could have given encouragement to an address, which to me seems big with the greatest mischiefs that can befall my country. If I am not deceived in the knowledge of myself, you could not have found a person to whom your schemes are more disagreeable. At the same time, in justice to my own feelings, I must add, that no man possesses a more sincere wish to see ample justice done to the army than I do, and as far as my powers and influence in a constitutional way extend, they shall be employed to the utmost of my abilities to effect it, should there be occasion. Let me conjure you, then, if you have any regard for your country, concern for yourself, or respect for me, to banish those thoughts from your mind, and never communicate as from yourself or any one else, a sentiment of the like nature."

Every line of this letter bears indications of a powerful internal struggle—a struggle to maintain that self-composure and moderation he was wont to exhibit, but which, under this new evil, threatened to forsake him. Incomparable man! intrenched so deeply in virtue, that temptations and the arrows of misfortune rebound from his bosom, without even leaving the mark of their contact. Yet this act seems so in keeping with Washington's whole char-

acter and conduct, that it hardly strikes us as extraordinary. Virtues we never expect to find in others,
we should be supprised not to see exhibited in him.
His actions are all so elevated above the common
track of life, that it would disappoint us to find any
one of them tainted with the imperfections of our
lower sphere.   So harmonious is his character in
every part, that its colossal proportions, can be understood only by comparing him in detail with other
men in similar circumstances.

The case of young Asgill continued to trouble
Washington exceedingly, and his whole correspondence shows a constant and severe struggle between
his feelings, and his sense of duty.   Sir Guy Carleton finding, however, that he was immoveable in his
determination to sacrifice the young man, unless
justice was done to Lippincott, had the latter arrested and tried by court-martial.   It appeared, or was
made to appear on trial, that the latter acted under
the authority of the "*Board of Directors of the
Associated Loyalists*," and hence was not *personally*
responsible.   This transfer of guilt from the individual to a body or corporation, has always been a
favourite method to escape responsibility.   Of course,
the Board of Directors could not be hung—they
could only be disbanded, which was done—a task
not demanding very great sacrifice on the part of
Sir Guy Carleton, as he had in his pocket the power
to make a treaty of peace with the colonies.   This
manoeuvre, however, complicated the matter so
much, that Washington referred it again to Congress, which seemed, by its tardiness, willing to let
death claim its victim in the ordinary way.   Washington wrote bitterly of this neglect of Congress, declaring that his own treatment of that body did not
warrant it, and justifies himself in making the complaint, by asking, "When no notice is taken of my
application ; when measures I might otherwise adopt
are suspended—when my own feelings are wounded,

and others are perhaps suffering by the delay, how is it possible for me to forbear expressing my disquietude?"

In the mean time, young Asgill's mother, crushed to the earth by the dreadful fate impending over her only son, a mere boy in years, appealed, with all a mother's tenderness and earnestness, to the French ministry to intercede with Washington to spare his life. The letter was shown to the king and queen, who were so affected by its pathetic prayer, that they directed the Count de Vergennes to request, as a favour to France, that Captain Asgill might be set at liberty. This spurred up the tardy Congress to action, and the young man was restored to his family.

Sir Guy Carleton at length, in August, gave notice that preliminaries for a treaty of peace had begun at Paris. The war was now closed, and the French troops marched north previous to their embarkation for France. Washington, to show a mark of respect to his allies, took his army down the river to meet them at King's Ferry. He ordered all the troops to be clad and equipped with the clothing and arms furnished by France, and those taken from the English magazines at Yorktown, which the French generously surrendered to the suffering Americans, and drawn up in two opposite lines some distance apart. Between these the entire French army passed, with colours flying—the Americans playing the whole time a French march. These gallant soldiers, with the sensitiveness peculiar to their race, felt this expression of gratitude and compliment deeply, and made the heavens ring with their enthusiastic acclamations. The two armies encamped on and near Verplanck's Point for a month, when the French departed for Boston, and the Americans returned to Newburgh. But just as the evils of war were disappearing, more threatening danger appeared in the attitude of the army. The prospect of relief and of prosperity to the country did not better their

condition, much less forebode any good in the future.
At the very time officers and men were entertaining
their French allies at Verplanck's Point, they were
in a state of the greatest destitution. At Yorktown,
old Baron Steuben had to sell his horse in order to
raise funds with which to give a dinner to the British
officers; and in the last meeting of the troops of the
two nations, the American officers were filled with
mortification that they were unable to return the
civilities of the French. Their families were suffering at home, while they had not the means to pay
for their own daily expenses. Says Washington, in
writing to the Secretary of War, "Only conceive
then the mortification they must suffer (even the
general officers) when they cannot invite a French
officer, a visiting friend, or a travelling acquaintance,
to a better repast than bad whisky (and not always
that) and a bit of beef, without vegetables, will afford
them." In speaking of the result of neglecting to
provide for the army, he says, with that clear foresight which at times almost amounts to the spirit of
prophecy, "Under present circumstances, when I
see such a number of men goaded by a thousand stings
of reflection on the past and of anticipation on the
future, about to be turned on the world, soured by
penury, and by what they call the ingratitude of the
public, involved in debts, without one farthing of
money to carry them home, after having spent the flower of their days, and many of them their patrimonies,
in establishing the freedom and independence of their
country, and suffered every thing that human nature
is capable of enduring on this side of death. I repeat
it, when I consider these irritating circumstances,
without one thing to soothe their feelings or dispel
the gloomy prospects, I cannot avoid apprehending
that a train of evils will follow, of a very serious and
distressing nature. * * I wish not to heighten
the shades of the picture so far as the reality would
justify in doing it— I could give anecdotes of patriot-

ism and distress which have scarcely ever been paralleled, never surpassed, in the history of mankind.
*But you may rely upon it, the patience and long
suffering of this army are almost exhausted,* and
that there never was so great a spirit of discontent as
at present. While in the field I think it may be kept
from breaking into acts of outrage; but when we
retire into winter quarters, unless the storm is previously dissipated, I cannot be at ease respecting the
consequences. *It is high time for a peace."* With
such words on his lips, and such gloomy thoughts
filling his heart, Washington had now marched his
army into winter quarters, and sat down to wait the
result. He wished to visit Mount Vernon, but dared
not leave the army. As in the field of battle, so in
every place where danger thickened, he interposed
his person and influence to save his country. His
predictions proved true; the army soon became unsettled, and from discontent proceeded to loud murmurs and open menaces. It addressed Congress,
but its appeals were met with an unsatisfactory
response, and there now seemed no means left of
obtaining justice except their swords.

At length, March 10th, an anonymous notification
of a meeting of the officers at the Temple* appeared,
followed by a spirited and stirring address, written,
as it afterward appeared, by Major, subsequently
General Armstrong. This address was well calculated
to arouse the army, already in a highly inflammable
state. The author, after speaking of the disappointment every one had felt at the indifference of government to the wants and rights of the army, saying
that "faith has its limits as well as its temper, and there

* A large log building had been erected on the camp-ground
in which to hold meetings of the officers. It was to be dedi-
cated the "Temple of Virtue," by a ball, which Washington opened with the beautiful Mrs. Warren as a partner.
But after the ball broke up, the officers spent the remainder
of the night in such scenes of revelry and riot that it was
called simply the "Temple."

are points beyond which neither can be stretched without sinking into cowardice or plunging into credulity," takes a survey of the past, and in a series of startling questions asks how their services have been rewarded—their toils and sufferings received. Rousing their indignation by the recapitulation of their wrongs, and the contemptuous treatment of their humble petitions, he exclaims—" If this then be your treatment, while the swords you wear are necessary for the defence of America, what have you to expect from peace, when your voice shall sink and your strength dissipate by division; when those very swords, the instruments and companions of your glory, shall be taken from your sides, and no remaining mark of military distinction left but your wants, infirmities, and scars ? Can you then consent to be the only sufferers by this revolution, and retiring from the field, grow old in poverty, wretchedness, and contempt ? Can you consent to wade through the vile mire of dependency, and owe the miserable remnant of that life to charity which has hitherto been spent in honour ? If you can—*go, and carry with you the jests of Tories and the scorn of Whigs, the ridicule, and what is worse, the pity of the world! Go, starve, and be forgotten !*" But if they revolt at this, and would " oppose tyranny under whatever garb it may assume," he says, "*awake, attend to your situation, and redress yourselves !* If the present moment be lost, every future effort is in vain; and your threats then will be empty as your entreaties now." He bids them assume a bolder tone—appoint men to draw up not a " *last remonstrance*"—tell Congress that with them rest the momentous question of war or peace between it and the army—that nothing but redress shall prevail on them to abandon their arms; and if the war, not yet settled, should be protracted, they would, in case their remonstrance was unheeded, " leave the government to its fate," and " retire to some unsettled country to smile in turn, and mock when their fear cometh on." Such language and sentiments fell like coals of fire on the wronged and embittered hearts of the troops, and portended a fearful explosion. The crisis that Washington foretold had arrived, but Heaven enabled him to meet it. He immediately issued an order, calm in its tone and without severity in its language, simply postponing the meeting till next Saturday.* By this sagacious movement he disarmed opposition and gained time. He spent the interval in personal conversations with the principal officers, and by his great influence, wise counsel and promises, allayed the agitation, so that, before the day of meeting, he had undone all the mischief caused by the address.

The Temple was thronged with officers long before the hour appointed for assembling had arrived. Washington, accompanied by his escort, rode over from Newburgh, some three miles distant, and dismounting at the door, walked slowly and solemnly to the raised platform at the farther end. The house was still as the grave, and every eye was bent on their beloved commander, who like a pillar of fire, had moved before them in the long night of their sufferings. Taking out his spectacles, he pleasantly remarked, "*You see, gentlemen, I have grown blind as well as gray in your service.*" This simple expression, falling as it did on hearts strung to the highest tension, thrilled like an electric spark through the assembly. As he glanced over the throng of officers, and saw the veterans on whom he had so often called, and not in vain, in the hour of battle and in the day of danger, he felt sure of support and of success.

The address, calm, kind, conciliating and sympathetic, was listened to with breathless interest. When it was finished, Washington, without adding another word, passed out and remounted his horse. Knox immediately arose and moved that the thanks of the

* This caused another address more moderate in its tone. These are known as the famous Newburgh addresses.

officers be rendered to the commander-in-chief for his address, "and to assure him that the officers recipro- cate his affectionate expressions with the greatest sincerity of which the human heart is capable." A committee was appointed to draft resolutions, which reported in half an hour, declaring " that no cir- cumstance of distress or danger shall induce a conduct that might tend to sully the reputation which they had acquired at the price of their blood and eight years' service." It was also resolved, that "the officers of the army view with abhorrence and reject with disdain the infamous propositions contained in a late anonymous address," etc. The conspiracy was ex- ploded, the crisis past, and the danger over.

Soon after the news of a preliminary treaty of peace, signed at Paris, being received, Washington issued an order fixing the 19th of April, 1787, as the day on which it should be publicly proclaimed to the army. At twelve o'clock, the Temple was thronged, and the joyful intelligence communicated amid deafening plaudits. In the evening the chaplains, in accordance with the orders of the chief, offered up their thanksgiving and prayers at the head of the several brigades. All the military prisoners were set at liberty in honour of the event, and the American camp shook till a late hour with the shouts and laughter of the soldiers.

Having addressed an able, patriotic circular to the several States, Washington made a tour north to visit the battle-fields in that section of the country. Visiting Saratoga, Ticonderoga, and Crown Point— he went west as far as Fort Schuyler, being absent nineteen days. On his return, by the request of the President of Congress, then sitting at Princeton, he repaired to the latter place to give the aid of his counsel, in measures to be adopted for the common welfare.

A large proportion of the officers and soldiers hav- ing gone home on furlough during the summer, Congress, on the 18th of October, issued a proclamation discharging them and all others from service. The army was thus disbanded, with the exception of a small force left at Newburgh. The scene presented at this final breaking up of the army was pitiable. Officers and soldiers were left without funds to reach their homes, and there were cases of individual suffering and destitution, which would move the coldest heart. Playing the tune of Roslin Castle, the mournful requiem, to the measure of which they had always borne their dead comrades to the grave, they paraded for the last time, and then turned sorrowfully away. The only consolation left the poor soldiers, as they scattered the over country, was the farewell address of Washington to them, in which he praised their valour and patriotism, and promised to guard their interests.

At length the orders arrived for the evacuation of New York, and Washington returned to West Point, where he met the few remaining troops, and moved down to Harlaem. On the morning of the 25th November, General Knox advanced to where the Third Avenue and Bowery now meet, and awaited the withdrawal of the British troops. As they retired he advanced, and as the last British soldier left the soil of freedom, cannon on the battery thundered out their joy. Washington and Governor Clinton then made a formal entrance, escorted by a corps of Westchester light-horse. The two rode side by side, followed by the Lieutenant-Governor, and Council four abreast, these by Knox and the officers on horseback, eight abreast, and they in turn by mounted citizens, the procession being closed by the Speaker of the Assembly and citizens on foot. The next Monday Clinton gave a grand entertainment to the French minister and officers, and the city rung to the clamours and joyful shouts of the people.

Thursday, the 4th of December, was fixed upon for the final leave-taking of Washington with his officers. This was the most trying event in his whole career,

and he summoned all his self-command to meet it
with composure; Knox, and Greene, and Hamilton,
and Steuben, and others, assembled in Francis'
tavern, and waited with beating hearts, the arrival
of their chief.   Not a sound broke the silence as he
entered, save the clatter of scabbards as the whole
group rose to do him reverence.   Casting his eye
around, he saw the sad and mournful countenances
of those who had been his companions in arms,
through the long years of darkness that had past.
Shoulder to shoulder they had pressed by his side
through the smoke of the conflict, and with their
brave arms around him, met every shock of misfortune with undaunted souls.   He had heard their
battle-shout answer his call in the hour of deepest
peril, and seen them bear his standard triumphantly
on to victory.   Brave hearts were they all and true
on whom he had leaned, and not in vain.   A thousand proofs of their devotion came rushing on his
memory—their toils and conflicts rose before him,
and the whole history of the past with its chequered
scenes swept by, till his heart sunk in affection and
grief.   Advancing slowly to the table, he lifted the
glass to his lips and said, in a voice choked with
emotion: *"With a heart full of gratitude and love,
I now take leave of you; I most devoutly wish that
your latter days may be as prosperous and happy as
your former ones have been glorious and honourable."*
A mournful, profound silence followed this short address, when Knox, the friend of his bosom, advanced to say farewell.   But neither could utter a word
—Knox reached forth his hand, when Washington
opening his arms took the stern warrior to his heart.
In silence, that was more eloquent than all language,
each advanced in turn, and was clasped in his embrace.   Washington dared not trust himself to
speak, and looking a silent farewell, turned to the
door.   A corps of light infantry was drawn up on
either side to receive him, and as he passed slowly

through the lines, a gigantic soldier, who had moved beside him in the terrible march at Trenton, stepped forth from the ranks, and reaching out his arms, exclaimed, *"Farewell, my dear General, farewell!"* Washington seized his hardy hand in both of his and wrung it convulsively. In a moment all discipline was at an end, and the soldiers broke their order, and rushing around him seized him by the hands, covering them with tears and sobs of sorrow. This was too much for even his strong nature, and as he moved away his broad chest heaved and swelled above the tide of feelings, that had at length burst the sway of his mighty will, and the big tears rolled unchecked down his face. Passing on to Whitehall, he entered a barge, and as it moved out into the bay, he rose and waved a mute adieu to the noble band on shore. A mournful cry was borne back over the water, and the impressive scene was over.

He had now severed every link that bound him to public life except the formal surrender of his commission to Congress. Passing on to Annapolis, where this body was in session, he was followed by the excited population, escorted by military, and hailed with shouts at every step of his progress. On the 23d of December he publicly gave in Congress his resignation as commander-in-chief of the army. A profound silence reigned during the address, and many an eye was suffused as he closed with the impressive words, "Having now finished the work assigned me, I retire from the great theatre of action, and bidding an affectionate farewell to this august body under whose orders I have so long acted, I here offer my commission, and take my leave of all the employments of public life." The next morning he left for his farm, having for eight years and a half served his country without reward, and achieved her independence without a spot on his name. As he slowly travels back to his quiet home, bereft of every title, a simple American citizen, neither asking nor wishing honour, he is an object of surpassing interest. The history of the world cannot match him.

After long years of toil, of suffering, and of danger, he arrived at the summit of power only to descend quietly again, leaving all his authority with that Congress which had so often distrusted, neglected, and even plotted against him. Superior to temptation, superior to passion, too lofty even for unholy ambition, he showed how unjust had been their suspicions, how impolitic and injurious their opposition, and how much above them he had been both in wisdom and in virtue. It required no effort for him to surrender power. Having wielded it solely for his country's good, he laid it down as a burden the moment his country's peace and liberty was secured.

Arriving at home, Washington found that during eight years' absence, his affairs had become sadly deranged, and he immediately set about their adjustment.

The executive council of Pennsylvania had instructed the delegates of the State to lay before Congress the question of remuneration for his long and faithful services. But the latter would listen to no proposition on the subject. Simple in tastes and habits, he had enough for his wants, and sought only repose. At first it was difficult to roll away the weight of care that had so long rested on him. He could not, he said, get better of the habit of reflecting on the business of the day immediately after waking, but as he became gradually accustomed to his freedom, he felt, as he wrote in a private letter, "like a wearied traveller, who, after treading many a painful step with a heavy burden on his shoulders, is eased of the latter, having reached the haven to which all the former were directed, and from his house-top is looking back and tracing with an eager eye the meanders by which he had escaped the quicksands and mires which lay his way, and into which none but the all-powerful Guide and Disposer of events could have prevented his falling." In a letter to Lafayette, to whom he always opened his heart, he said, "At length I am become a private citizen on the banks of the Potomac, and under the shadow of my own vine and fig-tree, free from the bustle of a camp and the busy scenes of public life, and am solacing myself with those tranquil enjoyments of which the soldier who is ever in pursuit of fame, the statesman whose watchful days and sleepless nights are spent in devising schemes to promote the welfare of his own, perhaps the ruin of other counteries, as if this globe was insufficient for us all, and the courtier who is always watching the countenance of his prince, in hopes of catching a gracious smile, can have very little conception. I have not only retired from all public employments, but I am retiring within myself, and shall be able to view the solitary walk, and tread the paths of private life with a heartfelt satisfaction. Envious of none, I am determined to be pleased with all; and this, my dear friend, being the order of my march, I will move gently down the stream of life until I sleep with my fathers."

How simple yet self-sustained—how elevated in his own grand thoughts above all that this world can bestow. Through all the mazes and darkness and storms of the last eight years—apparently chained and fettered by circumstances to the earth, he had nevertheless, in the might of a great soul, been steadily soaring up to the serene heights of contemplation, to the pure atmosphere of unworldly thought.

During the summer Washington devoted most of his time to the improvement of his farm and entertaining guests that crowded to see him from almost every quarter of the world. Lafayette again visiting this country in August, he had an affectionate interview with Washington, and then started on a northern tour, while the latter made his sixth and last expedition west to visit his lands in that section.

Supplied with tents, pack-horses, and provisions, he set out in September on a journey of six hundred and eighty miles through the wilderness. He went by the old Braddock route, where had occurred the most important events of his early life. What strange reminiscences that journey must have called up, and what a change had passed over his destiny and that of his country since he first trod that desolate region. As he stood by Braddock's grave, the past and present met, and presented strange and most striking contrasts. A mere stripling, dressed in an Indian hunting-shirt, he had first passed over this route on his perilous journey as a commissioner to the French. The second time he traversed it in search of his first battle. The third ended in the terrible defeat of Braddock; and now, after such a long interval, he trod it a portion neither of French or English territory, but of a free land of which he was the deliverer. Having surveyed his lands on the Monongahela, he returned by a long and tedious route through the wilderness. The result of his investigations were given in an able letter to the Governor of Virginia, in which he portrayed clearly the advantage that would arise from a water communication through the country. With that sagacious forethought which was so characteristic of him, he had from the first foreseen and foretold the advantages of such communications both in the north and south.

On his return he again met Lafayette at Richmond, where both were received with public honours. The latter then accompanied him to Mount Vernon, and the two friends enjoyed that sweet communion which is known only to pure and virtuous hearts. His visit being completed, Lafayette reluctantly took his departure, accompanied by Washington as far as Annapolis. The tender nature of the relation that existed between these great and good men, and the warmth of Washington's affection, may be seen in the following simple, touching etter to the Marquis after their separation, December 8th.

Says he, "In the moment of our separation, upon the road as I travelled, and every hour since, I have felt all that love, respect, and attachment for you with which length of years, close connection, and your merits have inspired me. I often asked myself, as our carriages separated, whether that was the last sight I should ever have of you? And though I wished to say no, my fears answered yes. I called to mind the days of my youth, and found that they had long since fled, to return no more; that I now was descending the hill that I had been fifty-two years climbing, and that, though I was blest with a good constitution, I was of a short lived family, and might soon expect to be entombed with my fathers. These thoughts darkened the shades and gave a gloom to the picture, and consequently to my prospect of seeing you again."

In consequence of his letter to the Governor on the importance of internal navigation, the Legislature organized two companies (the Potomac and James River) and gave to him as a compliment, fifty shares of the former and a hundred of the latter. These he refused to accept, unless he was allowed to appropriate them to some public use. This was granted, and he made over before his death the shares of the James River Company to Liberty Hall Academy, in Rockbridge county, now Washington College, which has been materially benefited by the donation. The fifty shares of the Potomac Company, were bequeathed for the endowment of a University in the District of Columbia. What has become of them perhaps the directors of the Chesapeake and Ohio Canal Company, into which they were merged, can tell. During this year he became interested in a scheme of Lady Huntington for the civilizing and Christianizing the Indians, but Congress declining to grant any land for the colonists that were to be sent out in accordance with this plan, it fell through. The past year Washington had devoted himself almost entirely to his farm, and having at length got it in a proper state, he the next spring [1785] turned his attention to ornamenting the grounds by transplanting forest trees. He saw every tree taken up, moved, and put down in the place assigned it. He also added to his stock of fruit trees, and might be seen almost daily in the season for pruning, with knife in hand, clipping his orchards. That hand, which had so long grasped the sword, and made its light terrible on the battle-field, now wielded with far greater delight the pruning hook.

Still the privacy and seclusion he sought were not wholly attainable, for, though holding no public place, he was the most public man on the continent. Hence, between correspondence, applications for aid or advice, and a constant throng of visitors, only brief respites of tranquil leisure could be enjoyed. Nothing but the regularity of his habits allowed him any privacy. Rising before the sun, he shut himself up in his study till breakfast time. After breakfast he mounted his horse, taking such guests as chose to accompany him, and rode over his farms. On his return he again withdrew to his study till three o'clock, when he dined, and devoted the rest of the day to amusement.

In October of this year, Houdon took the bust of Washington, previous to making his celebrated statue of him, which had been ordered by the State of Virginia. Chantry and Canova both executed statues of him, but Houdon's is considered the best ever taken.

While Washington was thus enjoying the comparative quiet of his home avocations, events were gathering to a crisis, which showed clearly that the arm that had saved the republic in war, would soon be needed to rescue it from as great perils in peace. The impossibility of governing the country by a

Congress, grew every day more and more apparent. With such a mediator as Washington between it and conflicting interests and sections, it had floundered through the war almost miraculously, but now, when left entirely to itself, it only got involved deeper and deeper in embarrassments. Besides, if the jealousies of the separate States prevented them from yielding competent powers to Congress, to save the country from an invading army, it was clear they would operate with stronger force in peace. This state of things Washington declared would, unless remedied, effect "*our downfall as a nation.*" "This," he says, "is as clear to me as A, B, C, and I think we have opposed Great Britian, and have arrived at the present state of peace and independence to very little purpose, if we cannot conquer our own prejudices." He declared that, although a simple citizen, and hence as liable as any one to feel the effects of tyrannical legislation, he had no fear of "too great an extension of Federal powers," but he "predicted the worst consequences from a half-starved, limping government, that appears to be always moving on crutches and tottering at every step." Again, in writing to Mr. Jay, he says: "To be fearful of investing Congress, constituted as that body is, with ample authorities for national purposes, appears to me the climax of popular absurdity and madness. Could Congress exert them for the detriment of the public, without injuring themselves in an equal or greater proportion? Are not their interests inseparably connected with those of their constituents?" On the contrary, he feared that they would be too timid in the use of authority, held back by the fear of losing their popularity. Without going into the particular measures in which jealousy of giving too much power to Congress exhibited itself, the result at length reached was—*a confederacy too weak to hold together.* Unless a change could be effected, therefore, a dissolution of the Union was inevitable.

This deplorable state of things filled Washington
with the deepest anxiety and grief. To see the
goodly fabric he had reared with so much toil and
care fall to the ground, and the nation he had saved
from bondage become the by-word and scoff of kings,
was a contemplation from which he turned away
with an aching heart. He strove by every exertion
in his power to avert such a catastrophe. Events at
length shaped matters so that the threatened peril
was escaped. Maryland and Virginia appointed
commissioners to form a compact relative to the
rivers Potomac and Potomoke, and part of Chesapeake bay. These proposed other commissioners to
make arrangements for maintaining a naval force in
the Chesapeake, and to establish a tariff of duties on
imports, to which the laws of both States should
conform.* This suggested to the Legislature of
Virginia to request other States to send deputies also
to the convention, to take into consideration the
trade of the United States, and adopt regulations,
and suggest laws to Congress for an harmonious arrangement of the whole question of internal commerce. Only five States sent deputies, and these
without power to settle anything. They, however,
accomplished one grand work—they made a report,
showing the evils of the present federal system—and
recommended a convention of deputies from all the
States to take the matter up. Virginia appointed
seven, Washington heading the list. He, however,
hesitated about being "swept back into the tide of
public affairs." Besides, he had written a circular
letter to the States, declaring his intention to resign
the presidency of the Cincinnati Society, and saying
he could not be present at their next meeting in
Philadelphia. Now this meeting was to take place at
the very time appointed for the convention. If he
should, therefore, go to the latter, after he had refused to attend the former, the distinction would

* Vide Marshall's Life of Washington.

seem to be invidious—in short, it would look like a desertion of his old companions in arms. Especially would this construction be natural, as the society was very unpopular—being denounced unsparingly as anti-republican. It had a badge like foreign nobility—it admitted foreign officers—membership was hereditary in the family of the members, while it allowed the accumulation of funds to any amount. Although Washington had through his influence shorn it of its most objectionable features, and thus silenced some of the heaviest attacks of its enemies, still it was unpopular. But Congress having sanctioned the convention, thus giving it a legal character, and so arranged matters that the meeting of the Society of the Cincinnati should be a week earlier, thus giving Washington an opportunity to attend it first and explain his views, he at length, at the solicitation of men earnest for the welfare of their country, yielded his scruples and accepted the appointment.

The convention assembled the second Monday in May, with every state but Rhode Island represented. Washington was appointed president, and the result of its deliberations was the CONSTITUTION OF THE UNITED STATES.

This is not the place to go into the history of that convention. Its deliberations lasted four months, and the conclusions it came to were the fruit of a compromise. That jealousy which had hitherto rendered the confederacy comparatively powerless, on the one hand, and the strong desire to see great power concentrated in the Federal head, on the other, operated as antagonisms, and produced at last that which neither party could fully approve. The constitution was not stringent enough for the Federalists, and too stringent for the Democrats—and thus being a compromise, had the most determined, positive men of both parties for its enemies. Such patriots as Patrick Henry, Colonel Mason, Gerry and others opposed it.

It was, however, submitted to the different States, and Washington waited with the deepest solicitude their decision. The prospects of its adoption were poor at first, but they gradually brightened, and at length it became the constitution of the United States.

The first step, as provided by the new constitution, was the election of a President. All eyes were immediately turned to Washington. But averse to entering again the cares of public life, unwilling to incur the suspicion of being ambitious, and loth to part with pursuits so congenial to his tastes, he was disinclined at first to yield to the general wish. Being plied, however, on the only weak point he possessed, love of country, he was at last persuaded to accept the nomination, and was elected first President almost by acclamation.

CHAPTER XIV.

Washington prepares to leave Mount Vernon—He Visits Fredericksburg, to take leave of his Mother—He departs for New York—The Journey—Triumphal Arch at Trenton—Reception at Elizabethtown—Arrival and Welcome at New York—Installation of Washington as first President of the United States—He declines Compensation for his Services—Illness, and Recovery—Debate on Titles—Death of the Mother of Washington—Organization of the Departments—Washington makes a Tour through the Eastern States—The Seat of Government is removed from New York to Philadelphia—Establishment of a National Bank—Washington Visits the Southern States—Development of Factions—He desires to retire at the close of his term of Administration—Is induced to serve a Second Time—Re-inaugurated President of the United States—The French Revolution—England Declares War against France—Washington issues a Proclamation of Strict Neutrality—Opposition and Enmity—M. Genet's arrival, and Assumption—Washington requests his Recall—Relations with England—Jay's Mission—Opposition to the Tax on Distilled Spirits—Proclamation to the Insurgents—Calling out of the Militia—Restoration of Peace—Jay's Treaty—Its Ratification—Resignation of Randolph, Secretary of State—Washington's Private Life—Description of his Appearance on State occasions—Imprisonment of Lafayette—Washington's Successful Intercession in his behalf—Washington's Farewell Address—Election of John Adams—Washington returns to Mount Vernon—His Life in Retirement—Difficulties with France—Washington appointed Commander-in-Chief—He returns to Philadelphia to Organize the Army—Interview with Dr. Logan—Napoleon—Terms of Accommodation at Paris—Washington at Mount Vernon—His last Illness—His Death—His Character.

THE election of Washington being in effect unanimous, he was perfectly aware of the result, as soon as mere newspaper returns could be received from different parts of the country, and hence at once began to make preparations for leaving Mount Vernon. Speaking of the long interval before entering on his duties, he, in a letter to Knox, said, "This delay may be compared to a reprieve, for in confidence I tell you, (with the world it would obtain little credence,) that my movements to the seat of government will be accompanied by feelings, not unlike those of a culprit who is going to a place of execution, so unwilling am I, in the evening of a life nearly consumed in public cares, to quit a peaceful abode for an ocean of difficulties." His last act before commencing his journey north, was one of filial devotion. His aged mother lived in Fredericksburg, and thither he directed his steps. After embracing her, he told her of his election to the office of President, and added that, before he entered upon his duties, he had come to bid her "an affectionate farewell." "So soon," said he, "as the public business which must necessarily be encountered in forming a new government, can be dispensed with, I shall hasten back." "You will see me no more," she mournfully replied. "My great age and the disease which is rapidly approaching my vitals, warn me that I shall not be long in this world. But you, George, fulfil the high destinies which Heaven has assigned you. Go, my son, and may Heaven and your mother's blessing be with you, always." Overcome by the solemnity of her manner and the declaration, which he knew to be true, he leaned his head on her aged shoulder and wept. That great grand heart, which made him so terrible on the battle-field, was yet full of the tenderest affections, and clinging still to that dear parent, whose love for him was deep and unfailing as the ocean tide, he wept like a child when told he should see her no more. Not when on the disastrous field he stops and gathers around him, by his majestic bearing, the broken fragments of his army, nor when he stands at the head of the republic which he has saved, does he appear so great, so worthy of the adoration of men, as here when he leans and weeps on the neck of his mother.

The scene and the characters furnish one of the noblest subjects for an artist found in American history.

From the time that the result of Washington's election was known, till his departure for New York, congratulations and warm expressions of delight poured in upon him in such a constant flow, that if anything could have reconciled him to the abandonment of private life, the pleasure he was evidently giving to others would have effected it. Still it required a great effort to surrender the quiet of his home, and the pursuits so congenial to his tastes, for the turmoil of public life. In a letter to Edward Rutledge, he says: "You know, my dear sir, I had concentrated all my schemes, all my views, all my wishes within the narrow circle of domestic enjoyment. Though I flatter myself the world will do me the justice to believe, that, at my time of life and in my circumstances, nothing but a conviction of duty could have induced me to depart from my resolution of remaining in retirement, yet I greatly apprehend that my countrymen will expect too much of me."

At length, on the 16th of April, he bade a reluctant adieu to his farm and rural occupations, and commenced, what was at that time the long, tedious journey to New York. Instead of being elated with the proud position he was to occupy, or of feeling his pulses quicken at the whisper of ambition, a touching sadness pervades his whole conduct, and he inserts in his diary: "About ten o'clock I bade adieu to Mount Vernon, to private life and to domestic felicity; and with a mind oppressed with more anxious and painful sensations than I have words to express, set out for New York in company with Mr. Thompson and Colonel Humphreys, with the disposition to render service to my country in obedience to its call, but with less hope of answering its expectations."

His journey was more like the triumphal march of a Roman conqueror, than the quiet progress of an

American citizen.   The news of his approach preceded him, and from every farm-house and shop and hamlet—from every valley and green mountain slope, the grateful delighted people came swarming in crowds along the highway to greet him—and shouts, and blessings, and delirious welcome marked every step of his passage.   At Trenton, the inhabitants wreathed with garlands the bridge of Assanpink, where he lay encamped the night before he marched on Princeton, and over it bent an arch on which was inscribed:

THE HERO WHO DEFENDED THE MOTHERS,
   WILL ALSO PROTECT THE DAUGHTERS.

At the farther extremity a crowd of little girls, robed in white, with garlands around their temples, and baskets filled with flowers in their hands, stood ready to receive him as he passed beneath the arch.   Behind them, at a little distance, was still another throng composed of maidens also, arrayed in white, and still farther in the back ground the aged fathers and mothers.   As the stately form of Washington passed through the arch, those children and maidens burst forth into a song of welcome.   The chorus was, "*Strew your hero's way with flowers,*" and as its sweet and thrilling melody rolled heavenward, they cast their flowers in his path.   The aged parents behind with glad tears streaming down their cheeks; the daughters in front, arrayed in white; the little children nearer still, their eyes beaming with excitement, and the associations connected with the spot, all combined to render the scene one of the most tender and touching in the whole life of Washington: and as the clear and ringing chorus, "*Strew your hero's way with flowers,*" rose and fell in thrilling cadences on the air, the enthusiasm broke over all bounds, and a long shout of exultation, and "Long live Washington," shook the banks of the stream. The beautiful ranks opened to receive the chieftain as he advanced, and looking down on the throng of sweet upturned faces, the tears gathered in his eyes, and with a quivering lip, he waved his hat and passed on. At Elizabethtown an elegant barge, manned by thirteen New York pilots, neatly dressed in white, was waiting to receive him. The shore was lined with people, and as Washington stepped into the boat, they sent up a long and deafening shout. At a given signal the gaily decorated craft pushed from the shore, and as the oars dipped into the water there went forth a blast of trumpets, and triumphant strains of martial music floated out over the water. Boat after boat from New York met and fell in the procession, and when the open bay was reached, a whole fleet of vessels, flaunting with ribbons and gay streamers, and crowded with spectators, gathered around the barge of Washington, singing pæans of victory, while shouts blending in with the pealing of bugles and strains of martial music swelled the enthusiasm beyond all bounds. The whole vast concourse swept on toward the Battery, each wharf as they passed sending up a wild welcome from its crowded head, while the thunder of artillery received him at the place of landing. As he stepped on shore, one united loud "LONG LIVE WASHINGTON" rose from the multitude. Passing through lines of military, he moved to the head of the troops, when the whole fell in and passed up Broadway to the Park, beside which was the house selected for his residence. At night the city was ablaze with illuminations and innumerable fire-works, and the streets shook to the shouts of the populace. Wholly unlike all other men throughout his whole career, so here the passionate enthusiastic welcome he received did not waken up one of those feelings of gratification or pride which seem inherent in our very nature. Intent only on benefiting others, thinking sadly over the disappointments he might create, he says: "The departure of the boats which attended me, and joined on this occasion, some with instrumental music on board—the decorations of the ships, the roar of cannon, and the loud acclamations of the people which rent the air as I passed along the wharves, filled my mind with sensations (contemplating the reverse of this scene, which may be the case after all my labours to do good) as painful as they were pleasing." The pageantry which usually intoxicates the soul, and the adoration which naturally awakens pride, had no power over him. Thinking only of the country he loves better than his life, his mind passes on to the time when his best efforts may be misjudged and his fondest hopes disappointed. Good as he was great, so good that virtue in him seemed not the result of effort, but the natural breath of his being, he seems not to know what it is to resist temptation.

I do not design to go into a detailed history of Washington's administrations, for that would embrace the entire range of the political history of the country for eight years, sufficient in itself to constitute a large work.

His installation into office as First President of the Republic, April 30th, was accompanied with imposing ceremonies. At nine o'clock in the morning all the bells in the city called the inhabitants each to his own place of worship, to invoke God's blessing on their future chief, and on the country over which he was to preside. In those days the superintending providence of the Almighty was believed in, and his pleasure or displeasure considered worth regarding by those who loved their country. At noon the troops paraded in front of Washington's house, when he, attended by the committees of Congress and Heads of Department and Foreign Ministers, entered his coach and rode alone to the Federal Hall. Chancellor Livingston administered the oath of office in presence of the people, who ratified it with long and loud acclamations of "Long live Washington, our President."

After delivering his inaugural speech to the two Houses of Congress, he went on foot to St. Paul's church, where prayers were read by the bishop. At night bonfires and illuminations and transparencies kept the city in a tumult of joy, and lighted out the day, which had so auspiciously begun.

Acting on the principle which had governed all his public life, Washington announced to Congress that he would receive no compensation for his services, and asked only that his necessary expenses should be paid by the State.

The different departments not yet being organized, Jay, Secretary of Foreign Affairs, and Knox, of War, under Congress continued to fulfil the duties of their respective offices, while a Board of Commissioners had charge of the Treasury. From these Washington obtained full reports, which he himself went over carefully and in detail, and condensed with great labour. He at once, with his usual method, set out to master every department of government.

From the first he was constantly overrun with persons calling to pay their respects to him, distracting his attention and occupying the time which he needed for public purposes. This embarrassed him much ; still it was a delicate matter to avoid the evil on the one hand, and yet escape the charge of imitating royalty in exclusiveness on the other. After much discussion and correspondence, it was finally agreed upon to set apart one hour on each Tuesday, between three and four, to receive visitors.

In June, he was taken seriously ill, and suffered much from an affection of one of his limbs, and for a time mortification seemed almost certain to follow. Dr. Bard was his physician, and while the danger was imminent, never left his side. From the anxiety manifested in the countenances of those who surrounded him, and the constant assiduous attentions of the physician, Washington became convinced that his case was a very critical one. One day, therefore, being left alone with Dr. Bard, he looked him steadily in the face, and then asked him to say candidly, what he thought would be the termination of his disease. The doctor replied that he had great hopes of his recovery, still there were serious grounds of apprehension. *"To-night or twenty years hence,* (calmly replied Washington,) *makes no difference; I know that I am in the hands of a good Providence."* He was ill six weeks, and it was a long time before he regained his usual strength and health. When he had recovered sufficiently to ride out by being bolstered up in his seat, it was touching to witness the sad and anxious countenances of the people as he passed, and the murmured blessings that followed his receding carriage were worth more than thrones and diadems.

From the first, there had been in the Senate a singular excitement respecting the title with which the President should be addressed, and a joint committee from both Houses, was at length appointed to report in this important matter. Their united report was, that no titles should be given. But this was too democratic for the Senate, and a hot debate followed in that body, which was stopped only by the previous question. The committee of the Senate, however, reported that it was proper to style the President *"His Highness, the president of the United States of America, and Protector of their Liberties."* The House of Representatives took no notice of this, but addressed a communication to the President simply as *" President* of the United States."

The excitement extended to the country, and the newspapers took up the subject with great warmth, but the republican spirit at length overcame all opposition, and the subject of titles was dismissed from the public mind.

In August, Washington received intelligence of the death of his mother, who had reached the advanced

* Life of Dr. Samuel Bard, by Professor Mc Vickar.

age of eighty-two. In reply to a letter from his sister, announcing the sad event, he said, "Awful and affecting as the death of a parent is, there is consolation in knowing Heaven has spared ours to an age which few attain, and favoured her with the full enjoyment of her mental faculties, and as much bodily strength as usually falls to the lot of fourscore. Under these considerations, and a hope that she is translated to a happier place, it is the duty of her relatives to yield due submission to the decrees of the Creator."

Washington carried into his life, as President, the same habits of strict economy that he practised at home, yet he found it impossible often to come within the sum of 25,000 dollars, which had been voted by Congress as his salary, and he was compelled to resort to his private income to meet his current expenses. Only the departments of treasury, war, and foreign affairs, were formed during this session of Congress, and it adjourned in the latter part of September. Hamilton was appointed Secretary of the Treasury. Jefferson was at the head of Foreign Affairs, which office also embraced that of Secretary of State, while Knox was retained Secretary of War. Edmond Randolph was appointed Attorney General, and John Jay placed at the head of the Supreme Court. The different appointments caused much perplexity, but the President, by adopting one principle, viz., to select men solely for their qualifications and capacity to fill the office in which they were placed, succeeded in convincing most of the wisdom of his course.

When Congress adjourned, he took advantage of the session to make a tour through the Eastern States. He was absent a month visiting various localities, but he studiously avoided Rhode Island, because she had not yet come into the Union. Every step of his progress was an ovation, and he could scarcely move without having his carriage surrounded by enthusiastic multitudes, while congratulations poured in upon him from every side. The proofs of rising prospects and increasing wealth which appeared in the New England States gratified him exceedingly, and he returned to New York not only much improved in health, but cheered also at the great satisfaction of the people with their new government.

The passing of proper laws, the payment of foreign loans and home debts, and all the machinery of a new government, by turns occupied Congress, and necessarily deeply engaged the mind of the President. A short visit to Rhode Island, which had at length come into the confederation, was the only relaxation he took during this session of Congress. At its adjournment he visited again Mount Vernon, but its quiet walls and secluded haunts could no longer distract his attention from public affairs. Our relations with England were not promising, while those with Spain assumed a still more unfavourable character. These two nations, one at the north and the other at the south, stirred up the Indians to hostilities, and kept our frontiers drenched in blood.

In his dealings with the Indians Washington always adopted a humane policy. He recognized all their rights, and treated them in every way as if they were civilized nations. His course would doubtless have been successful but for the intrigues of England and Spain. At length, however, forbearance became a crime, and he commenced open hostilities against them. The defeat of Harmar, and afterwards of St. Clair protracted the war, so that it continued through nearly the whole first term of his administration, and drew heavily upon the Treasury. There is an incident connected with the overthrow of St. Clair, which illustrates Washington's love of justice. An adjutant general, Sargent, who was wounded in the battle, escaped and hastened immediately to the seat of government with the disastrous news. Being a man of wealth he was enabled to get transported rapidly, and hence outstripped the courier several days.

Washington invited him to Mount Vernon, where
he remained till St. Clair's despatches arrived; yet
during all this time he never asked a question respecting St. Clair's defeat.   Although much distressed and
deeply anxious about the event, he was afraid he
might hear a partial account, and thus be induced to
decide unjustly.   Sargent said that during the whole
time he was at his house no one would have known a
battle had been fought but from Washington's inquiry
every morning respecting his wound.

At length, in 1793, Wayne was appointed commander of the forces in the north-west, and by one
terrible blow prostrated the Indians and restored
peace.

Congress having changed the place of sitting from
New York to Philadelphia—it met at the latter
place in the fore part of December, 1790.   The
National Bank, established this session, awakened
much opposition, but Washington, after mature deliberation, approved the project.   With Congress he
was deeply engaged during the winter in completing
various plans of policy, and laboured unceasingly to
perfect the government.

When Congress adjourned in the spring, he made
a trip to the Southern States, going as far south as
Savannah.   The whole journey of eighteen hundred
and eighty-seven miles, was made with the same
horses and carriage.   His presence everywhere was
hailed with delight, and he returned more and more
convinced that a great and glorious future was before
his country.

At the next session of Congress, the elements of
those two terrible factions, Federalists and Democrats, began to develop themselves more fully, and
filled Washington with the gravest fears.   Hamilton and Jefferson, represented those two classes of
opinions in the country, and soon assumed a hostile
attitude to each.   The former was for concentrating
more power in the central government, by removing

it from the federal states—the latter for taking more power from the federal government, and bestowing it on the states.   Seeing the bitterness of feeling which these different views caused between the Secretary of the State and of the Treasury, and fearing the animosity that it would create in the country, Washington used all his influence to bring about some reconciliation or compromise.   His letters and appeals to each breathed the spirit of kindness and patriotism, but nothing could allay the fire which had been kindled, and it blazed on fiercer and fiercer till the overthrow of the Federalists, in the war of 1812, ended the strife.   Against himself, as the leader of the Federalists, all the venom and malignity of the Democrates were levelled.

In a letter, speaking of the political animosity which had pursued him, he says, " Until within the last year or two I did not believe that parties would or ever could go the length I have been witness to ; nor did I believe, until lately, that it was within the bounds of probability, hardly within those of possibility, that, while I was using my utmost exertions to establish a national character of our own, independent, as far as our obligations and justice would permit, of every nation of the earth, and wished, by steering a steady course, to preserve this country from the horrors of a desolating war, I should be accused of being the enemy of one nation, and subject to the influence of another ; and to prove it, that every act of my administration would be tortured, and the grossest and most invidious misrepresentations of them be made, by giving one side only of a subject, and that too in such exaggerated and indecent terms as could scarcely be applied to a Nero, a notorious defaulter, or even to a common pickpocket.   But enough of this.   I have already gone further in the expression of my feelings that I intended."   It seems hardly possible, at this day, that men could have been found so lost to reason, truth and virtue, as to load Washington with aspersions such as he here himself declares were heaped upon him. But political malignity always becomes personal, and is just as deep and unsparing.

When the term of his administration drew to a close, he hoped he would be permitted to retire to private life, and spend the remnant of his days in quietness and peace. His known reluctance to accept the first nomination, created great fear among all parties, lest he should utterly refuse to accept a second. The hatred of faction gave way to alarm in view of the disaster that might follow his desertion of the helm of state. Those who afterward became his enemies urged him not to think of retiring, declaring that his commanding influence and wisdom were indispensable in order to fix firmly and for ever, that which had only settled in o transient repose, and if he did not remain the whole tottering fabric would fall. By all that was dear to the Union, they besought him not to expose it at last to overthrow. They knew that Washington's weak side was his patriotism, and they plied it with appeals and arguments in turn, till at length he yielded, and on the fourth of March, 1793, was again inaugurated President of the United States.

For the last three years the rumblings of the coming earthquake in France, had startled Europe from her long repose, and Washington watched the progress of events with the deepest interest, not only from the principles that were involved, but because the fate of Lafayette, he knew, would be that of republicanism. At length the Bastile fell, and Lafayette, through Tom Paine, sent to him the key of that strong fortress of tyranny and secret dungeon of oppressed men. The National Assembly also wrote to him a letter, closing with "May the individuals of the two nations connect themselves by a mutual affection, worthy of the friendship which unites the two men, at this day most illustrious by

their exertions for liberty, Washington and Lafayette." But the joy which the apparent regeneration
of France had occasioned, gave way to alarm as the
car of revolution rolled on in blood, and soon Europe
was in arms to arrest its further progress. England
at length having joined the crusade for the overthrow of liberty, declared war against France. This
threatened to augment most seriously the difficulties
that surrounded the commencement of Washington's
second administration. He immediately submitted
to the cabinet several queries respecting the policy
it was necessary and right for the United States to
pursue.

They having answered these inquiries, he by their
advice issued a proclamation of strict neutrality between the two powers. Not only from the fact that
France was struggling for liberty, the very principles of which had been transplanted from this country, but also as toward an ally and friend who had
just poured out her treasures and her blood in our
behalf, this proclamation kindled into fury all the
latent fire that had been so long partially smothered,
and from that moment the secret opponents of Washington became more and more his open enemies, and
a relentless war was waged against him till the close
of his administration. It was denounced as faithless
to France and obsequious to England, and worse
than all, declared a mere party measure adopted by
his advisers to secure a political end. The charge of
striving to force this country into a useless war, of
sympathising with wholesale slaughter of women and
children, were retorted on the democrats, and that
strife of factions rapidly gathered strength, and increased in ferocity, till it shook the federal government to its foundation.

While this state of feeling was dividing the country, M. Genet, minister from the French Republic,
arrived on our shores. Landing at Charleston, he was
received with such enthusiasm, that he believed the

United States were ready to rush to arms to help their sister republic, who was only striving to carry out the principles of liberty and equality which her armies had learned in our long and almost hopeless struggle. He went so far in his extravagancies as to order vessels to be fitted out as privateers in the very harbour of Charleston. These in time returned with prizes, which called forth a remonstrance from the British minister. The American government immediately forbade the fitting out of privateers, which brought forth angry and impertinent letters from Genet to the Secretary of State. He even disregarded the declaration of our government, and kept sending vessels to sea, which, in turn, caused more stringent measures to be adopted. This, of course, excited still more violently the French minister, and in the blindness of his rage, he dared to threaten Washington, declaring that he had usurped the power of Congress, and even hinted at an appeal to the people. Washington, feeling that the dignity of the country required that he should no longer tolerate this insulting conduct, directed that a request should be immediately forwarded to France, asking his recall.

This had become more necessary, from the fact that the French minister had begun to organize societies over the land favourable to his views.

Our relations with England were still more complicated. Morose from the loss of her fairest colonies, and determined to narrow down their limits as much as possible, she held forts on our soil, and sustained the Indians on our frontiers in their hostilities. She also impressed American seamen, and her privateers seized American goods on the high seas. To vex France, she also issued two orders, one authorizing the seizure of all American ships laden with breadstuffs, if bound to France; and another detaining all vessels freighted with goods or provisions, sailing from any port of France, or of her colonies.

These orders struck down, with a single blow, neutral rights. The President, in his annual message of 1793, took strong ground against them, declaring that the United States should claim and maintain its rank among the nations of the earth, and that the only way to secure peace, was to let it be known they were always ready for war. Fox, the leader of the opposition in the British Parliament, alluding to this message of Washington, drew a contrast between Washington and the ministers of Great Britain, in which he said, "How infinitely more wise must appear the spirit and principles manifested in his late address to Congress, than the policy of modern European courts. Illustrious man! desiring honour less from the splendour of his situation than from the dignity of his mind." He declared that the potentates of Europe sank into insignificance before him. "For him," said he, "it has been reserved to run the race of glory without experiencing the smallest interruption to the brilliancy of his career."

Erskine, afterwards Lord Erskine, wrote to him, saying, "I have a large acquaintance among the most valuable and exalted classes of men, but you are the only human being for whom I ever felt an awful reverence." As in the field, so in the cabinet, amid internal troubles and outward difficulties, his character shone forth with undimmed and constant brilliancy.

The difficulties with the mother country, however, kept increasing, and a second war seemed inevitable. As a last experiment, he determined to send Mr. Jay as minister plenipotentiary to England, to see if an amicable adjustment might not be made, and a treaty secured. Congress, turbulent with contending factions, at length adjourned, and the public mind turned to watch the effect of Jay's mission. But while much hope was entertained from his efforts, and the prospects of peace seemed to brighten, internal insurrections menaced us with more immediate and imminent dangers.

The tax on distilled spirits, which had been levied by Congress, a few years before, caused at this time great commotion. This, instead of subsiding with time, had kept on increasing, and now had reached a point threatening civil war. The officers were violently treated in the discharge of their duties, and bands of armed men set at defiance the authority of the general government. Painful as the alternative was, there was no choice left but to meet force with force. Preparatory to more serious measures, Washington issued a proclamation, commanding the insurgents to disperse before the first of September, or he would call out the militia to enforce the laws. The insurgents, numbering some sixteen thousand men, were congregated chiefly in the western part of Pennsylvania, but there were many also in New Jersey, Maryland, and Virginia. Washington was, at length, compelled to call out the militia. Accompanied by the Secretary of War, he visited the two places of rendezvous of his troops (Cumberland and Bedford), and then ordered them to march across the Alleghanies, and disperse, at all hazards, the insurgents. This imposing force overawed all opposition, and peace was restored without the shedding of blood.

The constitution requiring all treaties to be ratified by the Senate, Washington issued a proclamation requiring that body to assemble in June. I shall not here discuss that treaty. That it was such an one in its conditions as this country would at present make, no one believes. Washington did not wholly approve of it. He considered it incomplete and unsatisfactory, but the choice lay between this treaty and war. As the national honour had not been sacrificed, he thought this partial settlement of the difficulties between the two countries was better than an open rupture.

The Senate occupied two weeks in discussing this treaty, and finally only by a bare constitutional majority, advised its ratification. Nor could this vote be obtained except by excluding one article in it which prohibited American vessels from transporting molasses, sugar, coffee, cocoa, and cotton either from the United States or West India Islands to any other part of the world. Ships not exceeding seventy tons might carry the products of the States to the islands—nothing more. This of course the southern members would not for a moment listen to. The conduct of the Senate embarrassed Washington much. He was not certain that this could be called a ratification till the excluded article was re-submitted to the English government. If it was not, his signature to the treaty would be clearly improper. In the mean time a senator gave a copy of the treaty to the editor of a newspaper, and it was published. Thus cast before the public, unaccompanied by any of the diplomatic correspondence, explanations, &c., it kindled into sudden and fierce conflagration the angry feeling that had been partially slumbering. It was everywhere received with clamours, with taunts and fierce denunciations. Public meetings were called, and national pride and honour so vehemently appealed to, that a feeling was raised, which for a time threatened to sweep away the administration. Bold and threatening resolutions were sent to the President from Boston. To settle the question at once, and allay the disorders, and prevent public demonstrations against the executive, Washington called together his cabinet, and submitted to it the question of ratification. All but the Secretary of State advised it, and on the 18th of August he signed the treaty with the condition annexed, and sent it accompanied by a remonstrance to the British government against the obnoxious article, which had the desired effect, and it was excluded.

The day after Randolph, Secretary of State, resigned

his office.   A letter from M. Fauchet, the French
minister, deeply implicating his character, had been
intercepted at sea and sent to the British cabinet, and
by them forwarded to Mr. Hammon, British minister
at Philadelphia.   The latter gentlemen handed it to
the Secretary of the Treasury, who translated it.
Washington was immediately sent for at Mount
Vernon, and as soon as he arrived the letter was
shown him.   In it were plain intimations that Mr.
Randolph was working for the interests of the French
nation, and could be brought over still further, in
short was false to his position, and the trust reposed
in him.   Washington in the presence of his cabinet,
quietly handed Mr. Randolph this letter and asked
for an explanation.   The latter was indignant that
the matter had not been submitted to him privately
before it was brought before the cabinet, and the same
day handed in his resignation.   In a note to the
President, he requested that this letter, so deeply
implicating his character, should be kept secret until
he should have time to secure a thorough and full
investigation, which would establish his innocence.
His request was complied with, yet he seemed in no
hurry to have the investigation take place, and never
did exculpate himself wholly from blame.   He delayed,
hesitated, pretended papers were withheld, &c., when
he had free access to all of Washington's papers,
both public and private, with full permission to use
them in his own defence.   Mr. Pickering, from the
War Department, took his place, and James M. Henry,
of Baltimore, became Secretary of War.
   When Congress assembled (March 29th), it refused
to enact the laws necessary to carry the treaty into
effect, and by a large majority passed a resolution
requesting the President to lay before them his instructions to Mr. Jay, with all the documents bearing
on the negotiations.   To refuse would be regarded a
tacit confession of improper conduct on his part, by
his enemies, while to accede would be yielding the

prerogatives belonging to his office, and allowing encroachments which the constitution had guarded
against. That instrument placed the treaty-making
power in the President and Senate. Though much
troubled at the dilemma in which he was placed,
Washington refused to comply with the request, and
gave as his reasons the unconstitutionality of it, and
the dangerous and mischievous tendency of adopting
such a precedent. The House was confounded with
this refusal, and for days after the hall rung with
angry denunciations, which were combated with
solid reason and calm judgment. The members,
however, at last yielded. Still there was much bitter
feeling engendered throughout the country, and one
would have thought from the tone and language of
many of the papers, that Washington, instead of being the defender and liberator of his country, was its
greatest foe and oppressor. But as he had stood
amid a mutinous army, under the suspicious distrust
and neglect of Congress, and in the night of disaster
and gloom of the revolution, so now he stood calm
and unmoved amid the assaults of political foes, and
under the false accusations of unscrupulous detractors.

In writing to Knox, he says, in speaking of his
enemies, "The consolation, however, which results
from conscious rectitude, deprives their sting of its
poison;" and again, "Next to a conscientious discharge of my public duties, to carry along with me
the approbation of my constituents, would be the
highest gratification my mind is susceptible of; but
the latter being secondary, I cannot make the former
yield to it, unless some criterion more infallible than
partial (if they are not party) meetings can be discovered, as the touchstone of public sentiment. If
any power on earth could, or the Great power above
would, erect the standard of infallibility in political
opinions, there is no being that inhabits this terres-
trial globe, that would resort to it with more eagerness

than myself, so long as I remain a servant of the public. But as I have found no better guides hitherto than upright intentions and close investigation, I shall adhere to those maxims, while I keep the watch; leaving to those who will come after me, to explore new ways, if they like or think them better.'' In looking back from this distant point to the party feuds and political distractions of those times, how lofty, how infinitely elevated above all his traducers and enemies does the character of Washington appear. Living in an atmosphere of truth and sincerity, seeking no selfish ends, but with an eye single to his country's good, he by the mere majesty of virtue alone, triumphs over all opposition, and finds his way to the innermost heart of the people. Neither partizan leaders nor loud-mouthed demagogues, nor cunning detractors could shake the faith of the nation in him their more than father. That faith of the masses in his truth and integrity, rising over all the efforts of political leaders, is the highest eulogium on their own virtue, and shows that they were worthy of the freedom they had achieved.

In the mean time, Randolph had prepared his vindication, as he termed it. The pamphlet was characterized by great bitterness of feeling, and unjust aspersions of Washington. Ingersoll, of Philadelphia, happened to go into the apartment of the latter just after he had received it, and witnessed one of those sudden explosions of wrath which terrified the beholder. He found, he said, Mrs. Washington, and other ladies. cowering in a corner like frightened doves over which an eagle is hovering, and gazing with silent terror on the wrathful visage of Washington, fairly blazing with passion, while a torrent of invective poured from his lips. The duplicity, falsehood, and ingratitude displayed in this `` vindication,'' for a moment unmanned him, and he became the lion he sometimes was on the battle field.

The private life of Washington, at this time, was

characterized by the great formality which distinguished that period. He rarely, if ever, walked out alone, but, dressed in black, with a secretary on each side, and all three wearing cocked hats, would stride majestically and silently along, apparently no more conscious of the presence of those attending him, than of his own shadow. He often took drives in a handsome cream-coloured coach, with four horses, into the country; but on Sunday, in going to church, he used but two horses. The livery of his servants was white, trimmed with gay colours, and when, with his coach and six, he drove to the Senate, his appointments bore but faint resemblance to those of a republican President of the present day. The following description, by Richard Rush, of his appearance on great state occasions, is very graphic:—

"Washington was to open the session of Congress by going in person, as was his custom, to deliver a speech to both houses, assembled in the chamber of the House of Representatives. The crowd was immense. It filled the whole area in Chestnut street before the State House, extended along the line of Chestnut street above Sixth street, and spread north and south some distance along the latter. A way kept open for carriages in the middle of the street, was the only space not closely packed with people. I had a stand on the steps of one of the houses on Chestnut street, which, raising me above the mass of human heads, enabled me to see to advantage. After waiting long hours as it seemed to a boy's impatience, the carriage of the President at length slowly drove up drawn by four beautiful bay horses. It was white, with medallion ornaments on the panels, and the livery of the servants, as well as I remember, was white, turned up with red, at any rate a glowing livery—the entire display of equipage at that era, in our country generally, and in Philadelphia in particular, while the seat of government, being more rich and varied than now, though fewer in number. Washington got out of his carriage, and, slowly crossing the pavement, ascended the steps of the edifice, upon the upper platform of which he paused, and, turning half round, looked in the direction of a carriage which had followed the lead of his own. Thus he stood for a minute, distinctly seen by everybody. He stood in all his civic dignity and moral grandeur—erect, serene, majestic. His costume was a full suit of black velvet, his hair, itself blanched by time, powdered to snowy whiteness, a dress sword by his side, and his hat held in his hand. Thus he stood in silence, and what moments those were! Throughout the dense crowd profound stillness reigned. Not a word was heard, not a breath. Palpitations took the place of sounds. It was a feeling infinitely beyond that which vents itself in shouts. Every heart was full. In vain would any tongue have spoken.

"All were gazing, in mute, unutterable admiration. Every eye was riveted on that form—the greatest, purest, most exalted of mortals. It might have seemed as if he stood in that position to gratify the assembled thousands with a full view of the father of his country. Not so. He had paused for his secretary, then, I believe, Mr. Dandridge, or Colonel Lear, who got out of the other carriage, a chariot, decorated like his own. The secretary, ascending the steps, handed him a paper—probably a copy of the speech he was to deliver—when both entered the building. Then it was, and not till then, that the crowd sent up huzzas, loud, long, earnest, enthusiastic."*

To the embarrassments which surrounded him resulting from Jay's treaty, and his own refusal to send to Congress the papers relating to it, was added the deepest solicitude for his friend the Marquis de Lafayette. This nobleman was at first the idol of

* From the Republican Court, by Rufus Griswold.

the French populace, but in the opposing tides of
revolution he had been stranded, and was now lan-
guishing in an Austrian prison.   We had at that
time no representative in Austria or Prussia, and
Washington could not therefore appeal directly to
those governments, still through our ministers at
other foreign courts, he interceded unceasingly for
his deliverance.   He sent also to the British cabinet
requesting its powerful mediation, but in vain.   As a
last resort he wrote direct to the Emperor of Germany,
asking as a boon, a great personal favour, that Lafayette might be permitted to come to America, promising to regard sacredly any instructions under which
he might embark.   At length he had the pleasure of
hearing that Lafayette had been delivered over to
the American consul at Hamburg, and of communicating the glad intelligence to young George Washington Lafayette, who had been for two years a
resident in his house.   Harassed by the difficulties
with France and England, that seemed farther than
ever from permanent settlement—well convinced in
his own mind that unless the policy and spirit of the
British government changed, another war with that
power was inevitable, he saw with relief his second
term of office drawing to a close.   Turning a deaf
ear to all proposals for re-elction for a third term, he
devoted much of his thoughts to a Farewell address
to his countrymen.   Among the noble legacies which
he left to his country, none is more worthy of being
treasured in the heart of the people than this address.
Through all its wise counsels, noble maxims, and
elevated thought, the spirit of undying patriotism
breathes like the undertone of an organ, through
some grand soul-subduing anthem.   His bitterest
foes forgot for awhile the animosity they had entertained against him, and the hardest heart was touched
by this last proof of devotion to his country.   That
address will never grow old.   It cannot be read at
this day without awakening patriotism in the dullest

heart, and causing it to sigh over the ambition and selfishness of our modern rulers.

John Adams was elected to fill his place, and he waited to witness his inauguration. Afterwards a grand parting entertainment was given to Washington. Sparks relates the following anecdote as coming from Bishop White: "On the day before President Washington retired from office, a large company dined with him. Among them were the foreign ministers and their ladies, Mr. and Mrs. Adams, Mr. Jefferson, and other distinguished persons of both sexes. During the day much hilarity prevailed, but on the removal of the cloth, it was put an end to by the President, certainly without design. Having filled his glass, he addressed the company, with a smile, as nearly as can be recollected in the following words; 'Ladies and gentlemen, this is the last time I shall drink your health as a public man: I do it with sincerity, wishing you all possible happiness.' There was an end of all pleasantry. He who gives this relation, accidentally directed his eye to the lady of the British minister, Mrs. Liston, and tears were running down her cheeks."

A simple citizen once more, he turned his weary footsteps toward the quiet shades of Mount Vernon. But the people knew no difference, he was still their father, and military escorts, and crowds of men and women, blocked his way, and he was borne by the huzzas and blessings of the people, almost to the gates of his dwelling.

It is difficult, at this remote period, to review in detail his administration, for it is impossible to conceive the difficulties and embarrassments that surround an entirely new government, whose foundation stones and whole structure were so widely different from all others. Things which now appear plain as noonday, had to be worked laboriously up to the light, and the first rude form reduced from the chaotic elements before the details could be fur-

nished.   It is enough, however, to convince us of
the wisdom and sagacity of his administration, that
a glorious future rested on it as a base.   No other
man could have put us even on firm footing, much
less consolidated us into a sound government, strong
at home and respected abroad.

Much has been said of the hostile feeling entertained toward Washington by Jefferson, and many
charges and criminations grew out of this animosity.
These differences, however, were chiefly political—
the two stood at the head of the factions, Federalists
and Democrats, and of course differed *toto cælo* in
their views of government.   Political animosity, it
is well known, is the most unsparing of all hatreds,
and yet it could not weaken the personal regard in
which Jefferson held Washington.   Although, in
the famous letter to Maggie, it is said he included
Washington among those whom he affirmed were
forming the government on aristocratic and mon-
archical principles, yet he declared that "his integrity was the most pure, his justice the most inflexi-
ble" he had ever known.   "He was indeed," said
he, "*in every sense of the word, a wise, a good, and
a great man.*"   Still he let his political views warp
too much his conduct, and Washington might justly
feel, that the former had repaid kindness with ingratitude, and confidence with suspicion.

One who had seen Washington at the capitol, invested with power, and the head of a great people,
and afterward watched him an industrious farmer,
repairing his barns and attending to his crops and
cattle, would have obtained a vivid conception of the
genius of our institutions, and the simple grandeur
of him who had founded them.

The year that followed his retirement from office
was a quiet routine of daily duties, and he thus
makes one day describe the whole.   He rose with
the sun and breakfasted early.   His morning meal
being accomplished, he says, in a letter to a friend,

"I mount my horse and ride round my farms, which employs me until it is time to dress for dinner, at which I rarely miss to see strange faces, come, as they say, out of respect for me. And how different is this from having a few social friends at a cheerful board. The usual time for sitting at table, a walk and tea, bring me within the dawn of candle-light, previous to which, if not prevented by company, I resolve that as soon as the glimmering taper supplies the place of the great luminary, I will retire to my writing-table and acknowledge the letters I have received. Having given you the history of a day, it will serve for a year." This, however, is a very incomplete account. The numberless deeds of charity—the constant acts of kindness—the devotion to the interests of others, especially to those of his country, which revealed the soul and heart, are not recorded. The knowledge of them scarcely lived in his own heart, for with him to do good, was his natural life, so that acts of virtue were no more noted by him than his pulsations. But while engrossed in these quiet scenes, the driftings of that terrible storm which was rocking Europe to its foundations, began to be felt on these shores, and it seemed impossible that this country should escape being drawn into its vortex. The intolerant French Directory insulted our Minister, Mr. Pinckney; French cruisers plundered our commerce, and indignities were heaped upon us that rendered farther indifference impossible, if the country hoped to secure the respect of nations. Preparations for war were therefore set on foot, and all eyes were turned once more to the nation's great leader to take again his place at the head of the army. The President nominated him Commander-in-Chief, and the Senate confirmed the nomination. Just having struggled through a long life of toil and suffering, and now treading the verge of the grave, a re-entrance to that life and struggle was painful in the extreme, yet to the last, thinking

only of his country's welfare, he declared he would
not entrench himself "under the cover of age and
retirement, if his services should be required in re-
pelling the enemy." He therefore accepted the appointment, and repaired to Philadelphia, and was
soon again merged in public affairs.

While here a little incident occurred, which exhibits in a striking light one feature of Washington's character. Mr. Logan had arrived as a sort of
secret envoy from France, sent here, it was supposed, at the instigation of Mr. Jefferson. Our properly
appointed plenipotentiary had gone over to adjust,
if possible, the differences of the two countries, and
this private underhand policy disgusted Washington. The following account of the interview between him and Mr. Logan, as furnished by his own
memoranda of the visit, is interesting, from the
strong light in which it displays the characteristics
of the two men.

"*Tuesday*, November 17th, 1778, Mr. Lear, our
secretary, being from our lodging on business, one of
my servants came into the room where I was writing, and informed me that a gentleman in the parlour
below desired to see me—no name was sent up. In
a few minutes I went down, and found the Rev. Dr.
Blackwell and Dr. Logan there. I advanced toward
and gave my hand to the former; the latter did the
same toward me. I was backward in giving mine.
He possibly supposing from hence, that I did not recollect him, said his name was Logan. Finally, in
a very cool manner, and with an air of marked indifference, I gave him my hand, and asked *Dr.
Blackwell to be seated*, the other *took* a seat at the
same time. I addressed *all* my conversation to Dr.
Blackwell; the other *all* his to me, to which I only
gave negative or affirmative answers, as laconically
as I could, except asking how Mrs. Logan did. He
seemed disposed to be very polite, and while Dr.
Blackwell and myself were conversing on the late

calamitous fever, offered me an asylumn at his house if it should return, or I thought myself in any danger in the city, and two or three rooms by way of accommodation. I thanked him, slightly observing there would be no call for it." Then follows some account of a conversation on political matters, in which Washington, without departing from his freezing politeness, gave some home thrusts, all of which however failed to disconcert the imperturbable Logan. The whole interview evidently made a decided impression on Washington, and chiefly, one would infer, from being perhaps the only instance in his life in which his manner, usually so impressive, or if he chose, crushing, failed to disconcert the object toward which it was directed. This Logan was evidently an extraordinary man, in his way, making up in impudence what he might lack in character. The minute details, as given by Washington, show that the persevering politeness with which the fellow met all his studied coldness of manner, somewhat annoyed him. The climax of impudence, however, was reached when he replied to this lofty hauteur with the kind and charitable invitation of protection and an asylum in his house. One of these little bursts of light which sometimes falls on and enlivens a whole picture, is here thrown on Washington's character, when, after saying, he answered him coolly and laconically as he could, he adds, "*except asking how Mrs. Logan did.*" Here the true innate chivalry of the man leaks out.

The organization of the army was a difficult matter, and went on slowly, yet the energy and skill he exhibited in fitting it for active operations, showed that although verging on his threescore and ten, "his eye was not dim, nor his natural force abated."

In the mean time, however, Bonaparte had vaulted to power, and our plenipotentiaries at the French capitol found little difficulty with him in coming to terms of accommodation. But Washington never

lived to see this great object of his heart accomplished
On the 12th of December, he rode out to visit his
farms as usual. But the day was cold and rainy,
and after several hours of exposure, he returned wet
and chilled. The next morning the ground was
covered with snow, and he remained at home. Toward evening he complained of a sore throat, and his
voice grew hoarse. He was aware he had taken cold,
but thought little of it, and spent the evening reading the newspapers, and in social conversation with
his family. As he was retiring his private secretary,
Mr. Lear, advised him to take something for his cold.
He replied, "You know I never take anything for
colds ; let it go as it came." But in the night he
awoke with a chill, while the inflammation in his
throat had greatly increased, and continued rapidly
to grow worse, so that by morning his breathing was
laboured, and his voice became so choked, that he could
with difficulty articulate. He sent for one of his
overseers to bleed him, and then despatched a messenger to Alexandria, nine miles off, for his old friend,
Dr. Craik. The disease, however, made such rapid
progress, that the family became alarmed, and sent
for Dr. Brown, who resided near. But the remedies
of these physicians, together with the aid of Dr. Dick,
who arrived later in the day, were powerless against
the disease, which seemed from the first to have taken
complete mastery of its victim. He was in the full
vigour of life, and this sudden arresting of nature in
its course, made the last struggles doubly violent.
He lay and panted for breath, feeling, as the hours
wore slowly away, that each one carried him nearer
to the point of suffocation. But not a murmur escaped
him. Calm and resigned, he bore his sufferings with
that serene composure which had characterized him
in all the trials of life. At half-past four in the
morning he sent for Mrs. Washington, and requested
her to bring two wills from his desk. She did so.
He then bade her burn one and keep the other. At

eight he got up and dressed and sat by the fire, but was compelled immediately to lie down again.   At noon he made another attempt, but could not rise. As evening approached, he turned to Dr. Craik and whispered, "*I die hard, but I am not afraid to die. I* believed from my first attack that I should not survive it.   My breath cannot last long."   The efforts to relieve him aggravated very much his sufferings, while they were powerless to arrest the disease. Feeling that they were wholly useless, he in a feeble voice thanked the physicians for their kindness, but requested them to desist and let him die quietly. Nothing remained to be done, therefore, but to sit and watch the steady but rapid ebbings of life.   At ten he whispered in a low, husky, scarcely articulate voice, "I am going—have me decently buried, and do not let my body be put in the vault in less than three days after I am dead.   Do you understand me ? Well."   It was fearful to see with what ruthless power disease crushed that strong nature down.   But with perfect composure he withdrew his hand from that of his secretary and placed it on his own pulse, as if to count its last strokes.   In a few moments his face changed, his hand slipped from his wrist, and he ceased to breathe. Mrs.   Washington, who was sitting on the foot of the bed, turned to the doctor and asked, "Is he gone ?"   "Yes," was the reply.   "'Tis well all is over.   I shall soon follow him ; I have no more trials to pass through."   His breath grew shorter and feebler every moment, till a little after ten, when he ceased to breathe.   As they looked on the lifeless form, it seemed scarcely possible that one, strong and healthy the day before, had really passed away, and death seemed doubly terrible, when with one quick blow it could carry so much to the grave. He went out with the century that gave him to the world ; and as his life had gilded its progress, so his death darkened its close, and hung weeds of mourning round the one that was dawning.

The account of his sickness and death were received in almost every part of the Union, and the nation was paralyzed. Solemn ceremonies attended the funeral, and a long procession accompanied the body to the tomb. Minute guns were fired as it sadly wound its way through the wintry grove, and his old war horse, saddled and bridled, walked riderless beside the coffin. The noble steed he would never mount again, and to that cold cheek the sullen gun would never send the blood, as of yore. His work was finished—his battles were over—and the more than Emperor laid in the peaceful sepulchre. As the sad news slowly travelled over the land, a cry of bitter anguish followed it, for sudden darkness had fallen on the nation, a calamity overtaken it, for which there seemed no remedy and no solace. The people were his children—and they mourned him as orphans. Even the young Republic of France, then struggling for life, put on crape, and for ten days all the flags and standards wore mourning, as though some great national loss had been sustained. The young Napoleon, flushed with victory, issued the following order of the day to his army: "Washington is dead. This great man fought against tyranny; he established the liberty of his country. His memory will always be dear to the French people, as it will be to all freemen of the two worlds; and especially to the French soldiers, who, like him and the American soldiers, have combated for liberty and equality." On the same day the trophies brought from Egypt were displayed in the *Champ de Mars*. After the splendid pageant was over, Bonaparte, with all the civil and military authorites of Paris, and accompanied by the most illustrious generals of his army, repaired to the Temple of Mars, now the Hotel des Invalids, to hear a funeral eulogium on Washington, by M. de Fontaine. When the news of his death was received on board the vessel of Lord Bridport, then commanding the British fleet, composed of nearly sixty ships of the line, lying at Torbay, he lowered his flag half-mast in token of mourning. Every ship followed his example.* Nothing can illustrate the grandeur and elevation of Washington's character more, than these tokens of respect from nations with whom we were on the verge of hostilities. The history of the race furnishes no such instance. Over the hatred and prejudices engendered by war—over faction, and falsehood, and detraction—that character rises so pure and exalted, that the worst passions of man, his deepest settled prejudices, shrink from assailing it; nay, humbled and rebuked, reluctantly do it reverence.

CHARACTER OF WASHINGTON.

No one, in tracing the history of our struggle, can deny that Providence watched over our interests, and gave us the only man who could have conducted the car of the revolution to the goal it finally reached. That revolution, from its incipient movements to its final close, was the most remarkable that ever occurred in human history. The principle of personal freedom had its birth in the teaching of Christ. From that time on, through all the changes of religious and political life, man struggled to make this principle practical. But at the first moment of success he was frightened back by the pathless, untrodden, and boundless field that stretched out before him. On this continent it began in asserting that taxation and representation should go together. But passing from this narrow basis to freer and broader grounds, it at length made a clean sweep of kings and titles and privileges of every class, and a common farmer presided over the destinies of a republic that acknowledged no law but the will of the

* Vide Sparks' Life of Washington.

people.   From the time Washington entered on his duties as commander-in-chief, to the close of the war, he moves before us like some grand embodiment of virtue and power.   To quote the language used by myself on another occasion—whether bowed in fasting and prayer before God in behalf of his country, or taking the fate of the American army on his brave heart—whether retreating before the overwhelmed numbers of the enemy, or pouring his furious squadrons to the charge—whether lost in anxious thought, as his eye seeks in vain for some ray amid the gloomy prospects that surrounds him, or struggling amid the broken ice of the angry Delaware, in the midst of the wintry storm—whether galloping into the deadly volleys of the enemy in the strong effort to restore the fight, or wearing the wreath of victory, which a grateful nation placed with mingled tears and acclamations on his brow, he is the same self-collected, noble-minded and resolute man.

Perhaps there never was a public character so little understood in the various qualities that go to make it up as that of Washington.   He is called the father of his country, and that phrase is supposed to embrace the entire man.   We contemplate the perfected, finished character, never thinking of the formation state.   We look at the fruit alone, without asking what kind of blossom produced it.

Notwithstanding men's intimacy with human character, they will insist that an extraordinary one, whether good or bad, must be an exception to general rules—from the outset a monstrosity either in vice or virtue.   But a great and good man is as much the result of growth as a tree.   It passes through different stages, indeed through errors, acquires virtue by self-control, and wisdom by experience, and so matures gradually.

There are certain moral qualities which adhere to one through life, and do not change amid all the vicissitudes to which he is exposed.   An utterly elfish boy, is usually a selfish man; and a child of generous and noble impulses, no matter to what depravity he may in other respects descend, generally retains those characteristics to the last. So Washington had as high a sense of honour when a boy as when a man; was as elevated and unselfish in his feelings at sixteen, as at sixty; but in all other respects he was totally different. In later years, repose and calm dignity were his great characteristics—in youth, ardour, and enthusiasm, and love of adventure. In the former period of his life, peace was his desire and delight, while in earlier days, he loved the excitement of war, and the scope it gave to his untried energies. In youth, the clangor of battle was music to his ears, but in riper age there was no sound so sweet to him as the song of the husbandman.

Washington might have been just as good, but never so great a man, had he possessed the same mildness and quietness of character in his childhood that marked his later manhood. A certain amount of combativeness—destructiveness, some may term it—is absolutely necessary to give a man energy, self-determination, and power. Every good and great man, from Moses to Paul, and Paul to Luther, has possessed it—much more, every wicked, ambitious spirit which has succeeded in changing the world. A warm and fiery heart is indispensable to great resolution and force. This Washington possessed. Cool and correct in judgment, yet quick in his impulses; methodical and clear in all his business arrangements, yet bold and fearless in danger, he possessed the basis of a strong and elevated character. At times during his career, he was exceedingly impetuous, and on a few occasions his passions burst through all control. His whole appearance then became terrible, and the beholder shrunk appalled from his presence. But these volcanic exhibitions were of rarest occurrence, and served only to indicate the fire that was slumbering below. Without them we should never have known how marvellous was his self-control.   He that *ruleth* his spirit, and not he that has no spirit to rule, is the truly great man.   It is one of the astonishing features of his life, that amid the perfect chaos of feeling into which he was thrown—amid the distracted counsels, and still more distracted affairs that surrounded him, he kept the perfect equilibrium of his own mind.   The contagion of fear and doubt could not touch him.   In this respect he did not seem susceptible to the common influences which affect men. His soul, poised on its own centre, reposed calmly there amid all the tumult and turbulence that shook the land.   The ingratitude and folly of those who should have been his friends, the insults of his foes, and the frowns of fortune, could not provoke him into rash acts or delude him into error.

His constancy and firmness were equal to his self-control.   The changeless aspect and steadfast heart he maintained during those seven years of trouble and gloom, which make up the history of the revolution, will be a wonder to the end of time.   Cast down by no reverses, elated by no successes, he could neither be driven into despondency, nor carried away by extravagant hopes.   But doubtless the trials which tested his firmness most, were those which we are least able to appreciate.   Those outward public calamities which all can see, and in which we know we have the sympathies of the good, can be more easily borne than ingratitude, injustice, suspicion and slander, from those we are striving to benefit.   Amid disorganized, disbanding armies—amid cabals formed against him—falsehoods circulated about him, jealousies of Congress—amid open accusations and implied doubts of his virtue and capacity, he moved calmly yet resolutely forward in the path of duty.   This fortitude under calamities, firm courage in the midst of reverses, and unshaken

constancy in every trial to which human nature is
subjected, prove him to have possessed a soul of
amazing strength, and a faith in the right never
surpassed.

Another striking trait in Washington's character,
was the sway he exercised over other men. No one
approached him without feeling this magical influence. A vast and comprehensive mind, which
seems both to understand and embrace those about
it, must, of necessity, exert great control. Besides,
there was that evidence of slumbering power, of
transcendent elevation of character, of resistless will,
of fearlessness and strength, in his very presence,
that made every spirit bend before him.

As a military man, Washington stands in the first
rank of great commanders. He possessed every
quality that goes to the formation of one. *Courage*
was never more completely impersonified than in
him. The bravest, said Napoleon, had his *moment
de peur*—moment of fear. But one cannot point to
the spot in Washington's career, where his firmness
and coolness for an instant forsook him. To this
was added that high chivalric feeling prompting a
man in perilous crises to deeds of personal heroism.
When the hour demanding them arrived, the most
perilous and desperate feats of valour were performed by him, that are found recorded in the history of
war.

Another very important quality—the power in a
commander to win the love and confidence of his
troops, no one possessed in a more remarkable degree
than he. Such devotion and love, amid starvation
and want and neglect, were never before witnessed.
Washington, at Valley Forge, holding the troops to
him by the power of love alone, attracts the wonder
and admiration of the world.

Caution and promptness combined in a leader,
make him a strong adversary in the field. To be
tempted into no rashness, yet show no hesitation or

delay—to commit no error himself, yet be prompt as a thunderbolt in taking advantage of one committed by another—are requisites rarely found, and yet possessed by Washington in a remarkable degree.

A moral firmness, which neither defeat nor difficulties, nor the most protracted and exhausting labour can discourage or force into cessation of effort, is rarely possessed by any leader, yet this never for a moment forsook Washington.

In *moral* elevation, no warrior of ancient or modern times approaches him. Given to no excess himself, he sternly rebuked it in others. The principles of religion were deeply engrafted in his heart; and as there was no stain on his blade, he could go from the fierce fought field to the sacramental table. That brow, which would have awed a Roman Senate in its proudest days, bent in the dust before his Maker. A Brutus in justice, he did not allow personal friendship to sway his decision, or influence him in the bestowment of his favours. Sincere in all his declarations, his word was never doubted, and his promise never broken. Intrusted finally with almost supreme power, he never abused it, and laid it down at last more cheerfully than he had taken it up. Bonaparte, vaulting to supreme command, seized it with avidity, and wielded it without restraint. The Directory obstructing his plans, he broke it up with the point of the bayonet. Cromwell did the same with the Rump Parliament, and installed himself Protector of England, and even hesitated long about the title of king. Washington, fettered more than both, submitted to defeat and disappointment, without using a disrespectful word to the congress that abused him, and rejected the offered crown with a sternness and indignation that for ever crushed the hopes of those who presented it. Calm and strong in council, untiring in effort, wise in policy, terrible as a storm in battle, and incorruptible in virtue, he rises in moral grandeur so far above the Alexanders, and Cæsars, and Napoleons of the world, that even comparison seems injustice. But the crowning glory of his character was his patriotism. This was so pure, so unmixed with any selfishness, that the breath of suspicion never sullied it, and no ingratitude or wrong could for a moment weaken its force. It was like the love of a father for his son, that neither injuries nor neglect can shake. Exposing himself to present suspicion rather than peril his country—weakening and endangering his own army to aid his lieutenants —rejoicing in the victories and renown of others more than his own, so that the land he loved better than his life, might be saved, he stands before us in all the harmonious proportions that make a complete man.

It has often troubled good men that Washington made no mention of religion in his last moments. But a man's life, not his dying speeches, must be the criterion by which we judge him. One who has studied Washington's character well, would be more surprised to hear him express greater religious feeling on his death-bed than in ordinary life, than to hear him express less. To such a man as he, and one who had for his whole life faced death in every form, that last solemn hour could give no new revelations, awaken no new emotions. For years it had made no difference to him, he said, at what hour he was taken away. He had placed himself in the hands of God, and given the time of his departure no further thought. Besides, Washington never expressed to any one those emotions and thoughts which concerned himself alone. No man kept a more full and complete diary, and yet throughout, there never leaks out by any accident, any of those soul utterances which it seems impossible, under all circumstances, to suppress. His inward life he never revealed, and to expect that he would make the portion of it into which religion entered an exception, is evidently unreasonable. His *views* and belief he never concealed—they were all emphatically

religious; but his EXPERIENCE was his own, and it
was known to no one but God.

> " The quarry whence that form majestic sprung
>   Has peopled earth with grace,
> Heroes and gods that elder bards have sung,
>   A bright and peerless race ;
> But from its sleeping veins ne'er rose before
>   A shape of loftier name
> Than his, who Glory's wreath with meekness wore,
>   The noblest son of Fame."

THE END.

MILNER AND SOWERBY, PRINTERS, HALIFAX.

BIOGRAPHICAL SERIES,

PUBLISHED BY

MILNER AND SOWERBY,

HALIFAX;

AND SOLD BY ALL BOOKSELLERS.

—••◦❧◦••—

LIFE OF OUR LORD AND SAVIOUR JESUS CHRIST.

———

LIFE OF GEORGE WASHINGTON.

———

LIFE OF THE DUKE OF WELLINGTON.

———

LIFE OF NAPOLEON BONAPARTE.

———

LIFE OF OLIVER CROMWELL.

The New Heart
The Lion changed to a Lamb
The Seven Champions of Christendom
Thomson's Poetical Works
Tiler's Natural History
Todd's Student's Manual
Todd's Angel of the Iceberg, &c
Todd's Sunday School Teacher
Todd's Lectures, &c., complete
Tregortha's Bank of Faith
True Riches, or Wealth without Wings, and Riches have Wings, by T. S. Arthur
Two Years before the Mast
Twice-told Tales
Uncle Tom's Cabin
Vara, or the Child of Adoption
Wallsend Miner, by J. Everett
Wars of England (The)
War Path (The)

Watts' Improvement of the Mind
Watts' World to Come
Watts' Scripture History
Watts' Logic
Waverley, by Sir Walter Scott
White Slave
Wide, Wide World, by Elizabeth Wetherell
Wilson's Wonderful Characters
Wit of the World
Wonders of Nature and Art
Wordsworth's Select Poems
Wordsworth's Excursion, and White Doe of Rylstone, &c
Young's Poetical Works
Young Man's Book of Amusement
Young Man's Best Companion
Young Man's Own Book [ion
Young Woman's Best Compan-

FOOLSCAP 8vo.—NEARLY ALL GILT BACK, SIDE, AND EDGES.

Basket of Flowers, and other Tales. 8 beautiful Plates
    Do.,   do., 6 Plates
Bogatzky's Golden Treasury
Boys will be Boys. By Mrs. Sherwood. 4 Plates
Buchan's Domestic Medicine. Coloured Plate
Buffon's Natural History. 323 Engravings
Bunyan's Pilgrim's Progress. 3 Parts, complete. 8 Steel Plates, and 100 Woodcuts
Burns' Complete Works. 8 Steel Plates
Byron's Poetical Works. 8 do.
Cennick's Village Discourses
Clater's Every Man his Own Farrier
Clater's Every Man his Own Cattle Doctor
Clater's Farrier and Cattle Doctor, Combined
Cope's Outlines of Sermons
Cowper's complete Poetical Works. 8 steel Plates

Edgeworth's (Miss) Parents' Assistant. 9 Engravings
Edgeworth's (Miss) Popular Tales. 9 Engravings
Elisha, by the Rev. W. Krummacher. Frontispiece
Finney's Skeletons of Theological Sermons. Portrait
Finney's Lectures to Professing Christians. Portrait
Finney's Lectures on the Revival of Religion. Portrait
Foxe's Book of Martyrs. 18 Engravings
Life of the Rev. James Smith. Written by Himself.
Longfellow's Poetical Works. 8 steel Plates
Milton's Poetical Works. 8 steel Plates
Poetical Keepsake (The). 8 steel Plates
Scottish Chiefs (The). 8 steel Plates
Seven Champions of Christendom. 8 steel Plates

Shelley's Poetical Works. 6
Steel Plates

Sherwood's (Mrs.) Popular
Tales. 7 Engravings

Sherwood's (Mrs.) Juvenile
Tales. 7 Engravings

Smith's Believer's Daily Remembrancer; or, Pastor's
Morning Visit. Frontispiece

Smith's Early & Latter Rain.

Smith's Bread from Heaven.
New Edition. Frontispiece

Swiss Family Robinson. 24
Engravings

Walton and Cotton's complete
Angler. Portrait & Cuts

Watts' Scripture History.
New Edition. Frontispiece

Wordsworth'sPoeticalWorks.
8 steel Plates

POETICAL GIFT BOOKS.   ROYAL 32MO.   GILT EDGES.

Bloomfield's Farmer's Boy
Bridal Gift (The)
Bryant's Poetical Works
Diadem (The)
Evergreen (The)
Forget-me-not (The)
Gems of Sacred Poetry
Gems of Poetry for those we
Love
Heart's Ease (The)
Heber's Poems
Heman's (Mrs.) Songs of the
Affections
Hours of Thought
Language & Poetry of Flowers
Love Gift for all Seasons
May Flower
Moore'sIrishMelodies&Songs
Moore's Lalla Rookh

More's (Mrs. H) Miscella-
neous Poems
More's (Mrs. H.) Search after
Happiness, Sacred Dramas
More's (Mrs.)Fatal Falsehood
Orange Blossoms; or, Brea-
things of Love
Poetical Keepsake
Poetic Gift of Friendship
Poetry of Love (The)
Poetry of the Affections
Sacred Harp of American
Poetry
Sacred Harp (The)
Sighs of Love (The)
Thomson's Seasons, Castle of
Indolence, and Britannia
Wedding Gift (The)
Young's Night Thoughts

MISCELLANEOUS.   ROYAL 32MO.   GILT EDGES.

A Kiss for a Blow
Anecdotes—Religious, Moral,
and Entertaining
Aunt Emma's Stories from
History
Authentic Anecdotes of Chris-
tian Martyrs
Æsop's Fables, with 100 Cuts
Basket of Flowers
200 Pretty Little Tales
Baron Munchausen (The sur-
prising Adventures of)
Beecher's Lectures to Young
Men
Berquin's Children's Friend
Better Land (The)
Book of Family Worship

Book for the Lord's Day
Bunyan's ComeandWelcome,
to Jesus Christ
Byron's Tales
Byron's Don Juan
Clarke's Scripture Promises
Christian's Pattern, and Wes-
ley on Christian Perfection
Daily Food
Dictionary of Love (A)
Doctor Syntax in Search of
the Picturesque
Doddridge's Life of Colonel
Gardiner
Fawcett's Christ Precious
Flashes of Wit and Sparks of
Humour

Fleetwood's Lives of the Evangelists, Apostles, &c.
Gems of Thought
Gems by the Way-side.
Gems of Piety
Goldsmith's Vicar of Wakefield
Great Secret; or, How to be Happy
Heart and Hand
Juvenile Friends (The).
Kiss for a Blow
Law of Kindness
Life of Joseph & Death of Abel
Lilliebright; or Wisdom & Folly
Mamma's Pictures from the Bible
Mason on Self Knowledge
Memoirs of Mrs. H. A. Rogers
Memoirs of Mrs. Newell
Milton's Paradise Lost
Mitford's (Mrs.) Juvenile Tales
Nelson and his Times
Ovid's Art of Love
Pike's Earl-

Pike's Persuasives
Pike's True Happiness
Pike's Motives for Perseverance
Pleasant Hours
Paul and Virginia, &c.
Richmond's Annals of the Poor
Sabbath Morning Remembrancer
Sunday School Reciter, First and Second Series
Sunny Side (The)
Tales of Fairy Land
The Raven's Feather, and Mio and Nick, by Dr. Barth
Todd's Lectures to Children
Todd's Truth made Simple
Todd's Angel of the Iceberg
Todd's Great Cities
Todd's Simple Sketches
Todd's Student's Manual
Todd's Sunday School Teacher
Two Half-Crowns (The)
Wilson (Bishop) on the Lord's

BIBLIOTECA DE CATALUNYA

1001935500

MISS EDG
Basket W
Birth-Day
False Key
Forgive a
MISS EDG
Contrast (The)
Grateful Negro (The), &c.
Lame Jervas, &c.
Lotttery (The), &c.

Out of Debt Out of Danger, &c.
To-morrow
Will

MRS. SHERWOOD'S JUVENILE TALES
Boys will be Boys. 4 Plates
Caroline Mordaunt
Christmas Carol, &c.
Little Girl's Keepsake (The).
Little Henry and his Bearer
Joys and S

Juve
Maid
Susa
Swis
Two

ARTHUR'
Cedardale
Haven't-T
Maggy's
Our Little
Pierre, the
Poor Woo

&c.
Year's Gift
&c.
? &c.

BIBLIOTECA

A-9

4/89-

08260

Check Out More Titles From HardPress Classics Series In this collection we are offering thousands of classic and hard to find books. This series spans a vast array of subjects – so you are bound to find something of interest to enjoy reading and learning about.

Subjects:
Architecture
Art
Biography & Autobiography
Body, Mind &Spirit
Children & Young Adult
Dramas
Education
Fiction
History
Language Arts & Disciplines
Law
Literary Collections
Music
Poetry
Psychology
Science
…and many more.

Visit us at www.hardpress.net

Im The Story
personalised classic books

"Beautiful gift.. lovely finish.
My Niece loves it, so precious!"

Helen R Brumfieldon

★★★★★

UNIQUE GIFT

FOR KIDS, PARTNERS
AND FRIENDS

Timeless books such as:

Alice in Wonderland • The Jungle Book • The Wonderful Wizard of Oz
Peter and Wendy • Robin Hood • The Prince and The Pauper
The Railway Children • Treasure Island • A Christmas Carol

Romeo and Juliet • Dracula

Highly Customizable

Change Books Title

Replace Characters Names with yours

Upload Photo (for inside page)

Add Inscriptions

Visit
Im The Story .com
and order yours today!

CPSIA information can be obtained
at www.ICGtesting.com
Printed in the USA
BVHW041727230819
556656BV00010B/962/P